CHER

CHER

STRONG ENOUGH

Josiah Howard

Plexus, London

ALSO BY JOSIAH HOWARD:

Donna Summer: Her Life & Music

Blaxploitation Cinema: The Essential Reference Guide

For my mother

Gail Ann Blackmer

British Library Cataloguing in Publication Data
A catalogue record for this book is available
from the British Library

ISBN-13: 978-0-85965-484-5

Cover photo: Cher in 1975, Photo Fair
Cover and book design by Coco Wake-Porter
Printed in Great Britain by Bell & Bain Ltd.

CONTENTS

ACKNOWLEDGMENTS

To the following people I am most grateful. First, to Cher: thank you for the inspiration. Beginning in the summer of '75, when I first discovered you dancing, singing and looking gorgeous on *Cher*, I have considered you a family member; accompanying me–through your recordings, concerts, television and film work–during both the good times and the bad. Writing this book has been a personal joy.

It has also been a personal joy for me to talk, many times protractedly and on more than one occasion, to the select group of people whose spectacularly combined talents made *Cher* so special: Jimmy Dale, Ret Turner, George Schlatter, Lee Miller, Digby Wolfe, Ray Klausen, Tony Charmoli, Dee Dee Wood, Anita Mann, Bo Kaprall, Paul Galbraith and Donna Schuman.

I am equally indebted to the talented performers who talked to me about their craft, about Hollywood in the 1970s, and, in particular, about rehearsing, performing and taping their appearances on *Cher*: Gailard Sartain, Wayne Rogers, Lily Tomlin, Jimmie Walker, Janet Lennon, Kathy Lennon, Ruth Pointer, Nona Hendryx, Kris Kristofferson, Rita Coolidge, Billy Swan, Jimmy Webb, Mark Wilson, Ric Drasin and Jim Morris.

Rounding out the Cher story, before and after the *Cher* show, were my conversations, communications and/or emails with the following people, a stellar group that includes both familiar and unfamiliar names: Neil Sedaka, Les Dudek, Allan Blye, Rona Barrett, Gary Chowen, Liz Smith, Julian Wasser, Steve Barri, Bob Esty, Lenny Roberts, David Wolfert, John Durrill, Janis Ian, Alan O'Day, Les Reed, Dick Holler, Fred Mollin, Sandy Pinkard, Tom Snow, Allee Willis, Jim Lapidus, Renee Faia, Chad Michaels, Randy Cierley-Sterling, Chuck Braverman, Bob Karcy, Barbara Johnson, Tina Schultz, Sandy Griffin, Enrique Rodriguez Jr., Fred Thaler and 85 others–CBS employees, *Sonny and*

Cher Comedy Hour employees, *Cher* employees, and various close-proximity others including legal experts, industry professionals, artists, performers, dancers, agents, assistants, and technical craftsmen—who provided valuable information but did not wish to have their names appear in print.

"Special Musical Material" contributor Billy Barnes and series regular Teri Garr's original *Cher* shooting scripts were of immense help to me. So was producer George Schlatter's personal *Cher* notebook, a written confirmation of all the dates, times, facts, salaries, budgets, meetings, communications, negotiations, and activity that took place—on and off—the *Cher* show set.

Photo Fair's rare *Cher* pictures have made this book much more than it would have been otherwise. So have pictures from the TV Time and Nostalgia Network photo archives. Bob Mackie, Ray Aghayan and Fred Silverman's extensive filmed interviews in the Archive of American Television were immensely informative. So were the many privately obtained photos, contracts, memos, tapes, DVDs, and "confidential" CBS-TV, Warner Bros. Records, *Sonny and Cher Comedy Hour, Tonight Show*, John Engstead Photography, William Morris Agency, Katz/Gallin Agency, Dick Grant Intercom and *Cher* show documents. Also helpful were producers Chris Bearde and Allan Blye's *Sonny and Cher Comedy Hour* and *Sonny Comedy Revue* shooting scripts, and producer Nick Vanoff's *Sonny and Cher Show* shooting scripts.

Although they are not often seriously considered, the McFadden Group's three publications *Photoplay, Motion Picture* and *TV-Radio Mirror*, along with the Laufer Company's *Rona Barrett's Gossip* and *Rona Barrett's Hollywood*, provided a wealth of information. In an era before the internet, Twitter, Facebook and entertainment-centered television programming, information on Hollywood stars was, for the most part, gleaned from the press: the "high" and the "low." As relates to this project, I often found the "low" press—the weekly tabloids included—much more up to date, honest, accurate and informative than the so-called (carefully cultivated and filtered) "high."

The many gossip columns that provided a valuable alternative source of information about Cher, her show, and her day to day living, throughout the 1970s included, most importantly, John J. Miller's "In the Jet Stream" and "It Happened This Way," Rona Barrett's "Nothing But The Truth" and "Channel to Channel," and Sue Cameron's "Coast to Coast." Miller, Barrett and Cameron, although they were not the only ones, had unrestricted access to Cher, Gregg Allman, Sonny Bono, and producer George Schlatter throughout the entire length of *Cher*'s run.

Also of great help to me were the following monthly and weekly columns, each of which appeared—sometimes simultaneously—in newspapers as well as "movie" and "fan" magazines. Army Archer's "Hollywood" and "Behind the TV Scenes," Dorothy Manners' "Good News," Patrick Agan's "Star Gazing,"

Adrienne Baker's "Rockin' Man," Pat Campbell's "Inside World," Will Tusher's "Strictly Confidential," Doris Lilly's "More Than You Asked For," John Rellim's "The Latest Score," Shirley Eder's "Everywhere," Janet Charlton's "Info-Mania," Tony Rizzo's "Star Trekking," Pamela Mason's "Don't Breathe a Word of It," Dianne Bennett's "For the Record," Ron Scott's "The Naked Truth," Marcia Borie's "Celebrity Talk," and Cal York's "Remember You Heard it First in Photoplay."

Additional and no less important information came from Mary Ladd-McCray's latter-day Cher "zines"—*Cher Superpak Vol. 1*, and *Cher's Golden Greats*, *Cher's Friend's* President Susan Kane's collection of "Cher... ing the Limelight," the bi-monthly newsletter sent out by Cher's official 1977-1983 fan club, Cherzilla's "nothing-left-uncovered" Cher memorabilia collection, and the newspaper clipping files at the Academy of Motion Picture Arts and Sciences Library in Los Angeles, and the Lincoln Center Library for the Performing Arts in New York City.

Special appreciation to: Lindsay Scott and Lindsay Scott Management, Paul Brownstein and Paul Brownstein Productions, Claudia Menza and the Menza-Barron Literary Agency, Rosie Polzin, Joseph Schonowitz, Vicki Wickham, Stacey Soltis, Alan Mercer, Sue Retallick, Barbara Krynick, Charles L. Perdue, Adriana Alvarado, Jim Shea, John Harrington, Marta Lee, Jon Iger, David Holler, Ben Ohmart, Paul Ciulla, Jeff Connor, Susan Chana Lask, Michael Sayles, Nelly Neben, Robert Cotto, Lisa Kristofferson, John Epperson, Adam Rosen, Robin Siegel, Jeff Bleiel, Harvey Fenton, Coco Wake-Porter, LuvMyCher, DarkLadyUK and KidLove90s.

Sandra Wake believed in this project passionately. Her editorial leadership, keen eye, patience, and knowing suggestions completely transformed this book. So did Tom Branton's meticulous cleanup of this passionate writer's impatient and very clumsy hands.

Heartfelt personal thanks to my partner Artur Zebrowski who reviewed the text, made suggestions, and encouraged me to consider Cher as what he believes her to be first and foremost: "a musician."

Finally, a very special thank you to Tony Alansky, Scott Andrew Mortenson, Jed Root, Stephen Tashjian, Clarence E. Gamblin, Antonio Merenda and Brandon Lee Olson.

INTRODUCTION

"**I**'m scared of going it alone. Suppose I've lost it, whatever the hell it is I have," Cher told *TV Guide* shortly before her one and only solo variety series was up and running. She needn't have worried, as she was in good hands; and they were familiar ones. The CBS television network, on whose airwaves she starred for three years in the top-rated *Sonny and Cher Comedy Hour*, were behind her. So were million-dollar sponsors. And so were a phalanx of well-established professionals: a who's who of the entertainment industry's most talented writers, producers, directors, musicians, choreographers, art directors, dancers, background singers, photographers and beauty experts.

Following the demise of Sonny and Cher's personal and professional partnership—a full ten years after they first skyrocketed to fame with "I Got You Babe"—Cher headlined her very own *solo* variety show. Entitled simply *Cher*, the program aired on Sunday night, first at 7:30 and then at 8:00—from February 1975 right through to the end of December. What unfolded for 37 weeks (29 episodes in all) was nothing short of fascinating. "Cher is an original and we're making sure that she shines," said George Schlatter at the time. And in *Cher* she most certainly did—more brilliantly than she ever had before.

From her protracted battles with CBS, which included the network's unease with her "indecently exposed" navel, racy comedy sketches and "hip" jargon, to the break-neck schedule required to write, produce, rehearse and film an entire 60-minute program (sometimes two!) in just five days, *Cher: Strong Enough* offers an absorbing, behind-the-scenes look at Cher—on her own for the first time—and starring in her very own four-time Emmy Award-winning, Prime-Time television variety series.

"Everything seems to be happening to me all at once," Cher observed in early 1975. And it was. The story of what was going on in the background during the run of her solo series is as fascinating as what was going in front of the cameras. In the shadow of her fantastic solo success, and in the short period of just twelve months, Cher appeared in front of a grand jury to testify in a murder case, formally ended her two-year romantic (and business) relationship with media mogul David Geffen, finalized her divorce action against Sonny Bono, whom she charged with "involuntary servitude" and violation of the 13th Amendment which outlawed slavery, dealt with Sonny's $24-million counter lawsuit that charged "breach of contract" (as well as a custody battle for their daughter Chastity), married, filed for divorce (nine days later), and reconciled with rock giant Gregg Allman of the Allman Brothers Band, responded to her father John Sarkisian's $4-million "invasion of privacy" lawsuit, released the most fully realized (but almost totally overlooked) album of her entire career—the Jimmy Webb-produced *Stars*—made a "nude" appearance on the cover of *Time* magazine which resulted in the publication being categorized as "pornographic" and pulled from newsstands in Florida, delayed taping of her series for two full weeks—until sweeping behind-the-scenes changes were made—and negotiated an amicable, yet short-lived TV reunion with Sonny Bono—while pregnant with Gregg Allman's baby!

Featuring exclusive first-time interviews with *Cher* show (and *Sonny and Cher Comedy Hour*) intimates, creators, personnel and guest stars, as well as the many artists who wrote, produced and arranged Cher's vast catalogue of music (No. 1 hits in each of the last six decades—the '60s, '70s, '80s, '90s, '00s, and 10s), *Cher: Strong Enough* also documents a peak and under-examined period of performance that, ten years before she became an Academy Award-winning "serious" actress, foreshadowed her later career triumphs and left a lasting imprint on a generation.

Cher's (live) on-air television renderings of American Songbook classics like "Am I Blue?" "How Long Has This Been Going On?" and "Since I Fell For You" are among her very best. Her musical (and visual) collaborations with household name superstars like Michael Jackson, Elton John, Ray Charles, Tina Turner, David Bowie, Bette Midler, Patti LaBelle, Linda Ronstadt and Glen Campbell are among her most memorable. Her glittery, midriff-baring and boundary-pushing Bob Mackie costumes—and elaborately coiffed wigs—are in a category all of their own.

"My mother always told me, 'Be careful what you wish for because you just might get it,'" Cher has said. And in 1975, via *Cher*, her dream—as it turned out the first of many—to transcend "Sonny and Cher", to work with "relevant" singers, actors, comedians and musicians—people *she* admired—and to "be really big on all fronts" came spectacularly true.

Josiah Howard

PART ONE:

Cherilyn

1

THE SICILIAN AND THE "INDIAN"

During their admittedly brief tenure as 1960s pop stars, Sonny and Cher were a genuinely exciting musical act who, although not always convincing as "singers," proved themselves to be a distinctly American phenomenon: two high-school dropouts who no one thought would amount to anything but who, nevertheless, had honed their skills, persevered, and turned their outlandish dreams of show-business success into glittering, glamorous reality.

"Our life together was a good show, but the cast was all wrong," Cher would later observe, and perhaps that was the problem all along. Sonny and Cher's shared dream of entertainment-industry stardom, along with their palpable determination to please and not fail, was the only thing that they ever really had in common. It was enough for a while.

Cherilyn Sarkisian's early life and experiences are relatively familiar territory but bear repeating. Cher's mother was Kensett, Arkansas-born Jackie Jean Crouch. Jackie was born in 1927, the daughter of thirteen-year-old Lynda Inez Gully and seventeen-year-old Roy Crouch. Her ancestry was French, English and Cherokee Indian. Jackie's parents parted ways when she was five, and Jackie and her younger brother Mickey grew up in the care of their doting but alcoholic and often sickly father (he loved country music and encouraged his daughter to perform, even escorting her to radio stations and nightclubs). "Home was one room, a hot plate, lice and cold drafts," Jackie once recalled, and when her father moved the family from Arkansas to Los Angeles, things didn't get much better.

Throughout the 1970s Jackie described her father Roy as emotionally challenged but loving—even making the move to Los Angeles at the urging of Bob Wills and his Texas Playboys because Wills believed she could be a star. But, beginning with a 1988 interview with *The Chicago Tribune*, Jackie changed her story. "My father tried to kill my brother and me," she frankly informed writer Leigh Behrens. "I thought it was because we didn't have enough food and we were living in the 'skid row' section of Los Angeles. But then [through extensive therapy] I remembered that, at the time it happened, my father was working and we had money—but he didn't want my mother [whose new husband demanded she retrieve her children] to get custody of us." Jackie's newly-surfaced memories were harrowing. "I heard hissing. I thought it was snakes. All the gas jets had been turned on in the apartment. I saw a figure cross the room—it was my father. I heard him walk down the stairs and then walk away and then I knew we were going to die. I grabbed my younger brother [Mickey] and we ran next door to the neighbors. They called the police."

The police investigation didn't confirm Jackie's suspicions, but her relationship with her father was forever changed. At seventeen Jackie moved out and a year later, while on a short trip to Fresno, California with a girlfriend, met and married John Paul Sarkisian, a charismatic Armenian who made his living at various jobs including harvesting and delivering seasonal produce (watermelons), auto-shop manager, bartender, and hairdresser. For a time, Sarkisian and Jackie's brother Mickey even ran a popular Hollywood nightclub called the Haunted House, which was located in the space vacated by the old Arthur Murray Dance Studio.

Although Jackie and "Johnny" were "deeply in love," the relationship was, from the start, a rocky one. But not so rocky that Jackie didn't give birth, after a considerable amount of reflection—"I did consider an abortion. I remember sitting up on the table, the sweat pouring off of me. I can still feel the chrome"— to a daughter she named Cherilyn. Jackie was a huge Lana Turner fan and Turner's daughter's name was Cheryl. "I loved the name Cheryl, so I named my daughter Cherilyn—the first part 'Cheryl' was for Lana's daughter and the second part, 'Lyn,' was for my mother whose name was Lynda."

Cherilyn Sarkisian was born on May 20, 1946 in El Centro, California, a small town located 85 miles east of San Diego. The Sarkisians had relocated to El Centro after John's father purchased five trucks in hopes that his son would start his own produce business. The produce business didn't come to pass; Johnny lost the trucks, one by one, in a gambling match. "It was really scary having a baby and no stability," Jackie remembered. "After about a year I had had it. I traveled to Reno and got a divorce."

Jackie would marry several more times. "I'd been married three times by the time I was 21 because I was raised in a time when you didn't go to bed with someone unless you married them." Her union with an aspiring actor named John Southall produced another daughter—Georganne (called "Gee")—but only lasted four years. An even briefer marriage (five months) to Joseph Harper Collins followed. Up next, but not for long, was a man named Chris Alcaide.

Banker Gilbert LaPiere, who had previously been married and had custody of his two daughters—children who were close in age to Cher and Georganne—was remembered fondly, and Cher and Georganne even took his last name. But the marriage didn't last. Reconciliation, and a *second* marriage and divorce from John Sarkisian—"the most persuasive man in the world"—were also part of Jackie's story. So was a quick marriage and divorce from a man named Hamilton Holt. Craig Spencer, 21 years her junior, was a later love whom Jackie (who officially became known as "Georgia Holt" in the late '60s) remained with for five years.

As a child Cher spent an extended period of time in a "home for the needy," actually a fully staffed day and night care facility used, for the most part, by single working mothers. "After I divorced Johnny, Cher and I moved east," Georgia recalled. "For a long time I was supporting us singing in a nightclub in Scranton [Pennsylvania]. I had to have somewhere to leave Cher and I wasn't getting any money at all from Johnny."

"I didn't live full-time with my mother until I was like three years old," Cher revealed in 1996. "After I found out about that a lot of things that I didn't understand made sense. When I was a kid I was always waking up at night not knowing where I was. The long period of time that I spent away from my mother explained that for me."

When Georgia was able to take care of Cher and Georganne herself, mother and daughters moved from house to house, from apartment to apartment, while Georgia pursued her dream of making it big as either a singer or an actress. Occasionally she got work. She made cameos on *The Lucy Show* and *The Adventures of Ozzie and Harriet*, but the closest she ever came to movie stardom was when she won a supporting role in the 1950 film *The Asphalt Jungle*. "I was given the part of the blonde. But later my agent called me up and told me that this new girl named Marilyn Monroe had been given the part instead."

Like her mother, Cher entertained dreams of becoming a movie star. The animated films *Dumbo*, *Bambi* and *Cinderella* as well as the musical *Oklahoma!* fascinated her, and early on she began perfecting a signature that she deemed suitable to sign as an autograph. Mother and daughter frequently made trips to Hollywood Boulevard, where they sat in their car, enjoyed ice-cream cones and watched the parade of interesting people. "I didn't know how or what I was going to do but I knew that I wanted to be famous," Cher later recalled.

Hitting her teens, Cher's desire to become famous intensified, but was clouded by a rebellious stage that included smoking, cursing and "dancing all night on the [Sunset] Strip." Her nonconformist nature combined with a lack of interest in school (pronounced by an inability to focus—later diagnosed as a lower-tier case of Dyslexia) resulted in her dropping out of Fresno High School a year before she was to graduate. It was a decision that complicated her already contentious relationship with her mother—who was becoming increasingly concerned about her oldest daughter's "immaturity" and lack of direction.

At sixteen, Cher moved out of her mother's house and in with a girlfriend named Melissa Melcher. A succession of pay-the-rent part-time jobs made it clear that being on her own wasn't going to be as easy as she thought. Stints as a secretary, clerk (at Robinsons department store in L.A.) and a counter-girl position at See's, a confection shop, didn't leave her feeling fulfilled and didn't last for long. Then, out on a double date with roommate Melissa, Cher met a man named Sonny Bono. "When I first saw Sonny, everything around him got blurry and there was just him standing there—all in black. I was totally blown away."

Salvatore Phillip Bono was born on February 16, 1935—the only son among Italian immigrant Santo and second-generation Italian-American Jean's three children. Salvatore's (from the very beginning his parents called him "Sonny") early years were spent growing up in Detroit, Michigan. "My father was an honest, hardworking man who always held a steady job," Sonny remembered in his 1991 autobiography *And the Beat Goes On*. Even so, in order to make ends meet, mother Jean also worked—styling, coloring and setting neighborhood women's hair in the living room of the Bono home. "Our house always smelled of the last permanent," Sonny said, and when he was twelve, his family—Jean and Santo along with his two older sisters, Betty and Fran, moved from Detroit to Hawthorne, California, a blue-collar suburb south of Los Angeles, where Sonny's father established himself as a for-hire truck driver and mother Jean expanded on her beauty skills, eventually renting a downtown storefront.

It was true that Sonny's parents were passionately "traditional," hard-working and respected in their community, but it was also true that they were ill-suited for one another. Entering into an arranged union (Jean married Santo when she was fourteen), Sonny's mother was "all warmth and caring" while his father was "stern, taciturn and glowering." He was also a heavy drinker. "I don't think me or my sisters ever connected with our parents," Sonny recalled. "We didn't grow up bitter. We didn't sit around and complain about being mistreated. But each of us was more at peace whenever my mother and father weren't around." The Bonos' divorce came only after Jean discovered comfort and romance in the house next door.

Sonny and Cher's first encounter took place at Aldo's, a trendy Hollywood eatery. Sonny's friend Red Turner was "dating" Cher at the time and Red thought Sonny would like Cher's roommate Melissa. "I was attracted to Melissa instantly... Cupid had fired a bull's-eye," said Sonny who, by his own account, was initially unimpressed with Cher. "I've just met the girl I'm going to marry, her name is Melissa—Melissa Melcher." But, unbeknownst to Sonny, Melissa was not only thoroughly uninterested in him—she was thoroughly uninterested in *men*.

A few days after their initial meeting Red, Cher, Melissa and Sonny got together a second time and eventually ended up at Club 86—an L.A. lesbian nightclub. When Melissa and Cher got up and took to the dance floor themselves, Sonny and Red made a quick exit. A few weeks later Sonny encountered Cher a third time. "I saw her looking out the window of a neighboring apartment building. Her face registered the same response as mine—total surprise. We exchanged smiles and waves. Then we both motioned to meet each other downstairs."

Following their fortuitous reintroduction, Sonny and Cher began officially dating. Cher told Sonny that she had "sort of" run away from home (she told her mother she was living with a stewardess) and was now living with a group of not-too-dependable girlfriends. When she made it clear that her new living situation wasn't working out (and that she wasn't a lesbian), Sonny invited her to stay with him: "No funny business. No strings attached."

"Cher's eyes were as deep as dark tunnels. The longer I stared into them, the stronger their pull on me became," Sonny remembered, and it was only a matter of time before their platonic arrangement became both emotional and physical.

Sonny, whatever he might have assumed, was not Cher's first lover. In 1988 Cher candidly informed *Playboy* that she lost her virginity at the age of fourteen. "I was really in love with the guy. He was too old for me. He kept bothering me and bothering me and so we finally did it. I said 'Okay, is that it?' He said, 'Yeah.' I said, 'Now go home and don't ever talk to me again. I don't ever want you coming over here, and that's it. Okay?' So he left."

Cher had another romantic liaison before she met Sonny. "He was 35 and I was crazy in love with him. He was very handsome. He used to work around our house. He looked like Tom Selleck, but blond. Six-foot-four. He made all the women crazy. I was with him secretly for about a year."

Sonny and Cher's physical union came to pass following a brief separation carried out by Cher's mother who, when she found out that her underage daughter was living with a man, first made her move into a Hollywood girls' residence and then took her on a month-long trip to a relative's home in Arkansas. The move and the trip out of state didn't keep Sonny and Cher from wanting to be with one another—even if, according to Sonny, their sexual relationship was less than passionate.

"I wish I were able to say that I saw banners and fireworks the first time Cher and I made love," Sonny confessed in *And the Beat Goes On*, "but I didn't. More important than the sex was the love story that started to unfold between us." The love story was, as it turned out, a powerful one: it centered them, allowed them to feel less alone, and gave them both the courage and confidence to pursue their most heartfelt dreams. (Interestingly, throughout Sonny's autobiography, both of Cher's surnames are misspelled. Sarkisian is "Sarkasian" and LaPiere is "LaPierre.")

When Sonny first met Cher he was not only a full eleven years older than her, he had also been married, was separated from his former wife, and was the father of a little girl named Christy. "My marriage to Donna [Rankin] was doomed from the very beginning," Sonny later confessed. "It wasn't horrible and it wasn't good. It wasn't anything, and that was the problem. After Donna and I separated I rarely saw Christy." (He did, however, become her benefactor later in life. After Sonny and Cher hit the big time, he helped support Christy, put her through college, and got her a job on his and Cher's television series.)

When Cher first met Sonny he was an established, if not financially successful, songwriter. A veteran of Los Angeles recording studios, Sonny had, for a time at least, imagined that he could make it as a solo act. In 1955 he wrote and recorded his first song—"Ecstasy." The only home it ever found was in Sonny's apartment. "Ecstasy" was followed by other Sonny-penned and performed tunes with titles like "Calling All Cars" and "As Long as You Love Me," recorded under pseudonyms that included Davey Summers, Ronny Sommers, Prince Carter and Don Christy (a combination of wife Donna and daughter Christy's names). None of the singles were successful.

1958's "Koko Joe," written by Sonny but performed by someone else—Don and Dewey—provided him with his first residual check. When the Righteous Brothers also recorded the tune, things were looking up. "She Said Yeah" was recorded by Larry Williams and later included as a filler track on the Rolling Stones' *December's Children*. "Needles and Pins" (co-written by Jack Nitzsche) became a modest hit for Jackie DeShannon in 1963 and the following year was covered by the Searchers.

Selling songs to other artists made Sonny a semi-familiar name in recording circles, but it didn't pay the rent. That feat was accomplished by his position as a gofer for the legendary, and increasingly eccentric, music producer Phil Spector—a job he begged Spector to give him. It was Sonny's proximity to Spector that served his dreams best. Through Spector he had direct access to the music industry's top talent. He also had a bird's-eye-view of how *genuine* hit records were created, pressed, and marketed.

Cher offered Sonny even more opportunities to succeed. Young, hip, fashionable, willing and eager to take direction, Cher possessed qualities that, more than Sonny's ever did, had the distinct air of possibility about them. With Cher in his life, Sonny traded in his dreams of becoming a pop star for the dream of *creating* one. They were a perfect pair that came together at the perfect time. As Sonny put it in *And the Beat Goes On*, "I became convinced that this shy, skinny, teenage girl with bad skin, a big nose, and an unusually deep singing voice, was star material. All she needed was someone to channel her hidden talent." He was the one.

It was through Sonny that Cher made her debut as a singer, first as a substitute background vocalist at Phil Spector sessions and then on Spector-produced tunes that included the Righteous Brothers' "You've Lost That Lovin' Feelin'," the Crystals' "Da Doo Ron Ron," and the Ronettes' "Be My Baby." Sonny even got Spector to produce a solo record for Cher. "Ringo, I Love You" (its B-side the self-explanatory "Beatle Blues") featured Cher as "Bonnie Jo Mason"—a name Spector believed sounded "down-home American." A somewhat catchy teenage girl's love lament to Beatle member Ringo Starr, the song, though spirited and timely, was, nevertheless, a certifiable flop. Part of the problem was that Cher's voice was deemed too deep by many disc jockeys. The consensus was that she sounded like a man singing a love song to another man.

Another problem, one that became apparent only after the fact, was that "Ringo, I Love You" seemed a bit too exploitative; shamelessly attempting to ride on the coat-tails of another popular group's success. When the record was released Cher told the press that the Beatles were her favorite group. But creating a song and singing it to one of the group's members was a bit much. Cher's second single was the Sonny-penned (and produced) "Dream Baby" (B-side "I'm Gonna Love You")—a blatant and unapologetic Spector knockoff. This time around Cher was billed as "Cherilyn." A bit more ambitious and musically sound, "Dream Baby" was fully embraced by DJs, but didn't become a hit.

Keeping busy in the studio, Sonny joined Cher and recorded several tracks—"The Letter," "Do You Wanna Dance," and "Love is Strange" (all on one 45 disc). When it came time to issue the songs, Sonny decided that they should call themselves Caesar and Cleo. He, with his penchant for novelty and built-in publicity, hoped the record would be a successful-by-association tie-in with the soon-to-be-released and much talked-about Elizabeth Taylor spectacle, *Cleopatra*. The gimmick (and the record), like "Ringo, I Love You" before it, didn't wash.

So it was back to the drawing board. Bonnie Jo Mason, Cherilyn, and Caesar and Cleo were all failures. Perhaps "Sonny and Cher" (all agreed that it sounded better than "Cher and Sonny") a "new" singing team, wouldn't be.

2

I GOT YOU BABE

Sonny and Cher's first single, "Baby Don't Go" (B-side "Walkin' the Quetzal"), was an upbeat and peppy tune written by Sonny and released on Atco Records. The maudlin, Sonny-penned "Just You" (B-side "Sing C'est La Vie") was released shortly thereafter. Catchy, contemporary-sounding, reflective of the other songs released during the era, both "Baby Don't Go" and "Just You" became modest West Coast hits, enabling Sonny and Cher to hire a band and acquire some onstage experience. Although Cher was terrified of performing live, the "new act" appeared in small clubs—including the Purple Onion, an establishment managed by Cher's Uncle Mickey—and on multiple bills with other "local" bands. Sonny and Cher's "I Got You Babe" (B-side "It's Gonna Rain"), written by Sonny in a day and recorded just as fast, topped the *Billboard* singles charts, sold three million copies, and became their signature song.

"Charlie Greene [Sonny and Cher's manager] saw me performing at the Troubadour one night and asked me to show up at Gold Star Studios the following day," remembers guitarist and bass player Randy Cierley-Sterling (professionally known as Randy Sterling). "I had no idea who or what we would be recording, I just knew it was another 35 dollars [scale for union musicians] gig."

At the "I Got You Babe" session, Sterling's innovative guitar licks were recorded and expanded to great effect. "Sonny had that studio packed to the gills. I don't think I had ever seen so many musicians crammed into such a small space. I wasn't really sure that all the musicians he hired were needed, but all of us were certainly happy to be doing a paid gig."

"In one night our whole lives changed," Sonny said following the phenomenal success of "I Got You Babe", and it was a profound change; one that brought financial comfort, purpose and, finally, validation. If they never enjoyed any other show-business victory, never had another hit, faded into obscurity as swiftly as they had emerged under the spotlight's hot glare, their names were now forever a part of pop-music history. In the midst of "Beatlemania," Sonny and Cher, the odd-looking "married" couple, with their simple song about love seeing them through difficult times, made everything seem all right. (Although they told the press they were married on October 27, 1964, they didn't *actually* get married until much later, right before daughter Chastity's birth according to Cher in the '80s, but "not until Chastity was nearly a toddler" according to Sonny in 1991.)

"With 'I Got You Babe' all the right buttons were finally pushed," observed music historian Ken Barnes many years later. "From its vaulting bridge, to the rapturously resolved false ending, 'I Got You Babe' touched the hearts of the most curmudgeonly crew cuts... it was a stirring confidence that love would prevail over anything a vague, uptight societal 'they' might throw at it." And "I Got You Babe" never lost its appeal. Covered by everyone from Etta James and Tiny Tim in the '60s, to David Bowie featuring Marianne Faithfull in the '70s, and the Ramones in the '80s, in 1985 (the tune's twentieth anniversary) UB40 featuring Chrissie Hynde covered it and saw their version go all the way to the No. 1 spot on the British pop charts (No. 28 in America).

In 1993 the song's chart success was further extended. That year the lead character in the critically acclaimed film *Groundhog Day* repeatedly heard the song on his ever-ringing clock radio. Consequently, so did others. Twenty-eight years after it was first released, Sonny and Cher's original version of "I Got You Babe" re-entered the charts and went to No. 66 in Britain. In 2011 it was announced that "I Got You Babe" was the second most played song by American astronauts (ironically, the first was the Canadian band Rush's tune "Countdown"). In space "I Got You Babe" roused astronauts on the Atlantis, Discovery, and Endeavor space missions, while on earth television shows like *Good Times*, *The Golden Girls* and *The Simpsons* kept the song alive through performance and impersonation.

Sonny and Cher backed up their "Babe" success with a string of popular singles including "What Now My Love" (No. 14), "But You're Mine" (No. 15), "Little Man" (No. 21) and, later, "The Beat Goes On" (No. 6). As a solo act, Sonny scored with "Laugh at Me" (No. 10), and Cher carved out a solo market with "All I Really Want to Do" (No. 15), "Where Do You Go" (No. 25), "Bang Bang (My Baby Shot Me Down)" (No. 2), "You Better Sit Down Kids" (No. 9), and "Alfie" (No. 32).

It was during recording sessions for Cher's debut solo album that Randy Sterling first got to see Cher up close and personal. "After 'I Got You Babe' hit, Sonny called me up and asked me to work on Cher's first solo album [*All I Really Want to Do*]. I didn't get to talk with her much during the 'Babe' session but when we were doing her solo record it was different. I remember once seeing her all by herself outside the studio leaning against a car. She looked really upset so I walked over and asked if everything was okay. She said she was terrified; she didn't think she had what it took. She didn't think she was a good singer, she thought the whole session was a waste of everyone's time. I gave her a pep talk. I told her that she had already proven herself with 'I Got You Babe' and that was huge. I also told her that, perhaps, she wasn't the best judge of her own talent. Then I told her to stop analyzing everything and 'just get in there and sing your ass off!' She liked that. When I ran into her a few months later she pulled me aside and thanked me for my support."

During the "Sonny and Cher," "Cher," and "Sonny" craze—in essence three distinct and separate musical acts—Sonny and Cher had five singles in the top twenty (a feat equaled only by Elvis and the Beatles). Their albums, too, were everywhere. If record buyers didn't find anything in the "S" bin—*Sonny and Cher and Friends* (No. 69), *Look at Us* (No. 2), *The Wondrous World of Sonny and Cher* (No. 34), *Inner Views* (Sonny's uncharted solo effort), or *In Case You're in Love* (No. 4)—they only had to make their way over to the "C" bin and pick up *All I Really Want to Do* (No. 16), *The Sonny Side of Cher* (No. 26), *Cher* (No. 59), *With Love, Cher* (No. 47), or *Backstage* (uncharted).

From the very beginning Sonny and Cher used television as a tool. Their long hair and multicolored bell bottoms and fur vests—"the human equivalent of Afghan hounds," sniped one critic—did a great deal to cement a funky, anti-establishment image that young music buyers admired (and could copy). On music shows like *American Bandstand* and *Shindig!* they were cool; on variety shows like *The Ed Sullivan Show* and *Hollywood Backstage* they were endearing; and later on situation comedies like *Love American Style* and *The Man from U.N.C.L.E.* they were hip.

Sold-out concerts (mostly in America, but on a three-week European promotional tour they performed in London and Paris, and made headlines being "kicked out"—staged events to garner publicity—of some of England's most exclusive hotels), the piggybacking and cross-marketing of their solo and "team" albums, their journalistic forays (Cher wrote an advice column for *16 Magazine* called "Dear Cher"), a nationally marketed collection of "Sonny and Cher Fashions" and an assemble-it-yourself Sonny and Cher Mustang, kept them busy and in the public eye.

But not everything went according to plan. "I took the tempo [on 'I Got You Babe'] much too fast and the poor oboe player was playing the triplet at double time," remembers Les Reed, the musical conductor on the TV show *Ready, Steady, Go!*, a teen-oriented British television program on which Sonny and Cher appeared. The writer/composer (who helped discover Tom Jones and co-wrote and arranged a string of Jones's hits including "It's Not Unusual") managed to even out "I Got You Babe'"s tempo before Sonny and Cher began singing, but didn't escape Sonny's ire. "After the show Sonny collared me," remembers Reed. "He gave me a right roasting. I thought their appearance was marvelous but looking back, my experience with Sonny and Cher is one of distinct mixed emotions!" (A year after they appeared on *Ready, Steady, Go!*, Cher recorded Reed's "It's Not Unusual"—included on 1966's *The Sonny Side of Cher* album.)

Of all the rumors that circulated around Sonny and Cher during their ride at the top, including the persistent rumor that they were constantly fighting, the most outrageous must have been that Sonny and Cher were both men! The problem, it seemed, was both the way Cher looked (tall and thin) and her unusually deep singing voice. Just three months after they hit the big time, Sonny and Cher's manager's secretary was charged with responding to each and every inquiry, even those from fans, to refute the rumor. A letter dated September 8, 1965 from Judy Moll (secretary to Charlie Greene and Brian Stone, Sonny and Cher's managers) survives.

Dear Rosie,

Cher, we assure you, is a girl. She is nineteen years old and happily married to Sonny (who is 25) [*actually, Sonny was 30*]. She has a fourteen-year-old sister named Georganne. As for Cher's voice being too low: I think you will find that a lot of great female singers have low voices... just listen. Tell your mom that Cher is just a very slim, very pretty girl with a low voice. I think if you listen closer, you will find a lot of feminine quality in her voice, especially on songs like "Sing C'est La Vie," "Just You" etc.

Very truly yours,

Judy Moll

"After seeing Sonny and Cher make it really big I wondered if I really wanted that for myself," Sonny and Cher's arranger Harold Battiste (sometimes credited Harold Battiste Jr.) said after he accompanied them on their first sold-out concert tours. "I remember Cher on a beautiful summer day longing to go to the beach, but she couldn't because she'd most likely be mobbed. Now, here was this girl, probably the most successful little chick in the world, and she couldn't go to the beach! When we were in Europe they couldn't get out of the hotel without being mobbed. I felt sorry for them because I realized that a large segment of living was being denied them. I had a chance to see Europe and enjoy their success more than they did." (Battiste was the musical arranger on Barbara George's hit "I Know (You Don't Love Me No More)", a song Cher would later cover on 1976's *I'd Rather Believe in You*.)

But as big as they seemed, and even though they had their imitators—Bunny and Bear ("America's Sweethearts"), Friend and Lover ("Reach Out of the Darkness")—Sonny and Cher's success was fleeting. As the '60s drew to a close, so did their careers. The changing music and fashion scene, the "free love" movement, their endorsement of National Bible Week—"look who reads the Bible"—as well as Sonny's nationally distributed Public Service Announcement about the ills of marijuana (which played in school houses across America), resulted in Sonny and Cher's firm placement in the younger generation's "uncool" box. "We were getting a little old for the kids," Sonny surmised about their dramatic career downturn, "and that's the biggest mistake a performer can make—thinking he can stay young forever. Kids have a new idol every year." Cher, who actually *was* young at the time (in 1967 she was 21 while Sonny was 32), put it more succinctly—and more honestly: "The cool people thought we were square and the square people thought we were cool. It was over. Our careers went down the toilet."

Movies, it was thought, might keep the ball rolling. 1967's loosely plotted *Good Times* told the story of Sonny and Cher *not* wanting to make a movie. When the film was in the planning stages it seemed like a good idea, but by the time it reached theaters Sonny and Cher's popularity had substantially waned. *The New York Times* called the movie "a nice, colorful, sprightly bit of good-humored silliness," but no one went to see it, or for that matter bought the "I Got You Babe"-heavy tie-in soundtrack album.

1969's Sonny-penned *Chastity*, an attempt at social consciousness, told the not very interesting, necessarily melodramatic story of a tart-tongued teenage runaway. Cher got good notices—"She's onscreen for virtually the whole film and still handles herself with an easy flair," observed *Time*—but the movie, like *Good Times* before it, bombed at the box office.

"I took our wad, $500,000 and blew it on the movie [*Chastity*]," Sonny confessed, and since *Chastity* played to empty parking lots (it was distributed by American International Pictures, whose forte was the drive-in market), all their savings were gone. They also owed the government an estimated $200,000 in unpaid back taxes. Things looked bleak. But, still, they tried. For 1969's Cher solo album *3614 Jackson Highway*, Sonny handed Cher over to the talents of producers Jerry Wexler, Tom Dowd and Arif Mardin. Sonny and Cher traveled to Muscle Shoals, Alabama to record the project, but when the album's first single, "For What it's Worth," only made it to No. 125 and the album itself only made it to No. 160, an ugly truth was clear: opportunities for Sonny and Cher to make a living had all but vanished.

"People saw their big house and the Rolls-Royce parked in the driveway and everyone thought they were still successful," admitted Kapp Records head Johnny Musso in 1995. "But the truth was they hadn't had a hit in years and their refrigerator didn't have any food in it."

There was another truth: despite their money and career troubles, Sonny still deeply loved and admired his wife. In May 1998, a rare and highly personal Sonny and Cher document was published. Five months after Sonny died in a tragic skiing accident, his widow Mary provided *People* magazine with a copy of his and Cher's personal diary, a brown leather-bound journal that Cher had given him as a birthday present in 1968. From that time on, between 1968 and 1976, the two made semi-regular entries.

January 6, 1968.
Today is my 33rd birthday. I am never sans Cher. She lives inside my body. Cher is truly a star, from the top of her head to the bottom of her feet. Thank God I have Cher. She's my stabilizer. She's my generator too. She's my reason.

Joe DeCarlo, the man who replaced Charlie Greene and Brian Stone as Sonny and Cher's manager, provided them with a winning suggestion: they should remake themselves as nightclub performers. "Sonny just hated the idea. He kept saying, '[They think] we're freaks! Grown-ups hate us,'" remembered DeCarlo, but convinced that there was no other way, Sonny eventually succumbed.

It took time, two years; shorter than they expected but longer than they wanted, but Sonny and Cher would soon be back on top—not in the way they used to be, but on top nonetheless. For their new role as nightclub entertainers, they traded in their bell bottoms, bangs and beads for a tuxedo and an evening gown (Cher once boasted that she didn't own a dress). A store-bought dress on her lithe frame, a decision to let her trademark bangs grow out—Cher in her transitional period, hair newly parted in the middle but bangs not yet reaching her shoulders—signaled more than a new look; it meant a new outlook. The Sonny and Cher act was now officially and pointedly directed at an older, more middle-of-the road audience.

Along with music, Sonny and Cher now delivered marriage-centered one-liners and comedy patter—channeling Louis Prima and Keely Smith—that harked back to earlier times. Their status as parents was helpful, too. Chastity, born March 4, 1969 and named because Cher discovered she was pregnant while making the film, helped to make them acceptable on all levels and when they were signed to the Fairmont Hotel Circuit—performing in unimpressive yet respectable "showrooms" from Canada's Elmwood Hotel and Casino to New Orleans' Blue Room—there was a sense of accomplishment. Still, there were complaints. "We performed in places that you wouldn't believe," Cher informed *The Saturday Evening Post*, long after the fact. "You're used to 50,000 screaming, wildly enthusiastic kids and here are 125 people staring into their drinks saying, 'Okay, big shots. Entertain us.'" Sonny, too went on record discussing the challenging comeback trail. "You're standing in the kitchen of a restaurant in a tuxedo waiting to go on and the waiters are cursing and spilling their orders, jostling you, and then you're announced from the stage. You go from this kitchen into all the glitter and the lights. That's when you really become aware of entertainment as a *business*." (Photos confirm the bleakness of the situation: Sonny and Cher, lost in a netherworld of banquet tables, limp balloons, worn high-chairs and artificial wood paneling.)

Television played a large role in Sonny and Cher's comeback. "We did all the TV talk shows we could," Sonny explained. "We put in a year as professional guest stars, talk shows, comedies, game shows—everything. At first it was difficult because talk show hosts were afraid to ask us about anything but our hit records because they didn't know if we *could* talk about anything else."

A 1971 guest-host spot on *The Merv Griffin Show* totally changed everything for Sonny and Cher a second time. CBS's vice president in charge of programming, Fred Silverman, signed them on to do a five-episode summer replacement series. (Legend has it that Silverman "discovered" them on the show when, in actuality, he arranged the appearance—to see if Sonny and Cher had what it took to headline their *own* TV show.) When that proved to be a hit with audiences they were gifted with their very own Prime-Time, weekly variety series. *The Sonny and Cher Comedy Hour* debuted on December 27, 1971 and ran (in four different time slots) through to March 6, 1974.

"Before my first meeting with Sonny and Cher I really didn't pay much attention to them," remembers producer Allan Blye who, with his partner Chris Bearde, would go on to spend four years as producers, writers and creative directors of *The Sonny and Cher Comedy Hour*. Blye—who had been a juvenile singing sensation in his native Canada—previously wrote sketch material for *The Smothers Brothers Show* while his partner Chris Bearde did the same for *Laugh-In*.

"To me Sonny and Cher were former 'Hit Parade' recording artists; they had done well but were on the wane. I first saw them [at the Fairmont Hotel] in Dallas. They were appearing in the lounge with an eight-piece band—that makes ten people onstage. Well, I don't think there were ten people in the audience!"

Still, Blye and Bearde saw promise. "Their act was genuinely funny and they had the music to augment it. After the show we went backstage and met with them. Before Chris and I touched down back in L.A. we had a full outline of what would become *The Sonny and Cher Comedy Hour*."

Along with the "Vamp" routine—which featured Cher atop an upright piano while Sonny mugged and played the keys—*The Sonny and Cher Comedy Hour's* recurring segments included "Sonny's Pizza," a nod to Sonny's Italian ancestry, a fortune teller bit in which Cher delivered caustic put-downs (an extension of what would become the duo's trademark repartee), solo singing spots for Cher (in which she "displayed her theatrical inclinations") and Laverne—Cher as a gossiping "San Fernando Valley Yenta" (a character that she instinctively broadened; made less stereotypically Jewish). Also a staple was an elaborate multi-cast musical finale that poked fun at operettas and musical theater.

"The first time we taped the show we had to go out and find an audience," admits Blye. "I mean, at that time, no one really cared about Sonny and Cher and even fewer people were interested in going into a dark TV studio in the middle of a sunny day to watch them perform."

To fill seats (there were 250) Blye, Bearde and a few others descended on the expansive Farmers' Market—across the street from CBS Television City. "We bribed people with food and drink," says Blye. "We begged them to come across the street and sit for the taping. That was the very first *Sonny and Cher Comedy Hour* audience. People who just wanted a free meal!"

But during that very first taping something unexpected occurred. "We thought we had a chance, we thought we had a good show, but the audience response exceeded even our expectations," remembers Blye. "The laughs were constant, the applause deafening, the atmosphere was electric. After the very first show aired we never had to bribe another audience. The line of people waiting to sit for tapings ran around the building from the beginning of the series until it went off the air."

Influential *TV Guide* columnist Cleveland Amory confirmed *The Sonny and Cher Comedy Hour*'s sweeping appeal. "The songs, the jokes, the costumes, the skits, even the way the guests are used are all a cut above and beyond the average variety show. Is there anything she can't do? She can sing any song, do any skit, wear any clothes and, frankly, we'd tune in if all she did was sing that 'Vamp' song every week."

"I used to get fan mail about the hairstyles that I created for Cher," says Gary Chowen, Cher's personal hairstylist for the run of the series. "That show was really about three things: Cher putting Sonny in the toilet with her putdowns, her fashions and her hair."

And her hair, thanks to Chowen—who at seventeen was flown down from Canada to work his magic—was ever-changing. "At that time very few people knew what to do with long hair," says Chowen, who perfected his trade at Toronto's famed Caruso Salon. "With Cher I got to do everything. I made hairpieces. I'd take Dynell hair and use coat hangers, socks, sanitary napkins, styrophome, whatever it took to give her hair fullness, height, width and shape. I also did simple pullbacks—she looked great that way. I even made her look like Diana Ross!" Chowen's magic worked. Cher and her hairstyles—along with her costumes—were both imitated and the topic of conversation the day after each and every *Sonny and Cher Comedy Hour* broadcast.

Illustrator John Wilson also put his indelible mark on the show. His funky cartoon images of Sonny and Cher were emblazoned on more than a hundred white bulbs that graced the *The Sonny and Cher Comedy Hour*'s opening (and closing) set. Wilson's black and white portraiture became iconic: both a representation of Sonny and Cher's name-recognition and a product logo: used on scripts, stationery, CBS memos, tickets and throughout the actual show.

The more than 200 guests who appeared on *The Sonny and Cher Comedy Hour* included their daughter Chastity (who joined her parents in skits and came onstage during the show's closing segments), musical groups: the Supremes (minus Diana Ross), the Defranco Family, the Temptations; actors: Tony Curtis, Jack Palance, Jim Brown; comedians: Phyllis Diller, Jerry Lewis, Art Carney; and talents of dubious distinction: Miss Universe, Hugh Hefner and the Playboy Pets, Howard Cosell.

Singer and dancer Sandy Duncan appeared on the show. "She and Cher got into a huge fight," remembers a stagehand. "I don't think Cher could stand Sonny at the time but she also couldn't stand Duncan's making a pass at him—right in front of her face!" So did prolific writer Truman Capote (whose life was later deemed movie-worthy; 2005's *Capote* and 2006's *Infamous*). "I've always liked Sonny and Cher," the *In Cold Blood* and *Breakfast at Tiffany's* author confessed at the time. "I've never done anything like this and I thought it would be fun." (Although Sammy Davis Jr. [who recorded Cher's Sonny-written "You Better Sit Down Kids"] never appeared on the show, when Davis filmed his heavily-promoted appearance on CBS' *All in the Family*—taped across the hall from *The Sonny and Cher Comedy Hour*—he spent his entire off-camera time in Sonny and Cher's dressing room.)

The Sonny and Cher Comedy Hour also dabbled in politics. On March 14, 1973, former POW Air Force Captain John Nasmyth—who spent six years in captivity in Vietnam—made an appearance on the show. While imprisoned, Nasmyth had asked the press what had happened to his favorite singing group, Sonny and Cher. On the show Sonny and Cher presented him with a gift-wrapped collection of the albums they had recorded in his absence.

The Governor of California—and soon to be leader of the free world—also, as incredible as it might have seemed, showed up on the set of *The Sonny and Cher Comedy Hour*. "I remember everyone telling me that it was a really big deal that we got Ronald Reagan," Cher remembered in 2003. But Chris Bearde had the real story. "If you look at Reagan's appearance [the Governor was on-hand to receive "The Coveted Bono," a grotesque Oscar-like statuette], you'll see that Sonny is totally speechless. He stammers, he fidgets, he can't believe he's talking to *the* Ronald Reagan. Cher on the other hand doesn't seem to care. She isn't impressed, she isn't nervous. He's just another guest."

And, for some, the guests who appeared on *The Sonny and Cher Comedy Hour* were more interesting than Sonny and Cher themselves. In her book *Vincent Price: A Daughter's Biography*, Victoria Price remembered attending a *Sonny and*

Cher Comedy Hour taping that featured her famous father. "I'd seen Sonny and Cher on television and was casually interested in meeting them," remembered Price, who was nine at the time of her introduction. "But much more exciting to me than meeting Sonny, Cher and Chastity was meeting their guest star George Foreman. At the time I was a huge sports fanatic and he had just been crowned Heavyweight Boxing Champion of the World. I was absolutely thrilled to meet him." When Freeman King and Murray Langston, two of the "regular" comedians who appeared on *The Sonny and Cher Comedy Hour*, parlayed their success into an album deal–1973's *Freeman and Langston Featured on the Sonny and Cher Show*– it was clear to one and all that Sonny and Cher's return to the top via network television offered more than just a second round of popularity to an off-the-radar act, it was a far-reaching enterprise that proved advantageous to everyone associated with it.

3

GYPSYS, HALF-BREEDS
AND DARK LADIES

With 30 million people watching each week, the financial challenges of the '60s were a thing of the past and expansive magazine layouts documented the change. Along with their 21-room mansion (photos of which appeared in *Look* and *Life*), a palace whose cream-colored rooms were adorned with gold mirrors and cut crystal—"For me, modern furniture has no warmth. I like period rooms with the somberness of age," explained Cher—the couple owned, but rarely used, a Rolls-Royce, three Mercedes, a Ferrari, an Aston Martin, a Jeep (a birthday gift from Cher to Sonny), four motorcycles, a Cadillac convertible, and an electric mini-bike for Chastity. Located at 364 St Cloud Road in Beverly Hills, their home, as spacious as it was—seven bedrooms, nine bathrooms—was only useful for a time. In the summer of '72, after an extensive period of haggling, it was replaced by a larger one: much larger.

"I drove Sonny crazy to get me this house," Cher told *The Los Angeles Times* after they moved in. "I told him I wanted this house five years before we owned it. Tony Curtis lived here and he invited us to his birthday party. After we left I said, 'Son, someday we're going to live in that house.' He said, 'Maybe you're right.'" She was. The Tuscan-style residence was built in the '30s and was originally part of a three-home compound called "Owlwood"—which during the 1950s included actress Jayne Mansfield's infamous "Pink Palace" (demolished before they moved in). For a time the residence was occupied by movie mogul Joseph Schenck—head of Twentieth Century Fox. Other occupants included Esther Williams and Sonja Henie.

The "single family" (12,201 square feet) home was located at 141 S. Carolwood Drive in Holmby Hills (an exclusive Beverly Hills enclave) and surrounded by rolling hills, lush gardens, a guest house, a tennis court, a swimming pool, a massive motor court and a six-car garage. Along with nine bedrooms and ten bathrooms, the home's many amenities included an imported-wood entry hall, marble fireplaces, crystal chandeliers, Sistine Chapel-like ceiling paintings, a state-of-the-art professional kitchen, and maid and butler's quarters. Celebrity decorator Ron Wilson (as opposed to de rigueur celebrity decorator Phyllis Morris, whose clientele was the rock and film community and whom Time christened "la dame du flash") was charged with furnishing the house and his carefully coordinated appointments included signed 17th-century antiques, Scottish lace curtains, English paintings, and French petit-point carpets. Giant indoor palm trees brought life into the museum-like surroundings.

Sonny and Cher's new home cost $750,000 and (after Wilson redecorated it) was featured in an impressive six-page spread in Architectural Digest. Speaking about the house several years after their separation, Sonny confessed: "I saw the place as a monument to our status, but in reality the house was large and cold and good only for hiding out and hiding troubles." Sonny and Cher's return to the top was reflected in more than just their extravagant home: Cher, herself, became a model for consumerism. Along with a truck-load of gold, silver, and turquoise Indian jewelry, in interviews she confessed to owning 300 pairs of shoes. "What do you do with them?" Sonny chided. "I wear them." "No you don't." When a writer asked Cher what her favorite possession was, she provided a sound bite: "I don't have a favorite possession. I want to own everything and everything I own is my favorite."

Some magazines tempered reports on Sonny and Cher's wealth—and there were many—by informing readers of their charitable inclinations. "Talking about their good works embarrasses them," observed writer Henry Ehrlich in Good Housekeeping. "With little fanfare they contribute to cerebral palsy, the Junior Braille Institute, asthmatic children, American prisoners of war and the Los Angeles County General Hospital."

With the financial rewards of their new success on vivid display—and their television success confirmed on all fronts (an illustrated Sonny and Cher appeared in Mad and Sick magazines, and a cartoon Sonny and Cher appeared on the popular Hanna-Barbera television series, Scooby Doo)—Sonny determined to reclaim their former position as top-selling recording stars. 1971's Sonny and Cher Live was their first post-TV show album. More a program tie-in than a new collection of tunes—it clocked in at a slim 45 minutes and generated no single—Sonny and Cher Live nevertheless offered up a recorded documentation of both the duo's nightclub act, the act that got them their TV deal, and contained a hidden gem: Cher's thrilling live rendition of "Once in a Lifetime," a power ballad (the precursor of many) about seizing the moment, which they certainly had.

Released on Kapp/MCA, the label that picked them up after their contract with Atco—their '60s benefactors—lapsed, Sonny and Cher Live sold respectably

(No. 35) and paved the way for yet another live set; 1973's *Sonny and Cher Live in Las Vegas Vol. 2*. Two (actually three, considering the fact that *Sonny and Cher Live in Las Vegas Vol. 2* was a double-album set) live albums proved a bit much, even for Sonny and Cher fans. The second collection, which contained Cher's live rendition of "Gypsys, Tramps and Thieves," only managed to make it to No. 175 on the charts. 1972's *All I Ever Need is You* (No. 8) was Sonny and Cher's first collection of original studio-recorded material. Nominated for a Grammy for Best Pop Vocal Performance by a Duo or Group (it lost out to the Carpenters for *Carpenters*), the first single "All I Ever Need is You"—a tune that shrewdly expressed the same sentiments as "I Got You Babe"—was a crisp, clean, radio-friendly ditty that went to No. 7 Pop and No. 1 Adult Contemporary. The follow-up single, the Sonny-penned "A Cowboy's Work is Never Done," went to No. 8 Pop. Both tunes were performed on *The Sonny and Cher Comedy Hour*.

Along with their live sets and their Grammy-nominated original set, a sure sign that Sonny and Cher were back came with the quick issuing and reissuing of compilations of their earlier work. The deluge of "new" Sonny and Cher product included *Sonny and Cher: The Two of Us*, *Sonny and Cher's Greatest Hits*, *Sonny and Cher: The Beat Goes On*, *The Best of Sonny and Cher* and *The Hits of Sonny and Cher*. The "team" albums were joined by all-Cher product: *Cher's Golden Greats*, *Cher Superpak Vol. 1*, *Cher Superpak Vol. 2*, *The Very Best of Cher Vol. 1*, *The Very Best of Cher Vol. 2*, *The Golden Hits of Cher*, *This is Cher*, *Cher Sings the Hits*, and *Cher / Greatest Hits*. Amidst the Sonny and Cher fanfare, and in the shadow of *The Sonny and Cher Comedy Hour*, Cher released five albums of original songs: *Cher* (a.k.a. *Gypsys, Tramps and Thieves*), *Foxy Lady*, *Bittersweet White Light*, *Half-Breed*, and *Dark Lady*. From these original albums nine singles were issued. When all was said and done, she would hit the No. 1 spot on the *Billboard* singles chart three times (twice more than Sonny and Cher).

"Gypsys, Tramps and Thieves" (B-side "He'll Never Know") was her first No. 1 solo hit. Culled from 1971's *Cher* (after the song hit the album's title was changed to *Gypsys, Tramps and Thieves*), it was produced by Tommy "Snuff" Garrett—former head of A&R at Liberty/Imperial, Cher's '60s label. In 1961 Garrett produced Bobby Vee's No. 1 "Take Good Care of My Baby." In 1965 he repeated the feat with Gary Lewis's "This Diamond Ring." In early 1971 Garrett was hired by MCA Records' production head, Johnny Musso, to expand on Cher's already established—via "You Better Sit Down Kids" and "Bang Bang (My Baby Shot Me Down)"—story-song successes. One of his considerations was Cher's new singing voice. Beginning with 1969's *3614 Jackson Highway*, the teenage angst, whine and twang that endeared her to a generation of "hippies," was replaced with a sultry, low-register contralto accentuated by a dancing, instantly recognizable (and easily parodied) vibrato. It was this new-sounding, updated, and more mature Cher that Garrett was commissioned, against Sonny's will but at Musso's insistence, to fashion hits for.

"Gypsys and White Trash" was submitted to Garrett following an open call for material he deemed suitable for a Cher single. "I wanted a song along the lines of [Dusty Springfield's] 'Son of a Preacher Man,'" the producer informed *Billboard*, and after an unknown writer named Bob Stone met with him and heard him out, he got just what he was looking for. "Gypsys, Tramps and Thieves" (a simple tweaking of Stone's original title; later, when re-issued, the spelling would change from "Gypsys" to "Gypsies") told the tale of the illegitimate daughter of a gypsy who was "born in the wagon of a travelin' show" and whose "momma used to dance for the money they'd throw." After leading a hard-knock life, the unnamed vagrant meets a man with a "smooth southern style," has an illegitimate child and ends up herself a gypsy—with her *own* daughter looking bewilderingly on—as *she* "danced and sang."

Heavily orchestrated with violins, violas, cellos, and a full rhythm section—even a symlin ("It's like a piano with the top torn off," Garrett later explained)—"Gypsys" was pop perfection; an easy-listening, radio-friendly opus that offered a peek into the transient world of illicit gambling and road-side entertainment. "'Gypsys' was a brilliant marriage between the singer and the song with an outstanding Al Capps arrangement," remembers Lenny Roberts, who was the sound engineer on five Cher and three Sonny and Cher albums. "That song, as well as the entire album, was recorded on a 3M eight-track machine [at the time, sixteen-track was top of the line]. 'If it's a hit you can record it on wire,' Snuff once told me, and that's just about what we did. Snuff knew that 'Gypsys' was a great song and an automatic smash no matter how it was recorded."

At the time of its release, "Gypsys, Tramps and Thieves" was the biggest-selling single in the history of MCA Records, and the song, which Cher performed to great effect on *The Sonny and Cher Comedy Hour*, was nominated for a Best Female Pop Vocal Performance Grammy (the Grammy went to Carole King's "Tapestry"). The second single from *Cher* was the No. 7 power ballad "The Way of Love" (B-side "Don't Put It On Me"). It was a tune that highlighted Cher's newly (if sometimes begrudgingly) accepted versatility; she was just as effective singing a formally orchestrated torch song as she was singing pop.

Cher peaked at No. 16 on the album charts and was followed a year later with 1972's *Foxy Lady*. Not as strong as its predecessor, and not as popular (No. 43), the album's two singles were the collection's strongest. "Living in a House Divided" (No. 22; B-side "One Honest Man"—pulled from the *Gypsys* sessions) was a fast-moving jingle that accurately summed up Sonny and Cher's private life at the time. The follow up, "Don't Hide Your Love" (B-side "The First Time"), peaked at No. 46. "I loved Cher's version of ['Don't Hide Your Love,']" says singer/songwriter Neil Sedaka, who along with Howard Greenfield wrote the music and lyrics. "My publisher sent her my demo and I wasn't even aware of it. The inspiration [for the song] came from the beat of Anne Murray's 'Snowbird.' I thought it was perfect for Cher's voice. She did a great interpretation. It had a call and response in the chorus—a Neil Sedaka trademark—and Cher kept it. The single is exactly like the demo I made of it."

Sonny produced and even took the LP's cover shot, and it was his idea to fashion an entire Cher album around one of *The Sonny and Cher Comedy Hour*'s strongest segments; Cher's solo in the spotlight. 1973's *Bittersweet White Light* was the resulting product, a collection of ten mid-century pop standards—including "I Got It Bad (And That Ain't Good)," "The Man That Got Away," and "Why Was I Born?"—that came and went so fast, and with so little promotion, most people didn't even know it existed.

One of those people was *Sonny and Cher Comedy Hour* musical director Jimmy Dale. "I never knew that the [musical] charts I did for Cher made it onto an album," says Dale, who had come to *The Sonny and Cher Comedy Hour* via his previous work with Chris Bearde and Allan Blye. "I arranged six [of the nine] songs she sings on that album expressly for her solo TV spots." Although Dale's charts (complete with his distinct musical embellishments) were used by the 40-members-plus orchestra Sonny hired to play on the album, he received credit for only a single tune, "By Myself." (CBS music librarian Ted Dale [no relation], was falsely credited as "conductor.")

"['By Myself'] was a good piece of work in which I took a slightly adventurous rhythmic approach," says Dale. "When Cher heard it first played she ran over, grabbed me and kissed me. That was the only time that kind of thing happened during the four years I worked with her on *The Sonny and Cher Comedy Hour*. She just loved it!"

Perhaps, but record buyers didn't. *Bittersweet White Light* only managed to make it to No. 140 on the album charts, while the collection's only single "Am I Blue?" (B-side "How Long Has This Been Going On?") languished at No. 111. Part of the problem, it was agreed, was Sonny's over-the-top, exceedingly florid and "too busy" production.

"I can't believe what Sonny did with the music, and, for that matter, Cher's voice," admits Dale today. "[*Bittersweet White Light*] is a bad reminder of the late 1960s, with goofy synthesizer lines, 'swamp' rhythms, too much echo, and Cher sounding more like Sonny than herself. It doesn't do any justice to her talent and it's a shame."

Sonny was, as it turned out, one of the few who genuinely enjoyed *Bittersweet White Light*. He made it clear in the LP's liner notes.

I was asked to describe this album in words, I don't know if I can, I'll try.
A singer should make you *feel*. Every time I listen to Cher on this album I

feel sad, I feel happy, I feel lonesome, I feel love but most of all I *feel*. For the ten years I've known Cher she's always wanted to make people *feel*. She did it this time. SHE DID IT ALL THIS TIME.

Sonny

The very same year that *Bittersweet White Light* flopped, Cher came back swinging with her second No. 1 smash hit—"Half-Breed." "I didn't have Cher at the time," Snuff Garrett informed *Rolling Stone* about "Half-Breed"'s genesis. "It sat in my desk for three or four months." (Shortly after producing *Cher* and *Foxy Lady*, Garrett and Sonny had a "creative disagreement" that resulted in Garrett's firing). "But, to me, nobody else in the world could do that song. I held it back for Cher because I knew it would be a smash for her."

Written by Mary Dean (with Cher in mind), "Half-Breed" (B-side "Melody"), was bombastic and catchy; a song in which Cher shouted the tale of a bi-racial outcast who isn't accepted by either of her parents' relatives—"The Indians said that I was white by law / The white man always called me 'Indian Squaw.'" In an exaggerated, kitschy way, "Half-Breed," complete with (stereotypical, but no less exciting) war drums and "tribal chants," spoke to the disenfranchised, unrecognized, and/or misunderstood.

"Half-Breed"'s follow-up single was an equally engaging (and gimmicky) tune called "Carousel Man" (B-side "When You Find Out Where You're Going, Let Me Know"). "I have no idea why that song didn't chart," says singer/ songwriter John Durrill, who would later write Cher's No. 1 hit "Dark Lady." "Back in Oklahoma, where I'm from, there were a lot of carnival workers. I had a fascination with merry-go-rounds and I thought the sounds of a carnival together with merry-go-round sounds provided great symbolism. Life just keeps going round and round and more often than not you end up right back where you started." Durrill's writing combined with Garrett's swirling production was stellar, but few got to hear it.

Another tune from *Half-Breed* that didn't find much of an audience was "The Greatest Song I Ever Heard." "That song was inspired by [Barbara Streisand's] 'My Coloring Book,'" remembers singer/songwriter Dick Holler, best known for Dion's 1968 hit "Abraham, Martin and John." "I wanted to write a song that paired emotions with colors and 'The Greatest Song I Ever Heard' was the end result. I must say that I wasn't crazy about Garrett's production, but I thought Cher did a fine job. She has a really great vocal instrument. I definitely thought that if the song had been released as a single it would have been a great success; a perfect vocal showcase." Buoyed by its No. 1 title song, Cher's *Half-Breed* album peaked at No. 28. "Dark Lady" (B-side "Two People Clinging to a Thread") was Cher's third and final Snuff Garrett-produced No. 1 single of the '70s. Like

"Gypsys" and "Half-Breed" before it, both the arrangement and, by necessity, Cher's vocal, were shamelessly melodramatic—it opened with a lulling violin solo before kicking into a rolling thunder pop jam. It also, cleverly, played on the growing, and through her songs and image on television *buoyed*, perception of Cher—with her poker face, olive complexion and waist-long blue-black hair—as "exotic other"; first a gypsy, then a "Half-Breed," now a "Dark Lady."

"The first time that Snuff heard it he told me 'that song will be No. 1,'" remembers John Durrill. "That really made me feel good." Even so, Garrett thought the song, which told the story of infidelity discovered at the hands of a mysterious fortune teller, could be improved.

"The first ending I had for the song had the main character discovering that her husband was cheating and then just running away," says Durrill. "That wasn't enough for Snuffy: he wanted me to take somebody out! I was in Japan at the time playing with my band [the Ventures] and I got a frantic call. It was Snuff and he was screaming, 'Kill him! You've got to kill him!' In the end I had the main character kill both her cheating husband and the woman he was cheating with! Everyone just loved it."

Dark Lady peaked at No. 69 and spawned two more singles. "Train of Thought" (B-side "Dixie Girl"), the album's second single, was a song that everyone—Snuff Garrett, Lenny Roberts and the song's writer/composer Alan O'Day (best known for his *own* No. 1 hit "Undercover Angel")—was sure would be a smash. "How and why a song makes it to No. 1 no one really knows," says O'Day, whose forte was multi-layered and oblique story songs like "Angie Baby," a song intended for Cher but recorded and brought to No. 1 by Helen Reddy.

"'Train of Thought' is the story of a guy who finds out his wife is cheating and decides to kill her—but then, at the last minute, kills himself," explains O'Day. "When I first heard Cher's version I thought [Garrett's] arrangement was a bit fast and I wasn't crazy about the toy train whistle they used at the beginning but, I must admit, it certainly was a good 'pop' production." "Train of Thought" peaked at No. 27.

"I Saw a Man and He Danced with His Wife" (B-side "I Hate to Sleep Alone"), *Dark Lady*'s third and final single, sparked less interest than "Train of Thought." Another John Durrill-written tune (he also wrote *Dark Lady*'s "Dixie Girl"), the song presented Cher in arresting voice, surrounded by a big band, Glenn Miller-esque music production.

"I first approached Snuff with the chorus of 'I Saw a Man' and he just loved it," says Durrill. "So I went back and finished it. That song was one of those airplay hits [No. 42]. People loved it and called in and requested it all the time, but it just didn't sell. Regardless, I thought it was a wonderful song. I ran into Snuff a while ago and 'I Saw a Man and He Danced with His Wife' came up. Snuff said that he didn't get it right—that's why it didn't hit bigger. I told him he was absolutely wrong. The song and the *Dark Lady* album are perfect exactly the way they are." Others agreed. *Rolling Stone* said of *Dark Lady*, "Cher's voice is so attractive that one senses possible future direction, e.g., a commitment to country-soul..." *Creem* surmised, "*Dark Lady* is the best album Cher has done since *3614 Jackson Highway*."And *Billboard* claimed that "this set more than any she has done before, exposes just how versatile this lady really is."

To no one's surprise, all of Cher's '70s hits played well on TV. When she sang "Gypsys," she, literally, stood in front of "a wagon in a travelin' show." For "Half-Breed," she mounted a horse—a *real* horse—in full (Bob Mackie) war bonnet and sequined loin cloth. For "Dark Lady," she donned a black satin gown adorned with a bejeweled tulle mermaid bottom and topped off with a bizarre, gargantuan tulle veil/headdress.

In 2000, Cher talked at length about her Snuff Garrett years.

"I remember playing 'Dark Lady' for David [Geffen]... and Joni Mitchell was there, and a whole bunch of cool people. And David said, 'That song is horrible! Do they have to put it out?' and I said, 'Yeah, Dave they do.'" Asked what her favorite song from the period was she replied without hesitation: "'The Way of Love.' It was a really big hit for me and people really loved it. They still love it. I put it back in my show the last time I toured because people kept asking for it." When asked about the efficient way in which her early music was produced, Cher said: "I could do a whole album with Snuffy in three days. I'd sing each song through two or three times and, if we got it, it was on to the next one. You have to understand what it was like. We were on the road, I was recording, and we were doing *The Sonny and Cher Comedy Hour*—all at the same time! I did the best I could fitting each obligation into what little time was allotted."

But on *The Sonny and Cher Comedy Hour* Cher sang more than her Snuff Garrett-produced hits. She sang soft rock (the Beatles' "Yesterday," Bread's "If"), jazz ("Ain't Misbehavin'," "I Got it Bad [And that Ain't Good]"), standards ("The Man that Got Away," "Body and Soul"), blues ("Can't Help Lovin' Dat Man of Mine," "Cry Me a River"), torch songs ("Am I Blue?," "How Long Has This Been Going On?"), top 40 ("He Ain't Heavy, He's My Brother," "A Song For You") and even entered into the world of politics ("Working Together"). (Curiously, Cher opted not to sing some of the singles that her record company released. "Living in a House Divided," "Don't Hide Your Love," "Carousel Man," "Train of Thought" and "I Saw a Man and He Danced with His Wife," were never performed on *The Sonny and Cher Comedy Hour*.)

Cher's televised musical output, as varied and eclectic as it may have been, was viewed by different people through different lenses. "Cher's performances [on *The Sonny and Cher Comedy Hour*] are perfectly imperfect," says a sound technician who worked on the show. "If you look at the old clips the sound is abhorrent; it's tinny TV studio sound—not recording studio sound. The background singers are there, not to support Cher's vocals, but to cover up sound deficiencies—which include Cher's intonation problems as well as her missed notes. Sometimes when she drops to a lower register you can't understand a word she's saying. That would never happen today. Today there is Auto-Tune to correct wrong notes, the quality of sound in TV studios is seriously considered, and viewer expectations are much, much higher."

At the same time that Cher's solo hits were, quite clearly, setting her apart from—and above—the Sonny and Cher act, family-oriented magazines like *Ladies' Home Journal, Redbook, Good Housekeeping* and *Life* were pointedly—if only in print—keeping them glued together. Time and again, and with Sonny and Cher's complicity, the press expanded their joint public profile and made them a unit—what Cher would later call "the Siamese twin thing."

In fact, writer Starkey Flythe Jr. called his *Saturday Evening Post* article "That Amazing Creature the SonnyAndCher," and made the point that, to their audience, both TV watchers and music buyers, they were perceived as one and the same; "happily married" parents first, and performers second, who had weathered some difficult times but still managed to come out on top. What was under reported, especially in the "elite" press, was that the old difficult times had been replaced with new ones. Although Sonny didn't much notice, the long journey through the '60s had dramatically changed his wife. When she first met him she welcomed his guidance and paternalism, but time changed both her world view and her needs. The sixteen-year-old waif had become a grown woman, someone who had suffered four miscarriages (and knew "the anguish of having to make a decision not to have a child"), given birth, dealt with her husband's admitted ongoing infidelity, and, most pressingly, felt creatively and emotionally unfulfilled. "First I was Sonny's girlfriend, then I was his wife and, later, Chastity's mother," Cher said in 1975. "But, throughout it all, to Sonny, I was really never more or less than the older child in our family."

There was another problem. Even though Cher had rationalized the heavy workload necessary to maintain their newfound success—in 1973 she told *TV Guide*, "People say, 'How can you stand a whole summer on the road, all the one-night stands?' I thrive on it"—all the hard work took its toll on her. Just a year after the rosy portrait she presented to *TV Guide*, she verbalized a dramatically different view: "I want to take some time off and enjoy our success. We've got a schedule that would break a truck driver."

"He was very, very domineering," *Carol Burnett Show* writer Bart Andrews informed writer Mark Bego about Sonny's approach to dealing with his wife at this time. Andrews and Sonny and Cher had adjacent offices at CBS. "Even beyond fighting with [Cher], he was always telling her what to do, when to do it... and he always had to come out the winner."

Lark Baskerville, a journalism student and press-relations representative at L.A.'s Greek Theater who stayed at Sonny and Cher's home from April 1972 through January 1973 when they were on tour, also offered her frank behind-the-scenes view of things to the press. "By the time I moved out in '73 I noticed a big change [in Sonny]. He seemed to have a case of what I call superstar-itus. Even his relationship with his staff became strained. Sonny and I were once very good friends. We'd talk for hours about things and I would talk to Cher a great deal too. Eventually, though, I realized, for myself, that I could no longer communicate with him." So she moved out. She wasn't going to be the only one.

4

I GOT SOMEONE ELSE BABE

Without a doubt, 1973 was the most tumultuous year in the lives of Sonny and Cher. Although the couple had made an agreeable Best Soundtrack presentation on February 23, at the Academy Awards—holding hands, smiling for the cameras, appearing to be content—and later at the Actor's Studio Salute to Merle Oberon, the tabloid headlines told a different story. As early as November 1972, when the Bonos began but didn't complete an engagement at the Sahara Hotel and Casino in Las Vegas, the rumors started to swirl. "Sonny and Cher Fighting!" "Sonny and Cher Cancel Las Vegas Engagement!" and "Sonny and Cher: The Great Pretenders," painted the portrait of a relationship on the rocks.

And it looked like their hold on the record charts was too. Although no one much noticed, 1973 saw the release of what would turn out to be Sonny and Cher's final album. The laboriously titled *Mama Was a Rock and Roll Singer, Papa Used to Write All Her Songs* was issued during the summer months and didn't even make the top 100 (it peaked at No. 132). An edited version of the ten-song collection's title track (for the single, the grandiose 9:39 song was divided into two parts) peaked at No. 77. The single and album would mark "Sonny and Cher's" final chart entry.

Looking back, the album is remembered not for Sonny's noisy, long-winded, and apparently self-referential opus "Mama Was a Rock and Roll Singer, Papa Used to Write All Her Songs," or for the chillingly true to life uncharted second single "The Greatest Show On Earth" (B-side "You Know Darn Well")—the tale of an unhappy couple who put on a good show for their friends—but for the album's photos. On the front cover Sonny and Cher posed, surrounded by stuffed animals and dolls in Chastity's well-appointed bedroom. On the back the couple, stone-faced and with an air of obligation, sprawled out on their enormous four-poster bed.

Still, engineer Lenny Roberts (who is thanked in the liner notes: "special thanks to Lenny for his ideas and patience") holds the album in high regard. "This was Bono at his absolute best," says Roberts. "He booked probably 45 musicians into these two small studios. When he asked me where we were going to put the (surprise) Hawaiian stick players, I hadn't a clue. They ended up between the two studios in an area that was used for delivery. It was a session that I'll never forget. And I loved the record."

Although it failed to chart, "Real People" (B-side "Somebody"), an MCA single not included on any of their albums, is considered by many to be one of their very best recordings.

Almost a year to the date that Sonny and Cher cancelled their Sahara appearance, the same thing happened a second time—at the same hotel. Yet another cancelled appearance, their duties as presenters at the Golden Globe Awards, threw additional light on private matters (at the Sonny and Cher-less Golden Globes, Cher tied with *All in the Family*'s Jean Stapleton for the Best TV Actress Musical/Comedy award).

Cher told columnist Rona Barrett that on October 26, 1972, following a particularly ugly argument, she knew that her marriage was finished. "I went to San Francisco for the night but I felt too guilty. I figured that running away wasn't the best way to do it so I returned two days later." Upon her return Cher agreed to continue performing as "Sonny and Cher" under one condition: out of the spotlight they would lead separate lives. And, for a time at least, they did. "I was so happy to be free," Cher told *Ladies' Home Journal*. "There were so many things in our relationship that I thought were so oppressive to me, that I started going out immediately with a guy in our band [guitarist Bill Hamm] and having the time of my life." When the relationship with Hamm came to an end Cher became involved with songwriter/keyboardist David Paich (whose "David's Song" appeared on 1973's *Half-Breed*), who would later become one of the founding members of the band Toto.

Hamm and Paich may have been the first to take Sonny's place in Cher's personal life, but her attraction to musicians had been established many years earlier. As reported in Mark Bego's book *Cher*, when Sonny and Cher made their first trip to England to promote "I Got You Babe," much to Sonny's annoyance, Cher chatted up John Lennon and Paul McCartney at a party. Later, on their British tour, she flirted with Roger Daltry and her manager Charlie Green told Bego that she had an "eye" for Rod Stewart. "There's something about men in rock 'n' roll that I have an affinity for," Cher later admitted. And the attraction would continue throughout the years.

"When you enter into a total commitment with a sixteen-year-old girl I suppose you've got to admit to yourself that somewhere along the line that girl is going to ask herself if there isn't a part of her life that she's missed," Sonny later observed. "I think our eventual breakup was as simple as that."

During the waning final year and a half of their marriage, Sonny, too, was romantically busy with outsiders. After dating a young woman whom Sonny officially identified as "Joyce Smith," as well as a slew of dancer/model/actresses, Sonny became seriously involved with Connie Foreman (who looked strikingly like his first wife Donna), a rusty-haired, blue-eyed cocktail waitress and student at UCLA. Connie was identified in the press as Sonny and Cher's "secretary," and she and Sonny remained together, on and off, for two years. "My first knowledge of trouble between Sonny and Cher came at the conclusion of one of their Vegas gigs," remembers Lenny Roberts. "On the plane ride home Sonny and Cher didn't sit together." Instead Sonny sat with Connie. "Mid-flight Sonny came over to me and asked me to take Connie home when we landed at LAX. My assumption was that he wanted to be seen getting off the plane and going home with Cher."

Sonny's August 21, 1973 journal entry:
We still have a television show, and the public still thinks that we're married, so we're both very much involved in our careers. Connie and I live together as husband and wife. But my public wife is still Cher in order to maintain all the things I want right now. That's the way it has to be.

It was Sonny's relationship with Connie Foreman that blew the lid off of Sonny and Cher's clandestine separation and "business understanding." When pictures of Sonny and Connie dining intimately at L.A.'s Nicky Blair's and Ollie Hammond's Steak House surfaced and were published in movie magazines, the gig was up. Secretaries don't usually get dressed up and go out for a night on the town with their boss. They also don't usually live with their employer. And at the same time that the pictures of Sonny and Connie appeared in print, Cher had met and was dating a second David; record mogul David Geffen.

David Lawrence Geffen was born on February 21, 1943 in the Borough Park section of Brooklyn, New York. Before his introduction to Cher (they had informally met years earlier when he was briefly associated with Phil Spector) Geffen had already made his name as a formidable manager, talent scout and businessman. He was best known for discovering Jackson Browne (whose song "The Wizard of L.A." payed tribute to him), Laura Nyro (who was, for a time, his girlfriend), Crosby, Stills, Nash and Young, and Joni Mitchell (who also wrote a song about him; "Free Man in Paris"). When he met Cher for the second time, Geffen was the Chairman of the Board of Elektra/Asylum Records.

Cher and David Geffen first "connected" on September 23, 1973 at the opening night of the Roxy nightclub in Hollywood (an establishment in which Geffen was a co-investor). The opening night was a glamorous rock-world event. Along with seeing the venue's premier act, Neil Young, Cher spent time in On the Rox, an exclusive "members only" club located directly above the Roxy auditorium. Cher wasn't a member but, nevertheless, she had no trouble getting in.

Geffen was, on sight, smitten with Cher. Following a first date, which took place at Geffen's home the night after their Roxy meeting (and included producer/manager Lou Adler as a go-between), the two began seeing more and more of one another. "It didn't take long for me to like David," recalled Cher. "I could talk to him. Not only could I talk to him but he seemed to really be listening." During their very first evening together at Geffen's home that's exactly what they did; talk. Cher told him about her and Sonny's secret separation and spoke at length about her desire to transcend what she believed was her thoroughly mediocre recording work. Though she was an unqualified success, Cher told Geffen that her hit novelty tunes along with her role as Sonny's arms-folded, tart-mouthed television sidekick left her discontented, and her station in the music industry ("TV's tent show queen," wrote one reviewer) left her feeling self-conscious, stifled and hemmed in.

Geffen—whom *Newsweek* called "Hollywood's golden boy"—and Cher's relationship served them *both* well. The couple's newsworthiness (and Geffen's pull, especially in the music business) was on clear display at the 1974 Grammy Awards—Cher's much-photographed first public appearance without Sonny. Even though she wasn't nominated for anything that year, Cher and Geffen were given front-row center seats—directly in front of Bette Midler and rows ahead of Diana Ross—both of whom *were* nominated. At the event, Cher presented an award with *Kojak*'s Telly Savalas—who was supplementing his TV cop duties with a singing career (Cher's producer Snuff Garrett produced Savalas's self-titled debut album). When they walked to the podium Savalas turned to the crowd and quipped, "Sonny couldn't make it!"

The 1974 Grammy Awards turned out to be one of Cher's most photographed public appearances. Pictures from the event—Cher with Geffen, Cher hugging a jubilant Stevie Wonder, Cher with host Andy Williams and multi-Grammy-winning Roberta Flack—appeared everywhere. And Cher looked radiant. Dressed in a butterfly motif ensemble complete with long flowing hair and bare midriff, Cher's was the only picture that really mattered (to the press) that evening. (The following year, *Ms.* magazine used an illustration of Cher, wearing her butterfly ensemble, on its cover.)

"David knows this business better than anyone else," Cher said at the time, and part of his new "business" was taking the reins of Cher's career. "It's not that I want to do it," he assured *Esquire*, "but this is the woman I love... it's not a client. She needs help right now." Not only did Geffen take charge of Cher's career, he also took her on trips—Aspen, Hawaii—and presented her with diamond-encrusted gifts; a Rolex watch, a bracelet and, most notably, a ring. "I asked him to buy it because I wanted to feel someone loved me enough to give me something to wear," Cher explained. "My finger was so naked, because it had been covered for so many years. It's not really an engagement or wedding ring. It's just something to keep my finger warm." As the Cher/Geffen courtship intensified—and with rumors of marriage circulating ("I've traded one short ugly guy for another," Cher quipped), it was reported that Cher, in an effort to please her new Jewish companion, was considering converting to Judaism. "Converting [to Judaism] is not an impossibility," Cher explained. "I do have an open mind on the subject. But all I'm doing right now is learning and acquiring a better understanding of what Judaism is all about. David's family is devoutly Jewish. They accepted me with open arms, great warmth and love. But it occurred to me that they might not be comfortable with him marrying outside of his faith. They never said that, but I could understand them feeling that way. Right now I'm just looking into it."

During the early part of their relationship, with an eye toward pointing Cher in the direction of her revised career goals, Geffen asked to review Cher's contractual obligations as part of the "Sonny and Cher" act. The record mogul's assessment was scathing. He pointed out that all the money that Cher earned as a solo recording star—the bulk of the money the duo earned from records, especially in the '70s —was divided up *equally* by both Sonny and Cher. Furthermore, the company that bore her name, Cher Enterprises, had her contractually bound until January 1, 1977; forbade her to work for or collect monies from any outside source; and stipulated that any personal checks that Cher wrote (she never wrote checks, she paid cash or charged) were automatically null and void unless they were personally approved by Sonny and/ or his business partner/lawyer Irwin O. Spiegel. (Cher would later say that the most galling detail of her contractual obligations was the two-week "no more and no less" vacation that she was guaranteed.)

After examining Cher's personal documents, Geffen encouraged Cher to renegotiate with Sonny. When he refused, Geffen advised her to bring both her personal and professional relationship with him to a complete close.

And she did. Following Geffen's advice, Cher hired one of Hollywood's most powerful lawyers, Milton "Mickey" Rudin—Frank Sinatra's lawyer and the lawyer who handled Lucille Ball's complicated personal and professional split from husband and business partner Desi Arnaz. Acting on his client's behalf, Rudin, along with David Geffen, immediately notified Tony Fantozzi—Sonny and Cher's booker at the William Morris Agency—that personal matters between Sonny and Cher made it "impossible" for the duo to complete previously agreed upon "Sonny and Cher" commitments. "Geffen went to Fantozzi and screwed things up for me," Sonny told the press at the time. "Cher was with him so that indicated approval on her part." Also notified were executives at Sonny and

Cher's record label MCA, CBS-TV, Proctor & Gamble, Revlon and American Home Products (*Sonny and Cher Comedy Hour* sponsors), and a lengthy list of concert halls—most importantly Lee Guber and Shelly Gross, owners of a string of cross-country Music Fairs (theaters-in-the-round), that had paid Sonny and Cher in advance, sold tickets, and done promotion for future appearances.

"Cher Bono has filed suit against her estranged husband Sonny, charging that he and lawyer Irwin O. Spiegel, had tricked her into 'involuntary servitude,'" wrote *The New York Times*. "Mrs. Bono stated in February 27 court papers that Sonny and his lawyer had induced her to sign a contract giving them all rights to her future earnings, even if her marriage to Mr. Bono were dissolved. Cher was 'unsophisticated in business matters,' she said, and the defendants took advantage of that fact."

Cher's official divorce petition had actually been preceded by a litigious action by Sonny. Three weeks earlier, on February 14, Sonny filed for "legal separation" from his wife. At the time of Sonny's filing, the final episode of *The Sonny and Cher Comedy Hour*'s fifth season had yet to be filmed and the duo was just weeks away from having to perform four heavily-promoted and exceedingly lucrative ($150,000) live shows at the Houston Astrodome, America's largest arena. "I just don't understand how Sonny and Cher's type of act—an act where each keeps putting the other down—can help but get to them," observed a Sonny and Cher band member at the time. "It's bound to carry over somewhat into their offstage actions and attitudes toward one another."

Writer George Carpozi was in attendance at one of Sonny and Cher's Astrodome shows. "Onstage they lacked enthusiasm," remembered Carpozi. "Their patented crossfire of putdowns was a poor imitation of what audiences had gotten accustomed to seeing. They hardly spoke to each other, sang fewer duets, and seemed to be trying to avoid each other onstage as much as possible."

"There is no bitterness whatsoever between Sonny and Cher," publicist Dick Grant assured the public (and Sonny and Cher's backers) as the negative reviews for the Astrodome shows began to pile up. "Yes, they have some personal difficulties, but their problems are not affecting their work and they will keep all their other in-person commitments." It was wishful thinking. The Astrodome shows, as joyless, perfunctory and disjointed as they may have been, were the final four performances that Sonny and Cher, as a married act, would ever perform.

Astonishingly, especially given today's particularly litigious society, once official notifications were made and Cher's lawsuit against Sonny made it clear that the couple had advanced from a legal separation to a divorce, the larger part of Sonny and Cher's contracts were negated with little more than a second glance. A publicly squabbling and headed-for-divorce-court Sonny and Cher just didn't (at least at *this* time) seem to make much sense to anybody. With David

Geffen's assurance to CBS executives that he would give them first dibs on a solo Cher series, CBS canceled *The Sonny and Cher Comedy Hour*—even though they could have kept them working for another two years. MCA, too, agreed to release Cher from her contractual obligations—including all of her "Sonny and Cher" commitments—with the relatively friendly request that she simply finish the final tracks on her half-complete *Dark Lady* album. (Determined to get the most out of their final association with Cher, MCA mounted an expansive publicity campaign—posters, magazine ads, in-store life size stand-up displays—for *Dark Lady*.)

But not *all* of Sonny and Cher's contracts were torn up. On the advice of his attorney, Sonny filed a "breach of contract" lawsuit against Cher that asked for $24 million in damages (later reduced to $4 million). "Sonny and Cher remain good friends," assured Sonny's lawyer Howard L. Winton, "Sonny's lawsuit is purely business. Yes, it has to be resolved; there's a corporation that can't be thrown out and broken contracts that have to be settled. But this paperwork doesn't enter into Sonny and Cher's personal feelings for one another."

Throughout 1974, and through to the end of 1975, separate lawsuits by Sonny and Cher were filed, withdrawn, amended and re-filed. They included career-centered filings (a $14 million loss of income claim filed by Sonny), residency (who would live in their Holmby Hills mansion; in what Sonny called a "guerilla action" Sonny claimed that Cher, Geffen and Chastity, who had been living in a rented Malibu home, commandeered the mansion accompanied by two firearm-wielding security guards), financial allowances (Cher was awarded $25,000 monthly alimony along with $1,500 child support), and custody battles (Sonny, in an emotional court appearance, made a plea for dual custody—six months with Sonny and six months with Cher). When all was said and done—and a lot was said, not just by Cher, who was raking her soon-to-be former husband over the coals in interviews, but also by Sonny, who, in an effort to reduce Cher's alimony payments, provided the court with a list of her "extravagant" expenditures ($ 6,000 a month on clothing, $900 a month for her psychiatrist, $600 a month for her manicurist)—Cher retained full custody of Chastity and remained in residence at their home, which she immediately put up for sale.

Cher's very public custody battle for Chastity was one of those stories that "had legs." The March 9, 1974 edition of *The National Star* (which appeared on newsstands before custody negotiations) expanded on the story and featured a first-hand, uncharacteristically bitter interview with Sonny. More damaging than Sonny's comments about David Geffen—whom he said he wanted "to string from the nearest tree"—were his observations about Cher's in-need-of-help mothering skills. "Cher became cold and distant [following their agreed upon secret separation]. She seemed to be drifting into another orbit. If we were sitting at the dinner table with Chastity and Chas asked her a question, she would look at the kid as if she didn't know her." Sonny also informed *Star* columnist Michael St. John (the two met at the Polo Lounge of the Beverly Hills Hotel) that on New Year's Day 1973, Chastity's repressed emotions spilled out into the open. "Suddenly Chas, for no reason at all, picked up her dish of food and threw it at Cher... a half-hour later [after Sonny sent Chastity to bed], Chas was standing in the den-room door, crying and screaming, 'I love you mommy—I love you.' Cher didn't know how to cope with this. Whenever these outbursts occurred, she started yelling at *me* about doing something to discipline 'the child.'"

The National Star interview, which Sonny, for a time at least, denied giving— even threatening to sue—was picked up by the mainstream press. *Rolling Stone* brought the story to the music world and even reproduced the tabloid's cover. *Motion Picture*'s John J. Miller contacted Sonny to ask him about the ugly details of the *Star* piece—which included Sonny's revelation that a turning point in their relationship occurred when, during lovemaking, Cher called out another man's name.

"To take it [the *Star* article] apart specifically—I really couldn't do that," Bono told Miller. "I mean, to start—it's all really silly." But the *Star* piece did do damage. Following its publication a steady and alarming stream of anti-Cher mail began to make its way into Cher's CBS-TV mailbox. Cher did lose out to Sonny on one front: Sonny's loss of income claim. The court, disagreeing with Cher's rebuttal that she was "uninformed and unsophisticated in business matters," ruled that her signature on documents, no matter what she claimed or how it got there, was legal and binding. Cher was ordered to pay Sonny $4 million (later reduced to $1.2 million).

In 2010, 35 years after the fact, Cher talked frankly with *Vanity Fair* about her complicated breakup. "If Sonny had agreed to just disband Cher Enterprises... just split it down the middle, 50-50... and start all over again, I would have never, ever, left." When asked if she believed Sonny regretted his decision not to do so she surmised: "I'm sure he must have."

With David Geffen's help, by mid-1974, "Sonny and Cher" were very much a thing of the past. Newspapers and magazines confirmed it. Plastered everywhere were pictures of Cher—on the arm of Geffen—at the Grammys and Oscars, out on the town at glamorous premieres (*Chinatown, Lenny, The Rocky Horror Picture Show*), theatrical openings (*The Magic Show*), concerts (the Doobie Brothers, Diana Ross), benefits (James Stacy, the Union tribute to Henry Fonda), and exclusive parties (Elliott and Jennifer Gould, Bob Dylan's birthday).

A late-night trip that Cher and Geffen made to Fatburgers, a popular hot-dog stand on La Cienega Boulevard in Hollywood, also made the papers. That evening, with time on their hands and with Jack in the Box and Musso and Frank's Grill closed, the two drove up in Cher's turquoise Ferrari (her midnight-blue Jensen Interceptor, a high-end limited edition British-made sports car, remained at home), ordered two chili burgers, and attempted to pay with what was convenient: a hundred-dollar bill. When the waiter told them he didn't have change Cher replied, "Keep it! You've got the best burgers in L.A.!" With that, the couple made a dramatic screeching U-turn, tooted their horn, and headed back up into the sanctuary of the Hollywood Hills.

"Me and a girlfriend were visiting New York for the very first time," remembers Barbara Johnson, who got to observe Cher up close during a performance of the Broadway musical *Grease*. "At intermission, when the lights came up, we saw all these people gather around someone and then we recognized it was Cher! She was with David Geffen. Well, after the show, we were standing outside the theater and a limo pulled up to the curb. A minute later Cher popped out of the theater. She had on a hot-pink halter top, black satin pants and strappy silver high-heeled sandals; she looked just gorgeous. I remember thinking that she seemed really happy. She and Geffen were laughing and enjoying themselves. They made a really nice couple."

By the summer of '74, the big question on everyone's lips wasn't "Are Sonny and Cher really breaking up?" (An episode of the TV show *Good Times* included the joke delivered by matriarch Esther Rolle to her two bickering children: "You two get along like Sonny and Cher!") but "What's going to happen now?" Cher, it was assumed, would be the first to have her own solo TV show. Not only was she a music star, she was a fashion magazine favorite who had appeared on the cover of *Vogue* not once, but a total of five different times. "My dear, I believe your style, fashion sense, and distinct look will be particularly attractive to the contemporary woman," *Vogue*'s editor Diana Vreeland assured her. And it was.

But much to everyone's surprise, it was Sonny Bono, not Cher, who was the first to secure a post-*Sonny and Cher Comedy Hour* television deal. "I'm a late bloomer," Cher said when asked to respond to the fact that Sonny was going to beat her back to the airwaves. "I wish him nothing but the best."

5

LAUGH AT ME

Two facts helped pave the way for Sonny to be signed to the ABC television network as a solo variety-show host: producers Chris Bearde and Allan Blye had already proven they could successfully manage a variety show—they were *The Sonny and Cher Comedy Hour* producers—and, in the fall of 1974, ABC cancelled ten Prime-Time ratings losers. "For a while there I wondered whether or not I was going to be able to make it alone," Sonny said. "After our divorce, I kind of came out looking like the bad guy. But now, with my new show about to air, I think I really have a chance."

"Sonny has always been way ahead of his time," producer George Schlatter recalled. Schlatter had honed his skills ten years earlier on *The Judy Garland Show* and came into his own with the creation of the groundbreaking comedy *Laugh-In*—on which Sonny and Cher had guest starred. "People don't realize that the whole free form of Sonny's music was an innovation. Revolutionary really," assured Schlatter. "The rhythm patterns, the melody patterns, were ahead of everyone. Did you know Sonny is a great dancer? He studied ballet! He leaps, he's sensational and he's never even used it yet. He also has a trained voice—an operatic voice. He's never used that either. He's saving all that for the next cycle, the next surprise. The talent is endless..."

Speaking 35 years after the fact in her book *Secrets of a Style Diva*, Sonny's ex-wife Susie Coelho also sang the praises of Sonny's virtues. "Sonny never learned to play the piano or any other instrument for that matter. Some say he could barely sing. But he refused to let that stand in his way. He would get an inspiration in the middle of the night, go down to the piano, and bang out a song with the only five chords he knew. Sonny believed in himself when no one else did. That is one of the greatest lessons I learned from him."

The Sonny Comedy Revue, as it was called, made its debut on Sunday,

September 22, 1974—a mere three and half months after the final episode of *The Sonny and Cher Comedy Hour* aired. Heralded in magazines and television ads as "the comedy show that all America is talking about," ABC had high hopes for Sonny's show. And, at the time at least, their high hopes made sense; Sonny was inheriting almost the entire *Sonny and Cher Comedy Hour* staff. Along with proven producers Bearde and Blye, director Art Fisher, and series regulars Freeman King, Teri Garr, Peter Cullen, Ted Ziegler, Billy Van and Murray Langston also remained for what was essentially *The Sonny and Cher Comedy Hour* without Cher. Sonny confirmed it. He told *TV Guide*, "We have all the same players... all that is except one!"

"Sonny will retain the same image he had on *The Sonny and Cher Comedy Hour*—a kind of down-trodden, sad-sack kind of figure," said Chris Bearde at the time. "And we don't intend to hide the divorce either. We want to hit it head on. We want to be honest."

But honesty, especially in variety-show television, was an oxymoron. Was Sonny going to sit down and discuss his ongoing litigation with Cher? Was he going to frankly talk about his new, extremely precarious position in the entertainment industry?

The list of celebrities who agreed to lend a hand on Sonny's show (many of whom had already worked with Sonny on *The Sonny and Cher Comedy Hour*) included Glen Campbell, Frankie Avalon, the Hudson Brothers, Barbara Eden, Sally Struthers, Charo, Twiggy, Joey Heatherton, and the Penthouse Pet of the Year. More impressive, and an indication of the kinds of guests Sonny, himself, wanted, was the signing of some of soul music's biggest stars: the Spinners, the Staple Singers, the Temptations, the Jackson Five (featuring Michael Jackson), Rufus (featuring Chaka Khan), Billy Preston, and Smokey Robinson.

The custom-tailored material that Blye and Bearde supplied Sonny with played off of, and spoofed, his already established public persona. There was "Great Lovers" (Sonny as Casanova, Julius Caesar, et al.), "The Bono Brigade" (Sonny as an army private), "The Little Man" (a silent bit), and "The Bono Italian Family Theater" (a recurring musical-comedy production). Additionally (on-hand from *The Sonny and Cher Comedy Hour*) were the "Sonny's Pizza" comedy sketches, and the elaborate comedy-opera finales that featured the entire cast in period costumes. But even with original comedy material and characters, top-name guest stars, and a desire to give the public what they wanted, *The Sonny Comedy Revue* never clicked with viewers. It wasn't that his show was particularly bad—certainly no worse than any number of other variety shows and specials that came and went at the time, including *The Hudson Brothers Show*, *The Bobby Darin Show*, *The Andy Williams Show* and two other variety programs, one called *Hamburgers* and one called *American Bag* (the latter two produced by Blye and Bearde)—it was that Sonny's show seemed to rely too much on a litany of particularly unfunny references to Cher's all too obvious absence.

Two numbers stood out, and not in a good way. On the series' premiere guest Howard Cosell performed an obtuse lip-synch to Cher's "Half-Breed." The "musical bit" was both un-musical and unfunny. So was Sonny's (maudlin at best) performance of his latest composition—a quickie MCA single release that didn't chart—entitled "Our Last Show" (B-side "Classified 1A"). The number, meant to touch the hearts of viewers and reference Sonny's own feelings, left viewers feeling uncomfortable and unsure about his vocal talents.

"Together, Howard Cosell and Sonny Bono offer great hope to all the talent-less people of the world," wrote Kay Gardella in *The Daily News*. "It has always been our contention that Sonny Bono has absolutely no talent. To call Sonny's appeal 'Chaplinesque' [which promotional material did] is blasphemy. Sonny's hour, a blend of skits and song, easily drives the last nail into the coffin of variety shows." *The Washington Post*'s critic Don Shirley was a bit more charitable; but not much: "If Sonny's likeable grins and frowns are somewhat limited as comedic tools, at least he is blessed with the same resident cast from his old show [*The Sonny and Cher Comedy Hour*], and all he has to do is react to the Italian or short-guy jokes cracked by his cast and by the program's guest stars." An unanticipated swipe at Sonny and his show came from one of his guests. "I'm doing it [Sonny's show] because of Arthur, and *not* because of Sonny," Sally Struthers frankly informed columnist Army Archerd. Struthers, of *All in the Family* fame, was romantically involved with Art Fisher, the show's director, and had only agreed to appear on the program as a special favor to him.

Everyone, of course, was waiting for Cher's assessment. "I didn't like it," she told *The New York Post*. "I didn't think [Blye and Bearde] gave him a fair shake. They still did the 'Cher' jokes on him. They couldn't get going because they kept him under the weight of us." Cher also revealed that, as a sign of support (she attended a taping), she wanted to appear on the premiere episode of the show, but CBS (whom she was in discreet negotiations with) refused to let her.

The Sonny Comedy Revue's final episode aired on December 22, 1974—an unlucky thirteen weeks after it premiered.

Viewed today, Sonny's solo series holds up well enough. The comedy vignettes are fast-moving and brief; the costumes and sets are outrageous—both theatrical and colorful; and, just like on *The Sonny and Cher Comedy Hour*, the program makes clever use of animation, graphics and an upbeat musical soundtrack. If there is an ongoing problem, it is the decision to constantly belittle Sonny. An excerpt from the tenth episode was typical.

ZIEGLER: [To Frankie Avalon] Frankie Avalon, king of the Beach Movies. Wow, were those ever great flicks. Those scenes between you and Annette

Funicello, moon-lit nights on the beach. Just you and her in a tight embrace. Boy do I miss those.

AVALON: *You* miss them? I'm here working with Sonny Bono. How do you think *I* feel?

(Later)

SONNY: [To Cloris Leachman] You know, Cloris, you really are a great actress. No wonder you won an Oscar and two Emmys.

LEACHMAN: Well, Sonny, maybe it's because I love show business. You know, appearing before the public in a meaningful, fulfilling role, or making people roar with laughter at brilliant, clever material. That's show business.

SONNY: Hey! We could use you around here. How about teaming up with me permanently?

LEACHMAN: What? And give up show business?

Vicki Pellegrino interviewed producer Chris Bearde shortly after Bono's solo series was cancelled. "ABC forced us to use the old *Sonny and Cher Comedy Hour* format on him," complained Bearde. "That was a terrible mistake. If they'd let us be free, do something totally wigged out, I think we'd have had a chance. Also, don't forget we were up against *Kojak* and *Columbo*—both top-rated shows. The network should have at least given us thirteen more weeks. Instead, the press has pilloried Sonny and his solo show. It just makes me sick."

George Schlatter agreed. "I think that it was probably ill advised to make the show so similar to *The Sonny and Cher Comedy Hour*. It was a mistake; plain and simple."

Today, Allan Blye thinks there's another reason that Sonny's solo show didn't work. "No one really wanted to see Sonny without Cher; and it wasn't his fault. People had an emotional investment in them as a team. I personally think the show was fantastic, but it didn't matter. Sonny without Cher wasn't what viewers wanted to see."

In an extensive, highly-personal interview that was given to *The Hollywood Reporter*, Sonny talked frankly about his personal and professional challenges at the time. "I'm feeling really sad right now. I couldn't feel anything when *The Sonny and Cher Comedy Hour* went off the air because, at the time, I went right into preparations for my show. I didn't have the chance to feel the loss. But I really feel it now. I need to take a couple months off and re-evaluate. There really is no answer to what has happened to me in the past year. You just don't believe that something traumatic has happened to you until afterward, and it really has just now hit me." About the cancelation of his show he said: "I'm glad I did it because it helped me get over the awkwardness of not having Cher by my side. The first time you go on alone you feel like you've lost an arm. It's something that Cher is going to feel too."

But that wasn't the only trauma that befell Sonny during the final months of '74. The November issue of *Movie Mirror* carried a bombshell. On the cover was a picture of a troubled-looking Sonny alongside a copy of a California birth certificate. The headline: "Why Sonny Bono Had to Hide His Illegitimate Son for Ten Years! We Have the Proof! We Have the Real Story!" And it seemed they did. Rona Barrett (an impeccable source) had been the first to report on the story of Mimi Machu, a French woman who for all intents and purposes was a Hollywood groupie. In the early '60s Machu—who claimed to know Marlon Brando, and who, for a time, had lived with Jack Nicholson—had been romantically involved with Sonny. "We were living together and I got pregnant," Machu informed *Movie Mirror*'s Lynn Sandar. "But then he met Cher and started seeing her regularly. So I ran away."

On April 10, 1964 at San Vicente Hospital in Los Angeles, Machu, who by her own account was a globe-trotting "free spirit," gave birth to a son she named Sean. On the birth certificate, she named "Sonny Bono" as "father of child." Her age was listed as 20 and Sonny's was listed as 29 (his age at the time). Sonny's "present or last occupation" was listed as "record producer," and under "kind of industry or business" she described Sonny as "self employed." *Movie World* obtained and printed a copy of the certificate, complete with names, dates and the Registrar Recorder of the state of California's embossed seal.

"He's not denying it," said Marcel Machu, Mimi's grandfather and the man who raised her son. "Sonny recognizes Sean as his son, but the reason he doesn't want to admit it to the press is because he's afraid it will affect his ongoing battle for custody of Chastity." (*Movie Mirror* stood by its story—even revisiting it the following month with a second cover story: "Sonny Keeps His Vow to the Woman Who Raised His Illegitimate Son.")

In his autobiography, *And the Beat Goes On*, Sonny admitted to many romantic dalliances over the years—even while married to first wife Donna—but neither confirmed nor denied ever having a relationship or a son with Mimi Machu. "I would very much like Cher to make it on her own—in her own series," Sonny told a group of reporters as he emerged from the Santa Monica County Court House following one of his and Cher's many court dates. "I'd even like to produce her show." Their appearance on the court-house steps produced a much-published image; a moment when Sonny, making the point that despite their tiresome litigation he and Cher were still on friendly terms, grabbed her, threw her head back and gave her a big sloppy wet kiss.

6

NEW TEAMWORK

A full ten months before Cher's solo series was officially announced, and five months before *The Sonny and Cher Comedy Hour*'s final broadcast, Cher presided over a lavish surprise birthday party for David Geffen. The catered affair, which had a three-ring circus theme, was held at the Beverly Wilshire Hotel. As it turned out, Geffen's birthday fell on the final day of taping for *The Sonny and Cher Comedy Hour*. Jolene Schlatter, producer George Schlatter's wife and a good friend of Cher's since the '60s, was at CBS that day and watched Cher finalize her commitment to "Sonny and Cher."

"Sonny was in his dressing room with his girlfriend Connie, very happy and laughing, and Cher was in her dressing room with Chastity, her sister, her secretary and Chastity's nurse," Schlatter reported. "Cher was excitedly talking about the birthday party she was giving David later that night. She was so excited! I thought, 'Why am *I* sad?' Cher was happy and Sonny was happy."

Along with Warren Beatty, Bob Dylan, Robbie Robertson, Mo Austin, Ahmet Ertegun, Jack Nicholson and Ringo Starr (the object of Cher's affection on her debut single "Ringo, I Love You"), also in attendance at Geffen's birthday party was writer Mary Porter. When the columnist asked Cher how she saw her immediate future she replied: "For the last three years I've done nothing but work. The first year that Sonny and I did our show I had fourteen days off out of 365. The second year, between the show and personal appearances, I didn't have even one day off. Can you believe it? I developed all sorts of ailments—stomach trouble, skin rashes. I told Sonny that I just couldn't take it anymore. He told me that I could—I just had to try. He was right. I did try. I did make it. I was able to keep up with all the work. But I was miserable. I didn't want to work that hard again."

Originally CBS planned to introduce Cher in her own solo variety series in

September 1975, but, realizing that they would be foolish not to capitalize on her spectacular notoriety (along with her current hit "Dark Lady"), the network decided that Cher's show would be put into immediate production. *Cher*, as the series was to be called—not *The Cher Show* or *The Cher Comedy Hour*—would be introduced to viewers as a rare 60-minute mid-season "event." Cher was on a vacation in Europe when she received a frantic call from her press agent Dick Grant, informing her that CBS wanted her to return to the States immediately and begin pre-production work. "I thought hard about it for about five seconds. I really wanted to take some time off but then I said, 'Hmmm. That sounds good too. What the hell. I might as well do it!'"

The process of putting together her show started with a number of protracted conferences. "They're very funny, these meetings," Cher recalled. "It's like seventeen guys and me and we're always talking all at once... and when the writers are there too, it's total pandemonium." During an early meeting whose focus was how to handle Sonny's absence, David Geffen offered: "Maybe the first time, you could walk out with a midget!" To which Cher deadpanned: "I've been doing that for twelve years. Maybe a very tall man and I just look up and say, 'You don't know what a relief this is for my neck muscles!' The most important thing to me is that the guests who appear on my show have to be special. I'm tired of seeing the same old people who turn up on every single variety show. I've made a long list which my producers have, and we'll see what they come up with."

Cher's return to CBS without Sonny by her side harkened back to the glamorous days of old Hollywood. In many ways she was an updated version of a 1940s-era movie star (one reviewer called her "TV's Marlene Dietrich"), returning to the studio that made her name. Telegrams awaited her. So did "welcome home" notes (including one from CBS program director Fred Silverman) and a sea of flowers. More importantly, the network also supplied her with her very own custom-designed dressing trailer—a rarity at CBS. For the four years that *The Sonny and Cher Comedy Hour* aired Cher shared a dressing space with Sonny that *Redbook* described as "an overlit, drab, and overflowing jumble of wig stands and hanging costumes."

"She had it all done up like a really large bedroom," remembers Ret Turner who, along with Bob Mackie, designed costumes for *The Sonny and Cher Comedy Hour* and made the transition to Cher's solo show. He also served as Cher's personal dresser. "The main feature, aside from the makeup table and dressing area, was a bed especially made out of trees. It was like a twig bed made out of real branches. There was a large cabinet that was filled with Indian dolls, and there were Indian-inspired rugs, pillows and prints everywhere. When you went into Cher's dressing room you totally forgot that there was a huge, dark, totally intimidating television studio just outside the door."

"Cher loved her dressing room," agrees producer George Schlatter. "Not only did she love it—everyone else loved it too, so everyone was always hanging out in there with her, especially the guest stars."

Along with providing her with exclusive and expanded dressing accommodations, CBS took Cher's two-page guest request and "ideas" list seriously. They also looked the other way when their star insisted on performers—David Bowie, Labelle, David Essex, Gregg Allman, Billy Swan, Jimmy Webb—that many of them had never heard of. (There must have been a collective sigh when additional, off-their-radar guest requests—the Who, Chicago, the Average White Band, Rod Stewart, Alice Cooper—proved to be unavailable.)

"I'll be doing both old and new songs," Cher said of the musical direction she wanted her new show to represent. "A lot of ladies in this business can sing rock and roll, but not old songs, and vice-versa. I'm at home with both." Featuring daughter Chastity, who was a beloved regular on *The Sonny and Cher Comedy Hour,* was something that Cher gave careful thought. "I'd like to have her on but only on special occasions like her birthday or Easter or something. When I have her on I want it to be totally different than before. I'd like to sit down and talk with her on camera. She's really very funny and very special."

The impressive list of advertisers who lined up to sell products on *Cher* included Procter & Gamble, American Home Products and General Motors—all of whom were willing to pay $70,000 for a 60-second commercial. The most prestigious advertising spot went to Revlon, who, for an additional fee, were given "premier sponsorship" via a mid-show "billboard" in which Cher's image and the Revlon logo would appear simultaneously as an announcer informed the audience that "This portion of *Cher* has been brought to you by Revlon... the people who help make the world just a little more beautiful."

"It's the difference between Tiffany's and the local toy store," assured producer George Schlatter. "The entire hour is designed to stretch her a little bit, and I think you'll like the results. Viewers will find that Cher has become more versatile, more aware and well read. She's also become much more adventurous. She'll be doing her first monologue, and a segment in which she gives her thoughts about dating; from a woman's perspective." As for references to Cher's tenure as half of one of show business' most successful husband-and-wife TV teams, Schlatter declared: "There will be no mention, and I mean none, of Sonny Bono on *Cher*. That was her past—*this* is her future."

And into the future they went, but it was often a bumpy ride. Schlatter, whom Cher called "Hammer" (due to his blunt approach) and Cher, whom Schlatter called "Nails" (due to the fact that she once suspended taping because she broke a nail and wanted to have it mended before filming), had a working relationship that was, by all accounts, contentious. "George did a really good job on that show," says Hollywood columnist Rona Barrett, a personal friend of them both.

"But if I remember correctly, he and Cher were always having disagreements; they both had stories to tell about the other."

In fact, Schlatter and Cher's skirmishes began during the very first *Cher* show meeting. As reported in *The Operator*, Tom King's biography of David Geffen, Cher balked at Schlatter's ideas for the opening segment. "First you sing your song. Then you come down the runway and say hello to the audience," Schlatter informed her. Cher's response: "Oh, no. I'm not into that shit!" "Cher, you are the star of this show. You have to come down and acknowledge the people." "It's old-fashioned." "You're right," countered Schlatter, "and that's exactly what the audience wants to see." When Cher wasn't looking the producer turned to head writer Digby Wolfe and whispered: "This is going to be a *very* long season."

Today, Schlatter has no qualms about admitting that he and Cher did not always see eye to eye. "At the time, and I still believe it's true today, Cher wanted to be a rock and roll star. She thought that that was the biggest barometer of stardom; the only way she could be personally validated. I wanted much more for her than that. Selling Cher on ideas that were not rock and roll-centered was always very, very hard." Their differences aside, Cher personally campaigned to secure Schlatter. "Cher specifically requested me," says Schlatter. "When she and Sonny split she called me up and said, 'George, I need your help.' I was thrilled, I believed, and I still do, that Cher is one of the most versatile and talented performers that show business has ever seen. She's a star—that's it. She is undeniably unique, special, and in a category all her own.

"Producing is a combination of many elements—all of which I love," says Schlatter. "It's as creative as you want it to be; it's as business-oriented as you can tolerate; it's something that requires a lot of passion and a desire and willingness to sacrifice all of your time and energy. A producer is the guy that does 'everything else.' You have to understand scenery—even though you're not a set designer. You have to understand movement—even though you're not a choreographer. Even more than these things, if a producer hopes to be successful, he must appreciate, admire, respect and support talent. All performers need love, understanding and discipline and a producer must know how and when to dish it out or hold it back."

Cher director Art Fisher, who had worked with Cher for years on *The Sonny and Cher Comedy Hour*, had a knowledgeable understanding of Cher and her chances as a solo television hostess. "She is frighteningly new at so many things that we are doing on this show, especially the comedy routines, but I know she can do it," he said at the time. "For a show coming up she'll be performing with Jerry Lewis and Nancy Walker. It's like a kid getting in the ring with Muhammad Ali. But we all think she's up for the challenge."

"I believe Art was the perfect director for Cher's solo show," says head writer Digby Wolfe. "George was a very domineering personality who was often very difficult to work with because he *does* like to get his own way. And, unfortunately, George's way usually turns out to be the best way, which makes things even more challenging. But in terms of comedy, George and Art were in synch. The pacing, the material, the direction that they both wanted to go in was the same. And they both had Cher's best interests front and center."

Along with George Schlatter, Art Fisher, Digby Wolfe, and immensely talented art director Robert Kelly—who designed *Cher*'s innovative moving "home base" stage, the program's ultra-modern circular chrome "Cher" logo, and a totally different set for each and every one of Cher's solo numbers (on *The Sonny and Cher Comedy Hour* the sets for Cher's solos remained stagnant; a dark void illuminated by an oversized spotlight)—several other professionals were brought onboard.

Musical director Jimmy Dale of *The Sonny and Cher Comedy Hour* was a familiar and welcome face. He was joined by lighting designer V. Dale Palmer (*Match Game, Tattletales*), choreographers Tony Charmoli (*The Julie Andrews Show, The Danny Kaye Show*) and Dee Dee Wood (*The Judy Garland Show, The Andy Williams Show*), and Digby Wolfe's supporting team of "scribes," among them Ron Pearlman (*The Barry Manilow Special, Barney Miller*) and Nick Arnold (*Dean Martin's Celebrity Roast*). Iris Rainer also wrote for the series. The only female writer on the *Cher* show staff, Rainer later based the character Cecilia "Cee Cee" Bloom (played by Bette Midler in the popular film *Beaches*) on her memories, associations and experiences working with Cher.

"Special Music Material" providers Billy Barnes and Earl Brown's contribution to *Cher* is immense. Barnes, an accomplished lyricist and pianist whose credits included *The Danny Kaye Show, The Bing Crosby Show* and *The Hudson Brothers Razzle Dazzle Hour* (he also made contributions to *The Sonny and Cher Comedy Hour*), was known in the industry as "The Review Master of Hollywood"—additionally he penned the two jazz standards "Something Cool" and "(Have I Stayed) Too Long at the Fair?". His partner Earl Brown's credits were equally impressive. Along with his work on programs like *The Dinah Shore Chevy Show* and *Donny and Marie*, Brown wrote the late-career Elvis Presley hit "If I Can Dream." For *Cher*, Barnes and Brown joined forces and created memorable original music and songs for comedy sketches, blackouts, interludes, duets and extended multi-part finales. Their outstanding gift to the series includes the often-used tunes "Girls Are Smarter" and "Trashy Ladies," as well as the scathing but funny "He'll Do," and "Ladies of the Silver Screen."

"I can't say for sure that my show is going to be a hit or even that I'll be heartbroken if it's cancelled," Cher told *The Los Angeles Times* before her program aired. "But I can say that with all the great people I have working with me, I'm sure it's not going to be bad."

7

THE STAR TREATMENT

Cher and costume designer Bob Mackie first met in 1968 on the set of *The Carol Burnett Show*. At the time Mackie was already a household name and Emmy winner for the TV special *Diana Ross and the Supremes and the Temptations on Broadway*. "During rehearsals [of *The Carol Burnett Show*] I saw Cher admiring a piece of beadwork I'd done," Mackie recalled. "She dolefully asked me, 'Hey, could you do something like this for me someday—someday when I have some money?'" Mackie's response was an immediate yes. With a keen eye for body types and proportions, Mackie was taken with Cher's broad shoulders, tiny waist, missing stomach and flaring hips. It was *he* who wanted to dress *her*.

Two years after their first meeting Mackie received a call. "It was Cher," Mackie remembered in his book *Dressing for Glamour*. "She asked if I would do her and Sonny's show [*The Sonny and Cher Comedy Hour*] and I said 'no.' At the time I had my hands full with *The Carol Burnett Show* and so many other projects. But she persisted. She kept calling me. Finally she said, 'Look, if you can't take the whole show, couldn't you just do *my* clothes?'" Mackie agreed. Unbeknownst to either one of them, serendipity was at play. From the moment they began their creative partnership the names Cher and Bob Mackie would forever be linked.

A little-known fact is that the soon-to-be-celebrated pairing almost didn't take place. Producers Chris Bearde and Allan Blye, unaware of Cher's desire to work with Mackie, but fully aware of and having previously worked with designer Ret Turner, first offered all of *The Sonny and Cher Comedy Hour*'s costume duties—including Cher's—to Turner.

"I knew that Cher had her heart set on working with Bob," says Turner, "and I knew that she and Bob were a perfect match. So when they offered me that job I told them that they should approach Bob with the offer of doing Cher's costumes and I would be happy to do everything else that was needed. They did, and that's how Bob and I started working together." Cher's costumes, like so many others for television at the time, were created at Los Angeles' Elizabeth Courtney Costumes, a company formed by Mackie's longtime designing partner and personal companion Ray Aghayan. It was, in fact, Aghayan, one of the most prolific costume designers of the '60s, who gave Mackie his first big break. Impressed with his sketches, Aghayan hired Mackie as both a sketch artist and personal assistant on *The Judy Garland Show* (a program on which Aghayan famously replaced the legendary Edith Head). As a designing team Mackie and Aghayan won the very first Costume Design Emmy for 1966's *Alice Through the Looking Glass*, and on the big screen their combined efforts shone brightly in 1972's *Lady Sings the Blues* and 1975's *Funny Lady*—both nominated for Oscars. When Aghayan (twelve years Mackie's senior) decided to step back from designing, Elizabeth Courtney Costumes was launched.

"I took care of the business side and Robert did most of the designing," Aghayan informed the Archive of American Television. And the new Mackie/Aghayan configuration was a tremendous success. Today, Elizabeth Courtney Costumes remains Los Angeles' premier costume house; a production space where show-business dreams come true. Lily Tomlin confirms it: "Going to Elizabeth Courtney is like going to Disneyland. Anything you want, anything you want *to be*, you can be. It's all there for you." (Ray Aghayan died on October 15, 2011 at the age of 83.)

The budget for *Cher*'s costumes was first set at $5,000 an episode and then, more realistically, expanded to $30,000. "I understand that Cher's wardrobe budget is the biggest ever for a weekly variety show," Mackie said at the time. "But, then, of course, her gowns are very much a part of the proceedings at hand. Designing for Cher is the most fun I've ever had." Of Cher's body Mackie observed: "She has the best tummy in the business. She also has wonderful armpits—so bare shoulders are not a problem. She doesn't have particularly long legs, but she has a long, sinuous body, so when you see her navel and five inches below it, everyone gets real nervous. They're like 'what's going on here!'"

In a three-page color piece that appeared in *The New York Daily News Sunday Magazine*, journalist Carol Troy made clear the fact that Mackie's work for Cher, as extensive and precise as it was, was the product of intense collaboration. "The designer employs six cutters and fitters," reported Troy. "And each of these people have assistants, all of whom are conversant in the highest refinements of the couture tradition. Mackie can supply the perfect molded bias-cut dress because he has a little lady working for him who has done the same for Dietrich, Joan Crawford, Carole Lombarde and Jean Harlow." Troy also pointed out a few fantasy-bursting truths: "The [gowns] are absolutely tiny, the slightest movement and you are apt to fall out of your dress. Many gowns employ a see-through

Previous page: Cleopatra never had it so good! Having won full custody of daughter Chastity, residency at Owlwood—the mansion she'd shared with former husband Sonny Bono—and her very own television series, newly single Cher had everything to look forward to. (Photo Fair)

Above and below: My how we've changed: Sonny and Cher as tiara-wearing hippies in the '60s and polished casino/fairground performers in the '70s. By the time Cher was ready to begin taping her own solo variety series, Cher, both these looks were officially a thing of the past. (J. Howard Collection)

The Sonny and Cher Comedy Hour *brought Sonny and Cher out of music halls and into American households.*
Music (the couple released four albums during the show's run) was at the heart of their act–along with comedy and
guest stars–but most viewers tuned in just to see what Cher, a Vogue favorite, would be wearing each week.
(J. Howard Collection)

Glamour takes time (and patience): Ever the professional, Cher stands stock-still on the set of The Sonny and Cher Comedy Hour *as five crew members prep her for the camera. (TV Time)*

Designer Bob Mackie adjusts a slithering snake atop the head of a glittering star. Small wonder that when Cher began starring in her solo series, the prep-time increased tenfold. (TV Time)

Above and below: New show, new man: Cher met Gregg Allman of the Allman Brothers Band just as she started rehearsals for her solo series. Here they are in May 1975 arriving at the Emmy Awards (above) and little more than a month later on June 30: their wedding day (left). (TV Time; Photo Fair)

Opposite: John Engstead (Paramount's seldom-credited head photographer) was hired to take publicity photos for Cher. This shot–dubbed the "flower picture"–was Cher's personal favorite. (Nostalgia Network)

Another gorgeous John Engstead publicity portrait, another beautiful Bob Mackie creation: Cher first wore this champagne-colored dress in '73 whilst on the road with Sonny. (Photo Fair)

fabric called souffle which is not sold in America because it's highly flammable, the beads, rhinestones and glitter that make up the outfits weigh a ton—some dresses weigh fifteen pounds, and you can't wear a bra or too much underwear."

(In 1979 Cher, whose relationship with Bob Mackie famously continues, thanked the designer in song. On "Outrageous," a tune included on her *Prisoner* album, she sings: "I don't trust anybody else's taste but Bob Mackie... and me!")

"People always say that Cher, and particularly Cher's solo series, was all about the costumes and wigs that Cher wore and that nothing else mattered," says Ret Turner. "But there had to be someone *wearing* all those costumes and wigs. And there had to be someone that *could* wear all those costumes and wigs. Without Cher's compliance and willingness to be different, to take chances, to be creative and daring, none of it could have happened."

And the "happening" was documented by legendary Hollywood photographer John Engstead, who replaced *The Sonny and Cher Comedy Hour's* Earl Miller. (Later in life, Miller became *Penthouse* magazine's most published photographer.) During the film industry's golden era, Engstead, head photographer at Paramount Pictures, specialized in female glamour portraiture. His idealized presentaions of Hollywood's A-list actresses included Greta Garbo, Lana Turner, Rita Hayworth, Joan Crawford, Marlene Dietrich and Judy Garland. Cher, a pop star and a television star but not yet a film star, was now, by association, going to be presented as something much more than she was at the time: Hollywood royalty. Engstead and Cher first met when he took promotional photos for *The Sonny and Cher Comedy Hour*. Cher liked his work so much that she commissioned him to take 1973's *Half-Breed* album cover (his pictures appeared on the back). Yet another Engstead image featured Cher tanned, glamorously made up, and engulfed in outsize pink and white flowers. The flower shot—"one of my best," the photographer later recalled—was used during the opening segment of her show, on the cover of regional television guides, on the Mego "Growing Hair Cher" doll box, and printed up as postcards that Cher, herself, used to respond to her voluminous fan mail. Other memorable Engstead portraiture included a shot of Cher posed against a giant oil drum wearing a black satin gown with a flowing floor-length feather boa simulating an oil spill; Cher, body-perfect, in a flesh-colored spangled ensemble dragging her matching cape on the floor behind her; and Cher, head and torso wrapped in a white towel, holding a bright yellow rubber duck. (A year later, with her life in a dramatically different place, Cher commissioned Engstead to take a "family portrait" that included herself, Gregg Allman, Chastity and the Allmans' new baby boy, Elijah Blue.)

Along with costumes and portraiture, Cher's troubled complexion also had to be taken care of. In 1975 Dan Eastman was a 31-year-old beauty-industry professional whose Beverly Hills salon Daniel Eastman and Associates catered to Los Angeles' rich and famous. "Cher came to me because she was breaking out," the cosmetician informed *Coronet*. "The heavy consistency of her pancake makeup [on *The Sonny and Cher Comedy Hour* set]—under all those hot Klieg lights for hours and hours—was clogging her pores and causing skin eruptions. In truth, I think her chronic skin problems were a combination of stress, nerves and poor eating habits." Eastman's "diet advice," "cleansings," and "extractions" (he also confessed to performing electrolysis on Cher) prepared Cher for yet another beauty professional—Ben Nye II.

"Breaking up the planes of a face is what makes a face interesting, and that's what I do with Cher," CBS Makeup Department head Ben Nye II revealed at the time (Nye replaced *Sonny and Cher Comedy Hour* makeup artist Al Schultz). Nye had learned his craft from his father who, like John Engstead, was a film industry professional—head of the makeup department at of Twentieth Century Fox. The "tricks" the makeup artist used on Cher (featured in women's magazines at the time) included contouring her nose and cheeks, placing a white dot at the corner of her eye, by her nose (the effect was a brightening of the eyes), applying three components on her lips—gloss, frosted gloss, and color—and brushing up her eyebrows with spirit gum or false eyelash glue (the effect was a more open look that facilitated the use of more color on the eyelid). The final element of Cher's glamorous visage was the application of custom-made, individually cut top and bottom false eyelashes. Cher's "Christina" lashes—created by Canadian-born Christina Smith—were, themselves, dazzling miniature works of art; accoutrements that Cher and many other '70s stars—including Diana Ross, Ann-Margaret and, most notably, Liza Minnelli—considered essential throughout that decade.

"Ben was a terrific and very creative guy," remembers Ret Turner, who watched Nye prepare Cher for the camera, again and again, over the course of many, many years. "Cher always knew exactly what she wanted to do makeup-wise and Ben did it for her. She would say, 'I want rhinestones glued in the corner of my eyes,' or 'I want multi-color eyelids,' and then Ben did it. They worked great together."

(When Nye and Eastman's skills were not enough to conceal Cher's unpredictable skin, a camera trick was employed. "When Cher was broken out, we would often film her with the lens an eighth of an inch out of focus," remembers a cameraman who worked on the show. "It was like putting a piece of gauze over the lens... like they used to do in the old-time movies. It made her blemishes completely disappear and it gave her a wonderful softness... an ethereal quality."

"When I'm home I don't put on all that shit," Cher surmised to *Coronet* about her makeup routine. "But when I'm on camera I put on eyelashes and all the other stuff—I think you need that. When I'm on camera I want to look like I'm *on camera*—not like I'm sitting at home."

And part of what viewers saw when she was on camera was her beautiful hair. "Cher really knows what fullness, width and style best accommodate her nose, chin and teeth," said Jim Oertel, Cher's hairstylist and "hair maintenance person" at the time. "She's very handy with her own hair. She does most of those little top knots herself." Although he worked mainly out of a Beverly Hills salon, Oertel (who filled in on *The Sonny and Cher Comedy Hour* when Gary Chowen wasn't available) was on hand when needed. "I have her come in every three weeks to have the ends trimmed and darken her hair—a warm Armenian brown to blue-black. Then she has it conditioned and blow dried. Cher's waist-long hair is her trademark. I don't think she'll ever cut it. A trademark is a very important thing and Cher's a smart cookie."

Years before she became a spokesperson for Jack LaLanne Health Spas, Cher took an interest in health and exercise. "In my experience stars are usually much more disciplined than the everyday person," Cher's personal fitness expert Ron Fletcher informed *Coronet* at the time. Ron Fletcher's Studio was an "in" Beverly Hills "work out" space that counted Raquel Welch, Ali MacGraw and Steve McQueen among its many members. "Cher is in the gym working out three or four times a week—no matter how long and taxing her schedule might be. And Cher is lucky. Most women's bodies change dramatically after they have a child. Hers hasn't. She has the exact same body she had before she had Chastity."

Two other "handymen" contributed to the Cher look circa 1975. They were her wig-maker and manicurist. Renata Leuschner (often credited "Rena") was the Hollywood wig-maker to the stars. Her elaborate and often outrageous lace-front, human-hair and synthetic wigs—including page boys, afros, buns, braids, falls, "Freedom Puffs," stacked perms, ringlets and pony tails—added the finishing touch to Cher's glittering Bob Mackie ensembles. "We used Rena because there were so many changes in my show and it all had to be done so fast, and nobody knew what to do with my real hair," Cher said later. "Rena had this special way of wrapping my hair. She could just get it up there in no time at all. With Rena's help I could do like fourteen changes a show." Cher's partnership with Rena, still in place today, was such a substantial part of her visual presentation that *TV Guide* featured the wig-maker's work in a two-page color spread.

Minnie Smith (no relation to Christina Smith) was known in Hollywood as the "manicurist-to-the-stars." Smith first started doing Cher's nails in the late '60s. "Cher started the square look," Smith recalled in 1975. "She wanted something different and I said, 'What the hell different can you do with fingernails?' I thought about it for a while and then I took out the round and left them blunt [at the tip] and all of a sudden Cher started a new trend. Richard Avedon fell in love with Cher's hands and her nails. Every time there's a *Vogue* layout we always get a hand." Cher's relationship with Smith, who was on call day and night during the filming of her solo series, was best summed up by a personalized photograph that Smith prominently displayed in her nail salon. It read: "Minnie, you know every fucking thing there is to know about me! Cher."

With a body by Ron Fletcher, a face by Dan Eastman, makeup by Ben Nye II, eyelashes by Christina Smith, costumes by Bob Mackie, hair by Jim Oertel, wigs by Rena, and nails by Minnie Smith, the only thing left to cover was Cher's feet—and they were covered by Fred Slatten. Although he is not much remembered, in 1975 Fred Slatten's discreet Santa Monica Boulevard shoe boutique, Fred Slatten's Shoes, was frequented by everyone. Elton John and Diana Ross were regulars. So were Tony Orlando, Sally Struthers and Gene Simmons (who famously frequented the shop just to flirt with the beautiful young girls Slatten hired) of KISS. When Cher, a perfect size seven-and-a-half wanted something that she couldn't find in Beverly Hills or New York, she called up Slatten, told him what she needed, and dropped by the shop to pick them up. "After *TV Guide* did an article on me my shop was slammed," Slatten later remembered. "All the kids wanted a pair of the silver platform shoes that I made for Cher—but no one had the money to pay for them! I mean I hand-punched every single one of those rhinestones [2,000 in all] on those shoes!"

"Not since *Laugh-In* has there been a show that is more of a total team effort," George Schlatter said at the time. "We're all working together, overtime—day and night—on Cher's behalf. I believe the end result is going to be simply astounding."

8

A CAST OF CHARACTERS

Although CBS told Cher that her series was being rushed into production in order to capitalize on her popularity, in actuality, the network had a more pressing reason to quickly develop the show. *Apple's Way*, a family drama about the life and experiences of the Apples, good-natured kinfolk who had moved from Los Angeles to Idaho in search of a more relaxed way of life, was a flop. As *TV Guide* put it: "It's quite a jump from Apples to Cher but CBS is poised to make the transition." The 7:30 p.m. time slot that the network chose for Cher had the series competing with *The Six Million Dollar Man* on NBC, and *The Wonderful World of Disney* on ABC—two programs that had a strong and loyal viewership. Even so, CBS believed that Cher's contemporary relevance (as a newly liberated woman, as a newsstand staple, and as a performer who was just coming off of a No. 1 single), grouped together with her already proven success as a TV star, would attract both the singer's loyal fans and a large number of curiosity viewers.

One of the people that Digby Wolfe hired to help create sketches and write gags and comedy material for *Cher* was Don Reo. Reo had made his name playing at Harlem's Apollo Theater. His comic character, a straight white man who was the butt of African-American comedian Slappy White's jokes, was a hit with both black and white audiences. Also hired was Alan Katz, a stand-up comedian whom George Schlatter discovered. Reo and Katz worked together as a team. "This is the first time in a very long time that Alan and I have done something really fun," Reo told the *Village Voice*. "'Relevant' TV sitcoms have snowballed and now we need some relief. You want to laugh, have a good time, not be reminded of the high price of eggs. At the beginning Alan and I were saying, 'Who is Cher? What is she?' Now we're both in love with her."

Writing in *Newsweek*, columnist Harry F. Waters offered up an on-target examination of just how *Cher* was being developed. "First you mesh a rock-pop legend with a producer of proven appeal among the under-25s (in this case, *Laugh-In* creator George Schlatter). Next, recycle some pre-tested comedic characters—namely, Johnny Carson's 'Matinee Lady' pitch-woman (Cher's 'Donna Jean Brodine'). Finally, flavor the mix each week with something hot (Elton John, Bette Midler, the Jackson Five), something cool (Freddie Prinze, Tatum O'Neal, Flip Wilson) and something blue (Redd Foxx). The result should be a sure-fire hit."

Cher told Andy Warhol that she was pleased that her leopard-clad "lady of the launderette" character Laverne would also be a regular feature on the show. "It's the only thing from *The Sonny and Cher Comedy Hour* that I'm carrying over to my own solo series. The first time I did Laverne she wasn't written as she is now. She was an old Jewish lady. And, somehow I just thought that that wasn't exactly what I wanted to be doing, so I changed it around and got her all dressed up and she turned out to be what she is today. I think everybody knows Laverne, you know, there's a 'Laverne' someplace all over."

Several years later Cher talked further about developing Laverne. "The idea of Laverne's hairdo was my copy of a Lucille Ball hairdo—but we gave her really terrible roots. Slowly but surely Bob Mackie and I came up with the costume. The [hanging] bra strap was Bob's idea; it was so perfect. The bra strap makes it. It took me a while to come up with the voice. I tried doing it every which way. At the very last minute before we did her live in front of an audience, the prop man gave me some bubble gum. Now I can't do Laverne without a piece of gum in my mouth. The bubble gum went in and Laverne came out."

"Today, nobody remembers Teri Garr," reflects Ret Turner, "but she played Olivia, the other tacky lady in the Laverne sketches. I designed Olivia's costume and I decided that her character would always have her hair up in curlers and wear this little pink mini-dress. Teri wore that outfit week after week for years and it always worked." (On *The Sonny and Cher Comedy Hour* the segment featuring Laverne was called "Dirty Linen"; on *Cher* it was called "Life with Laverne.")

The most engaging character created for *Cher* was Cher as "Cher" in a segment called "Saturday Night." The sketch supposedly offered up a mirror to Cher's own life and featured her returning home to a modestly furnished, one-bedroom apartment. Speaking in the hip, jive-talking vernacular of the day—lots of "far outs," "mans," "super cools" and "I can dig its," Cher discussed men, girlfriends and the special challenge of being a single woman. "Saturday Night" was so strong, so well written, so comfortably delivered, that watching the segment, which usually ran ten to fifteen minutes, was almost like watching a stand-alone situation comedy; a television show within a television show. "The only thing on *Cher* that I can really take full credit for is coming up with that particular segment," recalls Digby Wolfe. "The 'Saturday Night' sketch turned out to be very, very successful for Cher. We were trying to think of a way for her to work as a monologist, to do stand-up in other words, in a way that wasn't just a series of jokes like Letterman, Leno or Carson. I don't mean to disparage those comedians or their particular technique because they are great too. With Cher we were just trying to harness her natural talent for comedy under some kind of a conceptual umbrella that allowed her to be the character that the audience already viewed her as."

One of the ways in which Wolfe capitalized on Cher's public persona was to directly respond to her newsstand notoriety. "Because Cher had been associated in the tabloids with so many different suitors it offered us an ideal opportunity to get *her* point of view across about those various dates she supposedly had. The ['Saturday Night'] segment was a self-contained piece with a beginning, middle and end that the audience could look forward to seeing each week. Cher felt comfortable doing it and she loved the idea. I think that's why she did it so well."

"I've got to admit that 'Saturday Night' was my favorite sketch from the series," says George Schlatter. "I thought it was a warm and wonderful look into the woman. We filled the set with copies of things from Cher's own bedroom; stuffed toys, pillows, pictures, things that were familiar to her, and it made her really comfortable. We also used first-hand material from our conversations with her—her own personal experiences about dating and being newly single. It was a funny segment, but at the same time it was very real and often poignant."

"What I saw in Cher—beyond her singing capabilities, was an enormous gift for comedy," recalls executive in charge of production Lee Miller. "George and I talked about it for a long time and we were both in agreement that the way we could make Cher's show stand out from the other variety shows on the air at the time was to concentrate on and further promote and develop her comedic gifts."

A "Cher Concert" segment in which Cher performed a medley of pop/rock songs or a duet/dance number with a musical guest was a program highlight. The segment took place in front of a giant, circular silver "Cher" logo (with the four letters of her name shaped into a circle) that was lowered from the ceiling. "The *Cher* series logo caused a bit of a problem," remembers Lee Miller. "From the very beginning Cher loved it. I think she said something like, 'Far out man, that's cool!' She was always talking like that. But CBS wasn't so sure. They thought it was too modern-looking. I think they would've preferred a handwritten 'Cher' script as her logo, or maybe giant block letters [along with the Cher logo, block letters *were* used on the first season opening number set]. That was what they were familiar with from their many other variety shows."

As glamorous, cleverly designed and "hip" as the Cher logo was, and even though it read onscreen as glistening metal, it was, in reality, light-weight plastic.

"Bob [Kelly] designed it and told us to go to work," says a craftsman who was employed by Kelly. "I just took a big piece of clear plastic, cut it up in strips, and bent it into the shape of the logo. It was about six feet tall all around. For a while we debated whether or not to just keep it clear, but then it was decided that it should be silver. So I just took some silver paper, like wrapping paper but with a sticky back, and wrapped each piece in it. It looked substantial and it was really fantastic, but that giant Cher logo weighed maybe ten pounds. At the end of the first season I remember watching one of the stagehands cut it down and roll it back into the warehouse like a donut." (The Cher logo was used on all program correspondence, memos and embossed on each of the show's scripts. Additionally, Cher featured the logo on postcards, fan correspondence, and cleared the way for it to be used by "Cher's Friend's," her official fan club.)

Lee Miller had come to *Cher* via George Schlatter. "George is one of the most gifted, dearest, talented people that I have ever had the pleasure to be involved with," remembers Miller. "Originally he wanted me to be the associate producer on *Cher*. The title associate producer and executive in charge of production are pretty much the same [Miller was credited as 'executive in charge of production' for the first season and 'producer' for the second]. But when George asked me to join the *Cher* staff I told him I didn't want to be associate producer—I had already been doing that for ten years. But George really, really wanted me in that position. I told my agent to make an offer to George that was so high that there was no way in the world he would be able to afford me. Well, my agent called George, told him my outrageous requirements, and George's response was: 'Fine. Tell him to be at CBS tomorrow at 10 a.m.!'"

Along with the crass, unpolished but exceedingly funny pitchwoman Donna Jean Brodine, several other recurring comedy segments were created for *Cher*. "The Complaint Department," a sketch in which Cher played a tart-tongued, uninterested, wholly unsympathetic clerk at a busy department store, was fun. So were "Mable's Fables," a twisted take on popular fairy tales; "Women Behind the Men," a salute to the wives of famous and infamous men (Mrs. Long Ranger, Mrs. Sigmund Freud); "Girls Are Smarter," a women versus men compendium; and "Trashy Ladies," Cher's look at influential but unorthodox women in history. (The program ideas and sketches that were considered but never used included: "Cher on the boom for a one-line joke or comment"; "Cher commenting on herself while a song or dance is in progress"; and "Crazy people coming through... wackos not regulars. Zanies.")

Add to her many guises Cher's weekly "solo in the spotlight" musical numbers, each performed on a custom-designed set, and the *Cher* show offered up a visual smorgasbord—kooky, deadpan, sexy, dramatic, unpredictable—of *everything* Cher. "Until Cher, women have *been* the joke, not done the joke," observed George Schlatter at the time. "I'm not a social worker, I'm not a philanthropist, and I'm not into that with Cher. And she's not particularly into the feminist movement, but she *is* a product of it. She's the first female star to carry a show in the same way that men have; the first real woman of the '70s."

Although it wasn't much noted at the time, Cher was also the only female entertainer on television who was delivering a full comedic monologue at the top of her program (Carol Burnett chose, instead, to field questions from the audience). "The monologue that I do at the start of the show was the hardest thing for me to do," Cher later recalled. "When Sonny and I were together he talked to the audience and I talked to him; I had that buffer. But on my own show it was just me and the audience." In time, and much to everyone's surprise—especially given her initial reluctance—Cher looked forward to doing her show's opening monologue. "The monologue is definitely me. I'm not one to go bla-blah-blah about ecology and inflation and all the problems out there. I don't want to get people into them. I think what I should do is take people *away* from them. My business is to sing, dance and entertain."

Cher stood apart from other variety shows in yet another way; the program employed an unusually large number of females in significant behind-the-scenes roles. *Cher*'s assistant director, stage manager, choreographer, grip, script person, director's assistant, producer's assistant, secretary and interns were all female—a rarity at the time.

"From black, the Cher logo spins forward from infinity and freezes when it fills the frame... images of Cher explode all over: beauty shots, comedy shots; an avalanche of Cher," read the first page of each of season one's scripts. And, indeed, the "Opening Billboard" of *Cher* presented her in a dizzying array of costumes, wigs, and guises. Original press material stated that *Cher*'s first episode was a "special" program, and that it would air on Sunday, February 9 at 7:30 p.m. Alerted to the fact that Cher, in her return to television, was sure to pull in a substantial audience, ABC scheduled a repeat broadcast of the blockbuster film *Airport* as competition. In response, and at the last minute, CBS moved Cher's first outing to a less competitive time slot; Wednesday, February 12 at 10:00 p.m.

"Just standing there in one of the twelve to fifteen costumes she wears out every broadcast hour, Cher inspires more, and infinitely richer, fantasies than all the plastics of *The Wonderful World of Disney* [her NBC-TV competition] and *The Six Million Dollar Man* [her ABC-TV competition]," observed *Time*. It was a "mission accomplished" summing up that validated everyone's hard work, and magnified their hopes for the series' success.

PART TWO

Cher

(Formerly of Sonny and Cher)

9

LET ME ENTERTAIN YOU

On January 6, 1975, at 8:45 p.m. in Studio 31 at CBS Television City in Hollywood, Cher and an entourage of friends and supporters stood backstage waiting for taping to begin on her very first solo television series. Less than a year earlier, in the very same studio with the very same director, Cher taped her final performance on *The Sonny and Cher Comedy Hour* in an atmosphere filled with anxiety, uncertainty, and dubious well wishes.

CBS Television City was located in the Fairfax district of Los Angeles' west side at 7800 Beverly Boulevard. Built on the site of a former race track, the state-of-the-art building first opened its doors in 1952. 7800 Beverly Boulevard housed four giant television sound stages—Studios 31, 33, 41 and 44 (the reason the studios were so un-uniformly numbered remains a mystery)—as well as offices, rehearsal halls, craft shops, and an underground technical facility. The 1950s were boom years in which CBS distinguished itself with shows like *The Jack Benny Show*, *The Jackie Gleason Show*, *I Love Lucy* and *Gunsmoke*. In the '60s *The Ed Sullivan Show*, *The Red Skelton Show*, *The Andy Griffith Show* and *Candid Camera* were viewer favorites, and in the '70s *All in the Family*, *M*A*S*H* and *The Mary Tyler Moore Show* kept the network on top. *Cher* was taped at the same time and in the same facilities as *The Carol Burnett Show*, *Match Game*, *The Price is Right*, *The Jeffersons*, and *Rhoda*. Although Cher's special was filmed in CBS Studio 31, the larger part of the series' first season was filmed in the adjacent Studio 33 (home to *The Carol Burnett Show*). Both Studio 31 and 33, the "twin" studios, had a seating capacity of 300 and stacked seating—allowing the audience to view tapings while three mammoth rolling cameras filmed.

"By the time I was doing *Cher* the business had changed quite a lot," remembers George Schlatter. "When I did *The Judy Garland Show*, Judy had her own [permanent] studio at CBS—she never moved around. But by the time I did *Cher*, the whole idea of having your own studio was an outdated kind of concept. You did whatever show you were doing in whatever studio was available that particular week. With Judy the trick was to film her from beginning to end—like it was a live concert. With Cher, by the very nature of the star and what she wanted to do—all the Bob Mackie gowns, hairstyles, makeup and costume changes—it was stop and go, repeat takes, and editing together the best of the lot."

Judy and Cher did have one thing in common. "They were both these huge, gorgeous, talented, glamorous, exciting child-women who loved to play dress-up," says Schlatter. "I viewed both their shows as adult playpens in which it was my job to make sure they had the room and freedom to realize, expand upon and act out all of their personal fantasies."

Cavernous though it was, the CBS complex did not have room for production companies. Consequently, *Cher*'s support staff was housed in a suite of nondescript offices a few blocks away. "That's where the *Cher* show was really created," remembers second season art director Ray Klausen. "To get to the offices you had to travel past a walk-in community health clinic. On one occasion I arrived at work, heard a gunshot, went looking, and found a woman cradling her bleeding boyfriend. She was screaming 'he's just been shot by his drug dealer'; the man died before the ambulance arrived. I was designing all these glamorous make-believe sets for Cher and, at the same time, dealing with life and death situations—all in the same building!"

"For some reason I remembered the first night I saw Diana [Ross] all alone onstage," Cher recalled of the moments before she went onstage for the first time as a solo act. "But now it was *me* instead of her." Standing with Cher backstage that first night of taping were David Geffen and Bob Mackie. Sitting in the first rows of the audience were Cher's mother, sister, daughter and personal secretary Paulette Eghiazarian. "The excitement in the studio was so thick that you could hardly breathe," observed Sue Cameron in *The Hollywood Reporter*. "Dancers filming *The Carol Burnett Show* next door were running over on their breaks to see what was going on. So was the cast of *The Jeffersons*."

Seating time for *Cher*'s taping was 6:15. Taping was scheduled from 7:00-8:30. Cher emerged under the glare of CBS's hot lights at 8:45—two and a half hours after the audience had been seated. "Not only did the audience have to wait forever," recalls Bo Kaprall, who was a series writer, bit player and "warm up" guy, "they also thought they were going to see performances by Bette Midler, Elton John and Flip Wilson—all of whom had recorded their segments earlier in the week. That was a really difficult night for me. Keeping an audience waiting for an hour is unusual. Keeping them waiting for two and a half hours is outrageous. The delays went on forever. I remember at one point—somewhere around the two-hour mark—my writing partner came up and handed me a note.

It read, 'Cher's dead—STALL!' That was pretty funny but I thought, 'Pretty soon I'll join her, the audience is going to kill me!'"

"The Cher look right now is a gelid blank," wrote Rowland Barber in *TV Guide* (Barber was on hand to record the event for a cover story), but, following a motion from the stage director, Cher took her place center stage and let out "a startling, unearthly cry—the cry of a cornered animal that has just decided to fight back." For what seemed like an eternity (actually 60 seconds), Cher stood alone in the darkness and waited for her cue. It was the first time during that entire day that she was alone—no assistants, no advisors, no one to tell her that things were going to be all right.

"All kinds of things were going through my mind at that moment," Cher recalled. "I thought of Sonny not being there, no Sonny to turn to and say under my breath, 'How am I doing?'" Then the stage manager's arm came down, the lights went up, and the red eye of the television camera glared. Over the PA system the announcer's voice boomed: "Ladies and gentlemen... Cher."

Cher began her tenure as a solo variety show hostess singing the appropriately chosen "Let Me Entertain You" from the 1959 musical *Gypsy*. "I was so nervous I don't know how my voice got out. I started with just the piano and then the full track came up and suddenly I felt good—real good." As scripted, Cher began the song under a solo spotlight, then, following a musical cue, the lights came up and then she threw off her beaded cape, revealing a spectacular nude tulle, rhinestone and white fur-trimmed costume. "Once I stopped singing and had to talk to the audience I was terrified. All the good feelings evaporated. Please, let me remember the words. And, watch it Cher—don't speak too quickly—bad habit when I'm nervous. Pick out faces. Talk straight at them. Don't be too sincere. Don't be somebody you're not. Don't be Mary Tyler Moore or Carol Burnett.'" Cher's approach to dealing with her return to the airways was simple and direct: "For those of you who haven't noticed I've been gone—and for those of you who have—I'm back!" Her frank, shoot-from-the-hip approach was met with thunderous applause.

"I don't remember the applause, or my getting offstage, but the next thing I knew I was off. I was in this white fog. I was there but not there. I remember Bob crying. Paulette crying. Bette Midler was there now and she was crying too. I had a delayed reaction; I didn't start to bawl until I got into the bathtub later that night."

For her special, David Geffen assisted George Schlatter in securing Elton John and Bette Midler—two guests who were, at this time, rarely seen on Prime-Time television. Supporting the two top musical guests was comedian Flip Wilson (Cher made an appearance on *his* variety special later in the year.)

Cher had met and become friendly with Bette Midler in the early part of 1974. In fact, the song "Miss Subway of 1952," included on *Dark Lady*—the tale of a down-on-her-luck former beauty queen—began with the spoken passage: "To my idol 'The Divine' [Midler's tag], let's hope this never happens to *us*!" At the time of her appearance on *Cher*, Midler was known as a raunchy-mouthed, soulful songstress who enjoyed glamour, camp, and had a large and ardent gay following. Her pairing with Cher on a "Trashy Ladies" medley—both wearing undergarments, garter belts and feather boas—was eagerly anticipated. "Billy Barnes came up with that number," remembers Tony Charmoli, who was the choreographer on the first four episodes of *Cher*. "Cher, Bette and I worked on the choreography together. Cher likes to move a lot. She's not a big dancer but she's a good mover. I was pretty well-known in the industry for getting the best out of celebrities who were not trained dancers and that's what I did with Cher." Cher and Midler's eleven-song number—including the tunes "Sister Kate," "Lulu's Back in Town" and "Put the Blame on Mame" (see Appendix for full listing)—was a great success. "I had the affirmation from both of them on that one," remembers Charmoli. "They had a wonderful time. They were singing, dancing, rolling on the floor, negotiating these huge feather boas, and, get this one—catching flying twirlers! The only thing I didn't make them do was hang upside down from the ceiling with a knife in their mouth!" The hard work didn't faze Cher. "She was a real pro," says Charmoli. "I never, ever, had the feeling that she was thinking, 'Oh, God, here we go again, I have to go into this rehearsal hall.' She was always ready and willing to do whatever was needed. She'd say, 'Do I have to do that?' and I'd say, 'Yep, that's what I've laid out.' Then she would do it exactly as instructed. I think Cher knew that I respected her and that I wasn't trying to change her or lead her in a totally unfamiliar direction. After all, there is only one Cher. I knew that, and I think *she* knew that I knew that."

Hollywood Reporter columnist Sue Cameron was present during the "Trashy Ladies" taping. "It's too bad that what will air on the show won't include the outtakes," wrote the columnist. "Watching Bette Midler tape a number is quite an experience. Her one-liners had the crew and audience [an uninvited packed house] doubled over. The number took several re-takes to complete... Chastity even kept coming out and giving her mom and Bette cups of water... at one point Bette waddled up to the camera and said, as only she can: 'I'm up ta' here, honey!'"

"I was thrilled when I saw Bette on the set," remembers Lee Miller. "I had met her a few years before when I was working on the Tony Awards. We worked well together on that show and when she saw me on the *Cher* set she just screamed. We had a grand reunion."

Midler shared her experience appearing on *Cher* with *In the Know* magazine. "I looked like death! For the whole two weeks of rehearsals my hair was frizzed out and I wore no makeup at all. Well, they [the CBS crew] all looked at me like, 'Oh, holy shit! What did Cher drag in from the east coast?' Then, when I finally showed up on the set looking like a human being, I swear to God there was an audible gasp from the control room. They were all *so* relieved!" Midler had agreed to appear on *Cher* with the promise that she'd be given a solo singing spot—"Hello in There" (from 1972's *The Divine Miss M*). It didn't happen. Midler expressed her disappointment for a full year in her stage act and, while presenting a Grammy Award the following year, told the audience that her glamorous gown was Cher's: "She didn't give me a solo, so she gave me a dress!"

Cher also met Elton John in the early part of 1974, and when her solo show was in pre-production made a special trip—with George Schlatter and head writer Digby Wolfe—to see one of his concerts and make a personal pitch that he be a guest on her show. It worked. On *Cher* Elton performed "Lucy in the Sky with Diamonds," at the time the No. 1 song in America (several months later his *Captain Fantastic and the Brown Dirt Cowboy* became the first album ever to debut in the No. 1 position on *Billboard*'s album chart), wearing a silver rhinestone studded jacket and a pair of pink-tinted diamond-studded eye glasses. "I just loved that costume—it was incredible," John said later. "I think Bob [Mackie] got a lot of his personal fantasies out in the creation of all those wild clothes!"

Columnist Sue Cameron had a bird's-eye-view of John as he taped his solo. "Elton isn't used to performing on television. You could see that he wanted to do a good job and he made a great effort to be extremely cooperative each time something happened and he had to re-do his number. One time he did the whole number perfectly except for a mistake on the second to last note and he was really upset with himself."

He may have been upset with himself, but he wasn't upset with his hostess. "I can't think of anyone else I would fly from London to Los Angeles during the Christmas holidays for. Cher is a universal talent and a great lady. Besides, I consider her a good friend." On the show, Cher joined John for a duet of his tune "Bennie and the Jets." Originally the pair had planned to sing John's "Take Me to the Pilot"—a Cher favorite—but the consensus was that "Bennie" (the first song by a white artist to make No. 1 on *Billboard*'s R&B chart) was the more familiar song. Their duet was special. John at the piano and Cher on a stool, the two performers, at the peak of their popularity, perfectly matched—both in vocal talent and visual splendor. (Before the year was out, both Cher and John shared a rare and coveted honor: appearing on the cover of *Time*.)

When Flip Wilson ambled onto *Cher*'s stage he had already made his name— in a big way. Four years earlier *Time* called him "TV's First Black Superstar." Wilson was the star of *The Flip Wilson Show*, toured the country in an SRO nightclub act, released a string of comedy albums, and had a Flip Wilson/ Geraldine doll (Geraldine was his sassy-talking female alter-ego) in toy stores.

On *Cher*, Wilson as Geraldine and Cher as Laverne met in a "Life with Laverne" segment entitled "Class of '65."

LAVERNE: Don't you remember me? I was your constant high-school companion.

GERALDINE: You're not the football team!

(Later)

LAVERNE: [Admiringly] Oh, honey, this dress hugs my figure like a scared monkey.

GERALDINE: Yeah, and I think I know what scared the monkey!

Offstage, Wilson was a volatile and unpredictable personality who was struggling with substance abuse. In her book *The First Time*, Cher wrote that Wilson "walked out in the middle of taping and never came back." The comedian did the same thing several years later while appearing on a TV special starring *Three's Company*'s Suzanne Somers.

Cher's solo number was her interpretation of Stevie Wonder's "All in Love Is Fair" (a rebirth of sorts as it was the final solo song she performed on *The Sonny and Cher Comedy Hour*). The musical arrangement for the tune, along with her vocal—a soft intro leading up to an impassioned finale—mirrored her hit "The Way of Love."

Comedy highlights on the show included Cher as TV pitchwoman Donna Jean Brodine, hawking a product called Break-O-Matic (a brick); "Saturday Night," which featured Cher returning home and discussing her "all hands on" date; a blackout in which Cher dramatically began singing the tune "What Kind of Fool am I?" only to stop mid-song and don a pair of eyeglasses with bushy eyebrows and a mustache attached to them; and an "Old Folks Sketch" featuring Cher, John, Midler and Wilson as a group of rambunctious elderly residents. The hour ended with a musical finale in which the whole troupe performed a medley of "Mockingbird," "Proud Mary," "Never Can Say Goodbye" and "Ain't No Mountain High Enough." Photographs of the four clothed in what *Newsweek* called "Enough ostrich feathers, spangles and sequins to sink a Busby Berkeley musical" were widely published.

"That finale with Bob Mackie's incredible costumes and Bob Kelly's incredible set, has yet to be topped by anyone," says George Schlatter. "Cher loved Elton and Bette and they loved her—and it shows. CBS was as thrilled with that special, it totally sold them on the *Cher* series." Apparently less thrilling to CBS executives were four segments that were filmed for the special, but never aired. A comedy sketch called "Women Behind the Men," featuring Midler as a newscaster doing an investigative report on The Lone Ranger (John), Mrs. Lone Ranger (Cher) and the couple's friend Tonto (Wilson), ended up on the cutting-room floor.

So did two more sketches. The first was a "Zingers" segment that featured Cher, Midler, John and Wilson exchanging one-liners, some of them caustic.

BETTE: I found a really cheap way to sweeten my coffee.

CHER: Yeah? What is it?

BETTE: Just before I'm ready to drink, I dip Karen Carpenter in it!

FLIP: What's black and white and has three eyes?

CHER: What?

FLIP: Frank Sinatra and Sammy Davis Jr.!

"Mable's Fables" (actually the very first segment Cher ever filmed for the series) also hit the cutting-room floor. The sketch featured Cher as kooky Fairy Godmother Mable and Midler as a (decidedly; by the CBS censors at least) too-sexy Sleeping Beauty. (The third episode featured Cher and Nancy Walker performing a re-written, tamed down version of the segment.)

Elton John's comic asides didn't pass the network censors either. A consummate storyteller and ad-libber—later in the year he scandalized American audiences when he hosted the first annual Rock Music Awards—Elton's "grandmother story" and "Queen Mother story" were never heard by anyone outside of CBS Television City.

"After the writers delivered a script, the first draft would go to George and me and we would sit down and go through it," explains head writer Digby Wolfe about the complicated process of developing material for the show. "George and I would sit down with Cher and go through it. Then slowly but surely we would kind of whittle away at it, change it, change the running order, consider the music people's suggestions, the wardrobe people's suggestions. For instance, sometimes the wardrobe people wouldn't have enough time to come up with a costume for a particular sketch so we would pull that sketch and plan to use it later. Then, finally, the finished draft would go to everyone; the network, the sponsors, the agencies, the guest stars, and the censors. If we were lucky, the script would be filmed as it was—but that usually never happened."

Cher's first television outing without Sonny came in at No. 5 in the Nielsen ratings and later in the year won an Emmy for Best Art Direction or Scenic Design—Robert Kelly and (set decorator) Robert Checchi. The series was nominated in four more categories; Best Director—Art Fisher; Best Costumes—Bob Mackie; Best Musical Material—Billy Barnes and Earl Brown; and Best Writing. "Combination of guests not familiar to TV viewers, a sense of liberated-woman freedom that should appeal to femmes, and an eye-catching wardrobe for the male girl-watchers auger well for the *Cher* concept," wrote *Variety*. "The hour moved rapidly and at times with genuine musical excitement. Working very much in the star's favor is an obvious desire to please—something that was not always apparent on *The Sonny and Cher Comedy Hour*, where her role was putdown artist to Sonny's braggart." *The Christian Science Monitor* (an especially important review given CBS's concerns about Cher's "suitability") called the special "One of the most glittering premieres ever seen on TV. Cher is at her best in the show's one non-glitter number, in which she does a quietly poignant monologue ['Saturday Night']. No Nefertiti hairdo, no wild Bob Mackie costumes, just a Cher we don't know too well revealing a whole range of facial expressions to match the emotions she proves she can project." And *The Los Angeles Times*, Cher's hometown newspaper, (thankfully) gushed: "Three cheers for Cher and her new CBS variety series. Sonny without Cher was a disaster. Cher without Sonny, on the other hand, could be the best thing that's happened to weekly television this season."

"This has got to be the greatest period of transition in my life," Cher said at the time. "I don't know how it's going to work out, either personally or professionally, but it's the real turning point. What happens to me in the next few months is going to decide the direction my entire life takes."

10

"IN IT UP TO MY NECK"

In the midst of rehearsals for the second installment of *Cher* a tragic incident that took place several months before came back to haunt Cher. On January 13, 1975 Cher was served with a summons to appear in front of a Los Angeles Grand Jury and tell her side of what exactly took place at a fatal gathering she had attended.

On September 23, 1974, following a performance by the Scottish rock group the Average White Band (best known for their hit "Pick Up the Pieces") at the Troubadour nightclub in Hollywood, Cher attended a private party for the band that was held at Kenneth Moss's (founder of the failed Freelandia Air Travel Club) Beverly Hills home. Cher was a fan of the Average White Band's music and had gone to see the group play at the Troubadour several times—once even joining them onstage for an impromptu medley. At the party an illegal substance, thought to be cocaine but in actuality heroin, was passed around. Although Cher declined to use the substance another guest, Robbie McIntosh, the Average White Band's 28-year old-drummer, did. Shortly thereafter McIntosh passed out. He died the following day of "acute morphine-heroin intoxication."

"While I was at that party I felt like Little Annie Fannie," Cher told *Playboy* later in the year. "I mean, this guy passed stuff around, and he said, 'Do you want some?' And I said 'no' and I was sitting there and ten minutes later, everybody was out of it."

Attempting to manage an out of control situation, Cher took another of the group's members—bassist Alan Gorrie, who had also partaken of the substance, —home with her and, following the advice of her gynecologist (her personal physician was unavailable), induced vomiting, applied ice packs to his body and forcibly walked him around, preventing him from losing consciousness and lapsing into a coma. (Following the deadly evening Moss fled the country for Belize, where he remained "unavailable to be questioned" for a full nine months.) At the January grand jury hearing Cher took the stand and spoke for 45 minutes about what exactly happened at the party. "She was a most cooperative witness," said a source. "She gave us chapter and verse on what happened that evening and the role she played." She also gave chapter and verse to CBS executives who, already concerned about her "suitability" for Prime Time, wanted to know why she attended the party in the first place.

"It was all so stupid," Cher would later say. "They kept asking me how I could go to a party where I didn't already know everyone. Has it come to this in America? Where you are not allowed to go out to a place where you might meet someone new?"

Along with Cher's grand jury appearance it was also reported that, acting on behalf of his girlfriend, immediately following Robbie McIntosh's death, David Geffen called McIntosh's wife and begged her to keep Cher's name out of the press. That didn't happen. Although at the time Cher made her appearance the incident remained pretty much under wraps, on February 4, when Moss was formally indicted, Cher's involvement became general news. *The New York Times'* headline, "Coast Jury Indicts Party Host in Death of a Rock Musician" was relatively sedate; but others were not. "Cher in Drummer's Death!" "Cher Saves Man from Dying of Overdose: What Was She Doing at Drug Party?" and "Cher Witness to Murder? Family and Friends Rush to Protect Her!" were plastered on the covers of everything from *TV-Radio Mirror* magazine to *The New York Post*.

The early lack of coverage of the events that happened on September 23—*The National Star* broke the story with their October 12, 1974 cover "Cher Bono at Death Party"—was a puzzle to many. Often looked down upon, but more often than not correct and the first to inform readers about Hollywood's seedier side, *The National Star* (occasionally titled *The Weekly National Star* and eventually just *Star*) asked their readers (and the public) a legitimate question: Why had *The Los Angeles Times*, the biggest newspaper in the area, waited until February 21—nearly five months after the fact—to carry a single line about the presence of a major show-business celebrity (Cher) at a mysterious party where another celebrity (Robbie McIntosh) had taken a fatal overdose?

"We were aware of the investigation," a *Times* representative told *The Star* after repeated requests for a comment, "but when we knew it was going to a grand jury we agreed to wait until that happened and also to see if they could catch Moss."

But with whom had *The Times* agreed? The Los Angeles County Sheriff's Office or the super-influential David Geffen—who was Cher's boyfriend at the time? Robbie McIntosh's wife Edith told *Star* editor Steve Dunleavy that Geffen called her and demanded, "'under no circumstances must Cher be linked with this.' Robbie didn't even want to go the party that night. He was too tired after the show. Cher was the one who insisted he go. She said they were throwing a surprise party for the band and grabbed his arm after the second show."

(On June 25, 1975 Kenneth Moss returned to the States and was formally arraigned. Seven months later, in January 1976, the "Death Party" story itself died. Moss pleaded guilty to the charge of "involuntary manslaughter" and was sentenced to four months in the Los Angeles County Jail—followed by four years of probation.)

More than any other tabloid at the time, *The National Star* made its name on Cher's back. Introduced on February 9, 1974 by publishing magnate Rupert Murdoch as competition for the top-selling *The National Enquirer* (ironically, today, both magazines are owned by the same company—American Media Inc.) from the very beginning, and with two reporters whose sole job it was to report on Cher, *The Star* used Cher—her mercurial life, loves and travails—to attract, expand and maintain a loyal readership. And *The National Star*'s six million weekly readers were generously rewarded. In less than a year, via inside sources, vigorous fact-checking, juicy stories, and the inclusion of color pages, the tabloid really was what they said it was—"America's favorite weekly." More than this, and contrary to popular belief, *The National Star* was also almost always right. It was *The National Star*, not *The National Enquirer*—or for that matter, *Midnight*, *The National Tattler* or *Modern People*, three other popular weekly newsstand tabloids—that first broke the news about Cher's attendance at Kenneth Moss's "Drug Party." It was *The National Star* that first alerted readers that Cher and David Geffen's relationship had come to an end—and then published a photograph of Cher with her new love Gregg Allman. And it was *The National Star* that, later in the year, published information that Cher, herself, didn't know: CBS executives had, without informing her, made the decision to cancel her solo television series.

With the success of Cher's special behind her, and with her concession to CBS that she would avoid associating with people like Kenneth Moss—people who might cast her or the network in a bad light, thereby scaring away her program's million-dollar advertisers—filming of *Cher* proceeded at breakneck pace. The series' second episode aired on Sunday, February 16, 1975—just four days after the special (and, ironically, on Sonny Bono's fortieth birthday). Like the first program, the second installment of *Cher* also featured guests who were not regularly featured on television; Tatum O'Neal and Raquel Welch. Wayne Rogers, one of the stars of CBS's hit comedy *M*A*S*H*, was also booked on the show. The script for the second show was completed on January 15 and the show was taped just four days later, on January 19 and 20. "Usually, each Friday you got the script for the following week's show," says Ret Turner. "You had to start working on the new one immediately. It was always a very quick, very hectic production; very hard work. You had a week to put everything together and that was it."

Unlike other variety shows on the air at the time, the greater part of *Cher* was not performed in front of a studio audience. Instead, only a small portion of the show—usually the opening, closing and, sometimes, a musical number—was filmed with an audience present. The remainder was filmed in a rehearsal situation and witnessed by only a handful of TV-studio employees. "Cher has a lot of ability but she's an instrument and is only as good as the person who is playing her," *Sonny and Cher Comedy Hour* producer Chris Bearde told writer Vicki Pellegrino at the time. "Cher needs to be told what to do. She's a Ferrari but she has to be driven right. In the right hands she's a marvelous performer. In the wrong hands she's just a dull girl."

The five-day work week the *Cher* show's writers enjoyed—"ten in the morning until whenever we were done," remembers Bo Kaprall—did not apply to Cher. She was usually present at CBS six or seven days a week. As she told *Rolling Stone* (while shouldering only half the workload on *The Sonny and Cher Comedy Hour*), "Sometimes I think my whole life takes place in here [the CBS Studios]. Just getting dressed and then going out to do another show..." Tedious meetings, never-ending rehearsals, pre-recording (for Cher, her guests, and the program's orchestra), walk-throughs, run-throughs, and two eight- to ten-hour days of taping (the portion shot in front of an audience requiring a much more complicated set up), meant that, though the atmosphere on the set of *Cher* was often playful, actual playtime was kept at a minimum. Hard work was the order of the day; every day.

Chris Hodenfield's May 24, 1973 *Rolling Stone* piece on Sonny and Cher offered readers a vivid and unflinching glimpse of the tiresome and workmanlike machinations that took place off-camera. "There she stood in Studio B [Studio 31] of CBS Television City, the high-heeled hippodrome, Cher surrounded by her fleet of lackeys—one seamstress kneeling, two cosmeticians performing relief work, and a hairstylist under a pink wig. When her solo number is over, she blushingly acknowledges from side-to-side the invisible applause that will be added later. Right now only the cameramen applaud, which is the way it's been going through all the skits... the prop men help the timing by laughing uproariously at lines they've heard a dozen times over. The unsung laughers."

But even after *Cher* was "in the can," the program still was not ready to be aired. Post-dubbing (sounds effects; doorbells, ringing phones, etc); "sweetener" (a laugh track); pre-recorded "Cher Film Bursts" (collages of Cher along with the spinning *Cher* show logo); "Guest Billboards" (videotaped images of the programs' guests filmed against a black backdrop); and the careful placement of fifteen-, 30- and 60-second commercials and CBS network promos and station IDs, made creating a broadcast-ready product a time-consuming and thoroughly painstaking endeavor.

Cher's costume fittings ("no small feat when your basic trademark is wardrobe," wrote *Time*), were particularly arduous. "Wednesdays were fitting nights," Cher recalled. "I would go to Bob Mackie's workshop and stand for three and a half hours while he, Ret and sometimes Ray [Aghayan] looked on and made suggestions. Just standing there for hours and hours on end was hard, especially since I had already put in a full day of rehearsals. But I understood that we were doing a costume-oriented show, and fittings were part of my job."

"Director Art Fisher used to scream and holler that we weren't getting Cher changed fast enough between scenes," remembers Ret Turner. (He also was in the habit of snapping his fingers and exclaiming "fuck" after each and every camera cut.) "Me and a lovely woman named Trudy were responsible for dressing Cher, and Cher's costumes were always so elaborate that it really did take the two of us to get her ready. Often we used spirit glue to keep some of the more revealing outfits on and in place on her body. It was also our job to make sure that her hair was wrapped correctly to go under her wigs, hats and beaded helmets. Certain wigs had to be glued down along the hairline. Others had to be perfectly placed on her head. Bob designed each of the wigs she wore to specifically go with her outfits, so that was all a part of getting her dressed and ready. It took a lot of time and wasn't particularly interesting or fun—especially for Cher. The end result may have been fun—but not the preparation."

"Offstage, when she didn't have to perform, Cher usually went without makeup and dressed in blue jeans and t-shirts," remembers Donna Schuman, who was the executive producer's assistant (playfully referred to in scripts as "Assistant to the Mogul") for the entire length of Cher's series. "Cher was always very low key. She treated everyone associated with the show equally and with a great deal of respect. I also found her to be decent, honorable, loyal, sensitive, caring, direct, street-smart and dead-on honest. In the words of 'ol blue eyes'— she was a really 'great broad!'"

But Cher wasn't always low-key. Lee Miller had a different relationship with the often beleaguered artist. "Cher and I were very, very close throughout the entire length of the series," says Miller. "Many times my phone rang at midnight or even much later. I always knew it was Cher. She stayed up late and thought nothing of calling up the people who worked for her. She would say things like 'I want to change the song,' 'I don't like the sketch,' or 'we've got to fix this—it's all wrong.' It was my job to listen to her, discuss the matter, console her, and then, the next day, try and make everything right."

At the time of her appearance on *Cher* Tatum O'Neal was fresh off of her 1974 Best Supporting Actress Oscar win for her role in *Paper Moon*. The youngest performer ever to be awarded an Oscar, O'Neal's accomplishment helped land her on the covers of magazines like *Rolling Stone*, *People* and *Newsweek*. But the child star's personal life was often played out in the tabloids. Her actress mother Joanna Moore (best known for her role in *Walk on the Wild Side* but also a featured player in *The Hindenburg*) was an emotionally troubled alcoholic who had surrendered custody of Tatum and her brother Griffin to their father, actor Ryan O'Neal—who was often away on film shoots. In her autobiography *A Paper Life*, O'Neal revealed that, as a young girl, she was always on the lookout for a mother figure and that Cher, "the ultimate high-powered, high-fashion diva of the time," more than fit the bill. Cher and O'Neal first met in the early part of 1974 and Tatum immediately "embarked on an intense campaign to win her over. I called her all the time and literally camped out on the doorstep of her mansion. I implied that I had nowhere else to go, which wasn't quite true... I fell totally in love with Cher—not in a sexual way of course, but with a desperate hunger for her attention, as in 'Please take over my life. Let me be with you.'" Cher felt sorry for O'Neal, indulged her, and often took her with her shopping—a *People* magazine photographer accompanied them on a shopping spree. Two days after taping the premiere episode of her series, Cher even took Tatum, along with Chastity, on a three-day trip to Hawaii. "And I lived at her house for a few weeks," remembered O'Neal, "It was heaven!"

On *Cher*, Tatum proved to be irresistible. She opened the show dressed in a silver and white sequined gown and long "Cher" wig. She also, as "Tatoom O'Neal," did a spoof of Catherine Deneuve's popular Channel No. 5 perfume commercials, and, with Cher, sang Billy Barnes and Earl Brown's "Girls Are Smarter"—a lead in to several comedy segments. In "The Divorce," O'Neal played a woman who had been married 500 times. The lawyer hired to represent her was Wayne Rogers.

WAYNE: So what happened to your marriage?

TATUM: I don't quite know. I guess it's the difference in our ages. You see, I'm twelve and he's only eleven and a half. We have nothing in common. You know... he can't even do long division.

WAYNE: So it's definitely not going to work out?

TATUM: Not at all. He stays out till all hours of the night. Last night he stayed out till 7:00. And when he came home I could smell Kool-Aid on his breath. There's just no hope.

Comfortable in front of the camera, engaging to watch, strikingly natural, O'Neal, in her network television debut, was a knockout; and it was noted. "With all due respect to Rogers, Raquel and Cher, the hit of last night's show was youngster Tatum O' Neal," observed *Variety*. "...at all times a sheer delight." Off camera, as confirmed by several sources, O'Neal, whom the entertainment press had dubbed "Tantrum," was bossy and problematic—often bringing taping to a halt to ask questions, "fix her makeup" or make suggestions. At one point, during a break in taping, Cher was giving an interview to a TV critic and Tatum, unhappy that she wasn't the center of attention, couldn't keep still. "Tatum kept interrupting them," recalls a stagehand. "She kept making faces, noises, sticking her tongue out. At one point she went over and pushed her way between Cher and the reporter. That was it; George blew his top. He yelled, 'Tatum, get over here and sit down RIGHT NOW!' Everyone in the studio turned and looked and Tatum just sort of slinked away. I don't think that girl had ever been disciplined in her entire life." (Three weeks after the episode with Tatum aired, *The National Star* published an investigative piece on the actress. The headline: "Tatum... What a Cute, Talented, Pretty, Loveable, Clever little BRAT.")

Cher became friendly with Raquel Welch in the latter part of 1974 (the two crossed paths backstage at the 1974 Academy Awards ceremony, at which they were both presenters). "She *is* strange," Cher told *Playboy*, "But I really like her a lot." Welch and Cher took exercise classes at the Ron Fletcher Studio and Welch was invited to Cher's exclusive 1974 Christmas Eve party (an event that she and Sonny, who was also invited, departed from early in favor of taking in a screening of *The Towering Inferno*). No stranger to television, Welch had already headlined her own special, and although the reviews for her show were mixed, throughout the '70s she remained something of a cultural artifact; one of Hollywood's last contract movie stars.

"Cher is, without a doubt, one of the most professional ladies I've ever worked with," Welch recalled. "She is a sweetheart and she is under a tremendous amount of pressure. When I was taping her show, I really felt attached to everyone. They all really care about Cher. I'm so impressed with her and I had a really wonderful time working with her." Welch's accolades changed dramatically when the show on which she appeared aired. On the program—dressed in "hers and hers" sequined outfits—Welch and Cher did an exuberant rendition of "I'm a Woman." The number began with the two talking off-camera about how awful they looked and how they were not yet ready to perform. After a beat, they emerged glittering and glamorous.

"I started that with Cher because Raquel wasn't available," remembers choreographer Tony Charmoli. "Then I worked with Raquel because Cher wasn't available. It went on back and forth like that for about a week. I had pretty much laid out the groundwork for the number before I met them. Then, when I finally got them together in the same room, I just revised things to fit. I believed it was my job as a choreographer to always let the personality of the star shine through. Cher should be Cher and Raquel should be Raquel and I made sure that that's exactly what they were."

George Schlatter also remembers "I'm a Woman." "Cher and Raquel were in competition to see who was going to wear the least. I don't remember who the winner was, but when the two of them came out under the bright lights, it just took everyone's breath away. The entire crew was staring at them open-mouthed!"

A reporter who was present during the taping made this matter-of-fact observation: "Cher relishes the whistles and catcalls of the attendant stagehands with the frank pleasure of a girl who grew up thinking she wasn't very pretty."

Perhaps it was true. "When I was younger I was... you know... really ugly," Cher informed Rona Barrett. "I remember once I went to my mom and said, 'How come I'm dark and have an ugly nose and these teeth?' And my mother said, 'Let me tell you something. When you grow up, you're not going to be the most beautiful. You're not going to be the most charming. You're not going to be the most anything. But when I look at you, there is something about you that is different and unique—so don't worry about it.' When I think back on it now, that was the hippest thing that my mother ever said to me." In later years Cher summed up her thoughts about her physical appearance. "I think my looks are functional, they work. But I wouldn't choose them if I had a choice."

Raquel Welch had agreed to appear on *Cher* with the expressed stipulation that she be given a solo musical number. But like Bette Midler before her (and to a lesser extent Elton John—whose racy comic stories didn't make the final cut), Welch's solo—a cover of Roberta Flack's "Feel Like Makin' Love"—never aired. (Instead she performed the song on *The McLean Stevenson Special*). Cher explained what happened to *Playboy*. "CBS pulled Raquel's number and I'm real pissed off about it. Raquel and I were becoming really good friends. We did 'I'm a Woman' together. We came out in dresses and sang a song—no horrible gyrations, no anything. And she did a solo number, which was really nice. Well, first we got a call that they were cutting our duet because the program director said it was too suggestive. Then they said we could keep the duet, but her solo number had to go because she was singing a suggestive song and she placed her hand, God forbid, on parts of her anatomy. Well, when she found out about it, God, she just freaked. She called the network and got some guy that didn't even have the guts to tell her that it was their idea; he told her it was *mine*. Then she called me up and she was furious. She read me up one side and down the other. I said, 'Raquel, I swear to God on my daughter's life, I had nothing to do with it,' and she hung up on me. Then *I* got really angry. I called up Freddie Silverman, CBS's programming director, and said, 'You guys have just ruined a friendship for me.' So he said, 'I'll call her myself and tell her it was because she touched herself,' and blah-blah-blah. He called her, but she was into such a role by then that it didn't pierce. Maybe she thought they were just trying to cover up for me. I don't know, but we haven't spoken since." (Angry with Cher, but not with the people she worked with on the *Cher* show, Welch asked *Cher*'s Billy Barnes to escort her to that year's Golden Globe Awards.)

Writing in *TV Guide*, Cleveland Amory wasn't impressed with Welch's appearance on *Cher*. "Let's put it this way, we liked Miss Welch better when she was awful, because then she was sort of awful-fun. Now, unfortunately, she's gotten a bit better. Not enough to be good but too much to be fun-bad."

For his part, Wayne Rogers, who had been a guest on *The Sonny and Cher Comedy Hour*, participated in three comedy sketches, "The Divorce" with Tatum O'Neal, "The Complaint Department" with Cher, in which he tried unsuccessfully to return a broken toaster, and in a "Women Behind the Men" segment playing Sigmund Freud. Rogers also performed a duet with Cher, of Olivia Newton-John's 1973 hit "Let Me Be There." "That number was particularly hard for us," remembers Rogers. "Cher and I had a problem figuring out who was going to harmonize below or above who. Cher has a very deep singing voice for a woman and we tried that number over and over again several different ways. I don't think we ever really got it right."

The time he spent on *Cher* involved more than appearing in a few comedy sketches and singing a duet with Cher; he also helped George Schlatter deal with a difficult situation: Raquel Welch. "Raquel was a very insecure performer. She didn't want to sing, she wanted to lip-synch—she didn't want to perform live, that whole thing," recalls Rogers. "She was also very pretentious. George and I, and for that matter Digby Wolfe too, who was this great crazy guy, had no pretenses at all. The three of us hit it off right away and were very comfortable with one another. So George comes up to me during one of our rehearsals and says, 'Raquel says that her dressing room isn't big enough.' He said, 'I just can't deal with this Wayne—you've gotta help me out.' I said, 'Jesus, George, I'm not the producer; who am I to tell her anything?' And he said 'I know but I just can't deal with her; help me.'"

"I told George, 'Okay, I'll help,' and I took Raquel on a guided tour of all the other dressing rooms at CBS. I was trying to show her that the dressing rooms were basically all the same. The largest of the star dressing rooms at that time was Carol Burnett's. Carol wasn't shooting that week so I brought Raquel into Carol's dressing room and showed her around. She wasn't impressed. Finally I said, 'You know what Raquel, I'll tell you where the next biggest dressing room is. It's on the Warner Bros. lot. If you want, they can take a truck and bring you over there. It'll take a half-hour to get there and a half-hour to get back. The decision is yours.' Finally she said' 'Okay, I guess I'll take this one.' So while she was appearing on Cher's show she got dressed in Carol Burnett's dressing room! When I went back and told George that everything was okay he said, 'What did you do?' I said, 'She's going to use Carol Burnett's dressing room.' And he said, 'Holy shit! That's going to cause me even more problems.' I just said, 'I can't handle everything for you George, she's all yours now!'" (Two years later Welch made her feelings about the entertainment industry and its inhabitants crystal-clear. "Look, this industry is a hard, rotten business, full of the toughest, most unscrupulous, insensitive, low-life people you will ever come across. Anybody who makes it anywhere near the top, like myself, has worked extremely hard and ought to be proud of it, which I am. I consider myself triumphant.")

Welch's insecurities were not the only difficult situation presented to Rogers. The actor, who by all accounts was not shy about airing grievances (he was soon to exit the popular role of Trapper John on M*A*S*H because he believed the show's writers were favoring his co-star Alan Alda), had a showdown with Welch, Tatum O'Neal *and* Cher.

"Everyone was showing up twenty, 30, even 40 minutes late and I just didn't get it," remembers Rogers. "Sometimes one of the three wouldn't show at all. I called them all together and told them, 'Listen. This program isn't going to change my life one iota. I am here as a service person. I am here in the best sense of the word to service the show and to service the three of you. If you're not going to show up for readings or rehearsals I'm going home because this is disrespectful to me as your guest. You're making me out to be the patsy here, and that's a role I won't play for you.' After I gave my little speech they all showed up on time and from that point on they were just wonderful. They worked hard, showed an interest in what we were doing, and we had a really great time together."

Other segments on show number two included a blackout in which Cher dramatically started to sing "Nothing Can Stop Me Now" only to be knocked out by a boxing glove, and a "Life with Laverne" sketch in which Laverne meets Raquel Welch, whose car has broken down outside of Kenny's Kafe, a small diner owned by Wayne Rogers.

RAQUEL: I've got a flat.

LAVERNE: [looking at Raquel's chest] A flat what honey?!

Outstanding Cher solo segments included Cher's opening number "You're Nobody till Somebody Loves You," an upbeat tune made famous in the '60s by Dean Martin (and performed on *The Sonny and Cher Comedy Hour*) as well as a second installment of the "Saturday Night" sketch in which Cher discussed her date with a nineteen-year-old.

The "Cher Concert" showcased "Soul Cher." Dressed in a short afro wig and Afro-centric jewelry, Cher sang a down-home 'n' dirty medley of the Doobie Brothers' "Long Train Running" and the much-covered Stephen Stills hit "Love the One You're With." The hour ended with an elaborately staged and impressively choreographed tap-dance production number to Irving Berlin's "Top Hat, White Tie and Tails." For the number, Cher, Welch, O'Neal, Rogers and eight dancers gave it their all; vamping, posing, singing and tap dancing their heads off. (Taped and "banked" for later use, but never aired because it was deemed "objectionable" by the ever-present CBS censors, was a segment featuring Cher as Donna Jean Brodine pitching a household product called Stick-It.)

DONNA JEAN BRODINE: I've got a revolutionary new product here which will bond together any two surfaces in five seconds flat... Just grab it, squeeze it, and watch it go to work... if you know what I mean. And I'm sure you educated viewers do!

With the completion and airing of the second installment of *Cher*, billed as the series' "debut," Cher's solo series was officially up and running. "Generally speaking, the quick-paced format worked even better on her premiere than on her special," observed *Variety*. "And Cher even displayed some unexpected upper register vocal range in her rousing opening number. The second installment continues the promise shown on her first network outing." Cher's network "special" placed fifth for the week in the Nielsens. Her "premiere"—featuring Raquel Welch—came in a bit lower in 22nd place (even so, it was the highest-rated program the evening it aired). *Cher* may not have started out by coming in at No. 1, but Cher, her producers, her million-dollar advertisers, and the CBS television network all remained convinced that, in time, the series would develop into a long-running, highly regarded Sunday-night mainstay.

11

UP, UP... AND AWAY

Cher episode number three was noteworthy because, along with *Rhoda's* Nancy Walker, Cher's "Special Guest Star" was comedian Jerry Lewis, someone with whom she had a casual friendship—she and Sonny appeared on Lewis's 1967 variety series—and who had twice appeared on *The Sonny and Cher Comedy Hour*. The long-time spokesperson for the *Muscular Dystrophy Telethon* had come to prominence in the '50s and '60s as half of the (Dean) Martin and Lewis comedy team. Winning in the 1963 film *The Nutty Professor*, Lewis successfully incorporated that picture's main character—a well-meaning but misguided goofball—into the larger part of his comedy routines. "Jerry loved Cher and Cher loved Jerry," remembers Schlatter, and their work together made clear that it was true.

During the program's opening segment, following Cher's rousing rendition of the Beatles' "Got to Get You into My Life" (a song she sang with Sonny when they toured in '73) and a monologue about how she was attempting to gain favor with the Nielsen Ratings families, Cher informed her audience that Lewis was on the show. "I've got to tell you that I'm really happy that Jerry's on the show tonight. He's a great performer, a great comic, and a really good friend." The script for the episode indicated that, after Cher's mention of his name, the camera was to pan to Lewis standing in the wings. He would then wave at Cher and smile at the camera. Instead, Lewis jumped up onstage with Cher, engaged in a bit of teasing, and then joined her in a reprise of "Got to Get You into My Life" (adopting an ear-splitting wail). A tongue-twister sketch, in which Lewis played a confused detective and Cher played a painfully indirect crime victim, was inspired.

JERRY: Now let me see if I've got this straight. Peter and Penelope Piper picked a peck of pickled peppers. The peck of pickled peppers were pilfered

Previous page: And we're off! The premier of Cher's solo series was billed as a "Special" and CBS spared no expense; Elton John, Flip Wilson and Bette Midler awash in a sea of sequins and balloons. Midler wore this same costume later in her concert act.
(Photo Fair)

Three scenes from Cher's special. Clockwise from top left: Cher and Bette Midler performing a "Trashy Ladies" medley (Midler later complained that she didn't get a solo number); Flip Wilson as sassy Geraldine and Cher as tacky Laverne at a high-school reunion; Cher and Elton John (who was as funny off-camera as on-) in an "Old Folks" comedy sketch (Elton did get a solo). (J. Howard Collection)

Opposite: Cher with the wizard behind the madness, Mr. Bob Mackie. Cher's feather and skull-cap ensemble was supposed to appear on the cover of Time but was replaced at the last minute with a more flesh-baring (and memorable) photograph.
(Photo Fair)

Opposite above: Cher in a CBS promo with guests Jack Chico and the Man Albertson and Cloris Leachman. Both won Emmy Awards for their appearances in "Dinner at Eight", a comedy segment which was supposed to feature Cher. Below: Cher and Wayne Rogers (of M*A*S*H) participate in a salute to the all-American hamburger. The segment was so visually stunning that Bob Mackie received an Emmy nomination for Best Costume Design. (CBS-TV)

A great deal of material that was filmed hit the cutting-room floor. Cases in point: Cher and Bill Cosby's spoof of The Six Million Dollar Man TV series (left), deemed "too racy" by the censors; Cher and the Spinners (below) performing the group's soulful No. 1 hit, "Then Came You" (originally a duet with Dionne Warwick). The Spinners complained to the African-American press when this and other segments they filmed never aired. (J. Howard Collection)

Opposite above: Make me laugh: Comedienne Ruth Buzzi as frumpy Gladys Ormphby and Cher as Laverne (her "lady of the launderette" and the only holdover from The Sonny and Cher Comedy Hour) *discuss the difficulties of getting a date. Below: Tom and Dick Smothers have "fun" with Cher in "The Pain Game," a game-show spoof. Returning to the TV studio they had previously occupied proved emotionally challenging for the brothers. (Photo Fair)*

Above: Trick or treat? Cher plays the Bride of Frankenstein to Tim Conway's Mad Scientist Doctor. From '75-'76, Tim was a regular on The Carol Burnett Show. *(Photo Fair)*

To placate the CBS censors–enforcers of the all-new "Family Hour"–Cher featured a number of pointedly family-friendly guests. Left: Cher, the Hudson Brothers and Chastity enjoy a magic show. Below: Cher is all smiles with Robert Keeshan, known to children everywhere as TV's Captain Kangaroo. (CBS-TV)

from the back of a big black and blue Buick with a bent bumper containing a black and blue rubber baby buggy bumper, a blue and brown rubber baby buggy bumper and a brown and black rubber baby buggy bumper. While Penelope Piper stood at the door of Burgess's fish sauce shop inexplicably mimicking him...

[Jerry grabs his heart and falls over dead. Cher turns to camera.]

CHER: You know, that's the sixth stupid sergeant I snared into saying several silly speeches in succession simultaneously causing a coronary convulsion climaxing with a cacophony of croaked coppers on the concrete.

A "Women Behind the Men" sketch written for renowned mime Marcel Marceau and Cher was, as it turned out, performed by Jerry Lewis and Cher. Best known for his tattered top hat and red flower-wearing, white-faced clown named Bip, Marcel Marceau had appeared on *Laugh-In* and both Schlatter and Digby Wolfe looked forward to working with him a second time. "Working Marcel Marceau into that episode was a special challenge for me," remembers Wolfe. "We had a great version of the song 'He Aint Heavy He's My Brother' [included on 1971's *Cher* album]. We planned to have Cher come out and sing the song—which was fairly dramatic—and then we would widen the screen and Marcel would be revealed behind her in his classic, mime-clown outfit. What we wanted to do was have Cher go on singing without acknowledging him. After a few seconds passed a glove would come out and punch Marcel in the face, and then just as he was about to fall we were going to freeze the frame. A few seconds later he would be back and then get hit by a plank of wood, or a bottle—each time collapsing but freezing in frame before he hit the ground. Then when Cher reached the end of the song we were going to unfreeze all the images of Marcel and let them all fall to the ground. Cher would then notice him on the floor by her side and bend down, help him to his feet, and they would both walk offscreen. We worked on that segment for a very long time and couldn't wait to do it. We were all really, really excited. But, don't you know, Marcel missed his plane in Paris, so the segment went to Jerry Lewis instead.

"Now when Jerry got the material, he didn't understand it at all. Instead of the subtlety and sensitivity that we wanted to highlight—in both Cher and Marcel—Jerry came out with this sort of overt clown shtick which completely changed the mood, feeling and concept of the piece. I'm not saying that Jerry wasn't good. I'm just saying that it wasn't, at all, what I had written or what any of us really wanted. As a writer and a creative person, those kinds of concessions are very hard to take."

Show number three also featured a brief interlude in which Lewis attempted to get a granite-faced Cher to crack a smile, and Lewis and Cher as Mr. and Mrs. Sherlock Holmes.

Nancy Walker, who was as familiar to TV viewers as the indomitable "Rosie" in Bounty Paper Towel commercials as she was in her supporting role as Valerie Harper's wisecracking mother on CBS's *Rhoda*, was a much-beloved older female comedian. On *Cher*, Walker (who would go on to direct 1980's ill-fated disco movie *Can't Stop the Music*) performed the "Mable's Fables" segment originally written for Cher and Bette Midler. A look at the way the sketch was re-written to conform to the CBS censors offers clear evidence of the network's preoccupation with remaining "inoffensive."

(Cher/Bette Midler Version)

MABLE: Well, I guess things really haven't changed too much. Like morals.We didn't have birth control in those days, did we?

SLEEPING BEAUTY: Sure we did. We used dragons.

MABLE: Dragons?

SLEEPING BEAUTY: Sure. You're in the bushes with some sexy prince and a dragon comes by and breathes fire on you. Works every time.

(Cher/Nancy Walker Version)

MABLE: Well, morals have changed too... in the old days there was less... hanky panky.

SLEEPING BEAUTY: There sure was... that's because we had dragons.

MABLE: Dragons?

SLEEPING BEAUTY: Sure. You're fooling around with some prince... a dragon comes by and breathes fire on you. You couldn't care less about hanky panky.

It is interesting to note that, even though the censors bristled at sexual innuendo, they gave scant attention to political correctness. During a future broadcast, show number five, "Mable's Fables" featured guest star Freddie Prinze as Prince Charming. On first seeing him Mable/Cher informs Prinze: "You look like a float in the Puerto Rican Day parade!" Additionally, on a later broadcast, "Mable's Fables" ended with this:

MABLE: On our next program I'm going to tell you the story of Ali Baba and the Forty Thieves. It's about a bunch of Arabs that get a lot of money through shady dealings. On second thought, you don't need Mable for that one—you can read it in the newspaper.

Show number three was rounded out with two more comedy segments. In "Life with Laverne" Nancy Walker played Laverne's equally tacky, misguided and thoroughly self-centered mother, and in "The Interrogation" appeared as the domineering mother of a crime suspect named Scarface (Jerry Lewis). Musical guests the Osmond Brothers (Alan, Wayne, Merrill, Jay and Donny) were TV perennials who, with their squeaky-clean good looks and toothy grins, were regularly featured in teen pin-up magazines. The following year Donny and sister Marie would host *Donny and Marie*, their own hour-long Prime-Time variety series. On *Cher* the brothers performed the tunes "I'm Still Gonna

Need You" and "Danny Boy," sang Billy Barnes and Earl Brown's "Law and Order" (a musical introduction to several comedy sketches), and joined Cher for an exciting finale; a tribute to Stevie Wonder. The meticulously staged and choreographed Cher/Osmonds medley included: "You Are the Sunshine of My Life," "Signed, Sealed, Delivered I'm Yours" and "Superstition" (see Appendix for complete list).

"Cher and the Osmonds together was one of the series' highlights," remembers George Schlatter. "The Osmonds were pretty young at the time, and not particularly worldly or sophisticated. I remember that Mama and Papa Osmond were always around during rehearsals. They were not prepared for Cher's rather irreverent vocabulary—she cursed like a truck driver, and of course she loved doing it. But it took the Osmond parents back a bit. They thought, 'Exactly what kind of show are we allowing our children to appear on?'"

For her solo, Cher, in fine sultry voice, performed one of her favorites—the '20s blues standard "Ain't Nobody's Business If I Do" (performed on *The Sonny and Cher Comedy Hour* as well as 1979's *Cher... and Other Fantasies*). An early draft of the script indicates that Cher first considered singing Barbra Streisand's show-stopping "Don't Rain on My Parade" from the musical *Funny Girl*, but, apparently, changed her mind. The third installment of *Cher* was a solidly funny success. Nancy Walker was perfectly cast in the comedy segments and during rehearsals proved to be so agreeable and so well liked that she was asked to make a return appearance. *TV Guide* writer Rowland Barber was on the set during the taping of the next episode of *Cher*—show number four; a program whose guest stars were Cloris Leachman and Jack Albertson. As Barber reported "The company from the star on down is getting looser by the scene; director Art Fisher, from the control booth: 'Cut! I've got mike-boom shadows all over.' Cher: 'Yeah? What're you taking for it?'"

As it turned out, show number four would be more than just a fun-filled hour of entertainment; it was also an episode whose two guest stars—Leachman and Albertson—would both win Emmy Awards for Outstanding Continuing or Single Performance by an Actor or Actress in Variety or Music. (Although few people knew it, Jack Albertson was Cloris Leachman's uncle by marriage. At the time she taped her segment, Leachman was married—and had five children by—George Englund, Jack Albertson's sister's son.)

In superior voice, Cher opened the hour with Jimmy Dale's intimate version of Irving Berlin's "All By Myself." The song's lyrics—"I've got to face the unknown / I've got to build a world of my own"—seemed to describe Cher's current circumstances perfectly. She followed with a monologue about how clumsy she was off-camera and then joined Albertson and Leachman for a sharp, quick-moving song and dance routine entitled "Do a Take." Albertson, the cranky garage shop owner on NBC's *Chico and the Man*, had previously worked with

Cher on *The Sonny and Cher Comedy Hour*, and the script for this episode cleverly played off of his renown. In "Life with Laverne" he appeared as Ed Brown, his character on *Chico and the Man*, attending to a squawking Laverne.

LAVERNE: Hello! Hello! We need a doctor out here for my baby [her car].

ALBERTSON: Hold on, I'll call a policeman to catch whoever beat you up.

LAVERNE: Nobody beat me up.

ALBERTSON: You mean you left the house looking like *that*? On purpose!

Additionally, Albertson, sitting with Cher on a park bench, delivered a stirring version of Mike Douglas's melancholy 1964 hit "The Men in My Little Girl's Life." (At the conclusion of Albertson's song, Cher is heard saying, "You're going to make me cry!")

Cloris Leachman was a critics' pet at the time of her appearance on *Cher*. An Academy Award-winner for her supporting role in 1971's *The Last Picture Show*, she was also a popular supporting player on *The Mary Tyler Moore Show* and would soon helm her very own sitcom—*Phyllis*. Leachman, whom Cher described on air as "a fun broad to work with," was also a champion of *est* (Erhard Seminars Training) a spiritually-minded "personal awareness" program that was, for a time, both immensely popular and equally controversial. On the show Leachman joined Albertson in a send-up of a Geritol vitamin commercial (Geritol was a second-season sponsor), and recited a Shakespeare-like soliloquy accompanied by contemporary Cher's simultaneous jive-talking translations. A memorable "Dinner at Eight" segment in which Leachman played an elderly, wealthy eccentric who gives an annual party for past suitors who never bother to attend (with Jack Albertson as her faithful butler and only friend) won both actors their coveted Emmys.

"Cher should have won that Emmy," says Schlatter. "Originally that sketch was written for her, but at the time she was uncomfortable dressing down, and playing dowdy. She didn't want to play a little old lady with no makeup, a grey wig, and spectacles. Because Cher didn't want it, the part went to Cloris and she was stupendous. In costume you didn't even recognize her."

"I'd seen that sketch done in different languages all over the world," remembers Digby Wolfe, "but I must admit that I've never seen it done better than with Cloris and Jack. That was, without a doubt, one of the high points of comedy on *Cher*—and both Leachman and Albertson *deserved* the awards they won." (Cher took a small part in the sketch as a contemporary woman who listens to the butler's story.)

Cher's solo performances on show number four are also outstanding. Along with her opener, she sang an adroit, handsomely orchestrated version of "Am I Blue?" (*Bittersweet White Light's* only single), the well-known blues standard popularized by Ethel Waters. For the number Cher wore a lavender bias-cut bugle-beaded gown and page-boy wig. Photos taken of her in costume (and seductively positioned on a modern-looking asymmetrical set) were widely published—printed as fold-out posters in both *The National Star* and *Dynamite*. The "Cher Concert" segment was just as good and featured Cher singing a gospel-tinged medley of the cleverly paired Kiki Dee Band's "I've Got the Music in Me" and the Doobie Brothers' "Listen to the Music." "Cher's voice can still accommodate all manner of musical material as neatly as Saran Wrap," observed *Newsweek*; and her passionately delivered medley proved it.

"Saturday Night" (taped and banked the previous week) was also superb. During the segment Cher talked about her latest date: a split-personality Gemini. "I thought that the comedy skits on that show, especially the bit where she played a single '70s woman ['Saturday Night']—really showed that Cher had acting talent," remembers Rona Barrett. "She had great comic timing but she was also very natural and believable. That really is the essence of good acting; making someone else's written words sound like they are coming from your own thoughts and your own mind. Later, when she had great success as an actress, and everyone was so surprised, I thought, 'What did they think she was doing all those years on television?'"

Although Cher continued to have dealings with David Geffen—he discreetly courted guests for her show, attended early tapings, and oversaw the production of *Stars*, her first album for his label Elektra-Asylum Records, their romantic relationship ended. One of the problems was Geffen's busy schedule. As an executive VP at Warner Communications he was deeply involved in the complicated details presented by the July 1973 merger of Atlantic Records with Elektra-Asylum Records. He was also dealing personally, and extensively, with three of his company's acts: Carly Simon, Joni Mitchell and, most importantly, Bob Dylan. By all accounts, David Geffen was devastated by his and Cher's breakup and, for him, there were constant reminders of what could have been. The February edition of *Esquire*, written months earlier, featured Cher on its cover but, inside, offered up a comprehensive David Geffen career profile. Author Julie Baumgold had trailed the "in love" couple for days, chronicling their spending sprees, nights on the town, and intimate moments, but when the issue hit the stands they were no longer an item.

That didn't stop the ever-persistent David Geffen. For a time, he kept phoning, dropping by the studio and sending gifts—all to no avail. In 1975, when asked why their relationship ended, Cher said, "We broke up because he wanted to get married and I didn't. He was ready and I wasn't. I'd been and he hadn't. It was a play-or-pay deal." Six years later, in an interview with *Forum* entitled "Talking Straight with Cher," she was even more frank: "David, as brilliant and terrific as he was, was also so, so stubborn. If it wasn't going to be David's way he was really going to know why. David made a lot of contingencies."

In 2003 Chris Bearde provided his own portrait of Geffen and Cher's relationship. "After it was clear to everyone that Sonny and Cher were not getting back together, I was told to have a meeting with Cher to see if she would be open to signing with CBS as a solo. I met her informally—she was out with Chastity. Well, I remember seeing a Bentley come barreling up Beverly Boulevard. Then the car was driving up on the sidewalk. Now it's stopping directly in front of Cher, Chastity and me. The door flies opens and out jumps David Geffen. He was screaming and cursing at the top of his lungs for Cher to get in the bleeping car immediately; to get Chastity in the bleeping car immediately. What the bleep was she doing there? I don't believe I've ever heard that much cursing and screaming in my entire life. In an instant my 'meeting' with Cher was over. Two seconds later she and Chastity were gone—speeding down Beverly Boulevard in David Geffen's Bentley."

Show number five once again presented Cher on top form. The guests for the hour were the Pointer Sisters, Freddie Prinze and Teri Garr. Cher and Teri Garr were friends throughout the '70s and the actress excelled in several different arenas. As a dancer she performed in nine Elvis Presley vehicles—including *Roustabout*, *Clambake* and *Viva Las Vegas*; as the "girl next door" she appeared in commercials for Crest, Safeguard, Greyhound, and Sure; and as an actress she appeared on episodes of *The Beverly Hillbillies*, *That Girl*, and *Star Trek*. "Teri and Cher were always wonderful together," remembers Schlatter. "They were good friends who brought out the best in each other. They were about the same age so they also had a lot in common. Teri knew how to 'play low' so that Cher, especially when she was playing Laverne, could 'play high.'"

In her 2005 autobiography *Speed Bumps: Flooring It Through Hollywood*, Garr talked about the respect and admiration she had for Cher. "[At CBS] my dressing room was, as they say in show business, 'a nail with a hanger on it.' Regardless, Cher would always come over... what impressed me most about her was that she always acted like one of the girls. She'd come and sit down with the dancers and talk about face cream, hairdos or men—whatever. Cher taught me to do needlepoint, and we'd sit around working on our pillows between scenes. When I got stuck I always wanted to know the by-the-books way to fix it. Cher would say: 'Teri, you just do what you have to do. It's like life—you don't have to play by the rules. Just get it done.'"

Life with Laverne:

OLIVIA: Oh, Laverne, you look fabulous. And the apartment looks divine. Everything is so artistic. Like that painting of a man... it's so fantastic... it's like he's really looking at us.

LAVERNE: He *is* looking at us. That's Mr. Hinkel next door. Pull your shades down Hinkel!

On the show, Garr also appeared in what would turn out to be the final installment of "Mable's Fables." She played Cinderella to Freddie Prinze's

Prince Charming. (Additionally, Garr and Cher filmed two comedy segments—a second "Life with Laverne" and a "Complaint Department" sketch—that were banked and included in show number fourteen.)

Freddie Prinze was appearing on *Cher* directly on the heels of Jack Albertson—his co-star in *Chico and the Man*. At the time the twenty-year-old comedian had a top-rated television series, performed for standing-room-only audiences, had just released a comedy album, had appeared on the cover of *Rolling Stone* and was very publicly dating Kitty Bruce, comedian Lenny Bruce's daughter.

In "That's a Lie," Prinze played Cher's ever-lying husband—a man who cries wolf one too many times, and in "The Complaint Department" played a customer trying to return a faulty electric blanket.

FREDDIE: Is this the Complaint Department?

CHER: No, this is the White House and I'm the President.

FREDDIE: I beg your pardon?

CHER: No more pardons. I got into too much trouble with the last one. Now, what do you want?

Cher and Prinze also did a comedy tap dance number called "Singin', Dancin', Clownin' Around." But, as lighthearted as things seemed in front of the cameras, behind the scenes things were unraveling for Prinze, who seemed to have difficulty handling his swift ascent to the top. Struggling with substance abuse, the comedian was also prone to wild mood swings and depression. In a *TV Guide* cover story, writer Rosemary Edelman captured the beleaguered star in a moment of frustration. After being followed an entire day by photographers, and accused of being late for a dress rehearsal, Prinze, believing he had no other outlet, kicked a hole in an NBC dressing-room wall. "Freddie was one of the first—I think he was *the* first American Puerto Rican or Latino comedy star," remembers Digby Wolfe. "He was very charming. A very lovely kind of gentle, sensitive guy. He made quite an impression on all of us." Exactly two years and six days after he taped his appearance on *Cher*, Prinze, whom everyone enjoyed working with (he was asked to make a return visit) was dead; the victim of a self-inflicted gunshot wound to the temple.

Viewed today, one can't help but take note of the comfort, ease and good time the comedian seems to be having on the *Cher* show. There is no visual clue, none whatsoever, of the many demons that plagued him when he was offstage.

Cher admired the Pointer Sisters and they her. Just a week after they taped their appearance, the soulful foursome—Ruth, Anita, Bonnie and June—took home a Best Country Performance by a Duo or Group Grammy for their song "Fairytale." "We were all really big Cher fans and whenever she was on [TV] we all wanted to see what she was doing and what she was wearing," remembers Ruth Pointer. "When George Schlatter called and expressed interest in booking us we were really, really excited." Along with joining Cher for a series of "Girls

Are Smarter" musical lead-ins, the sisters did a solo number, "Live Your Life Before You Die." "Looking back I think a better choice for our solo would have been 'Wang Dang Doodle' or 'Yes We Can Can,'" [both in the charts] says Ruth. "But we were always trying to pump our own stuff and 'Live Your Life Before You Die' was a song that we had written and we thought it showed off our versatility. So, at the time, we insisted on doing it."

Show number five's highlight was a tour-de-force musical finale that featured the entire cast: "Chattanooga Choo Choo," "(I've Got a Gal in) Kalamazoo," and "On the Sunny Side of the Street" were just a few of the songs performed (see Appendix for complete list).

"We always had a special affection for '30s and '40s big band-type music and fashions so we were thrilled to do that number," remembers Ruth. "It was right in step with what we were already doing and already known for."

Dee Dee Wood, the second choreographer hired to work on *Cher* (Tony Charmoli was only available for four shows) oversaw the musical finale. "The first thing that I wanted to do was to get to know Cher," says Wood regarding the challenge of replacing Charmoli. "I had never met her or worked with her before so I really didn't know what to expect. Our relationship began with me giving her dance class each morning; before she started her workday. I think it was from 10:00 to 11:00 on rehearsal days at CBS. Cher told me that she wanted to learn control of her body. She already could dance—she certainly had wonderful movement and rhythm. At one point during our early work together I said something like, 'At this point you do a small plié and then you glide over in this direction.' She said: 'Hold it! Hold it! Don't use any of those words or any of that shit with me. If you want me to squat, tell me—"Cher, squat!"' After that, once I was on the same page as her, as far as language goes, I was totally relaxed and we had a lot of fun."

Wood also looked forward to working with director Art Fisher. "Though Art was obviously there all the time, he didn't have much contact with the workers on the *Cher* show and that surprised me—he was always up in the sound booth. I remember that at one point while I was working on the show I got a letter in the mail from him. I was sure I was being fired; but the letter was full of praise and admiration for my work. It was really cool, and it totally floored me. I always wanted to thank him for taking the time to send that letter to me, but he was never really accessible."

Fisher might not have been a presence at CBS but he certainly was in the tabloids. At the same time that he was discreetly directing *Cher*, he was engaged to *All in the Family*'s Sally Struthers. The couple (who met when Struthers appeared on *The Sonny & Cher Comedy Hour*) had been living together for two and half years and the constant changes in their relationship were (via Struthers) regular gossip column reading. "We're getting married in January of '75," Struthers gushed throughout the early part of '74, but January '75 came and went without a trip to the altar.

"I feel particularly bad about our breakup happening now, what with Sally involved in her legal hassles with *All in the Family*," Fisher dutifully reported to the press in the early part of '75. And Struthers agreed. "I've now been engaged to two different men and when I get too close I just run away," she told a reporter. "I'm sure there are many different reasons, but one of them is that I just haven't found anybody who can take care of me any better than I can take care of myself."

Dee Dee Wood was nominated for an Emmy for Best Achievement in Choreography for the work she did with Cher, Freddie Prinze, Teri Garr and the Pointer Sisters on show number five's 1940s musical salute. "It was just a little Jitterbug number," says Wood. "I was surprised by that particular nomination—I didn't even look to see who else was nominated that year because I thought, 'What are they thinking? Why did they choose that piece over all the other work I did on the show?'"

Viewed today the finale is not only a standout, but wholly worthy of the praise and nomination it garnered. A high-kicking, arms-flailing, meticulously choreographed (and obviously extensively rehearsed) segment, the literally show-stopping number is so strong and so deftly realized that it plays like a long-performed section excerpted from a popular Broadway musical. Ruth Pointer agrees: "That '40s salute really sticks in my mind. It was such an intricate number and everyone had such a hard time learning it that I'm amazed that we ever got it right. Doing that number was like Broadway and high school all rolled into one. We just loved it and we thought it came out really great."

Along with show number five's opening number—the effervescent "When You're Smiling," a tune first popularized by Louis Armstrong in the '30s — Cher did a monologue about how her TV show resembled a newborn baby, and appeared in "The Clown," a brief and poignant pantomime in which she, dressed as a clown, receives a letter, reads it, and then draws a tear under her eye.

Cher's "Saturday Night" segment was called "Another Saturday Night Out with the Girls."

CHER: Sue organized the hen party. She said we that it was time we girls stood up against the dominating men in our lives. When I asked her to explain she said she couldn't; she had to get off the phone or her husband would kill her!

Cher's solo was a lilting and gracefully rendered version of George and Ira Gershwin's "How Long Has This Been Going On?" (featured on *Bittersweet White Light*). For the performance Bob Mackie designed a feathered skull cap, black beaded gown and a stunning floor-length iridescent black rooster feather boa. "I was there for days and days taking pictures of Cher in that costume," remembers Julian Wasser, who was charged with getting a glamorous shot of the star for the cover of *Time*. "Cher looked incredible in that costume and we took shots of her against a green backdrop, then pictures of her on-set performing ['How Long Has This Been Going On?'], and then more pictures of her and Bob Mackie together." Wasser's photo of Cher in "the bird dress" was never used. "I nearly had a heart attack when I saw *Time* on the stands. They went with a previously published *Vogue* picture [by Richard Avedon]. We were all really disappointed."

Not disappointing were the other photos that Wasser took during his week-long assignment. "I made a lot of money from photographing Cher, that's for sure. And the pictures I took of her and her new boyfriend [Gregg Allman] were their very first posed portraits." (Wasser's pictures of Cher and Gregg appeared on the cover of *People* and as an insert in *Time*.) "When I went out to Cher's place to shoot her I brought along my son who, at the time, was around Chastity's age," remembers Wasser. "They had a great day playing together. I've got to tell you that I, like so many other people, always really loved Cher. She was like this L.A. street kid who made it really, really big. I had worked with Sonny and Cher back in the '60s when they were associated with Phil Spector so she knew me—knew my work. She was really a hometown kind of star—a very simple, down-to-earth kid. But I could tell—especially when I shot her at her house, that she was very stressed out. There was ongoing trouble with Sonny and problems at CBS. Everything seemed to be hitting the fan at once. I just tried to make the shoot go well without any additional problems."

During show number five's scheduled taping, Cher also filmed a "Donna Jean Brodine" Wonder Bat segment that was banked and used the following week.

"Cher is about to do a complicated bit of comedy in which she must pick up a baseball bat and successively smash a rug, a rubber spider, a lock, an alarm clock, a bottle, a cantaloupe and a birthday cake," wrote *Washington Post* columnist Nicholas von Hoffman, who was on set. "The routine is pure slapstick. It can only be as funny as the comedienne can make it, and, although it may look easy, any actor will tell you that, to remain in character while handling so many props so quickly is an accomplishment. Whack, smash, bang—spiders, clocks and locks go flying. 'Wonderful,' the director's voice tells her from the control room, but then ads: 'Now let's do it again!'" Cher's compliance and eagerness to work and get things right were best summed up in the final sentence that appeared in von Hoffman's piece. After being informed that the routine needed to be filmed a third time Cher nodded, made a clown face, and resumed her place: ready to begin again.

Cher wasn't home the evening show number five was broadcast. As a favor to Bob Mackie she was busy taping an appearance on a 90-minute television special called *The Fashion Awards*. The program was produced by Mackie's companion Ray Aghayan and featured musical material by *Cher*'s Billy Barnes and Earl Brown, and costumes by Bob Mackie and Ret Turner. Hosts for the event were John Davidson and Diahann Carroll. "*The Fashion Awards* stands out from the recent glut of award shows," reported *TV Guide*. "Instead of the boring acceptance speeches and bad jokes, the program features dazzling production numbers that set off fashions from such designers as Bill Blass, Calvin Klein and Bob Mackie." On the show, Cher and Carol Burnett—wearing "hers and hers" complimentary silver and white costumes, introduced a Bob Mackie montage that featured sketches, a brief interview, and scenes from the films and television shows he had worked on. When the montage was finished, Cher and Burnett beckoned him to the stage and presented him with his award.

Yet another occurrence was taking place the night that show number five was broadcast: Cher was going head-to-head with Barbra Streisand. The two superstars (who often shared the covers of movie magazines) had crossed each other's paths many times throughout 1974 and even shared a table (with boyfriends David Geffen and Jon Peters) at a benefit for the United Negro College Fund. *Funny Girl to Funny Lady*, Streisand's "glittering spectacular" from the Kennedy Center in Washington, D.C. was, that evening, broadcast directly opposite *Cher*. Both a benefit for the Special Olympics for Retarded Children and a movie premiere for *Funny Lady*—Streisand's newest film—the special included a live set by Streisand that included "My Man," "Don't Rain on My Parade," and her signature hit "The Way We Were." But all the hoopla surrounding Streisand's special event didn't much matter to TV viewers. That evening *Cher* got a 33 percent share of the audience, *Funny Girl to Funny Lady* got a 25 percent share, and the *Wonderful World of Disney* (broadcast opposite both shows) got a 19 percent share.

The Hollywood Reporter made clear the evening's significance. Their weekly "Coast to Coast" column was introduced to readers with the all-bold-capital-letter headline: *OH, WHAT CHER DID TO BARBRA STREISAND LAST NIGHT!*

12

MAGAZINE QUEEN

On Saturday and Sunday March 1 and 2, Cher reported to CBS to film show number six. The guests for the hour were David Groh, Lily Tomlin and the Jackson Five. Anticipating what was sure to be an exciting taping, a photographer from the Australian magazine *Women's World* was on set (as were others) taking photographs of every single segment. Later in the year Cher's single image was placed on the magazine's cover behind the banner headline "Cher: How the Stunning Star was Created."

Cher opened the hour with "Friends" (a song enjoying a renaissance due to her friend Bette Midler), followed by a monologue about quitting smoking. She also sang an engaging solo—the jazz/pop standard "Since I Fell for You"—on an elaborate waterfront set complete with wooden planks, flowing waves and a twinkling skyline. As Donna Jean Brodine she pitched Wonder Bat (filmed the week before), and over a clever animated sequence—created by Sergio Aragonés, one of Mexico's leading cartoonists—recited Rudyard Kipling's poem "If." The Jackson Five (Jackie, Marlon, Tito, Jermaine and Michael) had worked with Cher before on *The Sonny and Cher Comedy Hour* (they also appeared on *The Sonny Comedy Revue*). The group's talent, good looks and catchy songs—along with brother Michael's otherworldly charisma—made them an act that were just as much in demand for TV appearances as they were in concert halls. On *Cher* they performed "I Am Love" (from their album *Dancing Machine*) and the Billy Barnes and Earl Brown-written "The World is a Mess." Another segment entitled "Invention of the Commercial," featured the Jackson Five with Cher and little sister Janet in Stone Age loincloths playing primitive instruments. Filmed but not aired was "The Committee on Committees," a sketch that featured Cher and the Jackson Five in a debate about American government bureaucracy.

CHER: Where's the Secretary of Urban Affairs?

COMMITTEE: He's out having one.

CHER: Where's the secretary of Mass Transit?

COMMITTEE: He couldn't get here... his bus broke down.

The catalogue of material that was never aired is vast. "We always over-filmed," says George Schlatter. "That was something I did on *Laugh-In* and when I did Cher's show it was the same thing. Sometimes the segments just weren't funny enough or sometimes we didn't have enough time to squeeze them in. Then there were times when the censors disliked them so much that we just cut them. From a practical standpoint it made sense to have too much material rather than too little. I don't know who has all the stuff that we didn't air, but it must be substantial."

David Groh was one of the stars of the hit comedy series *Rhoda*. As it turned out, at the same time that he was rehearsing his appearance on *Cher* he was also being interviewed by *TV Guide*. Groh was unimpressed with Cher: the woman and the show. "The *Cher* show is pretty sloppy," Groh flatly informed *TV Guide*'s J.R. Young. "The writing is awful. It isn't clever. It isn't witty. It's... juvenile. There were really no rehearsals, just sort of a walk-through. Cher showed up for about twenty minutes and then left complaining she didn't feel well. And nobody seemed to care. I couldn't believe it. No wonder they use cue cards! Can you believe it? Cue cards!" Regardless of Groh's feelings, on the show he is not only game, but well suited for the sketches he appears in. In "I Want a Girl," he played a discriminating participant in a blind date with an over-eager woman (Lily Tomlin). In "Adam and Eve," he played Eve, a thoroughly confused inhabitant of the Garden of Eden (with Tomlin as Adam).

Today, comedienne Lily Tomlin offers an opinion as to why Groh may have been unhappy. "It could be that David was just tired of being the second banana. That's what he was on *Rhoda* and that's what he was on *Cher*. The material was basically written for us—the women, and he was a supporting player. He may have expected that being a guest star on a variety show would offer him different opportunities."

Although the release of *Nashville*, for which she was nominated for a Best Supporting Actress Oscar, was a few months off, when Lily Tomlin appeared on *Cher* she was already a household name. Telephone operator Ernestine, five-year-old Edith Ann, homemaker Mrs. Beasley, along with several other characters from her vast repertoire, brought her both acclaim and respect. She had also already headlined two CBS variety specials of her own, *Lily* and *The Lily Tomlin Show*—both of which were filmed in the same studio as *Cher*.

"I felt really lucky to have been the one in the right place at the right time to give her more exposure than she had had before," says George Schlatter, who first booked Lily on *Laugh-In*. "Her talent was so obvious. I believe Lily did much more for *Laugh-In* than we did for her."

On *Cher* Tomlin did the Fast Talker. "I always talked really fast–free association without finishing sentences and ideas before going on to the next," says Tomlin. "I remember seeing a commercial where the announcer was talking really fast. I thought, 'That's exactly what I do!' Somewhere along the line George [Schlatter] picked up on it and encouraged me to make it part of my act. It worked and people loved it." Of the "Adam and Eve" sketch she did with David Groh Tomlin says: "All I remember is that I hated my wig! Renata ["Rena"] gave me this wig to wear and I thought it was too severe and didn't make me look very good. It wasn't a wig that was made for me. It was just some wig from her workshop. I was very uncomfortable wearing it. But I must admit, looking at the show today, it looks totally fine–I don't think anyone cared about me wearing that wig but me."

In "The Bus Stop," Tomlin played a troublesome bag lady with Cher and Groh as her beleaguered subjects. "I was working a lot on Trudy the Bag Lady at that time," says Tomlin. "Earlier I had done Trudy on *The Smothers Brothers Show* and she was very different. On *Cher* I really brought her into focus– what she should say, and how she would act in different situations. It was a great learning experience for me." "Ernestine and Cher" is Tomlin's favorite segment. It featured Tomlin as her nosy telephone operator Ernestine calling up an unsuspecting Cher. "It's always great to have someone to play off of and Cher was the perfect foil for Ernestine. She was casual and cool while Ernestine was prone to act up and not do right. I was very happy with the way that segment came out."

ERNESTINE: Hello, is the party to whom I am speaking? Is this Cher and share alike Bono?

CHER: Yes, this is Cher. Who's calling?

ERNESTINE: My name is Ernestine Tomlin, a duly appointed and grossly underpaid servant of Ma Bell.

CHER: You mean you're an operator?

ERNESTINE: Judging from the media, I'd say that *you're* the operator, sweetie.

"She is mind-boggling and amazing. I admire and was constantly astonished by her," says Tomlin of her first experience working with Cher (24 years later Tomlin and Cher worked together again in *Tea with Mussolini*). "She's just really cool."

Show number six's most memorable segment is the program's musical finale, in which Cher and the Jackson Five perform a medley of the group's hits. Although Cher and Michael are obviously (and awkwardly) lip-synching, the costuming, energy and choreography is outstanding. The songs in the medley include "I'll Be There," "Never Can Say Goodbye" and "I Want You Back" (see Appendix for complete list). For the number Cher wore silver and white sequin bellbottoms, rhinestone platform shoes, and a glitter-dusted stacked-perm afro wig. "The Jackson Five came to the show with their own choreographer and their own choreography," remembers Dee Dee Wood. "My job on that particular segment was to incorporate Cher into their already established work and routines. It came out great. They looked incredible dancing and singing together. Michael Jackson is still one of my all-time favorite dancers." Lee Miller's memories of the Jackson Five are ambivalent. "They were great TV favorites because they had a huge public following, but I must admit that they never interested me much, not even Michael. I understood why they were booked but, to me, they were just immensely popular noise."

The day after Cher taped episode number six, her former record label MCA issued a "from-the-vaults" promo single lifted off of 1974's *Dark Lady*–her final album for the company. "Rescue Me" (B-side "Dixie Girl") was a tune first recorded by Fontella Bass in 1965. Cher's spirited and sassy re-make brought back images of Cher sitting atop the upright piano during the *The Sonny and Cher Comedy Hour*'s "Vamp" routines. Spirited though it was, and released just as Cher made a glamorous appearance at the 1975 *People's Choice Awards* (host Bob Hope quipped: "And there's Cher. I think Sonny Bono got her clothes in the settlement!"), "Rescue Me" (simultaneously issued in Britain) failed to chart.

When *Cher* episode number six aired, Cher's single image was placed on the cover of *Time*. Richard Avedon's cover shot showed Cher wearing a semi-nude, beaded and feathered Bob Mackie creation. "The picture was more like something that *Playboy* might publish," observed George Carpozi, whose paperback book *Cher* also featured the Avedon shot on its cover. "The portrait showed the slender, brown-eyed, black-haired beauty in a sheer-sheer, skin-colored see-through gown, threaded with fingers of icy silver sequins. The generous spacing of the sequins gave America an uncluttered glimpse of rosy nipples, an opalescent navel, and certain other shimmering anatomical wonders..."

Bob Mackie (who was Cher's date when she first wore the dress to a Metropolitan Museum of Art costume exhibit five months earlier) defended his creation. "It's really quite a decent dress," he informed *TV-Radio Mirror*. "Everything blends into everything else and you're never quite sure what you're seeing. It has a high neckline, no cleavage at all except for the areas that you can see through, and the beads are placed so that you don't see anything. The back *is* low–down to the waist; but so is Cher's hair. The press really has made it into something a lot more sensational, as far as nudity goes, than is really warranted."

And they did. The tabloid headlines said it all: "What is Cher Trying to Prove? Thousands Stare as She Goes Bare!" and "The Untold Story of Cher's Fabulous Sex-cess!" led the way to candid pictures of Cher in the dress while Germany's *Stern* and the Britain's *London Observer* reprinted the *Time* cover shot–in full. The city of Tampa, Florida had a problem with Cher and her dress. Sighting an on-the-books anti-obscenity law, Tampa officials classified Richard

Avedon's "nude" photograph as "pornographic" and forced area newsstands to remove the magazine from their shelves. "Under threat of prosecution" wrote *The New York Times*, "police ordered stores in the Tampa area to remove from their shelves copies of the March 17, 1975 issue of *Time* magazine that featured a picture of the singer Cher Bono on the cover." Following Tampa's ordinance, a Florida magazine distributor filed suit against the city claiming the ban was unconstitutional and a violation of First Amendment rights. United States District Judge Ben Krentzman agreed and on April 4—a month after the issue came out and three weeks after it was replaced on newsstands—chastised Tampa for their "overzealous and unconstitutional action."

But executives at CBS were also disturbed by Cher's *Time* cover. "I remember the picture caused a lot of unease with the standards and practices people at CBS," recalls Digby Wolfe. "They didn't like it at all. They thought the image was much too daring... much too revealing. I don't think they called Cher in and talked to her about it because, what did it matter? It was too late and there was really nothing that they could do about it. The magazine was on and off the stands in a week and everyone in the world had already seen it."

Time's Letters to the Editor Page provided readers with their own forum in which to discuss the cover.

"Disgusting—your recent cover. I tore it off and threw it away all crumpled up." *Judith F. Bonnie, Louisville, Kentucky*

"A *Time* cover story? Is there anything else America can do to help this 'mildly talented creature totally fashioned by show business'?" *Maxine Steward, Mesa, Arizona*

"As one of the 'older boys' of the family, I found the edition with beautiful Cher on the front cover was a treat." *Bill Stanyar, Toronto, Canada*

Cher's newsstand notoriety often overshadowed her television success. Despite the fact that during the first five months of 1975 she was featured on the cover of frontline publications like *Esquire*, *Los Angeles*, *Vogue*, *People*, *TV Guide* and *In the Know*, the "gossip rags" too were a big part of her story. Three headlines from March paint the portrait of a woman whose name was definitely selling magazines: *Hollywood Hot-Line*: "Cher Rushes Home in Tears. Daughter Chastity Stricken by Rare Illness! Doctors Warn Chastity Will Never Again Be Like Other Children." *Movie Mirror*: "Cher Caught at Private Porno Screening! Sonny Furious! He Demands New Court Action! The Whole Shocking Story!" And *Photo Screen*: "Elvis and Cher Admit They'll Marry! 'I've Never Been So Happy in My Life!' She Cries. The Whole Story in Their Own Words."

The Cher/Elvis story had legs. At the time it was reported that Elvis "wooed" Cher with flowers, proposed marriage and, when Sonny balked, offered to pay her alimony. "I don't even know Elvis; I know his wife," Cher informed Rona Barrett. "I said, 'Priscilla if he's really serious it's okay with me; tell him to send over the money!'" On two separate occasions Cher actually passed on meeting the "King." The first almost-meeting took place in 1973 while Sonny and Cher were playing Las Vegas. Sonny wanted Cher to join him and catch Elvis's show but she declined. It might have been a good decision. "He was a lumbering... gross, overweight shadow of himself..." Sonny later reported, and it was *that* Elvis that Cher turned down when he, after she was separated from Sonny, called her and asked her to spend a weekend with him. (At the time that the Elvis/Cher stories circulated, Elvis and his wife Priscilla were separated and Elvis was living with a 24-year-old beauty pageant winner named Lynda Thompson. Thompson claimed Cherokee, Scottish and Irish lineage. When *Motion Picture* did a piece on her, journalist George Bernard observed: "she reminds me so much of Cher that I couldn't resist the question of the similarity." Thompson's response was declarative: "I don't ever want to be compared to Cher. We may have the same tastes, and may even buy our clothes in some of the same places [Thompson, who had an open account courtesy of Presley, had a penchant for belly-baring ensembles, turquoise jewelry and feathers], but that's as far as it goes.")

Several years later, when she appeared on the *Phil Donahue* show, Donahue asked Cher what it felt like to be "Queen of the Tabloids." "Those magazines are, no matter how little we may think of them, an accurate barometer of the public's ongoing fascination with you," he surmised. Cher remained nonplussed. "Being on those magazines feels stupid! Really stupid!"

Cher show number seven featured three comedians; Teri Garr, Jimmie Walker and Marty Feldman. Cher opened the hour with Linda Ronstadt's rocking admonition "You're No Good" followed by a monologue about the many strange letters she had received since she began headlining her own series. Later in the show she did her "Saturday Night" sketch and discussed how difficult it was for her to get a date.

With so many comedians on board, Cher provided all of show number seven's music. Her solo was one of her favorites—Paul McCartney's "My Love" (included on *Half-Breed*). The "Cher Concert" was the hour's high point. "I've been getting a lot of cards and letters asking me when am I going to do my hits," Cher said as she introduced the segment. "Well, these songs have been really good to me so I'm going to do them for you right now." What followed was a note-for-note live medley of "Gypsys, Tramps and Thieves," "Half-Breed" and "Dark Lady." In superior voice, rakishly exuberant, and not backed by a team of dancers or one of Bob Kelly's super-elaborate sets, Cher proved that she was able to transcend the built-in limitations of her "story songs" and make them lasting and memorable pop opuses. But even though Cher introduced her greatest hits medley with praise, her opinion about her music, especially her Snuff Garrett-produced story songs, has changed over the years. Just a year before her performance on *Cher* she told *McCalls*, "'Gypsys, Tramps and Thieves' and all those songs are million-selling songs but they are ridiculous because artistically they aren't very fulfilling. Money-wise, they're great, but I would like to spend four or five months on an album and do something really fantastic."

In an interview that appeared in *Vox* magazine more than fifteen years later, Cher offered another reason for her detachment from her '70s hits. "In the early days it wasn't my place to choose songs. Snuff [Garrett] would find them, he and Sonny would decide how to do them, and I'd sing them. That was that. I kind of liked 'Half-Breed,' 'Gypsys' was fun to do; 'Dark Lady' was a pain in the ass because there was no place to take a breath—there were so many words in that stupid song!"

"When an artist begins to grow, they sometimes question the material that made them famous," producer Snuff Garrett later observed. "That's the case with Cher; she thinks her early hits are beneath her. I don't care if she ever sings them again or not; that's her business. To me, a product is a product for the masses; you make it commercial, you make it sell. If that's a shortcoming, I'm certainly not going to apologize for it." (A little known fact is that Garrett also found "The Night the Lights Went Out in Georgia," a No. 1 hit for Vicki Lawrence [*The Sonny and Cher Comedy Hour*'s Al Schultz was Lawrence's husband], for Cher. "I don't know why Sonny turned that track down," Cher later remembered. "I would have done it if he wanted me to... if he had liked it. Obviously *he* didn't like it.")

At the time of his appearance on *Cher* comedian Marty Feldman was already a household name in his native Britain. The star of the British TV series' *Marty* as well as *The Marty Feldman Comedy Machine*, Feldman made a splash in America in that year's critically acclaimed *Young Frankenstein*. On the show he played a hapless door to door salesman, the Lone Ranger, and had a role in the Flying Garbanzos, a sketch that featured the entire cast as a group of bickering trapeze artists. In her second appearance on the show, Teri Garr did a duet with Cher on the upbeat and silly country tune "Ragtime Cowboy Joe." "That was my idea," says choreographer Dee Dee Wood. "I thought the two of them would be really good doing kind of a corny number together. Bob [Mackie] designed these furry chaps and both Cher and Teri wore very little else on top. They had a great time doing that number. It was just adorable and a lot of fun." Additionally Garr (who, like Marty Feldman, was also in *Young Frankenstein*) appeared in the Flying Garbanzos and the "Lone Ranger" sketches.

Jimmie Walker, by all accounts the star of CBS's *Good Times*, was, at the time of his appearance, one of the best-known comedians on the tube. His exclamation "Dy-no-mite!" had become a catchphrase, he released a comedy album, co-starred with Sidney Poitier and Bill Cosby in that year's film *Let's Do It Again*, and even had a talking "Jimmie 'JJ' Walker" doll in stores. Offscreen Walker's success had its downside; his immense popularity hadn't been anticipated. A family show, *Good Times* was fashioned as an ensemble piece that, as originally written, was to showcase actress Esther Rolle, who had graduated from the role of Florida, the shoot-from-the-hip maid on *Maude*. That didn't happen. The phenomenon that was Jimmie Walker eclipsed the entire cast, creating an on-set atmosphere of bitterness and envy. And Walker didn't help matters any. Consequently, when he brought his highly touted stand-up routine to L.A.'s Comedy Store, not a single person from the cast or crew showed up to support him.

"I've only been star-struck twice in my life," says Walker today. "Once was with Muhammad Ali whom I adored and wanted to be, and the second time was with Cher. When I appeared on her show the buzz was all about how she would transition to working as a single after being a duo for so long. She made it all look effortless and I loved working with her. For me, it made me feel really important. I was doing things and appearing on shows that no other *Good Times* cast members were." Walker, who admits that "anytime there was a lull or a question about whether or not something was working comedy wise, they told me to throw in one of my 'Dy-no-mites,'" is a pleasure to watch on the program. He appeared in the Flying Garbanzos, did a spoof of a popular margarine commercial (which ended with him exclaiming "Dy-no-mite!"), and played a trouble-making student to Cher's prim and proper school ma'am.

"To this day, I've never seen the segments I did on the show, I was just too busy at the time. All I remember was that everything was professional, it was a pleasure to be working with Cher, and I thought her secretary [Paulette] was gorgeous!"

George Schlatter also made an impression on the comedian. "I love George. He's an honest, no BS producer; a visionary and a living legend. In my opinion, both he and Cher are national treasures."

13

A SUNDAY NIGHT STAPLE

By the time show number eight was filmed, the newness that was so much a part of Cher's return to TV sans Sonny had all but worn off. Cher was now, on her own, a standard Sunday-night fixture. "Cher was someone who came into your home, as your friend, and you and the entire family were comfortable with her," surmises Schlatter. "Cher and the people at home watching each week got together and visited."

From the very beginning Cher wanted her show to feature "cool," modern and relevant music acts, and Labelle (Patti LaBelle, Sarah Dash and Nona Hendryx) was certainly one of them. The trio of exceptional singers had already hit the top of the charts with "Lady Marmalade" and were regularly featured in both rock and soul music magazines (their outrageous space-age, glam-rock fashions endeared them to rock fans). Shortly after they appeared on *Cher*, Labelle made the cover of *Rolling Stone*—one of the very few black acts to do so at the time. "We were all very excited about doing *Cher*," remembers Nona Hendryx. "Cher's show was a great place to hear current music. It was hip and on the cutting edge of what was going on at the time." But their appearance had its challenges.

"I thought forcing us to change the lyrics of 'Lady Marmalade' was really stupid," says Hendryx, referring to the fact that CBS censors told the group that they were uncomfortable with the song's sex-industry worker theme. "I mean the [French] lyric was 'will you sleep with me tonight?' not 'will you have *sex* with me tonight?' That's the literal translation [on the show the group sang 'will you *dance* with me tonight?']. Also, the song says that he met 'Marmalade'. It didn't explicitly say that he met a prostitute for sex. We weren't performing on a kids' show, it wasn't a song for children, so it all just seemed very stupid to all of us—Cher included." (Less than a year later Lola Falana sang "Lady Marmalade," unchanged, on ABC's *Lola Falana Show*.) But Labelle's battle with the network censors didn't end there; Nona Hendryx's costume was also deemed "objectionable" and she was asked to change. "It really surprised me because Sarah was usually the one who wore the most revealing clothes," says Hendryx. "The discussion I had with the CBS censors had to do with my breasts; and they're not even big! They thought they were overly accentuated." (Hendryx wore silver breast plates over a form-fitting glittery white leotard). In the end, Hendryx won her battle with the censors—and even managed to trick them. "They were all so busy talking about my breasts and how the *Cher* show was a 'family' show that they never even noticed the whips and handcuffs that I was wearing. I think my other gear was totally off their radar. We all had a big laugh about that!" On the show Labelle joined Cher for a duet of their social statement song "What Can I Do for You?." "To be able to do a song like that was very important to us, especially on a show like Cher's which was, generally speaking, light-hearted. At the time we were anxious to transcend our popularity as pop-club-disco divas. If I remember correctly, even though we knew it would be fantastic exposure, we only agreed to do *Cher* if they let us do 'What Can I Do for You?' along with 'Lady Marmalade.'" (Amazingly, especially given the fact that several acts before them never got to see their solo numbers air, "What Can I Do for You" made the final cut.)

Nona Hendryx came away with another lasting memory of appearing on *Cher*. "We were pretty big when we did the show and at the time our manager Vicki was always on us about spending so much money on costumes. Our outfits were the real thing, real brushed silver breast plates, real exotic bird feathers, and lots of super-expensive imported fabrics. Well, when we did *Cher*, Vicki was there every day nosing around. She discovered that all the costumes that Bob [Mackie] did were done really quickly and really cheaply, for like a quarter of the price of ours. The feathers they used were like a penny a piece; the silver effects were plastic—sprayed to look like silver; the fabrics usually polyester. Nothing was what it seemed to be. On TV, as long as it photographed well, and it did, we discovered that you didn't need the real thing. That was an eye-opener for all of us."

Sarah Dash opened other eyes. When the censors didn't get their way with Nona they turned to her. "They wanted to spray my silver bra with some duller, and I went ballistic," Dash later recalled. "Cher was there and she said, 'No, you can't do that, that's her "look."' That was great; I loved the way Cher stood up for me. Eventually Bob came out and pinned my cape to the top of my bra, so you could see it, but just barely. That was fine with me." Costumes aside, Dash came away with another lasting memory of her *Cher* show appearance. "I felt that Chastity was one of the more gracious entertainment children—showbiz kids. If you offered her a piece of candy she would turn to Cher and say, 'Mom, is it okay?' I thought that was so cool, being in show business and being so conscientious about how you're raising your children."

At the time of his appearance on *Cher* Ted Knight was a co-star on *The Mary Tyler Moore Show*. Three years later the actor helmed his own *Ted Knight Show*. In comedy sketches Knight played a tightwad who runs into Laverne while searching for a bargain cup of coffee, and played a despondent screenwriter having trouble composing his suicide note. He was also featured in a blackout in which he tried to get a stone-faced Cher to laugh.

Comedian Redd Foxx, too, was a top television star at the time. His NBC series *Sanford and Son* was a ratings winner, he performed for sell-out crowds in Vegas, had previously appeared on *The Sonny and Cher Comedy Hour*, and was the star of producer Schlatter's current film project, the gay-themed *Norman... Is That You?* (Shamelessly appropriating the film's script, Foxx had *Sanford and Son* writers come up with a "repeat performance" gay-themed episode entitled "Lamont [his TV son] Is That You?")

On *Cher*, in takeoffs on TV commercials, Foxx played a drunk who sings the praises of milk, and a financial advisor who makes a pitch for the Soul Savings and Loan Company. In skits he was a bookie who operates out of a police station, and in "The Complaint Department," a customer who was having difficulty returning a pair of pants. Foxx also joined Cher for "Attitude," a Barnes/Brown-written musical introduction to the program's comedy segments. Cher opened the hour with John Denver's "Take Me Home, Country Roads" followed by a monologue about how everyone she knew was trying to fatten her up. Her solo was an emotionally committed rendering of the melancholy ballad "Never-Never Land," which she performed wearing a white beaded headdress and floor-length white fur coat with a train (Bob Mackie would later design a variation of this costume—which he called "Empress of the Arctic"—for her 1980s concert act). Cher also performed in "Saturday Night," in which she talked about her thoroughly boring date.

At the same time that show number eight aired, the *Cher* show was formally reviewed in *TV Guide*. "Cher is a very special woman—and she introduced this series with a very special 'Special,'" wrote columnist Cleveland Amory. "The series, itself, on the other hand, has been good, but not that—well, special." Amory went on to discuss what he believed were the show's shortcomings—hit-or-miss comedy sketches and an emphasis on "torch songs" and "blues numbers"—but pointed out: "Cher can sing anything... and she is wonderful in the series' opening monologues."

The next show—program number nine, was filmed without a hitch. Guests Jean Stapleton, Kris Kristofferson, and Rita Coolidge had all previously appeared on *The Sonny and Cher Comedy Hour*. Along for the ride was pop singer Billy Swan. On *Cher* Stapleton, co-star of CBS's *All in the Family*, joined Cher for several "Girls Are Smarter" intros, and played a tipsy Julia Child-like TV Chef, an incompetent driver, and Laverne's pushy Mother-in-Law. Ret Turner remembers his first encounter with Jean Stapleton. "It was when I was working on *The Sonny and Cher Comedy Hour* and Jean was a guest. She told me that she was going to wear her own outfit. The day after I met her, my assistant Norman called and said, 'Would you like to know what Jean's outfit looks like?' I said 'sure' and Norman, who was a great comic and was always putting me on said: 'Well, it's a pair of pink hot pants with a little short billowy blouse and a pair of high-heeled, sparkly, silver boots.' I told him to stop kidding and hung up on him. Later in the day when I went into CBS, there was the outfit, just as he'd described it! When I saw Jean, I delicately tried to express that I didn't think the outfit was appropriate. She said, 'But, I want to change my image when I come on a show like this.' I said, 'Nevertheless, I think pink hot pants and high-heeled silver boots are a bit much!' She was very gracious and in the end we ended up doing a lovely gown for her; something that both flattered her and was age appropriate."

Aside from Cher's "Saturday Night" segment, in which she talked about her reunion with an old high-school crush, and a winning sketch that featured Cher and Kris Kristofferson as a poker-playing married couple, the rest of show number nine featured musical performances. Cher opened the hour with a rousing rendition of the Ozark Mountain Daredevils' country/rock tune "If You Wanna Get to Heaven" (the band was more famous for their current tune "Jackie Blue") followed by a monologue about her plans for a Hawaiian vacation. Her solo was Jimmy Cliff's "Many Rivers to Cross."

"All the sets designed for Cher's solo numbers were designed to work in tandem with whatever song she was singing that particular week," remembers Ret Turner. Accordingly, "Many Rivers to Cross" was performed on an elaborate desert-scape complete with boulders, cacti, a starry night sky and, of course, a flowing river.

Kris Kristofferson and Rita Coolidge, winners of the previous year's Grammy for Best Country Vocal Performance by a Duo or Group for "From the Bottle to the Bottom," performed a solo spot on *Cher*—"Late Again (Gettin' Over You)" and joined Cher for a well-matched medley of three country songs: "Oh, Lonesome Me," "Help Me Make it Through the Night" (written by Kristofferson), and "Oakie from Muskogee." "I was really comfortable with the way me and Rita's duet with Cher came out," remembers Kris Kristofferson, "though I wish someone had told me to button up my shirt! Cher is really creative people—and she was and still is beautiful. She was quick on her feet, intelligent and had a great sense of humor. We chose the songs in the medley together, worked on them, and made it happen. As for me and Rita's solo spot, for the life of me I can't figure out why the hell we sang 'Late Again (Gettin' Over You)'. It's such a hostile song. Looking back it doesn't seem appropriate for that show."

Rita Coolidge disagrees. "I absolutely love 'Late Again (Gettin' Over You)'.

It's a song about life after the fact—'I'm getting over you'—and it cuts a nice little groove. Perhaps Kris doesn't like it because he wrote it not too long before we split up; maybe he was thinking of me [laughter]!" The Cher/Rita/Kris concert, which took place on a homey set that included an old-fashioned brass stove, a wicker basket, stuffed chairs, pillows, plants and a "tex-mex" throw rug, is notable not only for it's solid harmonizing, but for the fact that Cher and Rita Coolidge look remarkably alike. "Cher and I are close in age [Coolidge is one year older] and we're both Taurus," says Coolidge. "We both had Cherokee Indian heritage, we both had long dark hair parted in the middle and we both sang in a lower register. When we taped the duet everyone kept telling us we looked like sisters, but I already knew that. In the early '60s I had a friend who looked like Sonny—except he was a little taller. Whenever we were at the airport together people would come up and say, 'Hi Cher, can I have your autograph?' My friend and I were signing 'Sonny and Cher' for years!"

Singer/songwriter Billy Swan, who had hit the No. 1 spot on the Pop *and* Country music charts with his rockabilly tune "I Can Help," sang a live version of his hit. "To tell you the truth, the only reason I was booked on *Cher* is because I was Kris and Rita's opening act," says Swan, whose musical style *Photoplay* called "a zany combination of yesterday and today." Kris Kristofferson remembers the particulars of Swan's booking differently. "At the time Billy, who is a great guy and a dear friend, had a bigger hit than me *or* Rita. 'I Can Help' was a smash—it was everywhere. I may have suggested that he come on, but he wasn't booked based on my suggestion. He was booked because of his own talent and success at the time."

Swan recorded his segment in one quick take but a particular memory remains prominent. "I'm not really a performer's performer," says Swan, "I must have been looking pretty glum or something. I was up there doing my thing singing and playing the organ, and all I remember is Cher and Rita standing on a platform behind one of the cameras waving their arms and mouthing the words 'smile, Billy, smile!' To be on Cher's show—or for that matter just to be in her presence—was just really fabulous. I loved her from the second she came onto the music scene. I adored her style, her voice, just every move she made. Kris and I did all the music shows at the time and I remember them all, but I remember being on Cher's show, singing with her, talking with her, laughing with her—the most."

Show number nine's finale was an elaborately choreographed production number featuring Cher and four bare-chested male dancers performing "This is Reggae Music" by the obscure band Zap Pow mixed together with Johnny Nash's "Stir It Up". "Reggae was my favorite music at the time," remembers Dee Dee Wood. "This was way before rap music. So one day I asked Cher, 'Would you be interested in doing a medley of reggae music—kind of a West Indian musical number?' I thought, 'She's not even going to know what the hell I'm talking about.' But she just said, 'Hell yeah—I love Reggae music—let's do it!' I really think that particular number was exceptional. It was well done and it was something that everyone else on TV wasn't doing." But not everyone liked Cher's salute to reggae. A Mrs. Judy Carlton of Houston, Texas was disturbed enough to write a letter to *The National Enquirer*. "Watch it, Cher!" wrote the incensed tabloid reader. "We are all used to seeing *you* appear on screen half-naked. But you don't need to have the male dancers almost nude as well. That Jamaican dance routine in your recent show was a bit much!"

14

BELLY BUTTON BICKERING

In 1975 the Family Hour (7:00-8:00 p.m. every night of the week) was a concept, policy and approach to programming that the three major networks, CBS, NBC and ABC, all embraced. Bowing to pressure from organized conservative groups who thought that American homes should, particularly on Sunday, be able to enjoy an early-evening hour of entertainment that was "suitable for all family members," CBS—already concerned about Cher, her wardrobe and what they saw as her freewheeling lifestyle—advanced their campaign to rein her in.

From the very beginning the Family Hour was controversial. Critics (most notably producer Norman Lear, who, on his series *Maude*, had actress Beatrice Arthur deliver the line: "Walter, there's nothing good on TV right now; it's the Family Hour—remember?") thought the idea was both ridiculous and a restriction of First Amendment rights. Supporters of the Family Hour—the U.S. Catholic Conference and an inter-faith union called Morality in Media—thought the designation of time to "family viewing" reflected Christian values and family togetherness. Speaking in an interview with *TV Guide*, CBS's president Robert D. Wood said, "The family viewing concept is an attempt to program a specific part of our schedule so that the whole family can enjoy television together without being disturbed or embarrassed. We are also going to advise viewers when we plan to present program material that may jar the sensibilities of some or may be considered unsuitable for children, so that the realities of our society can continue to be shown."

"I'm not violent, and I don't think I'm outrageous. I am modern. Still the network has become terribly afraid of me," Cher said at the time. "They're really uptight about sex and they're worried about my dresses. They think I have that reputation already and they don't want to do anything to emphasize it." And they didn't. A flesh-colored sequined gown embroidered with white flowers that

Cher wore during a solo number was, after it was filmed, almost completely "wiped out." "They fogged everything but my face!"

Attempting to find out what children *really* thought about her show, Cher paid a visit to daughter Chastity's school. "Chastity goes to a fine school," Cher recalled. "It's for kids six to eight. I went in and rapped with them. They love my show. They love the singing and they love when I talk to the audience at the beginning. They like what moves fast and they like to have a good time. Everyone gets things on the level that they understand. If a kid picks up on a so-called dirty joke that means that they know about it beforehand."

"Cher always had a large contingent of kids watching her show," remembers George Schlatter. "She was hip and cool, and everything they wanted to be. At the time, she was getting more fan mail from children than she was from adults, and when she did *The Sonny and Cher Comedy Hour* it was the same thing. The idea that her show was unsuitable for kids was just all-around ridiculous." But not everyone thought so. WCPO-TV Cincinnati's general manager Bob Gordon publicly protested and took action. "I object to the total emphasis the lady seems to have on her way of dressing. From the tone of her show, I think it's better to program it later at night." Accordingly, in Cincinnati, Ohio, *Cher* was moved from 7:30 to the 11:30 p.m. time slot.

"When I first started my show, CBS said, 'You cannot say "turkey" and you cannot say "far out"—America doesn't know what that means.' I said, 'Oh, bullshit!' *Tony Orlando and Dawn* are X-rated compared to what I can do. It's like you can have tits up to your neck, but God forbid you should show them from the side or from underneath—or anything America might not be used to seeing. When I was married to Sonny I could get away with a lot more. Sonny took the onus off of my sexiness or something."

Cher's navel was an even bigger problem than her wardrobe. "I was the first person to ever show their belly button on TV," Cher later recalled. "Even Jeannie on *I Dream of Jeannie* had to put a piece of cloth over hers. Someone at CBS came up with the idea that my belly button was corrupting American morals. They confiscated pictures of me in which my navel was showing and tried to force me to keep it covered. But the censors' argument never made any sense. I was already showing my navel on *The Sonny and Cher Comedy Hour* for years and people loved it."

"We have no objection to Cher's wardrobe, however skimpy it is," CBS broadcast standards chief Tom Swafford informed the press. "But when she ad-libs, she gets into trouble. One minute she begs the audience to applaud the back of her dress, when there isn't anything but skin. Then, she says, 'Let's hear it for the front,' where there's hardly anything either."

George Schlatter spoke with *The New York Daily News*' Kay Gardella about the issue. "With all the bikini bathing suits on beaches today I don't think

Cher's navel will destroy our young people. Everything is clean and pure in the Family Hour and then we return to the hookers, pushers and junkies and the cops-and-robbers shows. Why isn't the network talking about the high price of gasoline? That's public rape!" *New York Times* writer Thomas Meehan agreed with Schlatter. "Should the American family, from the tiniest toddler on upward, be allowed to gaze upon Cher's belly button? This is the semi-awesome question that has jittery TV executives at CBS divided these days into a pair of angrily warring camps. The battle over Cher's belly button is ludicrous in the extreme. I have the sneaky suspicion that the networks are using the Family Hour as a smoke screen. Now they have an unwritten license to put on anything they damn well please in the later hours of the evening."

Today, George Schlatter has revised his thoughts about the belly button debate. "In retrospect, I believe that if Cher didn't show her navel the network would still have had a big problem with her. She has great sensuality and the clingy fabrics she wore, the sequins, the bugle beads, her whole visual approach just scared them to death—especially because, now, she didn't have a husband standing by her side." So prominent was the debate over Cher's navel-baring wardrobe that Rona Barrett asked her *readers* to weigh in on the issue. "Has Cher Gone Too Far with Her TV Wardrobe?" Barrett asked. The consensus was yes—and no: 46 percent of *Rona Barrett's Hollywood* and *Rona Barrett's Gossip* readers checked a "yes" box, 42 percent checked a "no" box, and 12 percent expressed "no opinion."

For:
"People who don't like Cher or her clothes don't have to watch her show. All they have to do is switch the dial—so what are they all yapping about?" *Deanna Brown, Warren, Michigan*

"I'm a grandma and my 22-month-old granddaughter watches the *Cher* show all the time. We both think Cher wears great clothes!" *Ann Lake, Winchester, Virginia*

"The biggest thrill my lover and I get each weekend is to drop by our favorite gay bar and watch Cher's show. It's the best drag show we've ever seen!" *"Mr. Connery," Beverly Hills, California*

Against:
"I think her show should be X-rated. If I had small children I would never allow them to watch!" *Marie Trucks, Sikeston, Missouri*

"She isn't fit to be on TV, much less half-nude the way she is. She can't even sing!" *Paul Humrich, Smith Center, Kansas*

"As a dress designer myself, I must say that her wardrobe is too revealing in that it 'reveals' how she and her designer Bob Mackie have no taste. She looks so tacky—like someone who works at an all-night diner!" *Adam Blaine, Hollywood, California*

"One time I did this beautiful solo on my show and they said they were going to make me go and change my outfit," Cher recalled a few years later. "Bob Mackie made me this beautiful kimono, and underneath was this long slip. It was really pretty, and they said, 'No, no, you look like a hooker!' And I said, 'I'm just standing in front of a window!' So Norman Lear was walking outside the studio and I ran out and said, 'Norman, come in here and look at this number and tell the censor what you think.' I was singing 'Sunshine on My Shoulders,' and Norman turned to the censor and said, 'You must be really sick if you can find anything dirty in that!'"

Cher's guests on show number ten were Liberace, Linda Ronstadt and Nancy Walker. At the time of her appearance Linda Ronstadt was among the recording industry's most popular female vocalists (she was also on the cover of *Rolling Stone*). Cher was a big fan of Ronstadt and her music (she opened show number seven with the singer's "You're No Good") and was thrilled to have her as a guest. On the show the singer performed a note-for-note live version of her hit "When Will I Be Loved" and joined Cher for a medley of "Drift Away" and "Rip It Up."

"'With your stringy hair you should wear this [a wig],'" Ronstadt said one of Cher's hairdressers told her while preparing to film her duet with Cher. "I have such a terrible reputation for being uncooperative and they were running late so, ultimately, it was my decision whether or not to hold them up or look like a fool. In the end I thought, 'I won't have a fit I'll just put the wig on.'" But she didn't look like a fool at all. Although she had come to prominence as a no-nonsense "country girl" vocalist, and standing next to Cher she appears even less animated than she usually did when she performed, on the show Ronstadt looked fresh, young and lovely; her wig was undetectable and her dress quietly glamorous.

"Linda Ronstadt was great," says Lee Miller. "She was easy to work with, happy to be on the show, and comfortable with herself. I'm not a fan of rock but I was a fan of Linda Ronstadt's music. To me it seemed different than rock, more classic country or soul. I didn't know about the problems she had with her wig but every performer has an idea of how they want to look. If you tamper with that there may be trouble."

Liberace certainly wasn't a performer who was afraid of appearing overly done up. In the '50s the pianist/showman headlined his own variety series and then starred in a number of outrageous, over-the-top TV specials. Liberace's appearance on *Cher* marked the one and only time the show went on location.

"When we took Cher to Liberace's house she just loved it," recalls Schlatter. "I think, by that time, everything was becoming a bit routine so she loved getting out of the studio. From a filming standpoint it was a big hassle. Setting up lights and finding a place for cameras in someone's home, especially when there are million-dollar antiques around, is both difficult and dangerous. But for Cher it was a welcome change. It invigorated her and she had a ball." And it shows. On the show Cher (as Laverne) travels to Liberace's Beverly Hills home to pay him a visit and instead of being turned away by the showman's discriminating butler (played by Jack Harrell—Cher's announcer) is given a personal tour by Liberace himself. Fifty-four-year-old Liberace's home, not unlike Cher's, was something to behold. Called "the Palace," the 30-room estate was filled with treasures. Among them, a piano once owned by Frederic Chopin, a bed once owned by Rudolph Valentino, and a set of custom initialed plates once owned by President John F. Kennedy. On the show, Liberace performed "The Way We Were" on the piano. However, it was his interaction with Laverne that was memorable.

LAVERNE: This is really some fabulous place you've got here.

LIBERACE: Yes, I have millions of dollars of antiques in this house.

LAVERNE: Oh, Libber, for that kind of money, you could've bought all new stuff!

(Later)

LAVERNE: [*Singing*] You know, Libber, I've got music in my blood.

LIBERACE: Too bad you don't have any in your mouth!

"The suit that Liberace wore on that show launched my career," says costume designer Jim Lapidus, who outfitted the showman in a black velvet and bugle beaded ensemble whose main feature was a glittering sequined keyboard design on the jacket's lapels. "After Lee wore that on Cher's show I got all kinds of other work. Lee was very excited about appearing with Cher. I used to call Cher the 'Bugle Beaded Bono Broad of Beverly Hills' and Lee just loved that and he told her. He said she laughed but corrected him: 'I wear bugle beads, I'm a broad, and I live in Beverly Hills—but I'm no longer a Bono!'"

"Everyone loved Liberace and Cher together," says Schlatter, and his *Cher* notebook substantiates it: "Laverne and Liberace were fantastic," reads a handwritten note. "Ask him to make return visit—and let's try some more location things—Laverne at the Hollywood Ranch Market, the Railway Station, the Trolley Graveyard... Vegas, etc."

On her second visit to *Cher*, Nancy Walker played Wanda the Circus Fat Lady in a humorous, but by today's standards politically incorrect sketch about the difficulties of finding a date when you're morbidly obese.

WANDA: I've finally found the love of my life. It's Sabu, the elephant trainer. I remember how we met. I was strolling through the circus grounds wearing a grey dress and he tried to stick a peanut in my nose.

In "The Interested Principal Cooking Teacher" Walker played Miss Fitts, the crazed nutritionist of Lizzie Borden High School, who has to deal with the school's principal, Miss Primly (Cher), and performed a one-liner routine with Cher—which included the songs "The Trouble with Men" and "To Keep Our Love Alive"—the topic of which was how each got rid of their unloving spouses.

Cher opened the hour with the Rolling Stones' "I Can't Get No Satisfaction" and followed with a monologue about old wives' tales. She also performed in three comedy sketches: Donna Jean Brodine, in which she hawked Laugh-O-Matic (a kit that transforms its owner into a comedian), "The Frill is Gone," an airline commercial spoof, and "The Nurse," a hospital sketch in which she played a wisecracking critical-care nurse.

Cher's solo for the hour was John Denver's "Sunshine on My Shoulders" (the tune that knocked "Dark Lady" out of the No. 1 position on the *Billboard* charts). "Sunshine" ranks among the very best of Cher's on-air solo vocal performances; beautiful to look at, deftly executed, and performed on an elaborate "Paris Art Studio" set complete with a spiral staircase, paintings, a skylight and a sunset/ rain shower.

With ten shows under her belt, and although she didn't know it at the time, Cher was more than a third of the way through her solo series' run. Everything, it seemed, had been covered: comedy, music, dance, drama, even animation. But there was one surprise left. And viewers had only a week to wait to see it.

15

ALL IN THE FAMILY

Episode number eleven proved to be a fun-filled hour that was noteworthy because it marked Sonny and Cher's daughter Chastity's very first appearance on the program. The fact that Cher waited so long to feature Chastity, who was a viewer favorite on *The Sonny and Cher Comedy Hour*, was a puzzle to many.

"I asked Son if he thought it was okay and he said it was fine," Cher later recalled. "She enjoys it and she's been doing it ever since she was two. You know, Chastity used to think that everyone's mother and father was on TV. In fact, we had a war because she *wasn't* on my show right away. Chastity was really pissed off when I had Tatum O'Neal on and not her. But I didn't want to put her on until my series was a success on its own. I knew everyone wanted to see her, but I didn't want to use her to get any ratings points."

Cher's relationship with Tatum O'Neal caused even more trouble. "I remember picking Chastity up at school and driving her to Cher's set and on the way hearing how unhappy her mother was making her," Sonny wrote in *And the Beat Goes On*. "Chas told me she was feeling neglected by Cher. And I said, 'What's the problem? She's your mom.' Chastity's response was, 'No she's not. She's more a mom to Tatum than she is to me.'" (Ironically, at the time of Chastity's confession, a photo of Cher and O'Neal was featured on the cover of *Movie Mirror*. The caption: "Cher Fights to Make Tatum O'Neal Her Child! The Secrets She Used to Get Ryan to Agree! Why the News Broke Chastity's Heart.") After learning about his daughter's unhappiness, Sonny drove Chastity back to his house and called up his former wife. "Cher expressed surprise and claimed she had no idea that Chastity was unhappy. She wanted to know how *I* knew, since I spent less time with her than she supposedly did. I said, 'I know because she told me, Cher.'" At that point in the conversation, according to Sonny, Cher put David Geffen on the phone (they were still romantically involved at this time).

"Geffen told me, 'Cher asked me to tell you not to worry about Chastity, everything is going to be okay.' I never had a problem dealing with Cher or Chastity except when Geffen was around. It broke my heart to think of Chastity being yanked back and forth between Cher, Geffen and me." (In his 2011 book *Transition: The Story of How I Became a Man*, Chaz [formerly Chastity] talks at length about how, during this period of his childhood, he was emotionally closer to his father, who nicknamed him "Fred," and had no opinion about how he dressed [always in boys' clothes] or acted [unfeminine].)

Throughout 1975, perhaps because she was a newly single mother, or perhaps because the public perception of Cher was that she was a party girl, Cher often found herself in the position of having to field questions about Chastity's wellbeing. "Chastity's actually a much happier child now that Sonny and I have broken up," she said at the time. "She would have to be a happier child. She not only sees more of me since the breakup, but more of Sonny too. And now she sees the best side of both of us. It doesn't necessarily follow that when a couple breaks up the child must suffer. In our case, I think it's just the opposite." Cher opened show number eleven with a rousing rendition of her very first solo hit, 1965's Bob Dylan-penned "All I Really Want to Do," followed by a rundown of the show's guests. Her final introduction was written for dramatic effect.

CHER: I have a surprise for you tonight. As you know, for ten years, I was married to kind of a very special man. And in those ten years he gave me a lot of things—a lot of really nice things. I guess one of the nicest things he ever gave me is something that I would like to share with you right now. Her name is Chastity Bono.

What followed was an engaging mother and daughter exchange in which Chastity showed her mom how she would open "The Chastity Bono Show." For the opening, instead of dresses, mother and daughter wore hers and hers matching bell bottoms and bare midriff tops. The pants were a mandate. In 2011 Chaz revealed that, during the final year of *The Sonny and Cher Comedy Hour*, she told her mom and dad—and Ret Turner and Bob Mackie—that she would no longer wear dresses. "One of Chastity's pastimes was to comb and curl my hair," says Ret Turner, who bounced back and forth between the roles of costume designer, dresser and babysitter. "At the time, I had rather long hair and Chastity was my hairdresser. She would comb it, play with it, braid it, put it in ponytails—she and I spent a lot of time together. During breaks in filming I would take her with me over to the Farmers' Market. We'd shop for food to bring back to her mom's dressing room and we'd have a little picnic. Cher would come in, but she wouldn't eat much of anything. Instead, she would just watch all the rest of us eat."

"Whenever Cher went to the Farmers' Market she wore a short wig and no makeup," says a CBS employee who occasionally joined her. "Sometimes she even had white dots on her face to treat her blemishes. She usually had lunch with her sister Georganne and Chastity. After she was seated she would look at the menu, decide what she wanted, and then whisper it into her sister's ear. Then Georganne would order everything–including Cher's food. Cher thought that if people heard her voice they would instantly know it was her. I thought the whole idea of Cher pretending *not* to be 'Cher' was fascinating."

Jolene Schlatter, producer George Schlatter's wife, pointed out another problem that Cher encountered when she attempted to go unnoticed: Chastity. "When we went out with Chastity Cher liked it to be a private affair, a time when she and Chas could just relax and have fun. I remember one time Cher was totally in disguise; dark glasses, wig, a big hat, and it worked–no one noticed her. But they noticed Chastity! Like it or not, Chastity was a TV star in her own right. She had appeared on the *The Sonny and Cher Comedy Hour* almost as much as Sonny and Cher!"

"Cher was a wise and patient mother who took great pains to ensure Chastity's wellbeing," recalls producer's assistant Donna Schuman. "She took seriously her obligation as a role model for both her daughter and other children. Along with Chastity, injured or sick children also received her full and compassionate attention. I know this for a fact because I frequently shuttled the kids back and forth, to and from her dressing room on tape days. Cher went out of her way to accommodate the many demands placed on her by her fans." (She also responded, personally, to fanmail–the larger part of which was requests for an autograph and/or photo.)

The other guests on show number eleven were the Ike and Tina Turner Review and Kate Smith (both of whom had appeared on *The Sonny and Cher Comedy Hour*) and Tim Conway. Best-known for her patriotic recording of "God Bless America," Kate Smith had starred in not one but three television series of her own: *The Kate Smith Hour* (1950), *The Kate Smith Evening Hour* (1951), and *The Kate Smith Show* (1960). On *Cher* Smith performed "What Kind of Fool am I?" (a song Cher spoofed on her special), sang a musical-comedy duet with Cher entitled "Relationships," and performed in a segment as a mother bird who is reluctant to let her baby bird (Cher) leave the nest. Tina Turner and Cher had a great deal in common, and following Turner's first appearance on *The Sonny and Cher Comedy Hour*, the two became close. Both struggled with their marital relationships, longed to enjoy a larger (independent) entertainment industry success, and wondered what would happen to them if they broke up their husband and wife show-business teams. (Cher would later write the Foreword to Turner's best-selling autobiography *I, Tina*.) Although Turner (who at the time could also be seen on the big screen in the musical *Tommy*) had not made public the fact that husband Ike was a violent and unpredictable drug addict, and that she was the victim of chronic spousal abuse (little more than a year after she taped the segment she fled Ike, her marriage, and her role as half of the Ike and Tina Turner Revue), on *Cher* Ike and Tina's live performance of "Nutbush City Limits" is awe-inspiring. Turner is in great voice and, with the Ikettes, her background singer/dancers, performs a breathtaking shimmy and hair-throwing routine while Ike and the band groove behind her. Not quite hitting their mark, but no less exciting to behold, is Cher and Tina's duet on the 1974 Shirley and Company hit "Shame, Shame, Shame." Dressed in hers and hers sequined ensembles and both writhing, throwing their hair, and revving each other up, their pairing was, if nothing else, a feast for the eyes; two sexy, glamorous, showy—and leggy—women giving it their all. "Tina and I had such a great time together on that number," Cher later recalled. "It was so hard keeping up with her. It took every ounce of stamina I had. She was unbelievably cool!"

Tim Conway first met Cher when Sonny, Cher and he were guests on *Laugh-In*. A popular supporting player on *The Carol Burnett Show*, he also starred in the thirteen-episode *Tim Conway Comedy Hour*. On *Cher* Conway played Dr. Frankenstein (with Cher as his monster wife), and a servant who constantly bickers with his wife (Cher). Conway and Sonny shared a bit of history. "Tim is funnier off camera than he is on," wrote Sonny in *And the Beat Goes On*. "We hung out together [Conway opened Sonny's brief, and eventually aborted, post-Sonny and Cher nightclub outings] and I appreciated his sensitivity. He understood what I was going through and he used to say, 'Sonny, you're a really talented guy. It's a shame you're in a box like this.'"

Show number eleven's highlight was the musical finale; an eye-popping salute to the Beatles. The twelve-song medley, featuring the entire cast, included the tunes "All You Need is Love," "I Want to Hold Your Hand" and "Yellow Submarine."

"George [Schlatter] suggested that we do the tribute to the Beatles," remembers Dee Dee Wood. "We had these wonderful huge painted backdrops for each of the Beatles' faces and Cher, Tina and Kate [Smith] were scheduled to come out in front of them. Now, Tina and Cher made sense, but Tina and Cher and Kate was just outrageous. During the final part of their number they were supposed to lift up their left hand to indicate that the medley was over. Well, Kate kept lifting up both hands—high in the air like she was being saved! We had to stop the tape over and over because Kate had never used a hand-held mike before. She was from the old days and she was used to standing in front of a mike on a stand. She had absolutely no idea what to do with her hands or the mike in her hand. I had a really hard time keeping a straight face for that one." (Show number eleven is the only episode in the series in which Cher does not perform any of her standard sketches: "Donna Jean Brodine," "Life with Laverne," "Mable's Fables," "The Complaint Department," or "Saturday Night.")

Show number twelve featured Art Garfunkel, Jimmy Webb, Mclean Stevenson, Charo, Chastity, and a newly tanned Cher—just back from a brief trip to Hawaii (her second that year). Art Garfunkel appeared on *Cher* for two reasons; one: he wanted the exposure, and 2: he had worked with and greatly admired singer/songwriter/arranger Jimmy Webb. On the show Garfunkel performed "Bridge Over Troubled Waters" (a No. 1 hit in 1970 when he was half of Simon and Garfunkel; and a tune Cher performed on *The Sonny and Cher Comedy Hour*) and joined Cher and Webb for a medley of Webb's tunes.

Jimmy Webb, who just so happened to be the producer of Cher's forthcoming album *Stars*, was a jack of all trades—singer, songwriter, musician—whose well-known catalogue of music included "By the Time I Get to Phoenix," "Wichita Lineman," and "Galveston"—all of which he wrote and all of which became hits for Glen Campbell. Cher was a fan of Webb. Even before he produced her album she performed his melancholy "Didn't We" on *The Sonny and Cher Comedy Hour*. Years later, when *Newsweek* asked her how she prepared for dramatic scenes in her films she said, "I lock myself away with a compilation tape of my favorite Jimmy Webb songs." On *Cher* Webb sat at the piano and played a medley of yet two more of his tunes—"Up, Up And Away" ("Record of the Year" and "Song of the Year" for the Fifth Dimension in 1968) and "All I Know" (a top-ten hit for Garfunkel in 1973). Cher and Garfunkel are in great voice and their harmonizing—Garfunkel, high; Cher, characteristically low—is impressive. "I don't remember a thing about taping that segment," says Webb today. "I have an absolutely paralyzing fear of television; something about 80 million little eyeballs looking at you. What surprises me is that I was actually able to do it. That I was able to make my fingers move across the keyboard. God, I'd like to go back and relive that day and try to remember more of it. The only thing that I'm pretty sure of is that Arty [Garfunkel] and I smoked pot in the CBS dressing room before we went on!" (Alongside Garfunkel's name in producer Schlatter's *Cher* notebook is the notation "Confirmed: with a bag!")

At the time of his appearance McLean Stevenson had just exited his supporting role on the comedy series M*A*S*H. He had also appeared on *The Sonny and Cher Comedy Hour*, *The Sonny Comedy Revue* and was, quite notably, a frequent guest host on *The Tonight Show*. On *Cher* Stevenson played the husband of a woman (Cher) who has been stricken by a string of bad luck, and a married (to Cher) mouse who has a roving eye for a another mouse, a sexy cocktail waitress (Charo). "So many of the sketches started with the creation of the costumes," remembers Ret Turner. "The mouse sketch with Charo and McLean was one of those. That was really fun and it was typical of what we were doing. We would just get the oddest people to do the oddest things. We never knew who the guest stars were going to be from week to week, so we just created the costume designs and the visual concept to accompany the script for that week's show. Then whoever came in—we'd make the costumes to fit them. Looking back it's pretty incredible that all the guests we worked with were willing to do the things we had planned. Whether it was a giant mouse or Humpty Dumpty, everyone was game."

Like Stevenson, Latina spitfire Charo, had previously been a guest on *The Sonny and Cher Comedy Hour* and *The Sonny Comedy Revue* (she also headlined her own variety special the following year). On *Cher* the shapely, sprightly, 24-year-old performer, who was best known for her catchphrase "Cuchi-Cuchi" (and who was notoriously married to 75-year-old bandleader Xavier Cugat) sang a solo "Malaguena," participated in a sketch in which she played the prim and proper sister to swinging Cher, and joined Cher and the Dee Dee Wood Dancers for an elaborately choreographed finale of "America" from the musical *West Side Story*. "What a hoot Charo was," remembers Dee Dee Wood. "When you dealt with Charo, you dealt with her sister, who, in looks and demeanor, was exactly like Charo. They both had this crazy energy and it was infectious. I really enjoyed working with her."

In her second appearance on the series, Chastity was featured in a comic interlude in which Cher played a hobo, with Chastity as her eager-to-learn sidekick, and joined Cher for her solo of the Joe Cocker hit "You Are So Beautiful." Cher opened the hour with Carole King's "Where You Lead" (performed with Sonny on *Sonny and Cher Live in Las Vegas Vol. 2*) followed by a monologue about how much she hated getting up early for rehearsals.

Three days after show number twelve was broadcast, Cher made good on her promise to Flip Wilson: she appeared on his Prime-Time network special. One of the hour's highlights was a segment in which she played Laverne and Wilson played Geraldine—two "ladies" who were the heads of a charm school (a not-too-subtle rewrite of "Laverne Meets Geraldine" from Cher's special). On the show Cher also performed "Bell Bottom Blues," wearing a blue sequined bell bottom ensemble, a cut from her new album *Stars*.

"Right now I'm kind of like the queen of a mediocre medium," Cher bluntly observed regarding her omnipresence on the tube—her own show, award shows, talk shows and specials. "I mean let's face it. TV is the kind of thing that you can pay attention to if you wish, and if you don't, you can go and clean out your drawers."

PART THREE:

Cher Bono Allman

16

RAMBLIN' MAN

Cher show number thirteen, usually an unlucky number, is Cher's personal favorite. The reason: along with Carol Burnett—whom she introduced as "the person that I respect most on television"—and Dennis Weaver, the program's musical guest was Gregg Allman of the Allman Brothers Band. According to Gregg, he first met Cher on Jan 21, 1975 at Los Angeles' Troubadour nightclub (in *The First Time* Cher remembers the date as "at the end of '74"). At the time of their first meeting a provocatively posed—and shirtless—Gregg was leering out at passersby from the cover of *Rolling Stone*. As Cher told it she had gone to the Troubadour to see soul singer Etta James. Joining her that evening were Tatum O'Neal, David Geffen, her sister Georganne and her secretary Paulette. When James finished her set, Cher and her entourage stayed on and caught Allman's (unbilled) "jam," a performance he agreed to in the hopes of "tightening his chops" for an upcoming Allman Brothers Band tour.

Gregory Lenoir Allman was born on December 8, 1947 in Nashville, Tennessee. When he was two years old his father was killed by a hitchhiker. Early on Gregg displayed an interest in music and, after the family moved to Daytona Beach, Florida, he and his older brother Duane bounced around in several local bands before forming their own group. The original Allman Brothers Band lineup featured Duane Allman and Dickey Betts on guitar, Berry Oakley on bass, and Butch Trucks and Jai "Johanny" Johanson on drums. Gregg, a jack of all trades, took on the roles of lead vocalist, guitarist, and organ player. In 1972 *Rolling Stone* called the Allman Brothers Band "the best damned rock and roll band this country has produced in the past five years," and when the group went all the way to the No. 2 spot on the Pop charts with "Ramblin' Man" (ironically held from the No. 1 spot by Cher's "Half-Breed") they had hit the big time.

But Gregg's success was experienced in the shadow of tragedy. On

October 29, 1971, his beloved brother Duane died in a motorcycle accident: he was 24. Little more than a year later, on November 11, 1972, Allman Brothers bassist Berry Oakley, 23, also perished in a motorcycle accident—just three blocks away from the spot where Duane was killed. The two, almost back to back dreadful events shook Gregg to his core and, as it would turn out, had a profoundly debilitating effect on him. Even so, the heartbreaking cards that life dealt Gregg didn't stop him and the Allman Brothers Band from recording, continuing to tour, or keep Gregg from releasing a solo album—1973's critically-acclaimed *Laidback*. "I remember it today like it was yesterday," Allman told an interviewer 35 years after his big brother's death. "But I knew he would want me to keep going. So that's what I did." (Duane Allman's legacy lives on. In 2003 *Rolling Stone* cited him at No. 2 on their "100 Greatest Guitarists of all Time List." The virtuoso guitarist was placed one step behind Jimi Hendrix and one step in front of B.B. King.) "I looked at Cher and she looked like an Egyptian goddess," Allman told *Viva* about his and Cher's first encounter. "She stuck out her hand and her fingernails were about three inches long; boy was I hot to trot!" Following their introduction, Gregg had one of his friends give Cher a note. It read: "I only came here for two nights, but if you'll come back tomorrow, I'll play another night." The note also had Gregg's phone number on it.

"When Gregg came to the house to pick me up, I came down the stairs and saw him looking at himself in the mirror," Cher recalled. "I said, 'Hey, you look great to me.' And he mumbled, 'I was just checking something... I wasn't really looking at myself.' I'll never forget it." And neither would Gregg, especially as their first date didn't go as planned. "Everything was just awful," Cher later recalled. "He took me to Dino's on the Sunset Strip where it's really dark, and started to suck my fingers. And I thought, 'Wait a minute; back up.' I said, 'Why are you doing this?' Next he asked me to go with him while he met some guy [Edgar Winter of the Edgar Winter Group], but first he wanted to change his clothes, which he did every ten minutes. So we split, and a while later [at a party that *Laugh-In* comedian and self-confessed heroin addict Judy Carne was throwing] he started to kiss me. I just said the dumbest thing; I said 'I'm not that kind of girl.' I have no idea where the hell that came from. I just ran out the door. I told him not to bother to show me the way. 'Catch you later, nice meeting you, you're a terrific guy, so long.' And I split."

Allman's story was similar. "We went out to Dino's and we didn't say nothing to each other, absolutely nothing. I mean it was just the most mediocre trip you've ever fuckin' thought about. I grabbed hold of her little finger and put it in my mouth and it was just too much, too fast for her, you know. She said, 'Now why don't we just go.' So I said, 'Okay let's go.'" But Gregg also admitted that after that night he was determined to "conquer" Cher. Another phone call was made and another date arranged. "On our second date we were walking down the street and I said, 'Goddamn it, I can't think of nothing to say to you, man, nothing.' And she said that she was thinking about the same damn thing. And I said, 'Why don't we just give it a break and go dance.' So we went to the Candy Store, which was [a private Beverly Hills disco] and danced our asses off. And we had a good time, and from there we went home and made love." (In his 2012 memoir My Cross to Bear Allman wrote that Cher "ripped [his] clothes off" and initiated their first sexual encounter. "She was hot to trot. I later read that she said I was one of her best lovers. That made me feel good. I'm not particularly well endowed but I know how to use it!")

Although Allman's formal introduction to the public as Cher's new romantic partner came earlier in the year, via the March 8 edition of The National Star, which featured a composite photo of the two under the caption "Cher... Meet Her New Love," paparazzi photos of the two at an endless number of "in" places like the Rainbow Grill, Bistro, La Scala, Luau, The Palm, Tana's, Roys, Dar Maghreb and Chasen's—all in L.A.—brought the point home more powerfully. During a visit to Starwood to see the Swedish rock band Blue Swede (best known for their No. 1 hit "Hooked on a Feeling") Cher even hopped onstage with Gregg and the band and performed a rousing impromptu version of her hit "Half-Breed"—before an unexpecting and dumbstruck crowd.

At the time Cher was also seen outside the safe confines of Hollywood with Gregg. During a rare break in taping, she flew to Macon, Georgia to spend a few days with him. The couple was spotted holding hands at Macon's upscale Bistro restaurant. They also went dancing, cruised around town in Gregg's cream-colored Corvette, and visited Gregg's local hangouts. An impromptu performance of "Proud Mary" at the decidedly downscale Uncle Sam's Roadhouse made headlines. "Gregg always hangs out here," said the club's manager Ev Courson at the time. "When he walked in with Cher people did a double take. They weren't really sure it was her because all those celebrities look smaller in real life and she wasn't wearing any makeup." But when she took to the stage the club's revelers almost dropped their drinks. "Once she started to sing there was no doubt in anyone's mind," said Courson. "It was definitely Cher."

Gregg Allman's appearance on Cher was an important one. Although he was now, via Cher, a familiar face in newspapers and magazines, most Americans (especially Prime-Time television watchers) weren't quite sure what he did—or, for that matter, if he was even talented. On the show Allman did a mesmerizing live rendition of the melancholy "Midnight Rider" that was cleverly edited together with a provocative routine performed by Cher and the Dee Dee Wood Dancers. "Midnight Rider" showcased Allman's distinct and soulful voice—"a drawling, whiskey-flavored sound," surmised Rolling Stone—and made clear that he was worthy of the praise that swirled around him. A singer not a screamer—

or for that matter even a showman—Allman, it was abundantly clear, was a gifted musician, one of those performers who seemed to be doing what they were born to do.

But not everyone thought so. "I remember that segment well," recalls Dee Dee Wood. "When we were taping, I swear to you, not one of us could understand a word that Gregg was singing. We kept looking at each other like, 'What the hell is going on here?' But we had to do it. We had to go ahead and tape Gregg and his segment exactly the way he did it. Cher wanted him on the show and that was that." George Schlatter, too, remained unimpressed with Allman. "Cher wanted Gregg on the show. It was very, very important to her. She got to perform with someone she was in love with and someone whose music she liked and respected. But I must admit, Allman never really did light my fire. I just didn't get him or his and Cher's relationship." Lee Miller is the most up-front about Allman's appearance at CBS Television City. "Gregg was only important to the people who worked on *Cher* because he was important to Cher. I remember him being very nice and very pleasant, he was not a problem at all, but he was only booked on the show because Cher insisted. No one else—and I mean *no one*—not the *Cher* show staff, not the sponsors, not the CBS executives, thought it was a good idea."

On *Cher* Allman also performed a spirited duet with Cher (Gregg at the organ, Cher singing and dancing by his side) of the 1965 Fontella Bass and Bobby McClure soul favorite "Don't Mess Up a Good Thing"—a tune included on 1974's *Gregg Allman Live*. "Our relationship makes me feel at peace and that makes all the work for my TV show easier to bear," Cher said at the time. "Gregg is so easy to get along with. He's patient and lets me be myself. We have an equal relationship. I didn't have that kind of relationship with Sonny."

Someone who wasn't at "peace" with the Cher/Allman relationship was a female stagehand who worked on her series. "Gregg and Cher were so fucking in love that it made me sick," admits the source who, enviously, watched Gregg and Cher's relationship blossom. "They were always together. He came with her to rehearsals and tapings and they would often have lunch in her dressing room. At the time Gregg was really hot and I was young and was a huge Allman Brothers fan. I thought, 'That bitch has it all.' She got out from underneath Sonny, she was gorgeous, she was talented, and now she was in a passionate romance with Gregg Allman. I wanted to kill her!"

"Special Guest Star" Carol Burnett was also a guest on show number thirteen (in a trade-off Cher agreed to appear on Burnett's show later in the year). Burnett and Cher first met in 1967 when Sonny and Cher appeared on her show. Later, they shared a studio at CBS, and on one occasion, when Cher was unavailable, Burnett took Chastity, along with her own daughters, to the circus. Burnett's elevated status at CBS was reflected by both her dressing room—she had one of the two largest (*All in the Family*'s Carroll O'Connor had the other)—and by the fact that, unlike most guests who appeared on *Cher*, she received a personally embossed faux-leather *Cher* show script.

In the "$24,663.89 Pyramid," a take on the $10,000 *Pyramid* game show, Burnett appeared as a contestant, with Cher playing an over-confident starlet, and Dennis Weaver as the game-show host. In "Shirley Holmes and Wanda" Burnett played Dr. Wanda, Cher played detective Shirley Holmes, and Dennis Weaver played a turn-of-the-century Barrister who has reported a double murder. A blackout in which Cher dressed as Burnett (red bobbed wig, pleated dress, hands in pockets) and Burnett dressed as Cher (long black wig, low-cut sequined gown, showgirl makeup) was funny.

CAROL: [As Cher] Hey, listen, you guys, just sit there and be cool, stay loose, mellow out, and I'll be back in a very far out minute.

CHER: [As Carol] Well, golly gee, just wait a second. You didn't say anything about Harvey or nifty little Vicki, and gosh, gee whizz, there might be some questions from the audience and you didn't sign my book or anything.

"Although no one knew it, Cher and Carol were the exact same size and could wear each other's clothes," says Ret Turner. "For instance, if we were doing an Elizabethan sketch and Bob had already done something for *The Carol Burnett Show*, we would just pull it from wardrobe and use it on Cher. That's exactly what we did for the blackout—they just wore each other's clothes!"

In the latter part of the '60s, Dennis Weaver was familiar to TV viewers via his Emmy-winning supporting role on one of television's most popular shows, *Gunsmoke*. In the '70s Weaver, an outspoken conservationist, spiritualist and humanitarian, was both the star of his own series *McCloud*, the face of BankAmericard (later Visa), and president of SAG, the Screen Actor's Guild. He also was a budding country music singer. On the show Weaver played a not too bright turn-of-the-century barrister, and sang "Prairie Dog Blues" from his album *One More Road*. "I enjoy singing, it's just another way to express myself," explained Weaver at the time, and although he never released a song that charted, on *Cher*, with two fetching female Dee Dee Wood dancers by his side, he appeared both competent and agreeable. "The Legendary Ladies of the Silver Screen" production number was the show's finale. It began with Cher and Burnett as "themselves" on a backstage set. Through song—the Billy Barnes and Earl Brown-written "Ladies of the Silver Screen"—they sang the story of two once-heralded but now has-been stars, Lily Lamont (Carol) and Vera Duveen (Cher). Five different costumes and four different sets illustrated their tale spectacularly. As children—"The Little Darlings"—Cher and Burnett, dressed in pigtails and bloomers, sang "I'm Following You" while doing a tap dance. As members of an all-girl band—"Vera and Lil's Band of Thrills"—the two don flapper garb, sing "Nagasaki," and play instruments, including a sax, trombone, bass and trumpet. As patriotic "war girls" they are driven onto a giant flag-bound set in a Jeep and perform the '40s Johnny Mercer hit "G.I. Jive." (When a bomb explodes, they emerge, covered in soot, and wearing dirty versions of their earlier '40s girl garb.) For the finale, as their current-day selves swathed in sequins, jewels, and furs, Cher and Burnett sing Barnes and Brown's "Lonely at the Top" (inspired by *Mame*'s "Bosom Buddies"), a tune heavy with bitchy repartee and double entendres. The finale closed with a chromo-key composite shot (reminiscent of those used on *The Sonny and Cher Comedy Hour*) in which all the different Carols and Chers—the children, the band singers, the war girls, and the legendary ladies—take their bows.

Cher opened the hour with Stevie Wonder's "For Once in My Life," a tune that—with its lyrics "For once in my life I've found someone who needs me / Someone I've needed so long"—appeared to be a direct acknowledgement of her newfound romance with program guest Gregg Allman. She followed the number with a monologue about the retinue of beauty professionals that "put her together" each week. During the hour she also performed "Geronimo's Cadillac" (her latest single) in front of a giant blowup of her newest album cover, *Stars* (the script for this episode indicates that Cher originally planned to sing the song live with an interpretive vocal introduction, but later chose to lip synch), and reprised "Saturday Night," in which she talked about a "bummer" masquerade party.

Cher, who had arrived by herself at CBS Television City at 8:45 a.m. the day she taped show number thirteen (and parts of show number fourteen) exited the studio a full sixteen hours later at 1:20 a.m. On her way out she was spotted in jeans and a t-shirt looking weary, but happily holding hands with Gregg Allman. Helming your very own solo variety series was indeed, it seemed, a full-time job.

17

GIRLS WILL TALK

Show number fourteen was a familiar affair. Along with Teri Garr and daughter Chastity the hour featured the Hudson Brothers and Art Carney, both of whom had appeared on *The Sonny and Cher Comedy Hour*. Like Sonny and Cher, the Hudson Brothers (Marc, Brett and Bill) came to television via a CBS summer replacement series. The singer/comedian's *The Hudson Brothers Show* was produced by *The Sonny and Cher Comedy Hour*'s Chris Bearde and Allan Blye. So was the teen-oriented *The Hudson Brothers Razzle Dazzle Hour*.

On *Cher* the Hudsons performed "Rendezvous" (from their current album *Ba-Fa*) and played bill posters attempting to put signs up outside a dilapidated theater. Cher and the Hudson Brothers enjoyed working together. Four years later, in 1979, Cher and Marc Hudson co-wrote "Too Far Gone," a track on her *Take Me Home* album.

Art Carney, best known as goofy Ed Norton on the classic '50s television series *The Honeymooners*, was, at the time of his appearance, riding high on the crest of a late-career comeback. Just a month earlier he picked up a Best Actor Oscar for his role in *Harry and Tonto*. On the show Carney performed a light-hearted duet with Cher entitled "My Blue Heaven," tried to get a stone-faced Cher to laugh in a comedy blackout, portrayed a dentist who is credited with inventing dentures, and played a husband who was becoming increasingly frustrated with his wife (Cher's) forgetfulness. "Art Carney is one of the reigning geniuses of comedy" says Digby Wolfe. "I mean there was nobody, before or since, in my mind, that could reduce me to tears of laughter. I loved working with Art and he was just brilliant on the show; a truly inspired comic voice."

Teri Garr appeared in two segments. In "Life with Laverne," Olivia (Garr) asked Laverne for tips on how to keep her husband happy, and in "The Complaint Department" Garr played a customer who runs into trouble returning a baby-shower gift. In another sketch Garr played a witness in a courtroom who is being given the third degree by a challenging prosecutor (Carney).

Cher opened the show with a rousing version of Jerry Lee Lewis's "Great Balls of Fire" (a tune she would later feature in her nightclub act). For the opening she re-introduced the much-photographed lavender and white chiffon butterfly motif ensemble she wore to the 1974 Grammy Awards. Her solo—accompanied by the Dee Dee Wood Dancers—was a meticulously rendered version of "Hernando's Hideaway" the perky, jangly, tune from the musical *Pajama Game*. "I remember we rehearsed and then taped that number for what seemed like forever," says one of the show's dancers. "Cher was always great but there was a step that she just couldn't get right. The whole number was a lip synch, so it wasn't about her having to dance and sing at the same time, she just had to try and not fall down! She hit the deck more than once. If I remember correctly she was almost nude [Cher wore a beaded white fringed criss-cross top and bikini trunks]. Each time her feet got tangled up and she took a tumble, she just got up, dusted herself off, and we all started over again."

The "Cher Concert" featured Cher and four background singers singing a spirited medley of George Harrison's "My Sweet Lord" (which she reprised four years later in *Cher... and Other Fantasies*) and the Edwin Hawkins Singers' "Oh, Happy Day." Two other segments, a blackout with Cher as a bosomy stewardess touting her airline's many "extras," and a segment that featured Chastity attempting to buy a balloon, rounded out the hour. Taking a cue from Carol Burnett, Cher's opening monologue was followed by a question and answer session that was both funny and informative.

Q: Will you ever have Sonny on your show?

A: Yes. On the first show of the new fall season.

On May 19, ten days after taping show number fourteen, Cher shared a stage with ten other female television stars. The event was the 27th Annual Emmy Awards. Lucille Ball (*The Lucy Show*); Beatrice Arthur (*Maude*); Carol Burnett (*The Carol Burnett Show*); Teresa Graves (*Get Christie Love!*); Michael Learned (*The Waltons*); Mary Tyler Moore (*The Mary Tyler Moore Show*); Susan Saint James (*McMillan and Wife*); Jean Stapleton (*All in the Family*); and Karen Valentine (*Karen*) all took turns with Cher hosting the televised event. Cher arrived at the ceremony on the arm of Gregg Allman wearing an ice-blue-colored sequined gown and choker—her hair pulled up with several curls cascading softly around her face. Her entrance was marked by pandemonium. When her limousine pulled up to the theater, fans screamed, cheered and pushed up against barricades trying to reach her. "A middle-aged man grabbed for her expensive, exotic hairdo and pulled at two dangling curls before a security guard came to her aid," wrote one reporter. Although the Emmy stage wasn't *her* stage, it might as well have been. Along with the *Cher* show being nominated in nine different categories, everywhere she turned she saw someone that she knew—and someone who had appeared on her show. Along with Carol Burnett, Jack Albertson and Cloris Leachman, all of whom won Emmys that night, she shared time with Flip Wilson, Art Carney, Freddie Prinze, Dennis Weaver, Tim Conway, Nancy Walker and Lily Tomlin.

On a roll, on May 20, a day after she served as co-presenter at the Emmys, Cher held her 29th birthday bash at Pips in Los Angeles. In 1975 Pips, along with L.A.'s Spago—where agent Irving "Swifty" Lazar held his annual Oscar party—was *the* place to be seen. Co-owned by former Sonny and Cher manager Joe DeCarlo (Chastity's godfather), the establishment, with its muted lighting, thick carpets, and dark paneled walls, catered to the rich and famous. Cher's secretary Paulette manned the door for Cher's birthday party and watched as Sonny, Rod Stewart, Elton John, Britt Ekland, Tatum and Ryan O'Neal, Anouk Aimée, Michael Douglas, Brenda Vaccaro, Joni Mitchell, Carole King, Harry Nilsson, Elliott Gould, Lee Grant, and Brett Hudson (with his date, Cher's sister Georganne), all made their way into the club. Although the party—which topped off at 202 people and included a photographer from *Motion Picture*—started at 8:00 p.m., Cher didn't make her dazzling entrance with Gregg Allman until 10:30. For the "arrival" photos, Cher was swathed in electric blue and silver bugle beads (a picture of her emerging from her limousine later appeared on the June 26, 1979 cover of *Circus*). Once inside, after basking in the kisses and well wishes of her many celebrity friends, Cher was presented with an enormous birthday cake emblazoned with the number 29. "At last my bra size and my age are exactly the same!" Cher quipped.

On May 23, three days after her 29th birthday, Cher was awakened in the middle of the night by a fire that started when an unattended bedside candle toppled and set the cloth skirt of her night stand ablaze. Though no one was harmed, her bedroom was blackened, several cherished antiques were destroyed and her ornate floral-patterned four-poster bed (featured prominently on the back cover of *Mama Was a Rock and Roll Singer, Papa Used To Write All Her Songs*) was rendered unsalvageable.

Five days after the fire broke out in her bedroom, the television special *Rona Looks at Raquel, Liza, Cher and Ann-Margret* (taped in February; at the same time she was taping her series' first episodes) aired. Rona Barrett was more than a Cher fan (she regularly presented Cher in her magazines *Rona Barrett's Hollywood* and *Rona Barrett's Gossip* in a flattering feminist light), she was also a popular writer—the author of 1972's *Lovo-Maniacs*, and 1974's *Miss Rona*—as well as a budding singer; 1975's *Miss Rona Sings Hollywood's Greatest Hits*.

On *Rona Looks at...*, Cher and the other *decidedly* female guests represented the "new" Hollywood female star. "Hearing intimate stories, and seeing Liza, Raquel, Cher and Ann-Margret reveal themselves emotionally, makes for quite an hour," observed *The Hollywood Reporter*. "Thoughts on love, marriage, parents, childhood, sex, psychoanalysis, plastic surgery, babies, and gossip, prove to be fascinating viewing."

"As far as I'm concerned, while all the women on that special answered never-before-asked questions, Cher was, by far, the most open and honest," says Barrett. "With Cher it was no act. She just told it like it was. She knew I understood her and I guess you either trust a person or you don't. I trusted that she would answer questions directly, and she trusted that I would fairly handle the information she wanted me and her public to know." Barrett believes her TV special was a first. "I knew we were entering into a new era and that there were many men and women who wanted subject matter and questions that had not been covered or asked before. The timing of that special was right. It took me about nine months to convince them all to participate, but the show was a smashing success. It's something I'm very proud of."

Show number fourteen aired on Sunday, May 18 and was the final broadcast of *Cher*'s first season. It was followed by five weeks of repeats (episodes two, three, five, eleven and thirteen respectively). "There was some question about whether or not the *Cher* show was going to return in the fall," remembers George Schlatter. "When we finished the first season we were in the red. CBS told us that they weren't going to renew unless we paid back all the money we spent that went over budget. Well, we called their bluff. We told them that no matter what their decision was about bringing *Cher* back in the fall, *we* weren't going to return unless they cleared the slate. They did, and I must say that we were all really relieved and really happy that we would be returning to work later in the year."

18

"I DO," I THINK

June 1975 was a hectic month for Cher—and it had nothing to do with her television series. On June 20, she flew with daughter Chastity (Gregg declined) to Britain and attended Elton John's sold-out Wembley Arena concert. Seven days later, on June 27, she appeared in a Santa Monica courtroom, spent a scant five minutes on the stand, and received her final divorce decree from Sonny Bono. Three days after that, she flew from Los Angeles to Las Vegas and married her boyfriend of six months—Gregg Allman.

"Turning down the champagne for a soft drink, Cher Bono drank a teetotaling toast to her new husband," wrote *The New York Times*. In a private ceremony that took place at 12:15 p.m. on June 30 in the Caesars Palace, Las Vegas hotel suite of her attorney Milton Rudin ("The most awful-looking room in the entire hotel—all purple, gold and turquoise" Cher later recalled), Cherilyn Sarkisian Bono married Gregory Lenoir Allman. The witnesses to the event were District Court Judge James Brennan, former manager Joe DeCarlo, sister Georganne, secretary Paulette, and Cher's press agent Dick Grant. Cher's wedding gown was the ice-blue and white satin dress she wore during the opening number of *Cher* show number thirteen—the episode on which Allman had appeared.

"One Sunday morning I woke up and Cher said, 'I got this Learjet and Nevada ain't too far away; why don't we get married,'" Gregg told *Viva* two years later. "I said, 'I don't know if I'm ready to get into this, but okay, let's do it!'" At the ceremony Gregg later recalled that he remembered thinking: "I wonder what I'd be doing if I were back in Macon right now."

By all accounts, from the very beginning, the Cher Bono/Gregg Allman marriage was a mistake. "I was never in love with Cher," Gregg frankly told *Viva*. "As a matter of fact, on the jet ride back from Vegas, there was not a word spoken between us. And I heard her say to her friend, 'Oh, God, what have I done now?'" Cher told Rona Barrett a story that was equally disturbing. "Only minutes after this judge pronounced us man and wife, man, Gregg was spaced out! I'd never seen him like that before. He didn't even know who I was!"

Gregg's substance abuse wasn't the only unexpected challenge for Cher. "I'm beginning to feel like an old dishrag" she confessed at the time. "And, I'm starting to get an inferiority complex. Whenever Gregg and I are out I find myself just standing around looking dumb and unwanted while Gregg raps with all these really, really young chicks." Cher could have learned a lot about Gregg's lifestyle by taking a look at the January 1975 issue of *Rolling Stone*. In it, writer Tim Cahill documented entire days and nights of drinking, partying and carousing as well as Allman's many "bad experiences" and "close calls" with drugs. "Before I knew Gregg, I used to feel that drug addicts were on the same level as murderers," Cher confessed. "Now I know that the person they harm the most is themselves. When I met Gregg I was totally ignorant about the way drugs change a person's personality. It's like having a retarded child: you have to prepare yourself for the responsibility." Cher's own experience with illegal substances was swift and definitive. "When I was sixteen I took four Benzedrines and thought I was going to die. I chewed the same piece of gum for three days. And I told my mother—I swore, never, ever again will I do drugs." Later, she tried smoking marijuana. "I have smoked grass a couple of times. Pot made me laugh and it made me paranoid and since I can be paranoid and I can laugh without it, who needs it?"

Apparently a great number of other people. "Gregg told me that a lot of rock musicians are into drugs. I certainly know what he means because a lot of TV people are on something too. I can think of three people in television who don't take anything: Carol Burnett, Mary Tyler Moore and me [Moore would later admit that she struggled with alcohol]. And, for the three of us who don't do anything, I can think of fifteen stars—gigantic stars—who do." (In his memoir Gregg Allman reports that on their second date he pulled out a little bottle of coke, spread it across her piano, and snorted it. "I asked Cher if it bothered her and she said, 'No, not at all.' A little bit of blow was okay but not heroin or drinking—she hated drinking as much as heroin.")

One of the stars that Cher knew "maintained" on drugs—cocaine in particular—was comedian Redd Foxx. "The first time he was on my show I was in my dressing room and Redd came in and said, 'Cher, do you have any coke?' I said, 'No, but I have some Dr. Pepper in the refrigerator!' I swear to God that's how little I knew about drugs at the time."

"Coke, Stardust, Lady Snow—whatever you call it, 'the white stuff' is the newest sensation to conquer 'Follywood,'" wrote columnist Maxine Letterford in an extensive investigative piece that appeared in *Motion Picture*. "The drug is weaving its destructive way, not to seedy hotel rooms patronized by down-

and-out actors, but to mansions whose occupants rate a star on the door. From dressing room to movie set, from swinging nightspot to red-carpet premiere, the fine white powder leaves a trail of spaced-out, freaked-out, high-flying celebs." And it seemed it did.

"It was grim," recalled Allman of the period immediately following their marriage. "It was me staying out all night, me staying away for two or three days. I just couldn't handle what I'd done. I was sorry that I had done it and she was just as sorry that we'd done it." (Gregg later admitted Cher's inadvertent discovery of his "rig" [drug bag] complete with heroin, needles, and rubber bands, hastened their breakup.)

On July 6, nine days after they got married, Cher filed for divorce. "I've always believed it best to admit one's mistakes as soon as possible," Cher informed the Associated Press. "Gregg and I just cannot live together as man and wife." Speaking with *Motion Picture*'s John J. Miller, she was more frank. "Listen, I really screwed up this time. What can I tell you? It [the marriage] was a mistake and a mess. I'm not happy or even depressed. Let's just say I'm resigned to the fact that I made a mistake. And I think when you make a mistake you should admit it fast." Miller's exclusive post-divorce interview was a *Motion Picture* cover story and included interviews with Gregg (reached by phone in Macon, Georgia), one of the Allman Brothers Band members, and three other close-proximity confidential sources. "Let's face it; men have been making all my decisions for me all my life. Now I'm finally on my own, making my own decisions for the first time, and I'm bound to make a mistake here and there. Marrying Gregg was, as it turned out, a mistake. I guess he makes a much better boyfriend than a husband."

"Don't believe those divorce stories," Allman countered to Miller. "It's not that I don't think she actually went into court and filed, but it's all just an example of her little temper tantrums. I'll fly back to Hollywood over the weekend and I'll straighten her out. That's what she wants me to do. She wants me to go into a panic and get hysterical. What Cher has to learn is that I have my own career, and it's a pretty damned good one at that. Most of her friends, and I guess a lot of her fans, think that I'm just a drummer or something in some rock and roll band. For God's sake, man, I made two or three million dollars on my own in just the last 18 months. I've got 47 people who are dependent on me for their income. I can't let my whole world come to a complete standstill just because she wants to be off somewhere on a honeymoon like they have in storybooks."

Allman didn't make it back to Hollywood the weekend following Cher's divorce filing—or the weekend after that. Feeling very much like a laughingstock, and in need of a sympathetic male ear (she had plenty of girlfriends to talk to) during her estrangement from Gregg, Cher turned to Sonny. "Cher called me up and we met and talked for a long time about her situation with Gregg," Sonny said at the time. "I told her that if she really loved him, he deserved a second chance and she should do her best to make it work."

The third week of July offered Cher a positive sign; Gregg admitted himself into a Buffalo, New York rehabilitation clinic. Elated and convinced that he had the determination to deal with his substance abuse head on, on August 1, she withdrew her divorce petition.

"I think it was seeing him in Buffalo that made me realize how much I truly loved Gregg," Cher recalled. "It was like I was seeing him for the very first time. I had seen glimpses of the real Gregg, but in Buffalo he was completely rid of the narcotics in his system. He was so warm and wonderful that I completely forgot about divorce." Much to his credit, and at a time when celebrity confessionals were a rarity, Allman talked frankly with *People* about the rigors of dealing with his addictions; in particular heroin. "It's like having a cat in your body. His air is all used up, and his claws are out and he's running around inside you trying to get out. Then, bam, the old spike [needle] goes in and you can almost see the cat go to sleep at the bottom of your foot. But you know he'll wake up and try to get out again."

By August the Allmans seemed to have put most of their troubles behind them. Gregg was progressing well in rehab and the couple was seeing a husband and wife psychiatric team that Cher said "helps me, helps Gregg, and helps us together." In an apparent show of support for Gregg, Cher even informed CBS and her record label Warner Bros. that all of her official publicity photos were to carry the caption "Cher Allman." Additionally, when Cher signed autographs, and they are certainly collectors' items today, she signed both her first and *new* last name.

A story that Cher revealed to *Ladies' Home Journal* made clear her belief that her relationship with Allman made her a better, more evolved, and less egocentric person. "One night in a restaurant I began fooling with my false eyelash and ended up just pulling it off. That may not seem like much of a gesture to some people, but it was a big thing for me. The old Cher—the Cher of 'Sonny and Cher'—would never have done that. I was so used to playing a role, a role I believed I had to play, the role of being a doll—you know, the clothes, the makeup, the whole bit. I felt that without it all I was nothing. Bob Mackie used to tell me that I was his 'private Barbie doll' to make clothes for. I've stopped playing that role. I had to—dolls get old and broken and thrown away."

Still, the mean jokes about the Allmans persisted. Los Angeles columnist James Bacon wrote in his syndicated column that if Cher ever married again "she should ask her friends not to throw Minute Rice." On late-night television comedian Irving Schatz joked: "It sure is dull... Cher hasn't been married or divorced all week!" And even Sonny got in on the act. When asked if he was planning to marry his girlfriend Susie Coelho he quipped: "We'll see how it goes. I think I'll let Cher get married a few more times first!" Two widely circulated stories added additional sting. The first involved actor James Arness (best known for his twenty-year tenure as Marshal Matt Dillon on *Gunsmoke*). On May 12 Arness's 24-year-old daughter Jenny committed suicide. Jenny's body was discovered by a friend who rented the first floor of her Malibu beach house. "A final request by James Arness's lovely tragic daughter Jenny was for Gregg Allman to sing 'their song' at her wake," reported *Variety*'s Army Archerd. "Jenny Arness and Gregg Allman were once engaged." Arness, who was under psychiatric care for "severe depression," left a 23-page letter indicating that she was taking her life because Allman, whom she was still in love with, had fallen for and married Cher—instead of her.

Cher spoke candidly with *Playboy* about what she knew. "I honestly can't tell you if she [Arness] left a note or not. All I know from what I've heard is that she sent letters to two or three other guys telling them that *they* were the reason she was committing suicide. I never met the girl, but Gregg did tell me that he went out with her, like, two years ago, and that he honestly doesn't feel responsible for what she's done." A second story making the rounds was a report that one evening, as she and Gregg dined out in Beverly Hills, Allman, drug-addled, incoherent, and incontinent—nodded out into a plate of pasta. "Cher and Gregg were dining at Chianti, an 'in' and *très* elegant Italian restaurant," reported Cher's friend Rona Barrett. "It's the kind of small eatery where voices are hushed and good manners are *de rigueur*. It's definitely not the kind of place that looks kindly on folks doing what Gregg did. Namely, passing out in his plate of spaghetti."

"My network, CBS, even ran that story," Cher complained. "I called them up and said, 'I love you guys dearly, but I'm going to sue you.' Because it was totally untrue. Neither one of us had ever been to that restaurant, and Gregg has never passed out anyplace we have ever been. His mother was upset [by the story], his grandmother. I mean, it made Gregg feel really bad."

"I always thought this was not going to be a successful union," says Rona Barrett of the Gregg/Cher relationship. "I never quite understood Cher's fascination with Gregg except that musically he was very talented—and he had a legitimization by the rock press that Cher didn't believe she had. I'm sure they had a passionate sex life and that always clouds one's vision, but aside from the sex, I think the real reason they were together was that Cher was looking for someone to take care of. Sonny, had allegedly bossed her around so much, I think subconsciously she was looking to do the same thing with Gregg."

"Cher and Gregg came to our house for dinner," remembers Rita Coolidge. "This was right before they got married and around the time Kris and I taped our appearance on her show. I could see that there was a problem [with Gregg] and I thought that there would be trouble. But how do you say anything? She was my girlfriend and she was so in love—she was just wild about Gregg—and he was a great guy; charming, charismatic and so talented. I asked myself if it were me in her place, would I want someone to tell me about potential problems they saw? I came up with the answer 'yes,' but only if I had asked for the other person's opinion. There was nothing that I could have said that would have changed Cher's mind about Gregg and if I were in her shoes I'm sure it would've been the same thing."

"Cher did not appear to love wisely," concurs producer's assistant Donna Schuman, who met and talked to the "charmingly disarming" Allman many times at CBS. "But she had the determination to love fully and the courage to suffer the consequences." It is a sentiment that no one who knew Cher would ever question.

19

NEW ALBUM, OLD FATHER

The drama surrounding Cher's personal life and travails almost totally obscured the release of her first Warner Bros. album *Stars*. In an attempt to both warm up and test the record buying marketplace, in late 1974 Cher's voice was featured on two stand-alone singles (released on the short-lived Warner-Spector vanity label) that went nowhere. "A Woman's Story" (B-side "Baby, I Love You") was the first. "Cher is a bit like a pitching machine," wrote Robert Hilburn in *The Los Angeles Times*. "She gets the ball over the plate but seems incapable of striking anybody out."

Cher's second Warner-Spector single, "A Love Like Yours" (B-side "[Just Enough to Keep Me] Hangin' On"; the A-side covered on *3614 Jackson Highway*), didn't manage a strikeout either. For the single Cher was improbably teamed with Nilsson—best known for his hit "Without You." "We were just coming in to do some backing vocals," Cher later revealed. "The song was supposed to be for John Lennon." The duet, intentionally or not, sounded like a Sonny and Cher song. In fact, Nilsson told more than one reporter that "A Love Like Yours" was sung by "Nilssonny and Cher."

"The *Stars* album, or for that matter the single 'Geronimo's Cadillac,' was certainly not the overwhelming commercial success that Cher, David [Geffen]— who got us all together and made it happen—or I anticipated," recalls *Stars* producer Jimmy Webb. "Looking back I think a combination of things worked against it. First; it came out the week after Cher was on the cover of *Time* and I think it's fair to say that she was overexposed. I mean when the album came out there was literally no place in the world you could go without seeing a picture of her face. The other thing I think that worked against it was that the material was a bit over the heads of her usual record-buying audience, who were looking for cheap thrills, sex, drugs and rock and roll. We all worked really hard on *Stars* and Dave saw to it that we had the top musicians of the day, but the song 'Stars,' as beautiful as it was, was rather morose."

"I wrote 'Stars' about the brutal time I had following my very first success," says singer/songwriter Janis Ian. "After my initial success [with 1967's 'Society's Child'] I had no follow-up. Everyone thought I was a one-hit wonder. So, after a few years of writing—and a few years of therapy—I just sat down and spilled out everything I knew about fleeting fame. When I finished 'Stars' I thought, 'Now I *know* I'm a real writer.'" Ian, whose biggest hit was her heart-wrenching look at adolescence "At Seventeen" (No. 3 in 1975) first recorded "Stars" a year earlier on *her* album *Stars*. "I was surprised and immensely flattered that Cher not only did a cover of the song, but named her album after it," says Ian. "To me it meant that Cher found the song worthy. I loved what she and Jimmy [Webb] did with it. She shortened it [Cher doesn't sing two of the original verses] and that made me think that she was really making it a statement about her own journey and feelings. I thought her version rocked and I think she rocks too!"

"Cher's first Warner Bros. album should have been more fun," observed *Rolling Stone*. "Her light approach to material is better suited to pop like 'Gypsys, Tramps and Thieves' than to Jimmy Cliff's 'The Bigger They Come, the Harder They Fall,' and Neil Young's 'Mr. Soul.'" The magazine did, however, praise the album's obvious standout. "She does her best job on the only Webb song on the album, 'Just This One Time.' It's the third version in the last twelve months, and much superior to both Webb's and Glen Campbell's."

Stars only managed to make it to No. 153 on the album charts and the only single from the collection, "Geronimo's Cadillac" (B-side "These Days")—a look at the plight of Native Americans—didn't chart at all "I loved 'Geronimo's Cadillac,'" Cher confessed 25 years after the single was released. "I wish I had been a better singer then because I would have done a better job on it. I had the emotion, but I don't think I quite had the control that I needed. I just got so tired of people making fun of my vibrato that at that time I was working really hard with my teacher to get rid of it." Flop though it was (and as yet not released on CD), Cher continues to view *Stars* as one of her most musically sound endeavors. "It's the only album that I've ever done that I'm really, really proud of," she said in 1982. "I just think it's really, really special." So do her fans. *Stars*, adorned as it is with a glamorous close-up of Cher's glazed and glistening face (a Bill King photo that had previously appeared on the cover of the December 1974 issue of *Interview*), remains one of her most sought-after works.

Yet another disappointment befell Cher during her television show's summer hiatus: Her "long lost" father John Sarkisian resurfaced and gave out a series of contentious interviews that directly contradicted the portrait she gave to the press about growing up poor in Los Angeles. Earlier in the year, on April 14, Sarkisian had filed a $4-million-dollar lawsuit against his daughter claiming that comments she had given to the press (in particular the magazines *Time*, *People* and *Interview*) held him up to ridicule, hurt his business relationships and, regarding his personal struggle with heroin, constituted an invasion of his privacy. The headlines said it all: "Cher's Father Talks about the People She Hurts," "Cher's Father Speaks Out: 'She's Just too Big for Her Britches!'" And "Cher's Father Attacks Her for Revealing Those Shocking Family Secrets." Cher's point of view was best represented on the cover of the September 1975 edition of *Hollywood Exposed*. It read: "Don't Call Cher 'Daddy's Little Girl.' She Can't Stand Her Father!"

"Cher has given everyone the idea that I just took off and never cared for her in any way," Sarkisian told writer Vicki Pellegrino. "Well, that's just not true. This whole thing between Cher and me is a big shame. As for my lawsuit, let's set the record straight right now. I've never gotten a penny from Cher. I wouldn't ask her for anything. I never have and I never will. If I get any money from her on this lawsuit, it's all going into animal welfare to stop dog fighting in the United States or to build an animal shelter."

In extensive interviews that appeared in *Pageant* and *Motion Picture*, Sarkisian debunked a long list of popularly circulated stories about Cher's childhood poverty. One had her tying rubber bands around her worn-out shoes to keep them from flapping. "That sounds more like her mother Georgia's story," said Sarkisian. "Cher never did wear any worn-out clothes or old shoes and she was never in any poverty row. She was well above average. I'm tired of hearing her talk about all this pauper stuff. I guess her publicity men figure more people will identify with her if they think she had a hard time of it." (Cher retold the "rubber band" story to *Vanity Fair* in 2010.) "After Georgia and I divorced I didn't have access to Cher," John Sarkisian explained about his separation from his daughter. "They'd be in Florida, Texas, New York—all different places. From the time that Cher was five until she was eleven I lost complete track of her. I couldn't find her—and I did try. Perhaps I should have tried harder, but Georgia always had me thinking that she and the girls would be better off if I didn't come around." Sarkisian gave a vivid example of how disenfranchised he was from his young daughter: "When Cher was little she never thought she was pretty. When I paid a little more attention to her sister Georganne—and it was sort of natural because Cher was about eight and Georganne was about four at the time, I got some flack from Cher about it. Not verbally, but I could see it. Once she broke down and cried and ran out of the room. I walked over and picked up her sketch pad—she used to sit and sketch for hours. She had drawn a hand, coming out of the water—like someone going down for the third time—with a tomahawk in it!" As for his struggle with heroin, Sarkisian told *Pageant*, "During World War II, I enlisted in the Coast Guard. While I was in the service I used to get severe pains in my chest. The pains got worse and they X-rayed me and found that my intestines were wrapped around my heart. At that time they had no operation for the condition, so they discharged me. They couldn't operate; all they could do was give me various kinds of drugs to keep the pain down. The Veteran's Administration Hospital gave me morphine, codeine and Demerol all the time... this went on for years and eventually I became addicted." Sarkisian said that when an operation had been perfected (but with only a 60-40 chance of success) doctors stopped prescribing his pain medication, forcing him to turn to the black market. Eventually he ended up in jail charged with illegal possession of narcotics. "It happens to a lot of soldiers in every war," said Sarkisian. "I got busted for heroin possession and spent four years in San Quentin."

"I didn't really meet my father until I was eleven and I would guess that in my entire life I have spent maybe 100 days with him," Cher said at the time. "He has been giving out all these interviews about me—my childhood. How does he know? I was talking on the phone the other day with my mother and she said, 'Cher, don't be so hard on your father, he used to be a nice man.' I didn't know my father when he was a nice man, so it doesn't do me much good, does it? My father is probably the big reason I'm so turned off by people who do drugs."

Having made his case in the press, and with a very slim chance of winning in court, Sarkisian eventually dropped his lawsuit and continued on with business ventures that included the Hungry Alligator, a fast-food restaurant in Los Angeles, and Gindi, an Indian jewelry store in New York City.

Cher and her father never did work out their troubles. In *And the Beat Goes On*, Sonny wrote that toward the end of an extended illness, Sarkisian, someone whom Sonny liked and spoke to from time to time, asked if Sonny could reunite him with Cher. The reunion never took place. In 1985, at the age of 58, Sarkisian passed away without reconciling with his only child.

20

ALL IN THE FAMILY TOO

In December 1974, Cher's mother Georgia Holt held court at a grand opening party for Granny's Cabbage Patch, her new store in Brentwood, California. *Photoplay*'s Cal York attended the "champagne reception"—a photo-op that included her two daughters Cher and Georganne and her granddaughter Chastity. "I found lots of pretty items for sale, including handcrafted quilts, antique oak furniture, and handmade toys from Appalachia. A beautiful antique brass cradle was on display too, though not for sale, because one of Sonny and Cher's fans presented it to them before Chastity was born, and Cher is too attached to it to give it up."

In the shadow of her daughter's television success, Holt, who would later embark on a solo singing career and co-author *Star Mothers: The Moms Behind the Celebrities*, offered columnists her opinion about everything related to Cher. When she learned that Cher's father had filed a lawsuit against her, she laid out her side of the story. "Johnny came into my shop and was there for two and a half hours trying to get me to make a bridge between them," she told columnist Cal York. "I was sitting with a couple of people and my face just turned white; I hadn't seen him in years. He kept saying, 'Why doesn't she talk to me? What have I done to her?' I think Johnny's lawsuit is just a bid for attention. You know, in Armenian culture if your child doesn't speak to you, that's the worst possible thing that could ever happen. He can't have any respect among his fellow Armenians."

Of her two daughters' early years Holt said: "The girls had fathers—but not for long. Probably because of my background it was difficult for me to choose wisely when it came to marriage." The lean years were hard on both Holt and her children.

"I can be silly and act like a kid but I don't feel like I was ever really young,"

Cher told a columnist. "Being young means not having to worry about anything. One of my earliest memories is when I was six and my mother said to me, 'How are we going to pay the rent?'"

Cher and her mother had a complicated and sometimes stormy relationship that often spilled over into the press. In 1973, after leaving Sonny, Cher said, "I would have gone home to my mother—but I'm not that crazy about *her* either!" And to Andy Warhol she admitted: "The idea of mother is to be warm and friendly and loving and to take care of you... I wish someone would have told *my* mother..."

On a 1979 TV broadcast on which Cher and her mother were guests, talk-show host Merv Griffin addressed the matter directly. "Now, I don't like to start anything on any of my shows, but some of your feuds have been famous. What exactly ticks you off about your mother, Cher? In what area do you feud?" Even though her mother was sitting right next to her, Cher didn't hesitate. "Well, you see, mother is very strange. You say something and you don't know what's going on and then all of a sudden you get a letter from her saying 'I'm very angry with you.' You call her up and say, 'What did I do? What did I say?' and she says 'I'm not talking to you.' Then, all of a sudden, one day, she starts talking to you again."

Cher's frankest conversation about her mother appeared in print twelve years later. In a rare contentious interview with *New York Newsday*'s Hilary de Vries, an interview that left Cher so unsettled she called the journalist several days later and tried to smooth things out, Cher said: "...it's difficult to do an interview in one day. You got one side of me that's for sure. But you didn't get everything. As for your questions about whether I'm talking to my mother... I'm real defensive... my mother and I didn't talk for almost two years because she wouldn't accept me. She thought I was too big for by britches and that it was her job to point out every bad thing that I did. Either you accept me for who I am or you don't get to have me around. I'm not ten years old anymore and my mother can't control me. She has to like me in spite of that. Like I have to like my daughter in spite of the things that I don't like about her."

Throughout 1975 Cher's sister Georganne LaPiere (who was fourteen when she first gave an exclusive interview to *Tiger Beat* about Cher) also gave out interviews whose focus was, decidedly, Cher. At the time Georganne was pursuing an acting career. She found work in commercials and appeared in bit parts on nighttime television shows like *The Streets of San Francisco* and *Police Woman*. Her most memorable role was her portrayal of Heather Grant, "a guileful seductress" on the soap opera *General Hospital*.

"Let's face it, there are many doors that have opened for me just because Cher is my sister," she admitted to *Photoplay*. "But I've learned that once you're inside those doors, it's all up to you." Of her early life Georganne surmised: "We were never 'poor,' we had no money, but we were never poor. Poverty is a state of mind. My mother, Cher and I may not have had a dime in our pockets, but we faced the world as if we owned it. That's the kind of spirit my mom had, and she instilled it in both of us." And speaking about her sister's state of mind while she was headlining her own television show, Georganne confessed: "All the hard work *is* taking its toll on her. She's lost a lot of weight and she's working harder now than she ever did with Sonny—and believe me, they worked really hard. But it's *her* show, and whether it lives or dies, depends solely on her."

"We are alike in a lot of ways, but we are also very different," Cher said at the time. "Georganne was really good in school and I hated it. When she was little she would throw tantrums and I never got mad. She plays jokes and I don't. I remember when we were little, after seeing *Psycho*, I was in the shower and she came in with a butcher knife. I screamed my head off!"

On July 14, Cher made a "surprise" appearance that had nothing to do with promoting her latest album *Stars*, or for that matter, her TV series. That evening Sonny Bono (who earlier in the year had appeared on *The Mike Douglas Show* singing "You've Got a Friend" which, given the circumstances, seemed directed at Cher) was a guest on *The Tonight Show* with guest host George Segal. In the midst of Sonny's good-natured chat with Segal there was an audible murmur in the audience. In a second's time Cher emerged from behind the show's famed velvet curtain and made her way over to the platform on which Sonny and Segal were seated. When the applause died down Segal quipped: "So, what's up Cher?" She deadpanned right back: "Well, nothing. Nothing really new has been happening with me lately!" Sonny and Cher's TV reunion made headlines around the world.

But like so much else that goes on behind the scenes in the entertainment industry, the entire Sonny and Cher television event was staged. Earlier that day Sonny and Cher spent two hours talking about what they would say and do on camera. Sonny was appearing on the show, as he succinctly put it, "to see if I can get people to like me again," while Cher's reason was quite different: she was trying to refute yet another rumor; this one had Gregg beating her up and Cher being secretly treated at a hospital. One version of the story was that Gregg beat Cher up because she filed for divorce. A second version had her enduring a beating first and then, afraid for her life, filing for divorce.

"There wasn't the least bit of truth to the story no matter what version you listened to," says a CBS stagehand, "but it really bothered Cher. She thought that it was the kind of story that people *wanted* to believe. So she decided the best way to show everyone that she wasn't limping around, a mass of bruises with two black eyes—don't forget, her show was on hiatus so she wasn't going to CBS everyday—was to appear on live television." And the stunt did what it was supposed to do. The rumors subsided.

At the same time that she made her appearance on *The Tonight Show*, Cher was featured on the cover of *In the Know* beside the outsize caption: "Cher: Star of the Year... But Why?" The extensively researched piece included a four-page career profile, an interview with Cher's mother, and a Q & A column—"What Do You Think of Cher?"—featuring answers from a gamut of contemporary women including actress Diana Rigg, who called her "fabulous," modeling agency magnate Eileen Ford, who called her "a travesty," and Republican House of Representatives member Millicent Fenwick, who called her "a gifted entertainer." The most surprising part of the *In the Know* profile was a learned examination of Cher's enduring popularity. Responding to the question "Why is Cher popular?" six psychiatrists offered up their opinions.

In New York City, Dr. Joyce Brothers wrote: "Cher has a very special quality that Marilyn Monroe had and very few do. They are sexy and don't take sexiness seriously. She is playing at it. She appeals to the men and brings the women in too." In Louisville, Kentucky, Dr. James Miller attributed Cher's popularity to the fact that "she is over-dominant. There is an element of passivity in most men, and she is attractive to such men. I do not feel that dominant men who still hold the concept of women being subordinate would be attracted to Cher." And in San Francisco, Dr. Paul Lowinger opined: "Cher is the new, liberated woman. She is the distortion with which the public sees the movement. They see her representing the freedom of women, in an imprecise but effective way. Cher is the continuity with the symbols of the past. She is Marilyn Monroe and Lana Turner translated to the 1970s. She represents the kind of fantasies people have about women that they can't realize in their own lives and their own families."

Later in the year Cher commented directly on the *In the Know* profile. "I read this dumb article about why I'm the biggest star in America and they had, like, six psychiatrists saying what it was," she told *Playboy*. "Well they didn't say shit. And there is no reason. I'm not the best at anything I do. I come out and say that dumb little bunch of shit at the beginning of my show so that people know there's a person behind it all—someone who's having a good time singing and dressing up. For 60 minutes my show takes them away from the drudgery, the news and all the bullshit that's going on in the world. There's something about me that people like. That's all I know."

Although Cher and her program staff had gotten word early on that they would be returning for a second season, as 1975 moved into its second half, the variety-show format itself appeared to be on its last legs. "There are a number of reasons for the variety shows' decline," reported *Billboard*. "This includes the very framework of the musical variety show, which seems to demand the rarely varied mixture of star monologues, corny, tired skits written to cover the show's mixture of name guests, and musical numbers which try to blend un-blendable

Previous page: The media fascination with Cher—her beauty, fashions and music—began in the '60s. CBS' 1975 Cher show was a natural progression. (Nostalgia Network)

Above: Versatility: Cher joins Rita Coolidge and Kris Kristofferson for a medley of country tunes—including Kristofferson's own, "Help Me Make it Through the Night." Below: Hot-steppin': Cher keeps in synch with the Jackson Five. Unsurprisingly, the Jacksons brought their own choreographer. (J. Howard Collection)

Cher (sporting spangled bell bottoms and an outrageous stacked perm) and Michael Jackson do the "Bump."
(J. Howard Collection)

Above: A glowing Cher arrives at the 1974 Grammy Awards with her beau (and benefactor) of almost two years, David Geffen. Below: "C" is for "comfortable" at the top—even without Sonny Bono at her side. (Photo Fair; TV Time)

Opposite: Cher on-set, but lost in a special-effects fog created to assuage CBS censors' ongoing concerns about her "vividly on-display attributes." (Nostalgia Network)

Cher's solo numbers were as lavish as anything from the Golden Age of Hollywood. *Opposite: Elaborately done up for "Lime House Blues"–performed on an ornate mid-century casino set. (Nostalgia Network)*

Above left: Cher with Baby's Breath in her hair singing "Many Rivers to Cross". Her set would not have been complete without a flowing river! Right: Cher performs "Geronimo's Cadillac," the first (and only) single from her 1975 album Stars, *clad in a high-glamor, fantastical Indian ensemble. (J. Howard Collection)*

Left: Do you believe? Cher with '60s pop idol and "God in Your Life" columnist Pat Boone. Below: Cher performs "When You Wish Upon A Star" with daughter Chastity (who made four appearances on the show) perched atop Paul Galbraith's giant papier-mâché swan. (Photo Fair; CBS-TV)

styles of host and guest." Banging the same drum, television producer Marty Pasetta told *Variety*: "Twenty years ago variety television was vibrant, now it's stagnant. Tony Orlando and Dawn and Mac Davis might be cute but they are so, so boring. If we fail to see variety programs as a challenge and carry on treating them as an easy format with interchangeable hosts and guests, television variety programming will soon be totally dead."

Bob Mackie agreed. In his 2000 interview with the Archive of American Television he noted: "They all looked alike and everyone started using the exact same material and the exact same ideas. I would go to a meeting for a new show and they would tell you their ideas. Everyone would be all excited and I would say, 'Well, do you want me to do it the way I did it on *The Carol Burnett Show* last year? Or the way that Sonny and Cher did it last week? Or the way that Jerry Lewis did it or Uncle Miltie did it in the '50s?' The variety-show format was eating itself up. It stops working when you keep giving the audience the exact same thing over and over again."

A look at the top ten shows at the time makes *Cher's* popularity all the more remarkable. *All in the Family* came in at No. 1 and was followed by *Sanford and Son*, *Chico and the Man*, *M*A*S*H*, *The Jeffersons*, *Good Times*, *The Waltons*, *Hawaii Five-O*, *Rhoda* and *The Rockford Files*. (Notably, the stars of six of the top ten shows appeared on *Cher*.) At the end of its first season *Cher's* place on *Variety's* top 50 television shows list was No. 23. The long-running *Carol Burnett Show* came in below *Cher* at No. 28, and the upstart, *Tony Orlando and Dawn* bested them both at No. 22. In or out of fashion (variety "specials" proliferated), CBS decided that Cher's variety show was worth continuing. At the close of the first season the network even agreed to honor Cher and George Schlatter's request that the program air in a later time slot. Accordingly, following the first broadcast of the new season, *Cher* would be moved from 7:30 to 8:00 p.m. "Everything seems to be running smoothly now," Cher informed Rona Barrett. "We've had some troubles but now we're on track. When my show returns in September—man, everybody better watch out!"

21

MUSICAL CHAIRS

Cher learned through her experience on *The Sonny and Cher Comedy Hour* that a consistent presence in the same time slot was advantageous: viewers got used to viewing a show at a particular time and made it a part of their weekly schedule. But CBS removed *Cher* from the airwaves for the entire summer of 1975 and used the show's time slot to test other programming. On Sunday, July 6, *Joey and Dad*, a variety series starring singer/actress Joey Heatherton and her comedian father Ray (produced by *The Sonny and Cher Comedy Hour*'s Allan Blye and Chris Bearde), aired. "No one remembers that show and it didn't do very well, but it was a lot of fun," says Blye. After four weeks, *Joey and Dad* was replaced by a one-off CBS News "Special Report," and then a four-week run of *The Manhattan Transfer*—a variety series starring the four-member retro-singing group. Neither *Joey and Dad* nor *The Manhattan Transfer* was picked up for regular broadcast.

Despite her ten-week absence from the airwaves, when CBS brought *Cher* back in the fall the show was better positioned than it had been before. Along with a half-hour later air time, *Cher* now had a new lead in called *Three for the Road*—a "family drama" (in the Family Hour) about a cross-country traveling widower and his two teenage sons. Other programs debuting that fall—some short-lived and some long-running—included *Starsky and Hutch*, *Welcome Back Kotter*, *Medical Story*, *Phyllis*, *The Invisible Man*, *Ellery Queen*, and *Barbary Coast*.

The behind-the-scenes changes during *Cher*'s second season were broad and sweeping. Along with choreographer Anita Mann, who came in to replace Dee Dee Wood, and art director Ray Klausen, who came in to replace (the Emmy-winning) Robert Kelly, director Art Fisher was replaced by Bill Davis (*Hullabaloo*, *Hee-Haw*), and then Davis was replaced by Mark Warren (*Laugh-In*, *Get Christie Love!*). The most significant change was the loss of head writer Digby Wolfe.

"At the end of the first season there was a bit of a coup that went on with the creative people behind the scenes," says Wolfe. "I remember there was a lot of political in-fighting and people jockeying to change or get different jobs on the staff of the show. From my many years as a writer and a performer, I think I had a good sense of when it was time to leave the party: so I exited."

So did quite a few others. Writers John Boni, Ray Taylor and David Panich were replaced by Mort Scharfman, Tom Moore, Michael Barrie, Jim Mulholland and George Bloom, and musical director Jimmy Dale was replaced by Jack Eskew (*The Hudson Brothers Razzle Dazzle Hour*, *The Lorenzo and Henrietta Music Show*). "Losing Jimmy was a big deal," remembers Lee Miller. "He was Canadian and he loved doing the show but he got tired of the long commute back and forth from Canada to L.A. He had a family that he wanted to spend time with. Cher was very upset when she found out that he wasn't doing the second season. She had become very comfortable with him. When Jimmy exited I hired Jack. I told him it was his job to make sure that Cher was comfortable with the music because if she didn't like something, she absolutely wouldn't do it. There were a couple of times when Jack presented her with arrangements that she just hated. I would look at her eyes and just knew that she hated them. Then I would turn to Jack and very diplomatically say, 'Why don't we try something different?' And we did. That's how we all worked together."

Hollywood Reporter columnist Sue Cameron contacted George Schlatter directly and asked him to comment on the "out of hand rumors" she'd heard about the musical chair game that the *Cher* show staff, in particular the top-tier players—including him—were engaged in. "This is a positive and happy move," Schlatter told Cameron—referring to the fact that writers Don Reo and Alan Katz and executive in charge of production Lee Miller were, for the second season, all promoted to the position of producer while *he* was moved from producer to executive producer. "I think it's healthy to promote from within and it's all going to work out very well. We are just going through the normal process that happens on shows. As for me, I've been going non-stop ever since the show started and I welcome the opportunity to oversee what's going on rather than be totally in the middle of everything. Cher is happy and everything is great."

One of the things Cher was happy about was the fact that she finally got her own TV studio. Throughout the first season Cher and musical director Jimmy Dale had voiced concerns about the discrepancy in sound quality in Television City's four auditoriums. After hiring outside acoustic experts, all decided that Studio 41 had the best sound. CBS agreed, and allowed her and her staff to call Studio 41 home. *Cher*'s return to the airwaves resulted in several changes in front of the camera, too. Cher was now a newly married woman (she wore a wedding ring), the "home base" set was dramatically transformed by newly hired art director Ray Klausen—in the place of the first season's marabou feather-trimmed glitter curtains and *Flintstone*-like block letters was a set designed to match Cher's opening-number gown, and a stage that George Schlatter "populated" with musicians.

"I kept thinking, 'How can we change the opening? How can we make it look less like Carol Burnett's?' The answer: place the band onstage with her," says Schlatter. Subsequently, the second season featured the entire eighteen-member *Cher* show orchestra "in shot"—including musical director Jack Eskew, a pianist, an organist, a guitarist, a drummer, horns, sax and a rhythm section. Schlatter's innovation—no other variety show had this opening configuration—refocused the viewer's attention and underlined *Cher*'s main ingredient: music.

Another of season two's changes was clever, but only aired for six weeks. "I happened to like the new animated opening a lot," says Lee Miller of the animation company Kid Millions' 58-second program intro. "I thought it was colorful and I liked that it was accompanied by an instrumental of 'All I Really Want to Do,' but, I've got to admit that, other than Cher, I was one of the very few people who did. I remember the executives thought it was too weird. They were particularly concerned about one of the images of Cher that had her looking out over a crystal ball [with smoke billowing behind her and horns sprouting from her forehead]. It was sexy and atmospheric but, as ridiculous as it seems today, some of the more conservative executives thought it could be interpreted as Cher making an alignment with the occult."

During *Cher*'s summer hiatus rumors circulated that Sonny was scheduled to make an appearance on the very first episode of the new season. Cher, herself, confirmed it during one of her first season monologues. "I really want Sonny for my show," Cher reiterated in an interview. "I love working with him. He's a good singer and he's much better with an audience than I am."

"I saw it on television the same way everyone else did," Sonny said at the time. "It's the sort of uninhibited, sensational thing Cher's been doing lately. Nobody checked with me." When *Cher* producers did formally contact Bono, whose solo *People* magazine cover story was headlined "Sonny Bono: 'Cher Always Calls Me When She's in Trouble,'" he remained cool. "A single appearance on Cher's show doesn't interest me much. I don't think that would mean anything to me. I told them the only thing I'd consider would be a series of appearances where we could both have some fun and a piece of something. But that might run into some serious ego problems, and I think they might pass."

They did. Sonny informed *Cher*'s producers that he would work with Cher if he could appear on six shows and be paid $12,500 for each (top payment for a guest spot was $2,500). Eventually Sonny agreed to make three appearances at the lower fee, but CBS concluded that three appearances was two too many. "At first Sonny was going to do the show, then I was told that he was not going to do the show. I really don't know what the deal is," complained a frustrated George

Schlatter at the time. "I don't think they do either." (Sonny's autobiography *And the Beat Goes On* incorrectly states that, following extensive negotiations, he *did* appear on *Cher*.)

For the second season of *Cher*, George Schlatter continued to focus on the acquisition of acts that Cher expressly requested—in particular David Bowie, Ray Charles, and the Smothers Brothers. Another performer that Schlatter hoped to secure was Goldie Hawn, who was a featured player on his *Laugh-In* series and whom Cher was friendly with. As chronicled in *The Hollywood Reporter*, Schlatter and wife Jolene cornered Hawn at a party and made their pitch for her to make an appearance on *Cher*. Hawn declined, but agreed to star in her *own* Schlatter-produced special (written by Digby Wolfe and aired on CBS) the following year.

The taping of Cher's second season was delayed by a full two weeks. "Cher just disappeared," remembers Lee Miller. "The first and second episodes were totally scrapped. We called everyone—her agent, her manager—and no one knew where the hell she was. Finally I got a call and she said, 'I'm in New York.' I said, 'Okay, what are you doing there?' And she said, 'I came here for some medical treatments.' Then she said, 'Please come here and meet with me. I have to talk about the show.' So Don Reo and I boarded a plane and went to New York. We spent three days there locked up with her in her hotel room. She didn't want anyone to see her because her face didn't look so good. She had what looked like two black eyes and burned and severely peeling skin, the result, she said, of a botched skin peel." (Cher's faulty medical procedure also resulted in the cancellation of a much anticipated television interview with Dick Cavett.) "During our many meetings Cher told me that she was having problems with the network and that she was having problems with George. I knew about the problems with network, but the problems with George were new to me; I thought she got along well with him. She said, 'What are you guys going to do about my problems with the show?' And I said, 'The correct approach is not for you not to show up. Whether or not you show up *we* are all still getting paid—and *you're* paying for it.' She nodded and told me that she wanted [first season director] Art Fisher to return. That surprised me because both Cher and Art had spoken to me separately about their difficulties with one another. I got in touch with Art and told him that Cher wanted him back but he wasn't interested. He wasn't ready to return."

Cher show documents shed further light on the complicated outcome of Cher's unscheduled (and unreported on) two-week absence from Television City. Season two's first two tapings were to feature David Bowie and Tony Randall and then Ray Charles and the Muppets. All four acts were informed that their taping dates were moved from mid-July to mid-September. Additionally, due to Cher's "no show," filming of the new season's first two shows would have to be "piggybacked" with already scheduled tapings, necessitating extended periods of overtime; a situation that did not please the program's crew or CBS. "I was furious about all the extra work we had to do because of Cher's disappearance," remembers a *Cher* staffer. "We all thought, 'How dare she? Who does she think she is?' We all had families and lives of our own. None of us wanted to work on her show or *any* show fourteen or fifteen hours a day—no matter what we were being paid. Cher's personal problems had become *our* problems and I don't think that any of us thought that that was fair." (The entrenched CBS union workers may have rumbled about the extra hours but no one quarreled with the "golden time"—double their hourly rate—they collected for their extra efforts.)

"I know that a lot of the staff is unhappy with me now," Cher told her crew at the time. "But there really is nothing else I can do right now. I can apologize; and I have. Now it's time for all of us to put our differences aside and do the hard work necessary to keep this show afloat."

22

SOMETHING FOR EVERYONE

Cher's first episode of the new season had been preceded by an August 25 repeat broadcast of her special. For the second airing, Cher filmed two promotional segments that were inserted into the show. Dressed in a bias-cut black satin gown, she walked into frame and took her place in front of the giant circular Cher logo.

CHER: Coming up in a minute is a special we did last January and I think it's really a terrific show. My guests are the Divine Miss M., Bette Midler, Flip Wilson and everybody's old tart Elton John. You know, we really had a lot of fun doing this show and I hope that you can dig seeing it again. I've got to tell you one thing, when I was coming down the ramp, you're gonna think you hear the sound of drums beating, but it's not—it's my legs banging together! By the way, we've got a new season coming up and it starts September the 7th, Sunday at 7:30.

The first episode of the new season featured the Smothers Brothers, the Muppets (Jim Henson's stuffed stars of the PBS children's program *Sesame Street*), and "Special Guest Star" Bill Cosby. The CBS slogan for the fall of 1975 was "Catch the brightest stars on CBS." It was an apt summation of Bill Cosby who, even though it was years before his groundbreaking *Cosby Show*, was a formidable talent; a performer who regularly appeared on TV, made feature films, and had released a number of comedy albums. Not surprisingly, producers of *Cher* thought it best that the episode featuring Cosby be broadcast as the season opener (even though it was the second show taped).

In "Hong Kong Nose," Cosby (wearing a prosthetic nose) played a hustler of bargain nose jobs who was trying to find a way into Cher's dressing room. In "The Recording Session" Cosby was a demanding record producer who continually interrupts Cher and the Muppets, who are in the studio recording the Rolling

Stones' "I Can't Get No Satisfaction," and in "Annual Medical Exam" Cosby played a doctor charged with giving giant Muppet Sweetums a physical. All of Cosby's segments fall flat. George Schlatter agrees. "That particular episode was not one of my favorites. Bill was never present during any of the rehearsals so Cher never really felt comfortable in their scenes together; and it showed."

"Cosby never really seemed like he much cared," reiterates a stagehand. "It was almost like it was a chore for him to appear on the show. I know there was some last-minute rescheduling and he may have been pissed off about that, but, whatever the case, he just seemed like he didn't want to be there." (And it may have been true. At the time Cosby was involved in extensive meetings whose focus was his soon-to-air *The Bill Cosby Special*.)

Prior to their appearance, Tom and Dick Smothers had starred in two variety shows of their own. *The Smothers Brothers Comedy Hour* (filmed at CBS in the same studio as *Cher*) was filled with biting political parodies and not-too-veiled drug and counter-culture references, while *The Smothers Brothers Show* was a tamer, more accessible hour of family-friendly levity. Both shows were cancelled, but the brothers continued; touring, releasing comedy albums, and appearing on any and all variety shows that would have them. On *Cher* the brothers performed "Smoke Gets in Your Eyes" with an overly friendly stuffed dog, did a solo musical number, "Yo-Yo Man," played two men who were having a difficult time learning Karate, and participated in "The Pain Game," a TV game show whose contestants are painfully penalized for wrong answers.

Filmed for this episode but never aired was an elaborate spoof of *Cher*'s competition *The Six Million Dollar Man*. In the sketch, entitled "The Twelve Million Dollar Date," Bill Cosby played Steve, a bionic man, Cher played Evelyn, a bionic woman, and Jack Harrell played Colonel Hathaway, the man who brings the two super-powers together.

STEVE: Things haven't been the same since I lost my arms and legs in a plane crash. Were you in a plane crash too?

EVELYN: Worse than that. I was an extra in *Jaws*.

STEVE: If you don't mind my getting personal... which parts of you are plastic and which parts are real?

EVELYN: I'd answer that question but we're on during the Family Hour.

Cher opened her fall season with a medley of Carole King's "Where You Lead" and Marvin Gaye's "How Sweet It is (To Be Loved by You)" followed by a monologue about what she did during her summer vacation. Her solo was Steven Sondheim's "Send in the Clowns" from the musical *A Little Night Music*. "When I heard that Cher was going to do 'Send in the Clowns' I was ecstatic," remembers Ray Klausen. "I thought I would design this really great, colorful clown-themed set. But then Cher came to me and told me that she wanted to perform the number wearing blue jeans! I couldn't believe my ears—I don't think she had ever worn blue jeans on the show before. She wanted to make a statement; she wanted to make it clear that she was more than just her costumes. So I came up with the idea of giving the viewer both: the hip everyday young woman that she wanted to present, *and* the glamorous Hollywood star that viewers wanted to see." For the number Klausen had Cher perform atop a clear staircase. In the background was a giant blowup of her *Time* magazine cover. "The contrast between Cher in jeans and the giant photo of her in that spectacular gown was striking. That was the very first solo musical number I did for *Cher*. I was the new kid on the block and I believe I proved myself with that one. Cher just loved it."

Another musical segment featured Cher and the Muppet Sweetums performing the Beatles' "Something." "I submitted the idea for that number," says Anita Mann, who came in to replace Dee Dee Wood as choreographer during *Cher*'s second season. "We had Cher dressed in this beautiful gold bugle beaded gown [a dress she wore on tour with Sonny in 1973], singing very solemnly, and Sweetums was kind of walking around the set behind her while she was singing. Sweetums was this big, clumsy, sweet-hearted monster and he was in love with Cher, kind of pining for her and completely destroying the set behind her. But Cher didn't know he was destroying the set. Then toward the end [of the song] Sweetums walks over and gives Cher a pat on the back—but he's so huge and so clumsy that he almost knocks her over! It was very funny and the lyric in the song 'something in the way he moves' worked perfectly."

Jim Henson and Frank Oz were so impressed with the Cher/Sweetums segment that they pulled Mann aside and thanked her. "Jim said 'you know, this was really a very special idea that you came up with' and 'if you're ever available we would love to work with you again.' That's how I got to do the two Muppet movies! I have Cher and that particular segment on the *Cher* show to thank for all my future work with Jim Henson." (Henson also tagged Cher's makeup artist Ben Nye II to work on his films.)

Anita Mann had looked forward to working on *Cher*. "First of all, I was a huge fan of the show—I never missed it. Then, when I was hired, I was just thrilled. I told the producers, 'Whatever works for Cher please tell me and that's what I'll continue to do.' I found Cher to be an extremely gifted natural dancer—she loved to move and dance. It's always fun to work with a star who likes dancing because a lot of times stars view dancing as just more work for them to do. They see a choreographer coming and they think, 'Okay, now the fun ends.' Cher wasn't like that at all. She would just sit and watch what I wanted her to do, all the while doing lots of other things like learning her script or discussing the show with the show's producers, and then she'd get up and do what I showed her—exactly as I did it. I was never even really sure that she was paying attention to me, but she would just absorb it all and instantly play it back for me. The only other performer I can remember who could do that was Michael Jackson."

Show number fifteen's finale—"Shape Up America"—was a winner. With an original tune written by Billy Barnes and Earl Brown, "Shape Up America," was a musical salute to fitness that included Cher, Cosby, the Smothers Brothers, Gailard Sartain, Sweetums, four bodybuilders, and celebrity nutritionist Eulle Gibbons. (Gibbons, in declining health, died three months later.) The standout of the "Shape Up America" segment is Cher's song "He'll Do," a tongue-in-cheek tune that chastised four posing, bathing suit-clad bodybuilders (Jim Morris, Don Peters, Bill Grant and Ric Drasin) for their lack of personality. "I was the first of the bodybuilders to be hired," remembers Ric Drasin, who was a musician, bodybuilder and artist (the logo he created for the World Gym chain is still in use today). "I got a call at Golds Gym and went down to audition. Cher was really great. I enjoyed her humor and she made everyone feel comfortable. Of course the actual taping was a bore—constant stopping and starting and repetition. I had done TV and posing bits before so, to be honest with you, what I was really looking forward to was the food they had put out."

Professional bodybuilder Jim Morris also appeared on the show. "I thought the camera work, editing and lighting really showed me off to great advantage; something that a bodybuilder is always concerned about. And Cher, well, what can I say? I admired her then and I admire her now. I had met her almost a year earlier when I was working as a bodyguard for Elton John. When she saw me on the set she came right over and asked how I was. We talked for at least twenty minutes. I remember thinking that she was someone that you would love to have as a friend; funny, smart, and just really cool."

At the same time that show number fifteen was broadcast, Cher was featured on the cover of *People* with her arms wrapped around Gregg Allman. The headline: "Cher and Gregg: She Helps Him Stay off Heroin—and His Band is Hot Again." "The FBI has been following both of us ever since that article came out," Gregg told columnist John J. Miller at the time. "They [tabloids] all have to go for the really juicy stuff. Everyone wants to hear about me on drugs, or me kicking Sonny's ass, or me beating the shit out of Cher. I can just imagine one of those really trashy ones publishing a cover shot of me with a needle in my arm and a headline reading: 'Gregg Allman Shoots Up in Bathroom While Cher Recovers from Savage Beating in Bedroom!'"

CBS executives, too, were unhappy with the piece. "I really don't feel any particular need to explain my life or the choices I have made to the public or to CBS," Cher retorted. "People wonder what I see in Gregg but it's really none of their business what I see in *anyone*. By now everyone knows I'm not Carol Burnett. But I'm not Lizzie Borden either. I don't know how to explain the chemistry of falling in love but I really do love Gregg. It may turn out to be impossible for us to get along living together, but that won't mean that all of a sudden I'll stop loving him. I don't take relationships lightly. I stayed with Sonny long after I knew our marriage had had it."

George Schlatter shied away from the constant requests he received to comment on Cher and Gregg's relationship. Instead, he talked to several journalists about his revised vision for the show. "We tried something and it didn't work," Schlatter told *The Daily News*. "During the first season we asked ourselves, 'Where is there a vacuum in television?' and we came up with rock and roll music as the answer. Since Cher loves rock and roll, it seemed like a perfect direction to go in. But it didn't work. We learned that fans of Elton John, Labelle and the Rolling Stones listen to records. They don't necessarily watch television. This time around we'll stay focused on music but we'll make sure it's broad-based." Schlatter's mention of the Rolling Stones might have reflected Cher's very vocal disappointment at not securing the band as guests. In the May 28 edition of *The Hollywood Reporter*, columnist Sue Cameron was the first to reveal that the Stones were in talks with Cher about making an appearance on her show. "Will Cher Get the Rolling Stones? Negotiations are underway. If things work out, the Stones will tape their appearance the week of July 9-13, when they are here in Los Angeles for their Forum concerts."

Cher first met Mick Jagger and the rest of the Stones in 1965. "When they made their first trip to America they wanted to stay with us," she recalled. "At the time Sonny and I had just bought this big house but we only had enough money to furnish the bedroom. So we said, 'You guys can't stay with us because we don't have any furniture.' They said 'That's okay, we'll rent cots.'" The Stones didn't end up staying with Sonny and Cher, but Sonny and Cher tagged along on several of their tour dates. It was enough to convince Cher that the Stones were "real" stars and that she and Sonny were just slumming.

"Getting the Stones to appear was a really big deal to Cher," says Lee Miller. "I think they were probably at the very top of her musical guest list. She was always playing the Stones and singing songs by the Stones on her show [later in the season she did a musical tribute to the band]. I'm not really sure why it didn't work out; maybe it was just a scheduling conflict. But I am sure that Cher was very, very disappointed." (Along with the Stones, negotiations with the Beach Boys, Aretha Franklin, Stevie Wonder, Carole King, Diana Ross, and Ann-Margret fell through.)

"There really *is* such a thing as middle-of-the-road television," Schlatter reflected at the time. "Along with more standards and more familiar music, we want guests who have a long-standing national acceptance and who can handle comedy sketch material. There's plenty of time. Cher's only 29. She's still growing as an entertainer. And what's important, she's an original. She's not another Julie Andrews or Dinah Shore."

A look at a four-page memo that Schlatter sent to *Cher*'s writers at the end of season one makes for fascinating reading. Among his many suggestions on how the comedy could be improved was the introduction of new characters: a Cooking Lady, "she could be a super-elegant snob... a real rich bitch with a butler (Jack) or a maid (Allan)"; a Crazy Lady, "not like Lily [Tomlin's] lady in the park, but *close*"; and a Frankenstein Lady, "a continuing horror segment with Jack as the mad doctor... and it ends up each week with a cliffhanger."

Schlatter also thought that "theme" shows were a good idea. "Classic Comedians" (Phyllis Diller, Don Rickles, Henny Youngman), "Movie People" (Bette Davis, Gloria Swanson, Van Johnson), "All Sports Show" (Muhammad Ali, Wilt Chamberlain, Joe Namath), "All Kids Show" (Rodney Allen Ripley, Jodie Foster, Ricky Siegel), "'60s Music Stars" and "Magic Show." Only the latter two ideas were filmed. "The network was always tinkering, always trying to change things," says Schlatter. "I believe that Carol Burnett, in particular, made things tough for Cher and her show. CBS wanted her to be more like Carol. To come out and be homey and comfortable—hand in pockets, shuffling her feet, 'the girl next door.' Well, there isn't anything 'girl next door' about Cher, and why would you want another girl next door when you already had one?" (Eleven years earlier Judy Garland, on whose program Schlatter also worked, had faced the same problem. Her response: "CBS wanted me to be the girl next door, but they couldn't find the right house, or the right door!") Not only was Cher not the girl next door, her sumptuous surroundings, many of which were created by Paul Galbraith—art director Ray Klausen's assistant—constantly underlined the fact. Galbraith's road to *Cher* was the result of a chance meeting with Klausen.

"Ray and I met at a mutual friend's birthday party," says Galbraith. "At the time I was the display manager at Bullock's [an L.A. department store]. At the party we were all asked to bring a personalized birthday card rather than a gift. Well, I made this really elaborate card and everyone just loved it. At the end of the evening Ray came over and told me that he was looking for work as an art director in Hollywood. He asked for my number and a few months afterward he called me up and asked if I was available to work on Cher's show!" From a makeshift studio in the garage of his home, Galbraith supplied *Cher* with everything from boulders to butterflies, from a puppet stage to a giant swan. He also hand-crafted every single second-season "home base" set with detailed papier-mâché work that matched Cher's gown.

Comedians Steve Martin (not yet a name-above-the-title film star) and Martin Mull (a regular on variety shows at the time) were signed on as both writers and "continuing players" during *Cher*'s second season. Both took part in brainstorming sessions, helped create sketch material, and, as it turned out, performed in a large number of never-aired comedy segments. Comedian

Gailard Sartain, only a bit player during the first season, joined Martin and Mull as one of the second season's important players.

"I got the job on *Cher* because I had already worked with [producers] Alan Katz and Don Reo on *Hee-Haw*," says Sartain. "The character I did most often on *Cher* was Otis. Otis came about one day while we were all tossing around ideas about what my participation on the show would entail. I had a set of silly teeth with me. I put them in, and in a funny voice said, 'How about this for a character?' Everyone loved it so we went with it." Sartain's second season contribution is substantial. "I was finally more than just 'atmosphere'" (a term Sonny used to describe him a year later when he joined the cast of *The Sonny and Cher Show*). And he was. At the top of each show Cher announced his name along with that week's guests, he was given solo comedy sketches—many of which he wrote himself, and his name was newly featured on the *cover* of all *Cher* show scripts. Still, looking back, the comedian has mixed memories.

"If there was a 'family feeling' at CBS then I, along with several other unnamed performers, were red-headed stepchildren sitting at another table. The way I looked at it was that work was work and that being on *Cher* was a bird in the hand. I felt very fortunate to be a part of one of the last great variety shows. I met a lot of incredibly talented performers on that show. For instance I remember thinking, 'I can't believe I am standing in the same TV studio as George Burns.' But I must admit that working on Cher's show wasn't always fun. In fact, I don't think that it was ever 'fun.' There were indignities and disrespect. It never came from Cher, but it came nonetheless."

"Otis was everything that Cher wasn't—big, round, awkward, clueless, and that was just great for the series," says George Schlatter. "Cher played well off of Gailard and he played well off of her. He's a really talented and creative guy and we were all very, very pleased with him and his exceptional work on the show."

PART FOUR:

(Another) New Beginning

23

SALUTE TO A FRIEND

On August 9, after completing taping of show number fifteen with Bill Cosby (as well as a series of footage with singer Ray Charles that was banked for inclusion in show number 24), Cher remained at CBS and prepared for an exciting public appearance. She had agreed to be a presenter at the first annual Rock Music Awards (not to be confused with the MTV Video Music Awards that debuted nine years later), a live Prime-Time television broadcast that was produced by Don Kirshner of TV's *Don Kirshner's Rock Concert*. The show was hosted by Cher's friends Elton John and Diana Ross and featured performances and presenters that included Chuck Berry, the Rolling Stones, the Edgar Winter Group, Labelle, Roger Daltrey and Ann-Margret (stars of that year's movie musical *Tommy*), Olivia Newton-John and Ella Fitzgerald. At the event Cher presented the final—most important—award, "Outstanding Rock Personality of the Year" (which went to John). For the presentation, Cher was brought onstage—perched atop an ornate bed—by four scantily clad men. Her theme music: "All I Really Want to Do."

"So what have you been up to?" Elton asked Cher as she looked out over the podium. Her response (the same response she gave Sonny earlier in the year when she appeared on *The Tonight Show*) worked wonders: "Oh, nothing much!" Photographs from the event, in particular shots of Elton, Cher and Diana Ross posed together against a glittery gold backdrop, were published in newspapers and magazines for the next few years. (*Circus* published a full-page color "pin-up" and *High Times* used a candid of Cher and Gregg arriving at the ceremony on their cover.)

The second *Cher* show of the new season—show number sixteen—was a slick, funny, fast-moving hour that featured Edward Asner, Redd Foxx and the Pointer Sisters. Cher opened the show with a medley of the Beatles' "Yesterday" and

Elton John's "Crocodile Rock," followed by a monologue about getting her annual physical. (After taping the number Cher changed costumes and returned to the stage to tape show number 24's opening—utilizing the same white flower-encrusted set.)

In comedy segments Cher played a kennel manager who is reluctant to let a werewolf (Foxx) check in for the night. She also, while introducing guests the Pointer Sisters, took part in a sketch in which she was constantly interrupted by oafish "stage-hand" Otis (Gailard Sartain). Two separate segments were combined for Cher's solo musical number "Love Song," first recorded by Olivia Newton-John (and performed on *The Sonny and Cher Comedy Hour*). In the first segment, Cher sang the song live, looking directly into the camera. For the second, she and a male dancer did an interpretive dance. "Scott Salmon was Cher's partner for that number," remembers Anita Mann. "Scott was, without a doubt, one of the most talented dancers that I had ever worked with. He was also incredibly handsome, so it made sense that I chose him to dance with Cher in that segment. 'Love Song' showcased Cher's versatility. She could go from something very dark and threatening—as far as dance goes—to something completely soft and lovely. She was so incredibly versatile; a rarity."

"Love Song"—best know by its haunting refrain "Do you know what I mean / Have your eyes really seen?" stands out as a premier vocal performance by Cher—complete with spoken passages, pre-recorded harmonizing and an echo chamber.

On his second appearance, Redd Foxx, fresh from a standing-room-only run at the Las Vegas Hilton, did a spoof of an insurance company commercial, and played a man who is attempting to mail an unwrapped fish through the post office. For the "Raw Fish" segment, Foxx insisted that actor Noriyuki "Pat" Morita (a staple on '70s television and a semi-regular on Foxx's *Sanford and Son*) join him. Offscreen there was a side of Redd Foxx that viewers didn't see. Along with the fact that his disputes with TV executives over *Sanford and Son* had spilled into the press, his ongoing divorce proceedings from Betty Jean Harris—his wife of nineteen years—and his constant female companions, a string of hopeful young Asian beauties, his cocaine addiction had advanced to a disruptive stage. "Redd Foxx was like a light switch," says a stagehand who was on-set for each of Foxx's three appearances on *Cher*. "He was just fascinating. We all knew he was suffering. I remember he had a bad leg and it gave him a lot of pain. When he was off camera he would just slump. His shoulders would drop and he looked like what he was—a drug addicted or maybe drunk old man. But on camera—wow! He was wonderful. None of his troubles read. His back was straight, his eyes were clear, and he did everything he was supposed to do. I really felt for and admired that man."

At the time of his appearance, Ed Asner was one of the stars of the popular

Mary Tyler Moore Show. In a very funny "Life with Laverne" he played a beleaguered moving man.

MOVING MAN: [Bringing in a small bureau] Alright lady, where do you want your chest?

LAVERNE: [Looking at her bosom] I think I'll keep it right where it is, big boy. I haven't had any complaints yet!

MOVING MAN: Yeah, well why complain about the small stuff.

(Later)

LAVERNE: I should have hired a different company. They would have waited on me hand and foot.

MOVING MAN: I can see why. Those are your best parts.

"Today I still cringe when I remember how I decorated Laverne's apartment," recalls Ray Klausen. "I wanted a zebra rug so we got this huge white rug and painted zebra stripes on it; that was okay. We got the most god-awful furniture; that was okay. Now here's the problem. You'd think that finding ugly wallpaper wouldn't be that difficult. But for it to be really ugly, really outrageous and ridiculous—well, finding that isn't so easy. I finally found something—all orange and green and brown swirls; flowers, birds, everything. But I hadn't checked with Bob [Mackie]. When Cher walked out onto the set in costume she totally disappeared: Laverne's outfit was almost identical to the wallpaper behind her. I was mortified. A star should always pop. They should never be swallowed up by the set or the background. I learned from that experience and I've never made that mistake again."

In addition to his visit with Laverne, Ed Asner also performed in two more sketches. In the first he was an "idea man" trying to pitch a new game show to doubtful TV executive Cher. In the second he is a funeral parlor director who suspects that Redd Foxx and the Pointer Sisters are not the decedent's relatives. On their first visit to *Cher* the Pointer Sisters opted to sing a personal favorite rather than one of their hits. The second time around they chose "How Long (Betcha' Got a Chick on the Side)", a song that was in heavy rotation. They also joined Cher for the program's finale—a musical tribute to Elton John that included John's songs "Saturday Night's Alright for Fighting," "Rocket Man" and "Goodbye Yellow Brick Road" (see Appendix for the complete list).

"When we were doing that finale we were marching on this elevated platform that was painted to look like a keyboard," remembers Ruth Pointer. "Bob and Ret had made these incredible jumpsuits for us, they had keyboards going down one side. Cher's was pink and ours were blue. Well during the taping Cher and my sister Bonnie went dancing off the platform in the wrong direction. Me, Anita and June were going one way—the way we had rehearsed, and we turned around and Cher and Bonnie were nowhere to be found! We were just hysterical and Anita, June and I just thought, 'Okay, it would be those two.' And then

Cher said, 'Well I didn't know I was going the wrong way,' and Bonnie said, 'Don't look at me, I was just following the leader!'

"I really miss doing those '70s variety shows," says Pointer. "I mean, because it was a whole week of concentrated creative work and we were working with the top people in the industry. What I remember from working on Cher's show was that Bob and Ret let us keep the clothes. We just thought, 'Oh, my God—we get to keep our costumes, too?' We had such a good time working with Cher. My sisters and I like to have fun. We laugh a lot, we're loud, we're a fun group of girls to be around. I can't tell you how happy we were to discover that Cher was just like us." But, like Labelle before them, the Pointers remained unimpressed with the CBS censors. "I've got to tell you that me and my sisters had a lot more fun during rehearsals then we did during the actual taping. On taping days there was always someone changing things, giving advice, telling us what we could and could not do. Being as naive as we were at the time we thought that the way that we rehearsed it—and we spent a lot of time rehearsing, praying that on taping day we would get it right—would be the exact way we would do it for the cameras. Wrong! Censors would always be there, there were constant meetings about who knows what, and usually everything we thought we were going to do was thrown out the window. I remember thinking, 'Couldn't you have told us this before? We stayed up all night learning what you gave us and now you want to change it on the spot.'"

Along with the changes in the script, on their second visit to the show, Ruth Pointer also noticed a change in Cher. "Cher was definitely different the second time around. The first time she was just enjoying herself. She was carefree. The second time she was involved in that whole Gregg Allman mess and her heart was breaking. I could totally relate to her problems because I'd been involved in some similar relationships. I could see that she had the inclination to fall in love with these bad boys and I did too. I think that successful young women who fall in love with bad boys think that they can change their sorry asses. But of course it's not true. It's never true. People change when *they* want to change; not when *you* want them to."

The Cher/Pointers/Elton John salute remains one of the second season's highlights, and Cher's live rendition of "Don't Let the Sun Go Down on Me" is so strong it sounds like it could have been released as a single. "Every time I run into Cher it's a screaming match," says Pointer. "It's like we're old girlfriends. There's never been a time when that didn't happen. It's always been screaming, hugs and kisses and, 'Oh, god, you've got to come over.' That woman is, and always has been, an inspiration to me. I love her—I just do."

Show number seventeen re-teamed Cher with both Nancy Walker and Wayne Rogers. She opened the hour wearing a spectacular black alix jersey gown encrusted with a pink jewel and silver sequined butterfly (on a butterfly motif set). The top of the hour's songs were a medley of jazz and blues singer Nina Simone's "Feeling Good" and Carole King's "I Feel the Earth Move," which was followed by a monologue, appropriately enough, about the CBS censors.

CHER: Hey, how are you? I'm Cher... the only four-letter word allowed on the new Family Hour. Last season my navel really made CBS nervous. At one point they thought they might have to blindfold the CBS eye. They even tried to putty my belly button. But I didn't let them... it's the only cleavage I've got! I really don't know what the problem is... I'm the only star on television who still has her Chastity!

"I was there for the taping of Cher's opening number," remembers Wayne Rogers. "Cher was supposed to come out and sing and do her monologue. They had it all set up, everyone was ready, the cameras were rolling, the announcer said, 'Ladies and gentleman... Cher' and Cher came out and completely forgot all her lines, so the director yelled 'cut!' They started the whole thing again, and the same thing happened a second time. Well I remember George was getting crazy—just raising hell. Everything was set up a third time, the cameras were rolling and the announcer said, 'Ladies and gentlemen... Cher' and Cher was nowhere to be found! After a moment a sheepish stagehand walked out into Cher's spotlight and George is screaming, 'What the fuck is this?' The stagehand says, 'Um, I'm sorry. Cher and Gregg went off to look at a house in the Canyon. She says to tell you she'll be back in half an hour!"

Show number seventeen's solo musical segments included the much-covered "Until It's Time for You to Go," along with a medley of the Fifth Dimension hit "Puppet Man" and the Isley Brothers' "It's Your Thing." "'Puppet Man' was so much fun," remembers Anita Mann. "For that number I used six male dancers who were experts in this kind of popping dance movement. They were all from L.A. and were dancing on street corners with their friends. It was all very contemporary, very modern and new, and Cher just loved it."

On her third appearance Nancy Walker was cast as a temporary hotline worker who gives advice to callers with problems, teamed with Cher in "The Corsican Sisters," a sketch about twin sisters who have grown up learning to endure each other's aches and pains, and joined Cher and Wayne Rogers in an original Billy Brown and Earl Brown song entitled "Limericks." "It wasn't as nuts as the first time I was there," remembers Rogers who, on the show, played a scientist in "Underwater Wackos" and joined Cher in a segment about two clowns who can't get through their wedding ceremony without cracking jokes. "The first time it was just complete madness; like a circus. But the second time around things were tamer, much more ordered and much more professionally done."

One of the reasons taping went smoothly—Cher's opening number aside—might have been the calm and cool presence of Nancy Walker. "She was such a professional in the best sense of the word," says Rogers. "She showed up on time, she was prepared, she knew what she was doing. In my opinion she wasn't wildly imaginative, but she knew what to do and wanted to do it as quickly as possible. She wasn't there to explore anything, expand on anything, or prove anything. It was just a job to her and she wanted to do it without any problems—and then go back home."

Program number seventeen's finale, a "Salute to the Hamburger," is among the series' most elaborately written, staged and costumed. Divided into eight parts, the finale featured the show's guests, six male and four female dancers, Gailard Sartain, Jack Harrell, Scott Salmon and "Felix" (a dwarf). The segment began with "The All American Dish," a tune performed by Cher, Walker and Rogers, and then moved into a "Senate Hamburger Investigation," a "Burger King Salute," a "Hamburger Tour," "The Silver Arches," "The Forbidden Burger," "The Hamburger Finale Speech" and a "Soup and Vegetable Fashion Show" that featured Miss Pickles, Miss Lettuce, Miss Onions, Miss Meat, walking-talking-condiments, as well as a giant hamburger (Cher and Walker). Bob Mackie received an Emmy nomination for his work on "Salute to the Hamburger." He certainly was in demand; nominated in the same category he lost out to himself—for the costumes he designed for the Mitzi Gaynor special *Mitzi... Roaring in the '20s.*

The long-term viability of the variety-show format may have, especially in the press, been in question, but the *Cher* show, seventeen episodes into its run, continued to deliver many shining and praiseworthy moments.

24

TWO FOR THE PRICE OF ONE

The taping schedule for show number seventeen, like so many shows before it, proved to be long and arduous. On Friday, August 1, Cher arrived at CBS at 9:00 a.m. Taping for the day was completed fourteen hours later at 11:45 p.m. Along with the episode's sketches and musical numbers, Cher filmed two musical segments with the Muppets that were banked and used later in the season, as well as two "Cher's Talent Showcase" segments that featured composer/lyricist John Hresc. "The next performer is very special young man who I think deserves to be seen and heard," Cher said during her introduction. He wasn't. The segments that Cher performed with Hresc—"Yearning and Turning" and "Old MacDonald Had a Farm" never aired.

"After I was a guest on *Cher* a second time, I remember pulling George aside and telling him that someone was missing the ball with Cher," says Wayne Rogers. "She was a wonderful actress—just one of those people who understood behavior. She had a great natural quality about her and that's something that you have or you don't. Working side by side with her you just knew that much bigger things were going to happen for her in the future."

Following taping of show number seventeen, filming of *Cher* was suspended for the duration of a week so that Cher could make good on her promise to appear on *The Carol Burnett Show*. Earlier in the season, dressed in a gown embellished with a fat stomach, extended hips and a pair of waist-length sagging breasts, Burnett actually spoofed *Cher*'s entire opening segment.

On *The Carol Burnett Show* Cher did a send-up of popular TV commercials, performed in "The Not So Eternal Triangle," a sketch about a self-important wealthy woman who is forced to surrender her husband to a homely vagrant (Burnett), and appeared in "As the Stomach Turns," a spoof of the long-running daytime series *As the World Turns*. Cher also sang an abbreviated version of "Just

This One Time" from *Stars*, and joined Carol for a song and dance medley called "Variety."

BURNETT: You know Cher we have a lot in common. We're the same height.

CHER: Right.

BURNETT: We're both Taurus.

CHER: Right.

BURNETT: We both have our own TV shows.

CHER: Right.

BURNETT: We have the same initials.

CHER: Sometimes!

The Carol Burnett Show's musical finale was "Solid Silver Platform Shoes," a spoof of rock and roll music in which the entire cast participated. For the number Cher and Burnett wore hers and hers sequined dresses, platform shoes and glitter afro wigs. (A photograph of Cher and Burnett posed back to back in their costumes was widely published.)

The fourth episode of Cher's second season, show number eighteen, was a family-oriented outing that featured Captain Kangaroo, the Hudson Brothers, Illusionist Mark Wilson with his son Greg, and Chastity. Cher opened the hour with "Can You Tell Me How to Get to Sesame Street?"—the theme song from *Sesame Street*—and followed with a monologue about how Chastity served as talent coordinator for the episode.

CHER: I figured I'd consult with a real expert on who to have as my guests so Chastity gave me a list of all the people she'd like to see. Unfortunately, Santa Claus was unavailable, the Easter Bunny was out of town, and the Tooth Fairy was working in Phoenix.

Following her opening monologue Cher introduced Chastity, and mother and daughter partook in a delightful ad-lib session. "I always loved working with paper mâché," remembers Paul Galbraith, whose giant white swan constituted the set for Cher's solo, "When You Wish Upon a Star" from the Disney film *Pinocchio*. "I loved it because it could look like anything—wood, metal, rocks, a building or a bird. I really didn't think much of the swan; it was just what was needed that week. But years later, when I was working on another show at CBS, someone came up to me and said, 'I just want to let you know that I have your swan.' I said, 'What?' And this young girl said, 'I was a stagehand on the *Cher* show and when we were done shooting they just threw your beautiful swan in the dumpster out back. At the end of the day I got my car, went around to the back of the building, and fished it out. It's now the centerpiece of my bedroom!' During my entire career I don't believe I've ever received a more honest or moving compliment."

On the show Chastity, who appeared with Cher atop Galbraith's giant swan, joined Illusionist Mark Wilson and his son Greg for a series of magic tricks. Cher's "Saturday Night" sketch was particularly engaging. Along with introducing her new roommate—a dog named Yutz—she talked about the fact that she was always late. (In second season scripts, next to Cher's call time— usually 8:00 a.m.—typed in brackets was: "sure!")

CHER: The nerve of some people. My date said to meet him downstairs at eight o'clock sharp. So I washed my hair, put on my makeup and was waiting downstairs for him on time... at 8:45. Look, to me, 8:45 is on time. If he wanted me to be there exactly at 8:00 why didn't he say 7:15?

At the time of his appearance, Captain Kangaroo (Robert Keeshan) was the star of CBS's children's program *Captain Kangaroo*. On *Cher* he attempted to sell his idea for a children's television program to a skeptical network executive (Cher), and had fun with a three-headed monster named Stupillo. In their second appearance on the show, the Hudson Brothers sang a solo—"Lonely School Year"—and, with Cher, played toy soldiers practicing their moves. (Filmed but not aired was a production number entitled "Nothing Nicer Than a Nonsense Song," performed by Cher, the Hudsons and four Anita Mann dancers.)

"Cher didn't show up for the one and only rehearsal we had," remembers Mark Wilson. "I thought, 'This is not going to work out.' For the rehearsal we used a stand-in, I think it was one of the dancers. I met Cher for the first time on the day that we taped. She was late, but I was told to expect that. For some reason I remember her fingernails. They were long and multicolored and I had never seen anything like them before. Anyway, Cher was very nice and she was extremely quick. The physical things that she was required to do she did automatically. I came away thinking that she really didn't need to come to the rehearsal after all. *I* would have been more comfortable with her there but she obviously knew much more about her capabilities than I did." On the show Wilson chopped Cher in half ("Don't worry this is just a trial separation," he quipped), divided her up in a "zigzag" box, and then, for the finale, made her levitate, disappear and reappear. "The levitation was my favorite segment," remembers Wilson. "That trick involves several effects; the levitation, the disappearance and the reappearance. In my opinion the most spectacular effect a magician can accomplish is to make a person vanish while floating in mid-air. It just doesn't get much better than that."

Show number eighteen, the "All Children's Hour," was a solid success that allowed everyone working on the series to take a collective deep breath. No "unfamiliar" rock songs, no daring costumes, no risqué comedy sketches; it also kept the CBS censors at bay. "I remember that episode clearly," says a musician who worked on the series. "That was the only week—and I worked on every episode—that there wasn't a censor on the set. Not even for a moment. Once those censors saw the script and the guests, I mean what was Captain Kangaroo going to do—strip?! They just took a week off!"

Cher's absence from the first two weeks of taping season two's scheduled programs meant that she, in the span of just a week's time, was obliged to film two full shows—simultaneously. Thus on September 18, 19 and 20, Cher taped two *Cher* shows together. The hectic and extended filming schedule meant that both programs (shows number nineteen and number 25) were taped in a studio situation with no audience present.

Show number nineteen, featuring Mac Davis, Gailard Sartain and Labelle, was a quickly put together (it had a 66-page script) and briskly recorded music-heavy hour that was just as exciting as the many painstakingly thought-out episodes that had preceded it.

Singer/songwriter Mac Davis—the Academy of Country Music's "Entertainer of the Year" in 1974 —was a popular television personality and had previously helmed his own *Mac Davis Show*. On *Cher*, Davis performed a solo, "I Still Love You (You Still Love Me)." Later in the show he joined Cher for a note-for-note live medley of songs that he wrote, including "I Believe in Music," "Baby Don't Get Hooked on Me" and the late-career Elvis Presley hit "In the Ghetto".

DAVIS: Cher, why isn't my shirt as sparkly as yours?

CHER: Because this is *my* show—not yours!

Cher had worked with Labelle (Patti LaBelle, Sarah Dash and Nona Hendryx) during the first season, but time had changed things. "The second time we were on I remember we were really happy to see all the behind-the-scenes creative people again," says Hendryx. "The hair people were fun. The makeup people were fun; and they were all Labelle fans. We were like, 'Hey! We're back!' and they were like, 'Hey girls, glad to see you—sit down!' But I've got to tell you that, the second time, you could really see that Cher was under pressure. I mean she was carrying the whole show by herself and there were so many changes going on in her personal life. She had changed."

The pressures that Cher was under came to vivid life when, during rehearsals with Labelle, she flat-out fainted. After being revived and escorted to the sanctuary of her dressing room, she returned to the set and fainted a second time. Concerned about her welfare, sister Georganne (who was present at the rehearsals and told columnist Cal York about it) insisted that she take a trip to a nearby hospital. Cher was examined and released. Her fainting spell was attributed to "exhaustion."

Choreographer Anita Mann was also aware of Cher's debilitating personal challenges. "As a woman who had just had a baby, I was very in tune with other females and very aware that Cher was suffering," says Mann. "We were all out there in Hollywood; we were all reading the same papers and watching the same TV shows. We all knew what was going on in Cher's personal life. It made me profoundly sad because I could see how heavily her life and decisions were weighing on her."

On show number nineteen Cher and Labelle combined their talents and did a duet of "Are You Lonely?" "We were all surprised that Cher wanted to do that song," says Hendryx. "But thinking back about her personal circumstances at the time, it kind of makes sense." The Cher/Labelle duet was as visually dazzling as it was musically sound. Dressed in hot pink, red and white space-age gear (Bob Mackie described Cher's costume as "Space Madonna-Meets Science Fiction Lady"), the foursome performed the tune live on a "concert" set complete with moving cameras and flashing multicolored lights. On their own, Labelle taped two solo numbers; "Messin' with My Mind" (from their current album *Phoenix*) and "Can I Speak to You Before You Go to Hollywood" (from 1973's *Pressure Cookin'*). Only "Messin' with My Mind" aired. "'Hollywood' was kind of a calling card for Labelle in terms of us as a group," says Hendryx. "'Lady Marmalade' was pretty much Patti's song with Sarah and I singing background, but 'Hollywood' was a little mini-musical in which we all shared equal parts. I started the song singing it to Sarah, then she picked it up and sang back to me, and then Patti comes in and is like a mediator performing to both of us. At the song's conclusion it all comes together as a resolution about our shared conflict regarding someone who 'goes Hollywood' on you. I think it was a bit too advanced for the show."

Cher opened the hour with John Denver's "Take Me Home, Country Roads" (also show number eight's opening song). Her solo was "500 Miles," a melancholy '60s tune first made popular by Bobby Bare. "'500 Miles' is my favorite Cher solo spot," says Ray Klausen. "After I got the script and read the lyrics, I went over to Universal Pictures and rented a first-class period train car. It had inlayed wood, recessed lighting and a crystal bud vase. When Bob Mackie saw it he just loved it and he went out and rented this leopard coat for Cher to wear. Even way back then the coat was valued at $75,000, so it was a really big deal to get it. Set decorator Bob Checchi was jumping up and down when he saw what we were doing and he added twelve of the longest stemmed red roses that I have ever seen in my entire life."

There was, however, a problem. "One of the lyrics in the song was 'here I sit broken hearted—not a penny to my name!' George came into the booth and had a fit. He was screaming, 'What the fuck are you guys doing? She's singing about being poor and you guys are making her look like a fucking billionaire!' I remember Bob and I just turned to him and calmly said, 'George, what difference does it make? She looks fabulous, doesn't she? Aren't you paying us to make her look fabulous?' With that he just walked away."

Two of show number nineteen's comedy sketches stood out: Cher as an embittered former "Miss U.S. of A." pageant winner and "Life with Laverne."

"Miss U.S. of A."

CHER: I almost split my gut when Miss Virginia walked out and said,

"I'm proud to be a Virginian!" She hasn't been a Virginian since junior high school.

"Life with Laverne" (featuring producer Don Reo as Laverne's brother Larry).

LAVERNE: Larry, you're still the same as when we were kids... full of the devil.

LARRY: Oh, I know it... and when I turned eighteen, Dad said, "Larry, with you around life is *hell*—get out!"

(Later)

LARRY: Laverne you look *très* magnifique... what's your secret?

LAVERNE: It involves getting to sleep every night at nine o'clock.

LARRY: I didn't know you went to sleep so early.

LAVERNE: Not me... Harry. Soon as he dozes off, I hit the road. Keeps me younger than springtime!

Gailard Sartain appeared in two segments. In the first he, as oafish Otis, pretended to introduce his "good friends" Labelle. In the second, "God Bless the Food and Drug Administration," Sartain showed off his deft comic timing playing a beleaguered homeowner who, while going about his daily routine, hears a litany of product recalls—including toothpaste, sour cream and, finally, his car—over the radio. Cher closed the hour with a "Rolling Stones Concert." Standout tunes in the tribute to the band—that almost made it onto her stage—included "Ruby Tuesday," "Jumpin' Jack Flash," and "Under My Thumb."

At the same time that show number nineteen aired, Sonny Bono appeared as a guest on ABC's *The Six Million Dollar Man* series. The episode was called "The Song and Dance Man" and featured Sonny playing a singing star who hires the Six Million Dollar Man for protection. Also featured on the show, in a bit part, was Sonny's girlfriend Susie Coelho. That week, at least, Sonny bested Cher. Sonny's *Six Million Dollar Man* episode came in at No. 6; while *Cher* came in at No. 39. (Cher later told *The Daily News* that Chastity preferred *The Six Million Dollar Man* to *Cher*. "She says she just loves him and can't wait to see him kill someone with his bare hands each week!")

Show number twenty featured the Ike and Tina Turner Revue and Anthony Newley. In their second appearance on the program, Ike and Tina Turner—especially Tina—are superb. Tina and the band do "River Deep, Mountain High" and "Baby Get It On" and Tina joins Cher for a version of "Country Side of Life." In a comedy blackout Ike was featured remarking—in an expressly Jewish voice—about Cher and her show through his subconscious. "On that show Tina was just on fire" remembers Schlatter. "Cher and Tina were sparking off of one another—egging each other on, higher, harder, faster, and they loved it. They both were simply fantastic."

Urbane British musician/actor/composer Anthony Newley—perhaps best known for his supporting role in the 1967 film *Doctor Dolittle*, but also the writer of "The Candy Man," "Goldfinger," and winner of the 1963 Song of the Year Grammy for "What Kind of Fool Am I?"—performed a solo, "Quilp," spoofed two TV commercials, and played Cher's nouveau riche husband, whose beloved Rolls-Royce has been kidnapped and is being held for ransom. Newley also joined Cher in "Life with Laverne," in which he played an interior decorator hired to re-decorate Laverne's apartment.

Cher opened the hour with a song that perfectly described her program's second season; the declarative 1920s standard "There'll Be Some Changes Made." Her monologue was about how terrible she was at telling jokes. The opening segment, one of very few second season shows to be performed in front of an actual live audience, did not go smoothly. During the taping, after she threw off her cape and stepped forward onto the home-base set's moving platform, Cher missed her mark and took a tumble. The studio audience gasped as she went from haughty glamour to a jumble of arms, legs, hair and sequins. "I hit the deck," Cher later explained. "Then I just popped my head up, waved at the audience, and we did it again." (Later, on show number 23, Cher used a clip of the event to great effect.)

Cher's solo number was Ian Whitcomb's 1965 hit "You Turn Me On," and the hour ended with a musical finale featuring the entire cast. "When I got the script for that particular show I said, 'Uh-oh, how am I going to put together Anthony Newley, Tina Turner and Cher?' remembers Anita Mann. (George Schlatter's notebook reveals that before negotiations fell through, Sonny Bono was to appear on this episode—in Newley's place.) "They first told me to do a Broadway production number so we worked on that for a while, but it just didn't seem to come together. At the very last minute—I was with Ray Klausen, and there wasn't even enough time to do a set—I said, 'You know what? Let's do an old-time revival meeting.' With Cher and Tina it just seemed like it would be an easy thing to do. Because we were on deadline we just staged the whole number in front of the studio scrim. There wasn't a set at all, just a platform, some benches and a bunch of sawdust that we sprinkled on the floor."

"I remember that number well," says Ray Klausen. "There was no time to do anything and no money to do anything. I remembered seeing the stage crew move around a cyclorama. A 'syc' is a big expansive piece of fabric that creates a neutral background. Well, I noticed the crew pulling the fabric back one day and I noticed that it draped beautifully. So, with no other alternative, I convinced them to gather it all up and pull it into sways. That was our tent!" The end result of the last-minute preparations is a high-spirited, hootin' 'n' hollerin', arms-flailing medley of "Brother Love's Traveling Salvation Show" (included on the Sonny and Cher album *Mama Was a Rock and Roll Singer, Papa Used to Write All Her Songs*), "Resurrection Shuffle" and "Saved." The segment is a joy to watch. The following year Ray Klausen and set decorator Robert Checchi (unexpectedly) won an Emmy for Outstanding Achievement in Art Direction or Scenic Design. "Jean Stapleton presented that Emmy Award to me," remembers Klausen. "When I got up onstage the first thing I did was grab the envelope from her hand and look at it. I thought it was a mistake; I couldn't possibly have won an Emmy for something I put together at the last minute. Winning that award was so wonderful because it made me feel like I was really a part of show business. After I won that Emmy I thought, 'I must be doing *something* right.'"

"I just didn't *get* that Emmy," confesses Anita Mann, "But then, again, *I* didn't win it, and I wasn't even nominated—*and* the whole production number was *my* idea!" (Proof of the musical finale's enduring appeal came four years later when Beatrice Arthur restaged it—complete with the songs "Saved" and "Resurrection Shuffle"—on *The Beatrice Arthur Special*.)

The morning after Cher taped show number twenty, a limousine quietly pulled up to her Holmby Hills mansion and whisked her away to Los Angeles International Airport, where she boarded a flight to New York City. Later that evening she attended a sold-out Allman Brothers Band performance. "I was at the concert that night," remembers Tina Schultz, an Allman Brothers fan. "We couldn't believe that Cher was there, in Jersey City, New Jersey no less! She seemed so happy and she seemed like such a groupie—she was onstage throughout their entire set. At the time I thought of Cher as this Hollywood glamorpuss, but when I saw her that night I thought she was a real rock and roll chick. She was doing exactly what I would have done: staying by her man's side."

25

WITCHY WOMAN

Six shows into her second season, and even though it was seldom in the top ten, *Cher* remained one of CBS's most popular broadcasts. Demand for tickets to see the show being filmed was in excess of two years; exceeding both the long-running *Carol Burnett Show* and the heavily-promoted *Tony Orlando and Dawn* show. Sandy Griffin, a Los Angeles homemaker who during the '70s spent her free time attending television show tapings, says that the wait for tickets was just the beginning of an extended period of time spent waiting; especially when it came to Cher. "I saw Cher tape several shows and I have to tell you that it was always disappointing," remembers Griffin. "First of all, they had you wait outside in the boiling sun for what seemed like an eternity. After a couple of hours standing—there were no seats anywhere—about 50 percent of the people would just go home. I always stayed, and once you were finally ushered into the studio, you waited some more; a lot more. Finally, a producer or comedian would come out, tell a few jokes or stories, and then the taping would begin. I never, ever saw any of the guests that appeared on *Cher* [tickets for the show promised 'Cher... with guest stars']. It was always Cher taping the beginning and closing—sometimes the beginning and closing of *several* shows. She also sometimes taped promo spots and once I remember seeing her do a solo number. The tapings took forever; hours."

There may have been a waiting list to see *Cher*, but there was no waiting list to see Cher at the newsstands. In the fall of 1975, Beauty Secrets, Inc. published *Cher: TV's Dazzling Superstar*, a 72-page magazine that included a color insert and articles with titles like "TV's First Sex Symbol," "Showbiz Golden Girl," and "Cher's Luxury Starship"; while, at the same time, Sterling's Magazines published *Cher Superstar*, a 92-page "Collector's Issue" that included three "pin-ups" and chapters with titles like "The Cher Story," "The Men in Her Life," and "The Cher Look." Additionally Scholastic Books published an 89-page paperback entitled *TV Time* that featured a picture of Cher on the cover.

"We had a whole rhythm going," observes Ret Turner of the large part of Cher's life that the pubic knew about but *didn't* get to see. "We, Cher included, could do all the hard work necessary to keep her show going because we were used to doing it—not because it was easy." Bob Mackie agrees. "When I was doing *Cher* I was doing two shows at the same time and the only way that I could do it [*The Carol Burnett Show* and *Cher*] was the fact that the only thing that separated the TV studio that Cher was working in and the TV studio that Carol was working in was the men's room! I could run back and forth between the two sound stages and check in on both of them."

"While you're shooting and taping one episode, you're also always in pre-production for what you're going to shoot two weeks down the line," says Anita Mann. "That kind of forward planning and 24-hour commitment is necessary from everyone—especially the craftspeople. We had to know everything in advance so that we could start getting the sets, costumes, choreography and music together. There are constant pre-production meetings, discussions about what you shot the week before—what worked and what didn't, and post-production meetings. Mostly what creating a show like Cher's entailed was the ability to multi-task. If you couldn't do a million things all at the same time, and do them well, you were doomed to fail."

Show number 21 was heavy on comedy. The guests for the hour were the Smothers Brothers, Steve Martin (Martin was a regular on *The Smothers Brothers Show*), Ted Knight and Gailard Sartain. In their second appearance on the show, Dick Smothers played a chain-smoking prisoner being visited by his wife (Cher), and both Tom and Dick performed in a sketch in which they tried to sell a variety show starring Howard Cosell to a doubtful network executive (Cher). Ted Knight was familiar to viewers via his Ted Baxter newscaster character on *The Mary Tyler Moore Show*. In "Life with Laverne" Knight reprised his Baxter character and showed up on Laverne's doorstep looking for an interview. He also played a man trying to find a father at a "Big Daddy" foundation, and performed a comedic song entitled "I'm in Love with Barbara Walters." Years before hitting his stride and becoming a film star, Steve Martin (who had appeared on *The Sonny and Cher Comedy Hour* and occasionally served as an opening act for Sonny and Cher when they toured) was a comedian of note. Only a year after he appeared on *Cher*, HBO broadcast *On Location: Steve Martin*, a filmed documentation of his one-man show. On *Cher* Martin performed the larger part of his stand-up routine (which was cut up and used in two more broadcasts—shows number 23 and 25). "It is one of my biggest regrets that we really didn't get to use Steve [Martin] or Martin [Mull] that much," says George Schlatter. "We brainstormed, wrote, and even filmed a great deal of material

Above: Over the top and past their prime: Cher and Carol Burnett ham it up as two former leading ladies of the silver screen. Below: "Girls are Smarter": All in the Family's Jean Stapleton and Cher turn up the sass for a rousing rendition of Billy Barnes and Earl Brown's apt girl-power anthem. (TV Time)

Opposite: Oceans apart: Cher flanked by guests who ran the gamut of her program's demographic. On her right, British heartthrob David "Rock On" Essex; on her left, American comedian and film star Jerry Lewis. (J. Howard Collection)

Above and left: According to producer George Schlatter: "Cher was never happier than when she was able to get legitimate rock stars on the show." And they don't get more legit than David Bowie. The same week he taped his appearance on Cher, "Fame" was the No. 1 song in America. (J. Howard Collection)

Above: Singing the blues: At the time of his appearance on Cher, country legend Glen Campbell was embroiled in a messy divorce. He and Cher performed a medley of hits penned by Campbell himself, including "Wichita Lineman" and "Galveston." (J. Howard Collection)

Opposite above: Magic moments: Cher and Ray Charles deliver a dizzying, show-stopping finale, including Charles favorites, "Hit the Road Jack," "What'd I Say" and "Look What They've Done to My Song Ma." Below: Lady Marmalade: Cher proves she can hold her own onset with feisty girl group, Labelle. From left to right, Nona Hendryx, Sarah Dash and Patti LaBelle. (Photo Fair)

Left: From left to right, Tina Turner, Cher and British singer/songwriter Anthony Newley perform "Resurrection Shuffle" on the Emmy-Award-winning set crafted by art director Ray Klausen. Below: Witchy woman? CBS executives thought this image (played over the second season's opening) aligned Cher with the occult. It was consequently pulled after just six episodes. (CBS-TV; Photo Fair)

Left: On July 10, 1976, Cher and Gregg Allman welcomed a son. Elijah Blue Allman made his television debut on The Sonny and Cher Show's *Christmas episode. Below: And they said it could never happen: Singer/songwriter Neil Sedaka joins Sonny and Cher on their post-divorce/reunion series,* The Sonny and Cher Show. *(CBS-TV)*

And the beat went on... Cher in 1979 at Caesar's Palace, Atlantic City, NJ, performing in her very first solo nightclub act, (left) and in 1987 as Moonstruck's merry widow Loretta Castorini—a role that won her the coveted Best Actress Academy Award. (J. Howard Collection; Photo Fair)

with the both of them, but, somehow, it never made it on the air. If I remember correctly Martin Mull was really disappointed by the way things turned out—that he had put effort and creativity into things that no one was ever going to see. But I don't think that Steve much cared. He was just passing through. Steve was secure in the fact that if it didn't happen for him on this show it was going to happen somewhere else. And, of course, it did."

"I think Steve Martin and Martin Mull were a bit ahead of their time," says Anita Mann. "I don't think the network understood or appreciated them. Cher's gut instinct about what was new and exciting was brilliant, but CBS wasn't always in step with her." For his part, comedian Gailard Sartain performed in a stand-alone "Man vs. Machine" sketch in which he had problems getting a cup of coffee from a vending machine, and, with the entire cast, participated in a comic look at "Big Time Crime."

Cher opened the hour wearing a pumpkin-orange bias-cut satin gown and black and white Egret-feather cape. Her opening songs were a medley of Janis Ian's melancholy "Stars" (the title track from her latest album) and Paul Simon's more upbeat and to the point "Keep the Customer Satisfied." The medley was followed by a monologue about Halloween. Cher's solo was a lovely version of Gordon Lightfoot's "If You Could Read My Mind." For her "Saturday Night" sketch she talked to her dog Yutz about her latest "loser" date.

George Schlatter's *new* vision for the series was only partially successful and show number 22 proved it. The hour featured Teri Garr, Martin Mull and George Burns and was billed as "An Old-Fashioned Vaudeville Review." The show was entertaining, but you would have never known it by the ratings. That week *The Six Million Dollar Man* came in at No. 10 while *Cher* only managed to rise to No. 49. At the time of his appearance, 79-year-old "Special Guest Star" George Burns was enjoying a late-career renaissance. Just a few months after appearing on *Cher*, he took home a Best Supporting Actor Academy Award for his role in *The Sunshine Boys*. Burns had also previously appeared on *The Sonny and Cher Comedy Hour*. "I'm busier now than when I was twenty," Burns said at the time. "I've never felt more like working and it's a good thing because I've never been more in demand."

On the show Burns and Cher did a soft-shoe to the tune "I Ain't Got Nobody," a slow dance to "Tea for Two," and a "Burns and Allen" comedy routine. He also had two solo spots; "The Baby Song," and "Where Did You Get That Girl?"—each punctuated by his unique comic interludes.

GEORGE: I must tell you, I'm dressing right next door to Cher, and there's a hole in the wall between our dressing rooms. I was going to plug it up, but why bother, let her enjoy herself!

"If I had to pick five performers in my life who I worked with and who touched me deeply, George Burns would be one of them," says Lee Miller. "I had a hand in booking him and we were all so thrilled to get him. I absolutely idolized George Burns. He was the most successful straight man in history—in fact, with *Burns and Allen*, George *invented* the straight man. Everyone copied his approach to comedy—even Sonny and Cher."

Original though he was, Miller says that it didn't much matter to Cher. "Cher was never ever intimidated by anyone. Jerry Lewis, Bill Cosby, George Burns—it didn't matter. I think Cher felt, 'In my own way I'm as big a star as they are, after all, they are appearing on *my* show.'"

Although he was a year away from his star turn on *Mary Hartman, Mary Hartman*, at the time of his appearance Martin Mull, like his contemporary Steve Martin, was a sardonic, push-the-buttons comedian who had released several albums—with controversial routines like "Jesus Christ Football Star" and "The Blacks Are Giving Me the Blues."

On *Cher* Mull performed a comic monologue (his one and only on the series), a solo, "The Humming Song," and appeared with Teri Garr in two sketches; "The Interpreters," in which he and Garr played interpreters who are trying to arrange a marriage between a pair of mismatched royal subjects, and "The Complaint Department," in which he, with Garr, played a just-married couple attempting to return their wedding rings to an incredulous store clerk (Cher). Mull was also featured in a brief spoof of the TV game show *To Tell the Truth*. In her third appearance, Teri Garr appeared in "Dave's Wine" (with Gailard Sartain), a spoof of a cheap wine product, and in "Life with Laverne" reprised her kooky Olivia role:

OLIVIA: Burt and I just got back from our first real honeymoon.
LAVERNE: But didn't you go on a honeymoon when you first got married?
OLIVIA: Yeah, but on that one we had one extra piece of baggage that ruined the whole trip.
LAVERNE: What was that?
OLIVIA: Burt's mother.

The program's finale was staged on a vaudeville set and featured Cher and Garr as the Folly Sisters, two scantily-clad mistresses of ceremonies. Cher opened the hour with a clever medley of the Carpenters' "Rainy Days and Mondays" and the 1930s jazz standard "On the Sunny Side of the Street," followed by a brief segment in which stoic comedian John Holland joined her onstage and presented her with several "questions from the audience." Cher's opening number gown—a see-through, mermaid-like creation—is one of the series' most phantasmical.

The significance of Cher's solo, "Lime House Blues," a little-known 1924 instrumental, was lost on most viewers. The Lime House Basin area of London was, in the early 19th century, notorious for its opium dens, bars, illegal gambling, prostitution, and violence. The area, often frequented by seamen, was also London's Chinatown. Displaying an acute awareness of the song's obscure references, Ray Klausen designed an elaborate set complete with a vintage roulette table, a poker table, a bar, a black etched marble floor, sparkling chandeliers and giant Oriental screens. Milling around the ornate set were nine extras—including sailors, prostitutes, gamblers, and a female impersonator—all smoking, drinking and having what looks like a seedy, good 'ole time.

For her part, Cher entered the set through a cast iron door. Wearing a hot-pink satin gown slit up to the waist, she then descended a staircase. Emblazoned across her gown was a glittering multi-colored dragon. Atop her head sat an ornate, hot-pink, gold and lime-green beaded headdress. In the span of just four minutes she sang, danced, was featured in a flashback—performed with Scott Salmon—and exited. "I was really happy with 'Lime House Blues,'" remembers Ray Klausen. "I don't think anyone in the world 'got it' but those of us who were working on it. I mean who knows what a Lime House is? But it didn't matter. Cher wanted to do it. She loved old songs and that was certainly one of the oldest ones we did!"

And Cher loved other things too. "Cher, as everyone probably knows, loves to shop," says Ret Turner, remembering a break that happened during taping of "Lime House Blues." "She came up to me and said, 'Ret, we're going shopping—now!' And I said, 'What do you mean we're going shopping now? There isn't time; you have to be back onstage in ten minutes.' She just grabbed my hand, looked me in the eye, and said, 'They'll wait!'

"I remember Cher went in her dressing room and put on a short blonde wig. She said, 'This way, no one will recognize me.' Wishful thinking! Everyone recognized her wherever she went—blonde wig or not. It was just Cher wearing a blonde wig. Well, anyway, we drove to this place in Hollywood called Palace Costumes. There was a woman there named Melanie who was really nice. Cher found this wonderful pair of embroidered boots, and when Melanie saw her with them she said, 'If they fit you, you can have them.' Cher tried them on and they fit perfectly. She was ecstatic, and with the shopping bug now finally out of her system, we were able to make our way back to CBS and finish taping. Those were the days!"

According to Teri Garr's original shooting script for show number 22, Gregg Allman and the Allman Brothers Band were scheduled to make an appearance and sing "Can't Lose What You Never Had" complete with two drum sets, a Rhodes piano, an organ, a guitar, and bass. Later in the show Gregg, without the band, was to join Cher for an "undetermined" duet. Cher's introduction of the band is scripted: "With only a small amount of prejudice, I'd like to present my favorite group... the fantastic Allman Brothers Band!" The appearance and the introduction never took place. In Teri Garr's script the actress drew an "X" through the rehearsal and videotape times for the Allman Brothers Band. And over the Cher/Allman duet she scribbled "Interpreters 10:00 a.m."–the comedy sketch she performed with Martin Mull. Today, it remains unclear who decided that Gregg Allman and the Allman Brothers Band would not appear on the show, but it is safe to surmise that when the decision was made, Cher and Gregg were not getting along.

The next episode of the series–show number 23–proved noteworthy; for all the wrong reasons. The guests for the hour were Wayne Newton, Steve Martin, Gailard Sartain and the Spinners. All of Martin's material had been previously filmed (show number 21). His segments included a sketch in which he played a mad hypnotist who terrorizes a doctor's office, and a blackout in which he tries to get a stone-faced Cher to laugh. Wayne Newton–"Mr. Las Vegas"–so much wanted to appear on *Cher* that he flew in from Casa de Shenandoah, his 40-acre ranch, on his one day off from his long-term duties as headliner at Las Vegas' Sands Hotel and Casino. Although he was most associated with his 1963 hit "Danke Schoen," Newton, who, like Cher, was proud of his American Indian heritage, had, in 1972, managed to go all the way to No. 4 with "Daddy Don't You Walk So Fast." On *Cher* Newton sang a solo, the much-covered "Feelings" and performed in a "Mr. Grinds" comedy skit. "Wayne Newton was particularly impressive in handling comedy," observed *The Hollywood Reporter*, "as good as any I've ever seen, especially in his mock commercial bit, where he deadpanned a commentator caught with an infernal machine that just won't quit in the pouring department." The hour closed with a rewarding three-song medley– "Rock-a-Bye Your Baby," "The Birth of the Blues," and "You're Nobody 'Till Somebody Loves You"–performed by Newton and Cher.

Daily News columnist Bob Lardine was on the set during the taping: "Wayne Newton has just finished singing 'Feelings,' and now everyone is waiting for Cher to emerge from her nearby trailer in the CBS studio," he wrote. "The only people present are the crew and a few hangers-on. Two bored crew members are discussing their upcoming flu shots, and the boom man is absorbed in reading *The Los Angeles Times*. One of the cameramen sports a sweatshirt with 'Dinah!' emblazoned on it, and he's arguing football with a prop man. When Cher finally saunters out she is wearing a bare midriff black halter and slacks. She kisses Wayne on the cheek and says: 'Nice going.' She looks a head smaller than Newton but he's wearing high heels and she isn't. Another drag on her cigarette and she is center stage. Cher appears remarkably bony, thin almost to the point of malnutrition, and while the camera adds ten pounds she could use at least twenty. Cher reaches into her halter and scratches subconsciously, then inhales deeply and shouts at the crew: 'Hey! Look at these boobs!' One of the soundmen yells back: 'Which one?' Everybody laughs, including Cher."

Filling out show number 23 was a look at television evangelists called "Money Works Miracles." The sketch was adroitly written by Gailard Sartain, who played Reverend Billy Joe Bob Sweeney, with Cher as his wife LuLu May. Looking very much like the Reverend Billy Swaggart, and adopting a preacherly tone, Sartain's Sweeney was shown to be having an affair with Libby Sue, one of the program's background singers, and openly hawking merchandise—including an album entitled *There's a Goldmine in the Sky and We're all Just Prospectors*. Sweeney's "thought for the week" said it all: "Friends, if I had a nickel for every time I have thought about you I would be a rich man. So help my dreams come true—send money!"

"That sketch was a lot of fun," remembers Sartain. "It was based on a televangelist character that I had created in 1970 for my own locally-based Tulsa, Oklahoma television show called *Dr. Mazeppa Pompazoidi's Uncanny Film Festival*. It was great fun for me to revisit that character and rework it for Cher and the show. I think it came off really well."

Cher opened the hour with "Ain't Nobody's Business" (performed on show number three) and followed with a monologue about how clumsy she was off-camera. Her solo was an exciting medley, of the Eagles' "Witchy Woman" and the Rolling Stones' "Honky Tonk Woman" performed with the program's dancers. "That 'Witchy Woman' medley is my all-time favorite production number from the show," says Anita Mann. "I was the one who suggested that the male dancers all be topless, which I thought was exciting, and of course it upset the censors. We were always pushing the envelope a little bit but they let that one slide. Can you imagine, Cher was lowered down from the ceiling on a rope to an underground cave! Cher *is* a honky tonk woman and a witchy woman. Those two songs were about *her*."

"I remember that number, too," says Ret Turner. "How could you forget it? Cher was dressed in a feather headdress, net body stocking, and thigh-high boots. That was really an example of how in tune Bob and Cher were with one another. She would say things like 'make me look like the Road Runner gone mad' and that's exactly what Bob did. He knew what she meant and he did it. In all the time that we all worked together, I don't think Cher ever once said 'no' to anything Bob made for her. There may have been a few things that she didn't particularly *love*, but she wore them anyway. She trusted his judgment, and she trusted that he would never dress her in anything that did not flatter her or did not work in tandem with her image."

Other segments on the show included Cher's on-target rendering of Aretha Franklin's "Do Right Woman, Do Right Man" (included on *3614 Jackson Highway*), "Life with Laverne," in which Laverne fantasizes about having her own variety series (Laverne sings an excruciating "The Lady is a Tramp"), and Cher as Donna Jean Brodine, who pitches an all-purpose gadget called Mug-O-Matic.

Top-selling group the Spinners (Philippe Wynne, Billy Henderson, Pervis Jackson, Henry Fambrough and Bobbie Smith) had previously appeared on *The*

Sonny Comedy Revue. At the time of their appearance the group was riding high on the tails of their No. 1 hit "Could It Be I'm Falling in Love." For the show, the band taped a stirring live medley of four of their hits; "Mighty Love," "Then Came You" (with Cher), "Games People Play," and "Could It Be I'm Falling in Love." Only "Could It Be I'm Falling in Love" aired.

"We are all insulted and very disturbed by this slight," Wynne informed the African-American publication *Jet* (the story was picked up by *Sepia* and *Black Stars*). Wynne reported that he and his band had agreed to appear on *Cher* as a special favor to George Schlatter, and that they had forfeited $30,000 in personal appearance fees to do it. On behalf of the Spinners he demanded a public apology.

"It wasn't done intentionally" *Cher* producer Alan Katz told *Jet*, assuring both the Spinners and the magazine that the group's recorded segments would air on a future broadcast. That never happened.

The flap with the Spinners was ironic. In 1975, when *Playboy* asked Cher whether or not she had any sense of the makeup of her audience, she revealed an acute awareness of her fans as well as the special connection she had with African Americans. "Well. I'm certainly not the 'hip' person's ideal," Cher admitted. "But, for instance, I have a really big black following. I went to the Apollo Theater in Harlem one night and someone asked if I wanted to be introduced. 'God, no,' I said. You have to be heavily into soul music or do something really terrific at the Apollo or they just tell you to go fuck yourself. But someone introduced me anyway and the audience gave me a standing ovation. I thought, 'Jesus Christ, this is terrific.' Another time, when I was in a market in Macon, Georgia, this little black girl, about three years old, tugs at my leg and looks up and says, 'Cher, I love you.' And I just couldn't believe it. But it happens to me all the time. I've always done a lot of black looks on my show because I happen to think it's a terrific look. If I were to be anyone else that's what I'd be. I'd be Diana Ross."

Cher's husband at the time, Gregg Allman, also expressed an affinity for black culture. He told *Rolling Stone*: "When I was little I used to hang around the little black churches in my neighborhood. I still do. I just stand outside and listen to their singing. I've never gone inside, though. I always think that if I do that I'll ruin it." In the article Allman also revealed that Ray Charles, Otis Redding and John Coltrane (all African Americans) were his three biggest musical influences.

26

WHO BECOMES A LEGEND MOST?

Four days after the episode featuring—or *not* featuring, depending on how you look at it—the Spinners aired, Cher was hit with bad news of a personal nature. On November 14 in Macon, Georgia, Gregg Allman filed for divorce.

Lawyers presented Allman's papers at Macon's Bibb County Courthouse. His documents informed the court that he and Cher had formally separated on November 11 and that he believed the marriage was "irretrievably broken." Cher heard the news from her press agent Richard Grant. "It was one of the worst things that ever happened to me. It was a Friday... Richard called me up around six o'clock, and he said, 'Cher, do you know that Gregg's divorcing you?' And all I could say was, 'No. Can you hum a few bars?'"

Cher's surprise was compounded by her (limited) commitment to *est*, the spiritual awareness program that Cloris Leachman [while appearing on *Cher*] encouraged her to explore. "The week after Gregg filed for divorce I was in the midst of a second weekend session of *est*," Cher told *People*. "It was really difficult to go in that room with 200 people after just being dumped."

Several months later Allman spoke with columnist John J. Miller about the "real" reason he filed for divorce. According to Allman, he had agreed to participate in a Federal investigation whose focus was the rock-music industry and its connection to "payola" (the illegal practice of paying disc jockeys to play songs) and drugs. When news of Allman's dealings with the Feds (and the fact that he had been granted immunity for providing names, one of which was Allman Brothers road manager Scooter Herring) made its way around rock-music circles, he said he received death threats. "They told me to keep my mouth shut or my life wouldn't be worth a dime. I filed for divorce because I wanted to protect Cher and Chastity. I didn't want them to be in danger so I did the only thing I could have done under the circumstances."

"I'm terribly afraid that he's going to end up in an alley someplace," Cher said. "I don't know if they still call it a 'hit,' but I do know that what Gregg's involved in is a serious and deadly business." Allman survived, and so did Cher and Chastity. On December 11, a month after filing for divorce, Gregg withdrew his petition and he and Cher agreed to continue working on their relationship. "Marriage is such a hassle," Cher observed. "It's just a label to wear so that people can figure out how to relate to you. It has nothing to do with the real relationship between two people. I didn't love Gregg, or Sonny for that matter, any more the day after we got married than the day before."

Cher show number 24 remains one of the series' most musically sound. The guests for the hour were the Muppets, Chastity Bono and Ray Charles and the Raelettes. Cher opened the show with an ironic medley (especially considering her personal life) of the Turtles' "Happy Together" and the Captain and Tennille's "Love Will Keep Us Together." She followed with a monologue about how pleased she was that Ray Charles and Kermit the Frog were guests on her show. Her solo number was Neil Diamond's thoughtful and dramatic "I Am... I Said"—a tune so well-suited to her vocal style that one wondered why it was never covered on any of her albums. Ray Charles was, even by this mid-career point, a living legend: an African-American jack-of-all-trades who had weathered many storms and, quite incredibly, remained on top throughout. His catalogue of music was vast and influential (later, his life was deemed motion-picture worthy—2004's *Ray*) and Cher was, most definitely, a fan. Charles signed a contract to appear on *Cher* on March 20—four and a half months before he reported to CBS to tape his segments.

CHER: [To Ray Charles] One time when I was fourteen or fifteen years old, I came home from school and turned on *American Bandstand*. I sat down and Dick Clark said, "Today we are going to hear a new hit from Ray Charles and it's called 'Georgia on My Mind.'" Georgia is my mom's name. Anyway, I was sitting on the floor in front of the TV and the song came on and it just knocked me out. I cried throughout the whole number.

What followed was an inspired Cher/Ray Charles duet of "Georgia on My Mind" (performed on *The Sonny and Cher Comedy Hour*). Charles at the piano, Cher comfortably standing by his side, the two made a striking pair. Charles also performed two solo numbers; "America the Beautiful" and Stevie Wonder's "Living for the City." (Only the latter aired.) He also joined Kermit the Frog for "It's Not Easy Being Green," and, during the show's finale, was featured with Cher, the Raelettes—his five female backing vocalists—and the *Cher* show orchestra for a thrilling soul jam. The medley of songs in the "Cher/Ray Concert" included "Hit the Road Jack," "Look What They've Done to My Song, Ma," "What'd I Say?," "Take Me Home Country Roads" (already performed twice on the series—shows number eight and nineteen) and "Just for a Thrill."

A memorable comedy sketch featured Charles as a robber and Cher as a bank teller. "That particular sketch is among the funniest pieces of comedy that I've ever seen," remembers Lee Miller. "Ray was playing a bank robber and George gave him this incredible line. It was, 'Stick 'em up,' and then after a beat Ray quietly asked, 'Are they up yet?' Well, the audience just went crazy. They literally stopped the show. They stood up, cheered, laughed and applauded for at least five minutes. We had to do that bank robber sketch over and over again, because Ray was so good, the writing was so sharp and the audience was so responsive."

Funny though it may have been, and even though Ray Charles was game, to some the sketch had the air of unseemliness about it. "I don't remember exactly what I felt," recalls a stagehand who was present during the taping. "But I just know that something didn't feel right." Others agreed. "Blindness is a tragedy and nothing to use to milk laughs from an audience," wrote an incensed *People* subscriber. "Perhaps next week the *Cher* show will have a ball getting laughs out of someone who is afflicted with cancer."

The merits of the bank robber sketch aside, producer Lee Miller did more than respect Ray Charles: he also *learned* from him. "Dealing with blind people is not the kind of thing that comes up often, or the kind of thing you ever really think about unless you're actually doing it. Ray, like every other guest on the *Cher* show, needed a script. But he was blind. So that meant that I had to figure out how and where to get a script printed in Braille. I had never done that before. It was a great learning experience for me. Not only did I get Ray a script in Braille but I had cue cards made for him in Braille. They were six-by-eight cards that he could run his fingers over whenever his hands were out of the camera's range. What a wonderful man he was; a spectacular talent, friendly, kind, blessed with a sense of humor. He made a lasting impression on all of us."

George Schlatter agrees. "Uncle Ray was everyone's favorite—he was pure magic. I had so much respect for that man and Cher did too. It was really, really special to Cher that Ray agreed to come on, and because he had signed his contract so many months in advance, we were all like kids waiting for Santa Claus to arrive. What I remember about Ray was that he had an outstanding sense of humor. He was always cracking jokes. It struck me that he seemed to be enjoying life more than we were. And more than people who had sight. He was the type of man that you just wanted to throw your arms around, and I did—many times. I think we all did."

In their second appearance on the show, the Muppets were featured in a sketch with Cher in which Waldorf, Mildred Huxtetter, Sam the Eagle, and Kermit the Frog were all working together to raise money for a TV station. On his own, Kermit appeared in a send-up of CBS's educational segment *Bicentennial Minutes* in which he spoke about the important role of frogs throughout history. Chastity and Kermit were also featured in a pleasant exchange about being tickled, and Cher with the Muppet Sweetums did a comical version of "That Old Black Magic." A blackout featuring Cher and Kermit divided the first and second half of the show.

KERMIT: So Cher, do you fool around?

CHER: [Laughter]

KERMIT: I didn't think so. I just thought I'd ask.

CHER: Well, what did you have in mind?

KERMIT: Well, uh...

CHER: Go with you to the hop?!

"I remember that particular segment clearly," says a stagehand who was present at the taping. "Cher and Kermit did what they were supposed to do for the camera and then, without stopping, they launched into this really raunchy back and forth about dick size, vaginas, oral sex, orgasms and multiple partners! It was hysterical—we were all rolling on the floor laughing—especially because it was Cher, dressed to the nines, trading quips with this ten-inch green puppet! Of course the segment never aired. What I wouldn't give to see that confiscated footage today!"

Show number 25 (the entirety of which was taped more than two months earlier, during Cher's marathon "catch-up" week) remains both one of the series' best remembered and most talked-about episodes. The guests for the hour were Steve Martin, Tony Randall and David Bowie. Cher opened with Linda Ronstadt's "When Will I Be Loved" followed by a monologue about how she was making an attempt to appear more refined and dignified. (After taping the opening, Cher left the stage, changed costumes, and returned and taped the opening of what would be aired as show number nineteen—on the same minimalist gold, brown and silver "home base" set). Cher's solo was Leon Russell's soul favorite "A Song for You" (also performed on *The Sonny and Cher Comedy Hour*). For the number Cher used the ornately orchestrated music track that accompanied the version included on 1971's *Foxy Lady* album. "Saturday Night" featured Cher preparing for a "romantic evening"—with her faithful dog Yutz.

Cher and *The Odd Couple*'s Tony Randall (a guest on *The Sonny and Cher Comedy Hour*) performed a brief medley of the comical "Silver Dollar" and "More of Her on the Chair," and took part in two sketches. "Commercial Lady," featured Cher as Tony's TV-addicted wife, and in "The Language Barrier" Tony appeared as a stuffy bank officer trying to communicate with a slang-talking hippie Cher. The sketch was a hit, but off-camera, Cher and Randall were not. Cher told her side of the story to *TV Guide*. "I had this guest—it wouldn't be fair to mention his name—a real star: movies, stage, TV series, the whole lot. I was playing like a hippie and he was a very straight guy. Well [during the taping] I threw him an ad lib and he got uptight, really ticked off. He said, 'You can't say that because I don't have a line to come back with, so unless you write me a

WHO BECOMES A LEGEND MOST?

line, I'd appreciate it if you'd just cut that out.' After that I just could never get comfortable with him again."

Cher and Randall might not have clicked for another reason—the actor's publicly stated conservatism. "I'm against sex as a tool because it's too easy. That's not entertainment. That's not using talent, it's just cheap... I think I'm above it." (Randall had a short memory: he came to prominence in "sex" comedies like *Will Success Spoil Rock Hunter?*, *Pillow Talk* and *Let's Make Love*.)

Steve Martin's participation in show number 25 consists of snippets from his stand-up act; a trick with a napkin and a purposely corny joke (all recorded earlier, during taping of show number 21). Speaking on a British television show more than 30 years after the fact, David Bowie (who made his Prime-Time American television debut on *Cher*) described Cher as "cold and distant" during their first meeting. "She did have these incredible eyes though... they kind of looked right through you." Bowie chalked up Cher's reserve to what he believed was his "strange, emaciated, drugged-out" appearance. At the time of Bowie and Cher's first meeting, Cher was negotiating her relationship with Gregg, dodging the censors, mediating trivial, but no less distracting behind-the-scenes "personality hassles," and was fully engaged in filming two complete episodes in the span of just three days. (Although he didn't know it, Cher's commitment to having Bowie on is best illustrated by his $5,000 performance fee—twice the $2,500 standard rate.) Their pairing is superb. Writing in *Creem*, Lisa Robinson observed: "Cher was obviously ecstatic doing a number with someone 'relevant,' hip and her own age. Finally she was paired with someone who she thought she might have something in common with."

And it was true. On the program Bowie, who, two years earlier, performed "I Got You Babe" (taking Cher's part) with Marianne Faithfull on *The Midnight Special*, sang a live version of his hit "Fame" (the No. 1 song in America on the day that he taped his segment) and joined Cher for a medley of his melancholy tune "Can You Hear Me?" Cher and Bowie closed the hour with a literally breathtaking medley of fourteen songs. The tunes in the Cher/Bowie concert included Bowie's "Young Americans," as well as "Ain't No Sunshine When She's Gone," "Day Tripper" and "Blue Moon" (see Appendix for complete list).

Columnist John J. Miller was on the set during Cher's first week back at CBS following her two-week no-show. "Things are going to have to change around here," Cher declared during an on-set meeting that was called to quell the growing behind-the-scenes discord. "It's time to stop all the nonsense. I know that we've all been under a great strain working the way we have to catch up. I also know that it's all my fault. I've got to straighten my life out now, right now. And I'm going to do it, but I need your help." (Gregg Allman was in the studio at the time of Cher's speech—hanging out in the empty seats of the CBS auditorium.)

Two sketches filmed for episode number 25, like so many before them, hit the cutting-room floor. The first, "War Toys," paired Jack Harrell and Tony Randall in a segment about a toy company's controversial products—toys with names like "Arty A-Bomb," "Nicky Napalm" and "The Firing Squad Game."

TONY: Would you like to see our new line of "happy time" toys?

JACK: Yes. What is this round object here?

TONY: Oh, this one... we think it's going to be a big seller this Christmas. It's called "Johnny Land Mine."

JACK: How does it work?

TONY: It's very simple. Even the smallest child can operate it. What you do is dig a shallow hole in the yard... place "Johnny Land Mine" in ... cover it with a thin layer of dirt, twigs, you know... then call over your friend. You say, "Hey, Billy... would you mind stepping over here!" He steps on the mine, triggers the explosive, and "Pow" he's *wasted*.

The second sketch featured Gailard Sartain as a forest ranger giving animals a lecture on how to behave in front of park visitors. "I wrote that sketch myself," remembers Sartain. "But I think it may have been a bit too much for the show. I hoped it would make the final cut, but I wasn't at all surprised when it didn't."

GAILARD: Guys, one final thing... we have some new owners for the park this year. The Mitsu-bashi Recreation Company... so let's be nice to the Orientals... I hope you all know what they look like. Remember the movie we showed on the side of cabin six, *Bridge on the River Kwai*? They were the bad guys... only now, they're the *good* guys. I can't tell the difference between the good and the bad.

On the show, Cher also filmed a brief segment in which her introduction of David Bowie is interrupted by goofy Otis (Gailard Sartain). It, too, ended up on the cutting-room floor. To fill out the suddenly short hour, a banked Donna Jean Brodine Jack-O-Matic comedy segment was used. "Cher was never happier than when we had what she though were legitimate rock stars on the show," says George Schlatter about David Bowie, who by all accounts seemed shy, unlike his public persona, and kept to himself during tapings. "They were what she wanted to be. That was her idea of *real* stardom."

Lee Miller agrees. "I wasn't always comfortable with the musical guests that Cher sought out, or the kind of music she wanted to sing. But I respected the fact that that was the musical style to which she committed herself and in which she felt most comfortable. She loved rock and roll, she loved rock and roll performers, and she wanted to be a rock and roll star—not a pop star. It was a case of surrounding yourself with the thing that you want to be, but aren't."

27

CHER SHARES "CHER"

As Cher's second season progressed, rumors circulated that the show was going to be cancelled. As *Screen Stars* indecorously put it: "Can Cher's backless, frontless costumes hold up the ratings of her show?" A look at the Nielsen ratings for *Cher's* second season revealed that, although she remained an entertainer and personality that many people enjoyed seeing on television each week, during her summer hiatus, viewers *had* turned to the competition—and never come back. The Nielsens for November 2 were typical. That week, in the 8:00 p.m. time slot, ABC's *The Six Million Dollar Man* came in at No.10, NBC's *The Wonderful World of Disney* came in at No. 24, and CBS's *Cher* came in at No. 49.

"Why did a girl with everything going for her last season suddenly land on television's skid row?" asked *The Daily News*. "When a lady who looks like an Egyptian queen and who has talent plays second fiddle to a mechanical male—Lee Majors as 'The Six Million Dollar Man'—something is terribly wrong."

At the time, George Schlatter had his own ideas about why *Cher* had slipped in the ratings. "One immediate and obvious reason that the show is not doing as well as it did last season is Cher's lead in *Three for the Road*, which is the lowest-rated show on the air." When *Three for the Road* was uneventfully cancelled (thirteen episodes were filmed but only eleven aired) and replaced with *60 Minutes*, Schlatter deadpanned: "Now, at least we'll be inheriting an intelligent audience."

"Right now I'm after CBS to put my show on in a later time slot—maybe ten o'clock," Cher told columnist Bob Mallory. "I simply can't do the type of show I think is best in the early evening. If CBS doesn't let me do it, then I guess we'll all have to face the consequences."

But Cher was not just unhappy with her program's time slot, she was also greatly disturbed by what she believed was the distorted image that the public—especially the TV-viewing public—had of her. "I was reading this thing about me being this sex goddess and I thought, 'My God, what a dumb thing that is.' I go around in jeans and a t-shirt almost my whole life, except when I'm working," Cher told *Playboy*. "I don't relate to the sex goddess stuff at all. I've been thinking about going on my show in a dress made out of an old army blanket. I don't give a shit. I honestly don't. Sometimes I think there are two Chers—the one people write about and the real me. The one people write about, the one on the television show, is after everybody's husband. All *I* want to do is—I want to have a man, and I want to have a life, and I want to do my gig. I figure it's almost like being a bank clerk. I go and do my job, and now, I guess, that's my job—the sex goddess stuff."

In her talk with *Playboy*, Cher also attempted to put to rest the perception that she was promiscuous—or as she put it, "an easy lay." "For the record, I think sex is a dumb thing unless you love somebody. I mean, I see some of these magazines with naked guys standing around looking like real assholes and I wonder how in the world any woman could get turned on. They all look like Ken dolls. I would never make it with some guy I just met. The only thing that sees you through life is a relationship with someone, so to fuck without any feeling or love is, to me, just plain stupid."

Not stupid at all, and in spite of the fact that her show had diminished ratings, were the many offers Cher received to expand on her solo television success. As reported in *The Hollywood Reporter*, producer/director Roger Corman approached Cher with the idea of having her star in a remake of the 1915 Theda Bara film *A Fool There Was*. Other offers, all of which she turned down, included television producer Barry Weitz's proposal for Cher to play a "cross-country lady trucker" on the TV series *Movin' On*, and requests for Cher to do commercials for cigarettes, hair care products, makeup, designer fashions and feminine hygiene products.

An offer that Cher *did* accept was Mego International Corporation's request to manufacture, promote and internationally distribute a Cher doll—complete with 32 elaborately designed Bob Mackie outfits. "Most of our dolls come from TV shows," explained Mego's Frederick Pierce at the time, "because that's what kids who buy dolls watch—television. Every toy company wanted to get Cher, but we got her. You have to have the star's faith that you'll properly promote the product."

And they did. It was through saturation TV ads—"Cher the doll with long hair / Cher the doll with gorgeous clothes to wear"—that the Cher doll, a twelve-inch figure with blue-black hair down to the ankles, sold two million units. Writing in *Creem*, columnist Lisa Robinson had a field day talking about the doll. "[Cher] arrived in the mail gowned in long pink polyester, sleeveless and halter necked.

Pink plastic high-heel shoes complete the ensemble, such as it is. The rubber-like skin color is somewhere between hepatitis and mulatto; facial makeup consists of red lipstick, blue eye shadow and blue eyebrows. You could brush your teeth with her eyelashes." In her page-long assessment Robinson also told readers that the Cher doll looked like "one of those voodoo dolls you buy in New Orleans to stick pins in," had "no nipples, the crotch is very Bionic Woman—imprinted on the ass is 'Made in Hong Kong,'" and that she was anxiously awaiting purchase of "the same spectacularly tacky wardrobe that the real Cher has."

Robinson may have been unimpressed with the Cher doll, but young girls felt differently. The doll was so successful that it spawned a cottage industry. Along with a Sonny doll (complete with *his* own wardrobe) there was a "Cher Makeup Center," "Dressing Room," "Travel Trunk," and "Theater-in-the-Round." Also up for purchase was Cher jewelry, a Cher brush and comb set, a Cher makeup box, and a Cher tote-bag. As Mego president Marty Abrams accurately surmised at the time: "When you're dealing with Cher, it isn't the toy business you're talking about; it's *show* business!"

(In 1975 a *paper* doll book illustrated by Glorian Bluhm—who had created books on everyone from Greta Garbo to Mary Tyler Moore—was presented to the Whitman Publishing Company complete with twenty outfits and a redesigned Cher circular logo. The project never made it to print.)

"While she was doing the *Cher* show Cher told me that she had been approached to do her own show in Vegas," remembers Ray Klausen about yet another offer that was sure to be a financial windfall. "I was like 'great' and Cher just looked at me and said, 'It's not going to happen.' She said they were offering her a ton of money but she had no intention of doing it. 'The time isn't right,' she said. 'You don't go to Vegas unless you have a really, really good show.' When she said that I thought, 'Oh man, this really is one sharp woman.'"

George Schlatter, too, wanted to make good use of Cher at her zenith. "I thought she would be perfect in a remake of *Annie Get Your Gun*. On my own, I optioned the property specifically for her. She could sing, dance and look really good. But Cher would have none of it. She thought that musicals were old hat. She didn't see herself doing a period piece. When I told her that I thought she was wrong, that it was a perfect opportunity for her to make the transition from television to film, she said she wanted to stay contemporary and focus on rock and roll. Being a rock and roll star was all that Cher really cared about."

Cher was also courted for the lead in the Barbra Streisand/Kris Kristofferson remake of *A Star Is Born*, as well as the Faye Wray role—ultimately given to newcomer Jessica Lange—in the Dino De Laurentiis 1976 remake of *King Kong*. Of the *King Kong* project, Cher told Rona Barrett, "I thought, 'I'll only get one chance as a serious actress, so I better not waste it playing opposite a giant ape!'"

Show number 26 featured David Essex, Jerry Lewis, Gailard Sartain and Jack

Harrell. It is, without question, one of *Cher*'s most visually stunning episodes. Cher opened the hour with a rousing medley of the Dorothy Fields classic "I Feel a Song Coming On" and the Carpenters' "Sing," followed by a question and answer session with Jerry Lewis. Her opening-number dress was a nude chiffon skirt and criss-cross top with embroidered white Venice lace in a snowflake motif (worn during her solo "All in Love Is Fair" on the premiere episode). In stellar voice, Cher performed her solo, Glen Campbell's "Rhinestone Cowboy," on an elaborate cityscape set complete with neon signs that read "Bail Bonds," "Bar," and "Hotel," expressively conveying the tune's melancholy and looking gorgeous in a head-to-toe rhinestone ensemble.

Twenty-seven-year-old David Essex's appearance on *Cher* generated a great deal of excitement. In his native England he was a teen idol, pin-up boy *and* genuine talent who broke through when he appeared in the 1974 film *Stardust*, and then hit the top of the Pop charts with his eerie-voiced "Rock On." His popularity in the UK was such that five members of the British press were flown in to cover his appearance on *Cher*. On the show Essex performed his newest single "Hold Me Close," and joined Cher in a superior rendition of Paul McCartney's "The Long and Winding Road" (covered by Cher on 1973's *Half-Breed*).

The Cher/Essex duet was as exciting to watch as it was to listen to. Standing amidst a forest of towering white trees, the two dashing figures were positioned center-stage on a fuchsia-colored set. Writing about his memories in his autobiography *A Charmed Life*, Essex said: "Cher was fine. I can't remember the duet that we did together but I do remember that I had to do this comedy sketch with Jerry Lewis, with me dressed as a cowboy. It was lousy."

Jerry Lewis (in his second appearance) provided most of the episode's comedy. He played an unsuspecting moviegoer in a theater that was showing a film that featured "Feel-Around," a new technology that enabled viewers to actually experience what is happening on the screen, and did a pantomime with Cher in "Two Lost Souls: Silence Is William Holden," a sketch about two lonely people who meet in a park. A trio of "Trashy Lady" sketches (divided by musical interludes featuring Cher singing Billy Barnes and Earl Brown's "Trashy Ladies" from show number one) was also fun. Cher and Lewis played in "Tarzan and Jane," "Samson and Delilah," and performed with David Essex in "Ma Barker." The trio also performed in a western-themed sketch (the one that Essex characterized as "lousy") in which Jerry Lewis played a Jewish Sheriff, Cher (in full war bonnet and loin cloth) played Running Bear—an Indian Princess—and David Essex played a cowboy.

CHER: Listen, are we still getting married today?

JERRY: Are you asking me if we're still getting married today? Are you asking me that? Me? Are we getting married today? Is that what you want to know, Running Bear?

CHER: No, I want to know it standing here with all my clothes on.

(Filmed and banked for use later in the season was a "Saturday Night" sketch in which Cher prepared for a dinner date at her apartment.)

Cher show number 27 (filmed in an empty studio in just eight and a half hours) offered viewers a who's who of 1960s pop/rock acts. The guests for the hour were Frankie Avalon (who had appeared on *The Sonny and Cher Comedy Hour* and *The Sonny Comedy Revue*), Pat Boone, Dion, and Frankie Valli (who appeared on both *The Sonny and Cher Comedy Hour* and *Joey and Dad*, the program that replaced *Cher* during the summer of 1975).

Cher opened the show with a medley of Three Dog Night's "An Old Fashioned Love Song" and Peter, Paul and Mary's "I Dig Rock and Roll Music" (performed on *The Sonny and Cher Comedy Hour*) followed by a monologue based on the popular jargon of the '50s and '60s.

The hour's three comedy sketches all centered around the episode's music-related theme. In "The Blackboard Jungle," Cher played a high-school teacher in charge of an unruly classroom. In "Elvis Army Sketch," Gailard Sartain played a long-haired hippie named Elvis Presley. And in "Graduation Party," the entire cast spoofed '50s *Beach Party* movies. (A blackout featuring Cher as the winner of the National Beehive Hairdo contest of 1958 was filmed but never aired.) Pat Boone was no stranger to television. In the '50s he was a singing star and the star of *The Pat Boone Chevy Showroom*—his very own variety series. Looking back, and especially considering the controversy that Cher's revealing costumes had engendered, it's surprising that Boone agreed to appear on *Cher*. At the time, the staunch conservative preacher and Christian activist wrote a monthly column for *Photoplay* entitled "God in Your Life," in which readers wrote in, explained their troubles, and asked for "Christian" advice. One of his columns was called "Sex and Satan on TV", and when *Photoplay* ran the piece they put Cher's photo on the cover! On the show Boone performed a solo, "Magnificent Sanctuary Band," and joined a sedately dressed (a flower pantsuit she wore on *The Sonny and Cher Comedy Hour*) Cher for a duet of another one of his hits, the soul cover "I Almost Lost My Mind."

Dion, formerly of Dion and the Belmonts, was a soulful crooner who, on February 3, 1959, narrowly escaped death when he made the last-minute decision to travel by bus (he wanted to save money) rather than by plane to a concert. The plane on which he was to travel crashed shortly after takeoff, killing everyone onboard; including Buddy Holly, Ritchie Valens and J.P. "The Big Bopper" Richardson.

On *Cher* Dion performed his early hit "The Wanderer" and was joined by Cher on one of his mid-period tunes, "Abraham, Martin and John." "I remember seeing Dion and Cher sing that song on the *Cher* show," recalls songwriter Dick Holler. "Of course I already knew Dion and his work but I've got to tell you that

I was surprised and impressed that Cher was interested in performing such a politically potent song. Their duet made an impression on me and it changed my opinion of Cher."

Frankie Valli, formerly of the Four Seasons, sang a note-for-note live medley of his two current hits: "My Eyes Adored You" and "Swearin' to God." And Frankie Avalon sang his No. 1 hit "Venus" and was joined by Cher on his fun, quirky, purposely nasally novelty tune "Dee Dee Dinah." The program's highlight was a dizzying "'60s Finale" in which Cher, Boone, Valli, Dion and Avalon all participated. Songs included "All I Really Want to Do" and "The Beat Goes On," by Cher, "Love Letters in the Sand" and "April Love," by Boone, "Let's Hang on to What We've Got" and "Working My Way Back ro You, Babe" by Valli and "Ruby, Baby" and "Runaround Sue" by Dion.

"Go Go dancing and '60s dance styles were pretty much my area of expertise," remembers Anita Mann. "I started out as a dancer on shows like *Shindig* and *Hullabaloo*, so it was really fun for me to take a trip back with that episode. We had the dancers all dressed in '60s style clothing and doing '60s moves like the Swim, the Wobble and the Jerk. It was all really visual and really exciting. I thought the number came out great."

Today, Mann remembers more than her concentrated work on the show. "I was there every day looking at what we were blocking and what we were shooting and I must say that the camera just loved Cher. If being a star entails knowing what to do when a camera is filming you, then Cher was always a star—even at this early stage. She gave the camera everything that it wanted and needed. I think that's what people, women in particular, identified with and liked so much about her. In my opinion Cher, as a solo act, came along at just the right time. Her life, her success, and everything she did was a great inspiration to the modern independent-minded woman."

Cher never saw show number 27 When the episode aired she was en route to Buffalo, New York, where, on December 8, she attended yet another sold-out performance by her husband Gregg Allman and his Allman Brothers Band.

28

IT WAS A GOOD YEAR

Cher show number 28 aired just as a major story broke. During November and December Cher had given out two interviews whose focus was her displeasure with CBS. What she didn't know, according to the December 9 edition of *The National Star*, was that, even as she was bad-mouthing the network, CBS executives had already made the decision to cancel her series. Under the banner headline "CBS Bosses Will Ax Cher's Show at the End of Its Run," the paper, whose writers got an exclusive interview with an unnamed CBS insider, informed readers that a combination of bad ratings and Cher's "turbulent marriage" caused millions of viewers to "switch off," thereby making *Cher* a losing commodity. Cher's show, it was agreed by CBS executives, would run through to the end of its second season (May 1976) and then quietly not return in the fall. As *The Star* indecorously put it: "The girl that was launched as one of the brightest stars of the new season, will end it as one of the industry's most astonishing flops."

Cher saw the article, whose inside headline read "The Collapse of Cher's World," and was furious. She called up the paper's editors and vehemently denied that the story was true. "Don't you think they would have told me that the show was going to be chopped?" Cher asked columnist Benjamin Douglas, who printed her response in the newspaper's next issue. "Your story is an outright lie... my show has not been axed."

But even if the story was a lie, it was a lie that had the ring of truth about it. The ratings *were* low, the public *had* switched off, and, to many, Cher, as a solo TV star, had outlived her usefulness. Fresh from her divorce from Sonny, America heralded her as a new liberated woman and waited to see if she could— especially given the fact that Sonny hadn't—make it on her own. When she did, the "curiosity factor" that was so much a part of the buzz around her had significantly diminished. As she later surmised; "After a while, after all the headlines and all the talk about my show, I think a lot of people just wanted me to go away."

But Cher, in *Cher*, didn't go away: at least not yet. *Cher* show number 28 was a comedy-heavy hour that starred Hal Linden, Ruth Buzzi, Glen Campbell, Gailard Sartain and Jack Harrell. Cher opened with a clever medley of the Ray Charles hit "Georgia" and bandleader Ben Bernie's jazz standard "Sweet Georgia Brown," followed by a segment in which she chatted with Ruth Buzzi. Rubber-faced comedienne Buzzi (twice a guest on *The Sonny and Cher Comedy Hour* and a regular on Schlatter's *Laugh-In*) was a TV variety-show favorite. "Laverne Meets Gladys" was filmed on Thursday, November 6, 1975 at 7:30 p.m.–twelve hours after Cher had arrived at the studio. The pairing of Laverne with Buzzi's Gladys Ormphby, a frumpy, homely, hair-netted outcast (a costume designed by Ret Turner) was a great idea. Though not as tight as the similar heavy-on-visuals pairing of Laverne with Flip Wilson's Geraldine, it was, if nothing else, a stellar photo op.

GLADYS: I come here each day to feed the pigeons and the squirrels and the wildlife.

LAVERNE: Well, I haven't seen any pigeons or squirrels around sweet cheeks but I'm very familiar with the wild life.

(Later)

GLADYS: Oh, Laverne, can you fix me up with a date? What about this first number in your little black book.

LAVERNE: I'll give you his number. But don't say I told you to call. I haven't spoken to him in years.

GLADYS: Why? Who is it?

LAVERNE: My husband Harry.

In "Gusto" Buzzi played her character "The Swizzler," a woman who rummages through garbage cans looking for discarded alcoholic beverages, and in "Motorcycle People," Buzzi played a biker dealing with her clumsy biker boyfriend (Gailard Sartain). "Trashy Ladies" featured Buzzi as Scarlett O'Hara in a *Gone with the Wind* spoof—with Cher as Scarlett's befuddled maid Butterfly, and Hal Linden as Rhett Butler.

SCARLETT: [To Rhett] Butterfly and I are gonna stay here and plant the corn, plant the 'taters, pick the cotton, scrub the floors, clean the windows, birth the babies.

BUTTERFLY: Hold it! I don't do floors... I don't do windows... and I don't know nothin' 'bout birthin' no babies.

(Later)

SCARLETT: Rhett! Why are you leaving? Aren't you going to say anything to me?

RHETT: Frankly Scarlett... I don't give a darn. You see, it's the Family Hour, so I can only give a darn. Or a hoot or a heck. I have to wait till nine o'clock until I can give a damn. And I'll be damned if I'm gonna wait that long.

At the time of his appearance Hal Linden was the star of CBS's *Barney Miller*. Like *Cher*, *Barney Miller*—because it aired in the Family Hour—was a program whose scripts were constantly scrutinized. "At 9:00 p.m. you can call a whore a whore, and at 8:00 p.m. she has to be a 'shady lady.' That's all I ever learned from the CBS censors," Linden later observed.

Linden appeared in "The Flying Garbanzos," a return to the kooky troupe of trapeze artists that also featured Cher, Buzzi, Gailard Sartain, Steve Martin, Martin Mull and Jack Harrell, and two more "Trashy Ladies" segments; one featuring Buzzi as Mae West and Gailard Sartain as W. C. Fields, and one featuring Cher as operatic vocalist Jeanette MacDonald and Linden as her singing companion Nelson Eddy. The hour also contained a blackout featuring Jack Harrell and Steve Martin as a judge and a defendant who is accused of stealing sugar.

Cher first met Glen Campbell in the summer of 1965, when Campbell was a session guitarist for Phil Spector. When the singer/songwriter made his way onto *Cher*'s stage he was a pop/country favorite who had also hosted his own television variety series—*The Glen Campbell Goodtime Hour*, on which Sonny and Cher had appeared. In turn, Campbell had been a guest on both *The Sonny and Cher Comedy Hour* and *The Sonny Comedy Revue*. Campbell was as busy on camera as he was off. At the time he was struggling with cocaine and alcohol, in the midst of a divorce from his wife of sixteen years, and carrying on an affair with Sarah Barg, singer/songwriter Mac Davis's wife. He was also, by his own account, homeless. "I lived in a hotel apartment, in downtown L.A., but mostly I lived on the road," he remembered in his autobiography *Rhinestone Cowboy*. "It was no more than a glorified closet. I found myself booking personal appearances to be working. To be doing anything except thinking about my life." Campbell's "busy work" on *Cher* was inspired. He performed "Country Boy (You've Got Your Feet in L.A.") and was joined by Cher for a medley of his tunes "Galveston," "By the Time I Get to Phoenix," "Wichita Lineman," and "Gentle on My Mind"—the latter three of which would all become Grammy Hall of Fame Award-winners.

The show's finale was a musical spoof of soap operas called "Marsha Welby's General Hospital and Boutique." For the extended number Billy Barnes and Earl Brown wrote four original songs: "Marsha Welby's Happy Hospital," "My Heart Is in Your Hand," "Psychomatic Tango" and "Rhythm of the Operating Room." The cast of characters in the finale included Cher as the glamorous and self-centered Dr. Marsha Welby, Hal Linden as her equally self-absorbed husband Dr. Steve Stunning, and Ruth Buzzi as Miss Laverne Blossom, a hapless elderly former movie star.

Before she started filming show number 29, and contrary to her statement to *The National Star*, Cher was aware that a dramatic change was at hand. Although it wouldn't be revealed until the next year, following the taping of the fourth episode of her second season (show number fifteen), she was struck by a bright idea. "All of a sudden I knew what I had to do," she told *TV Guide*. "I picked up the phone and tracked down Sonny who was out doing one-nighters, in Denver, and said, 'Son, I've got this crazy idea… let's work together again!'" Sonny's response: "I thought and I said, 'As long as I know you, Cher, I will never cease to be amazed by you.' Then I said, 'Well, why not?' Doing a show together made a lot of sense. I wasn't having any fun by myself, and I knew the terrible demands on Cher doing a single."

At this new juncture in her life and career, Cher found the idea of working with Sonny again to be both attractive and advantageous. She could return to doing half the work while at the same time retaining her status as a top television star. "I'm no bra burner, I needed his help badly," Cher confessed. "Carrying a show alone every week was exhausting. The ratings weren't that terrific, there was a lot of petty infighting that wasn't doing anyone any good, and the pressures were really, really getting to me."

After Sonny gave the go-ahead, Cher contacted (new) CBS president Robert Wood and made her case. Always on the lookout to repeat what had been successful in the past, the network agreed. Though it would be a bit unusual to have a formerly married couple hosting a TV variety show, they were sold on the idea that a newly-divorced but still friendly Sonny and Cher might accurately reflect the real world and the changing nature of romantic relationships. If Sonny and Cher were game, so was CBS.

Cher's negotiations with Sonny and with CBS remained private: exclusively so. She may have discussed what she was doing with family and friends, but no one who worked on *Cher* knew about them. "Even though I had worked side by side with Cher, and I believe she both trusted and respected me—she personally told me that she did—she did not inform me and I did not find out that she was negotiating with Sonny until we were already deep into what would turn out to be the *Cher* show's final episode," says Lee Miller.

"I knew there was something going on, I just didn't know what. Toward the end there were all these new people hanging around the set; [agents] Ray Katz and Sandy Gallin were among them. Nick Vanoff, a producer who enjoyed taking center stage, was one of the new faces too." In the past, on the *Cher* show, especially during tapings, no one was allowed on set that wasn't needed. The presence of the high-powered Katz, Gallin and Vanoff changed the energy in the studio.

"At one point Vanoff pulled me aside and said, 'When are you going to be through here?'" remembers Miller. "I said 'Tomorrow is the last taping day of the season,' and he said, 'How long will it take you to shut down the show?' I said, 'It depends on exactly what you mean by "shut down."' He looked me sternly in the eyes and said, 'I mean shut it down—let everyone go—it's finished.' I looked right back at him and said, 'Well, I think I could do that for you in a week; five days at the most.' I also said, 'Are you aware that this is going to cost you a lot of money?' And he said, 'Yes, certain people will be paid off; you're one of them. The people who don't have to be paid off, well, they won't be. It's your job to cut them all loose.' And I said, 'You know, this is really cold. No one has been given any advance warning or notice about this,' and Vanoff just said, 'I don't care if it's cold. I'm telling you to do a job. Are you going to do it or not?'" (Katz and Gallin were later hired as Cher's managers; Vanoff would produce the new Sonny and Cher Show.)

The final episode of *Cher*, show number 29 was filmed on Thursday and Friday November 13 and 14. As it turned out, the program was the series' Christmas episode. The guests for the hour were the Hudson Brothers, the Lennon Sisters, Redd Foxx and Chastity Bono. "That last show was a hard one for Cher to finish," remembers Ret Turner. "It wasn't that she was sad about it being the final episode, far from it. It was that she was physically sick the entire week." In fact, during the final week of work on her series, Cher was largely absent. "She didn't want to do costume fittings, she didn't want to rehearse, she didn't want to do any of it anymore."

For those who had spent the past year working with her, the indifference, impatience and edginess that Cher displayed when she did show up that week was out of character. "Because she didn't want to do fittings she told me to pull things that we already had from wardrobe and she would wear them," recalls Turner. "So I pulled this beautiful bias-cut bugle-beaded gown. I knew she had loved it the first time she wore it so I thought there would be no problem. When I brought it to her she dismissed it and said, 'No, that won't work.' And I said, 'What do you mean it won't work—it's absolutely perfect for the show.' She said, 'Give me the damned dress and I'll show you why it won't work.' And she put it on and suddenly I realized why it wouldn't work; the lady was more than a little bit pregnant—and she hadn't told anybody at CBS!" (Every costume that Cher wears on show number 29 was previously worn on *Cher* or *The Sonny and Cher Comedy Hour*.)

Lee Miller had learned of Cher's pregnancy earlier in the season. "I remember she called me in one day and she said, 'Lee, how many more shows do we have between now and the end of the year; how many more dance numbers?' And I said, 'Well, we usually do one for each episode and we've got eight shows left so, between six and eight.' She said, 'Can I do them all at once?' And I said, 'Why would you want to do that?' And she said, 'I'm not going to look that good in a month—I'm pregnant!' So I went and spoke to Anita [Mann] and we doubled up on a few of the production numbers and banked them. I'm glad we did, because just a short time afterwards Cher told me she didn't want to do them anymore. It wasn't that she thought she looked bad, she was just through with it all."

Ironically, at the time she was secretly pregnant and taping her Christmas show, Cher was featured on the cover of two movie magazines with made-up pregnancy stories. *Movie Life*'s cover read: "Cher's Delivery Room Heartbreak—'They've Taken My Baby Away!' Doctors Forced to Reveal Truth About Infant's Birth! Sonny Called In!" While *TV Radio Talk* "informed": "Cher Has Child in Secret Visit to New York! Sonny Rushes to Her Side! Husband Forced to Leave Them Alone!"

Cher opened her final broadcast hour with a medley of Bing Crosby's classic "White Christmas" and "We Need a Little Christmas" from the musical *Mame*. For the number Cher wore a green velvet gown with white-fur trim. Lively, committed, present on camera, there is no clue whatsoever that she is physically ill (due to her pregnancy), cantankerous, or uninterested in the proceedings at hand. Following a monologue about the holiday season, Cher introduced Chastity and their brief mother/daughter exchange was a delight.

Show number 29's segments included "Life with Laverne," in which Laverne is visited by the Ghosts of Christmas Past, "The Complaint Department," in which she was overwhelmed by a hoard of unwanted gifts, and a lovely solo of Alfred Burt's "Some Children See Him." "For that solo number I used poinsettias," remembers Ray Klausen. "I knew this guy in the Valley who grew them and he wanted to get them on a TV show so that he could generate more business. I said, 'Okay,' and I had him bring them to the studio. We surrounded Cher in a sea of bright red poinsettias. It looked absolutely beautiful. After Cher finished taping she went over to her assistant and got a cigarette. She lit it, took a few puffs and then walked over to me. She said, 'I just want you to know that I really liked what you did for this number. Everything looked great.' Then she wished me a happy weekend and walked off the set." Fourteen years would pass before Klausen would talk to Cher again—at the 1989 Academy Awards, which he art directed (in the '80s the title art director was replaced with production designer) and on which Cher capped the evening by presenting that year's Best Picture Oscar.

In his third appearance Redd Foxx, as actor Karl Malden, did a spoof of Travelers Checks commercials and played in two comedy blackouts; one in which he gives Santa Claus directions to Virginia, and a second in which he describes his "best wishes" to all the bigots of the world. Foxx's strongest segment was a sketch in which he played Elmer the Elf discussing the gifts on Santa's VIP list. For Cher, Elmer had "A tablet of marriage licenses—each one made out to

'Whom it May Concern,'" for bigot Archie Bunker of *All in the Family*, he had "a year subscription to *Ebony* magazine and two tickets to a fun-filled vacation at the Harlem Hilton," and for the ever-present CBS censor, he had a giant pencil "and a note telling him where to stick it!"

At the time of their appearance, the Lennon Sisters (Janet, Kathy, Peggy and Dianne) were staples on *The Lawrence Welk Show*. On *Cher* the four sisters were introduced with a black and white clip of them making their TV debut—twenty years earlier. They sang "Star Carol" and performed "Jingle Bells," adopting a variety of foreign accents. "Being on *Cher* was very exciting for us," says Janet Lennon. "Through our many years of performing on TV we had already worked with George Schlatter, Bob Mackie, Ret Turner, Earl Brown, Anita Mann and most of the behind-the-scenes people. The only person on the *Cher* show that we hadn't worked with was Cher!"

"During most of our time together Cher wasn't feeling very well," remembers Kathy Lennon. "Although she had a great attitude she was often nauseous and dizzy. If I remember correctly I think she fainted once. We didn't find out until much later that she was pregnant with Gregg Allman's child."

Making their third appearance on the show, the Hudson Brothers sang "Here Comes Santa Claus" and, behind the scenes, added comic relief. "Cher and the Hudsons were obviously really good friends," says Kathy. "They were always joking around with her and she seemed very happy that they were there. I remember Cher had just come in from shopping at a vintage clothing store. She had found this beautiful old velvet jacket with this exquisite embroidery and she had just finished modeling it for us. The Hudsons came up behind her and, as a joke, took a roll of gaffer's tape and started circling her. They were wrapping her up like a mummy. We all just froze. Of course when they pulled the tape off, the jacket was completely ruined. There were bald spots where the velvet used to be and the embroidery was in tatters. Kathy and I just looked down at the floor while Cher's mouth fell open. She was speechless."

For her part Chastity, as Theresa Twinkle, performed a tap dance. The number didn't go as planned. "Chastity came out wearing this lovely Shirley Temple-type dress," remembers Janet. "She had bows in her hair and a ringlet wig on her head. When it came time for her to perform she shook from head to toe and just stood and cried. Cher quietly went over, sat down, put her on her lap, and in a very soft voice said, 'You don't have to do this honey. Mommy really doesn't care. If you don't want to do it you don't have to.' Even though she, herself, was not feeling well, Cher was so sensitive and so sweet. She never once pushed Chastity. She said, 'If you want, you can just sit right here by mommy's side and we'll both just announce this next number.' I was very touched by how patient and loving Cher was with her daughter."

For the Christmas finale, Cher (wearing the very first gown she ever wore on the show—the white, tulle and rhinestone opening-number ensemble from show number one) is in excellent form, vamping with the Lennons, who sing "Santa Baby" and "Silent Night," having fun with the Hudsons, who sing "I've Got Your Love to Keep Me Warm," and cuddling with Chastity. Other tunes in the "Old Fashioned Christmas Ball," which was performed on a 1940s nightclub set with a snowy cityscape visible in the background, included: "Here Comes Santa Claus," "Let It Snow," and "Santa Claus Is Coming to Town (see Appendix for complete listing).

"After we finished the Christmas episode, I kept waiting and waiting for the new script to come but it never did," remembers Ray Klausen. "I thought, 'Oh, no. It's going to be another one of those weeks where I have to do everything in three days.' I certainly had no idea that there was never going to be another script. I remember asking Lee, 'What's going on with the new script?' and he said it wasn't ready. Then, sometime later, he came to me and told me that we were all fired. I couldn't believe my ears. I said, 'What are you talking about? Is this a joke?' Lee told me that it had nothing to do with my performance, or any of our performances, but that the series had been 'discontinued' and that Cher was probably going to reunite with Sonny. It was terribly upsetting to me. The idea that all these people at CBS had known what was going on—they were all talking about it, negotiating, planning—but they didn't tell any of us. It made me sick. I had learned so much on that show and I was proud of my work. I loved Cher, and the series had given me my very first Emmy. I didn't want it to end. But it was a done deal."

"There was no party or anything like that. How could there be? Nobody told us anything," says a stagehand. "When we finished taping that Christmas number the director told us to strike the set, and we did. We all went home completely unaware that the *Cher* show was finished."

29

THE BEAT GOES ON

Following the broadcast of Cher's Christmas episode and with filming of the series "suspended," CBS found themselves in the unusual position of having to instantly fill five hours of Prime Time. The five weeks that followed *Cher's* final original broadcast were filled with two repeat *Cher* episodes, numbers 18 and 28, repeat broadcasts of two films—*Tom Sawyer* and *Addie and the King of Hearts*—and already-in-the-can coverage of *The Monte Carlo Circus Festival*.

"There was no closure on the *Cher* show," remembers Ray Klausen. "That's for sure. One day it was on and the next it was off." And the lack of closure extended to TV viewers. Cushioned from the truth by the two repeat episodes that played after the final original broadcast, it was *TV Guide*, rather than Cher, CBS or her show's producers, that delivered the news that *Cher* had been deleted from the CBS lineup. The edict, included in *TV Guide's* synopsis of the final (repeat) airing, was plain and simple: "This is the last show of the series. Next month, Cher is scheduled to be joined by Sonny Bono in a reprise of their variety series."

Writing in the March 1976 edition of *Creem*, Lisa Robinson praised Cher and her solo series. "On her own Cher was becoming a truly interesting performer and a really good comedienne... sexy... fascinating. It's always interesting to see how she copes, and where she fits. The fact remains that *Cher* was the closest thing to 'rock' regularly broadcast on Prime-Time TV."

But there were those that remained unimpressed. "Tragic how they pumped her into grotesquerie, poured her into two tons of Moll Flanders and outsize wigs," wrote Marie Brenner in the February 1976 edition of *New Times*. "They made her kabuki theater and tried to clean her up. For comedy she threw bricks at a Frigidaire or pretended that she couldn't get a date... her solo TV series was ludicrous."

Neither ludicrous nor tragic was the fact that Cher, via her solo series, succeeded at what she had set out to do. Operating within the strict confines of a cut-throat industry, Cher proved both her versatility and her survival skills. Additionally, during *Cher*'s year-long run (and without Sonny by her side) she completed 29 monologues, 26 solo musical numbers, five solo concerts/medleys, seven choreographed music/dance numbers, 59 duets, and 117 comedy sketches. "Cher's show went off the air because, in the end, it just wasn't consistent and it wasn't very good," surmised Bob Mackie in 2000. "One week we'd have Jean Stapleton and George Burns and the next week we'd have Gregg Allman and some other rock band—which was a totally different audience. Viewers were never quite sure what they were going to see when they tuned in and that wasn't a good thing. They didn't want a show that was *that* varied."

George Schlatter's feelings about the series' cancellation are best illustrated by a handwritten note found in his *Cher* notebook. It reads: "Fifteen shows done this season. New show with Sonny in February. Drop everybody."

Originally the "press" announcement that Sonny and Cher were professionally reuniting was planned for Wednesday, December 3, 1975, but protracted negotiations resulted in a 24-hour delay. Part of the deal to bring the two together again included an agreement that both parties drop their lawsuits against one another. Cher also agreed to go on tour with Sonny in the spring of 1977 (and make a minimum of 101 personal appearances over a three-year period). Cher's half of the proceeds made from the Sonny and Cher reunion tour (he was guaranteed $1.5 million via performances or in cash via Cher) would go directly to Sonny to make up for the financial loss he claimed he suffered when the Sonny and Cher act was negated.

"I'm producing a show but I'm living a soap opera," admitted George Schlatter, who like Lee Miller and Ray Klausen was one of the last to find out about the reunion. "Cher is a little bit like a Roman candle—unpredictable. Three divorces and three reunions—one with her former husband—in the span of a year, has got to be something of a record, even in this town!" Schlatter was not asked to work on the new Sonny and Cher show but, in print, he wished her well: "I still love Cher, and I firmly believe that she and Sonny belong together. I wish them both nothing but success."

Lee Miller was another top-tier *Cher* staffer that did not make the transition to the new show. "I remember Cher and I talked about me coming on board for the new series," says Miller. "She told me that she really wanted me and [writer] Iris Rainer to continue working with her. I told her that it would be very hard for me to continue, especially given the way the cancellation of her solo series was handled. I told her, 'I don't see myself resurfacing as part of your new show after hiring and then firing all these people. They are, at least *were*, my friends.' Then she told me that Nick Vanoff was producing the new show. That was the very first time I had heard his name associated with her. I had seen him hanging around the last taping of *Cher* but had not been informed about exactly why he was there. I told Cher that working with Nick would be difficult. Years later he and I were friendly, but at the time we didn't connect. Cher asked Nick to call me and discuss the matter. He did. He told me that he wanted me to work on the new Sonny and Cher show as executive in charge of production and that he was going to be the producer. I said, 'So, let me get this straight. You're asking me to take a step backwards—to accept a demotion?' and he said, 'Yes, that's essentially true.' And I said, 'Well my goodbye is essentially true too—so goodbye!'

"I called Cher the next morning and told her that I loved her and that I loved working with her, but I didn't think it was right to ask me to go backwards. I said, 'I just can't do that—it's wrong.' Cher told me that she was unhappy I wouldn't be joining her but that she understood. We parted as friends and she and Nick found someone else."

Sonny and Cher announced their reunion at a press conference that was held at the Beverly Wilshire Hotel in Los Angeles. "Surrounded by agents and lawyers, and apparently realizing that nothing, not even divorce, should stand in the way of a profitable partnership, the couple have been reunited before the altar of potential ratings," reported *The New York Times*. The press conference was a well-attended media event that produced photos of the couple standing at an ivory-colored podium—both dressed in white suits. At the gathering a reporter asked Cher how she felt doing her own show after splitting with Sonny. "Speaking for myself, I enjoyed the show." Sonny then quipped: "You better speak for yourself!" And Cher came back with: "I know—I saw yours!" The old repartee was certainly there. Were they nervous? Cher was matter of fact: "I feel more nervous with you [the throng of reporters] than I do with Sonny."

"You know why Cher and I are so interesting?" Sonny asked *TV Guide's* Rowland Barber. "It's because our lives are laid open for the public. Cher and I have no secrets. When we go out there for the first time, we'll be telling them everything they already knew about us but were afraid to ask."

Presenting the now-divorced couple in the same format that they inhabited while married put everyone involved to the test. "If *you* think it's confusing, imagine what the show's writers are going through," said Nick Vanoff at the time. "They've been locking themselves in a conference room for eight hours a day trying to sort out their ideas. The overall concept of the show will be similar to the old *Sonny and Cher Comedy Hour*, but of course the many new influences in their lives have to come into it as well."

Cher's newly announced pregnancy was a major concern for everyone. "It was still all unresolved as we went into rehearsals," Vanoff informed. "We have looked at the problem from all possible angles and decided that we should play it as it broke. We didn't want to lay down any hard and fast rules."

In a *Washington Post* article entitled "Cher: Great Expectations," Cher's agent Dick Grant offered up *his* opinion about Cher's newly "delicate condition." "I don't think Cher will show until the eighth or ninth month because she's so slender and so tall. I just saw her over the weekend and she's still bone-skinny. If it does show Cher will dress accordingly." When asked whether or not Sonny and Cher would trade on-air quips about her pregnancy, Grant replied: "Maybe, maybe not." They did:

SONNY: I'm worried about you performing in your delicate condition.

CHER: Oh, really? I thought I was putting up a pretty good front.

As the many discussions about how to handle Sonny and Cher's reunion continued, the deadline for taping their premiere broadcast was rapidly approaching. In fact, the format in which the "new" Sonny and Cher were going to be presented had not been agreed upon until the day before the actual taping. "Obviously a one-week lead-in time doesn't allow much room for mistakes," said Vanoff. "But I must say that I believe we've assembled one of the best teams ever packaged in Hollywood."

At the same time that Sonny and Cher's reunion was making waves, *Sonny and Cher Comedy Hour* producer Chris Bearde was doing the same. Apparently he had a falling out with the duo—and he went to the press with it. "I wouldn't work with Sonny and Cher again for a million dollars," Bearde, who was riding high on the success of the syndicated *Bobby Vinton Show*, fumed. "They were nothing but trouble. The problem is that Sonny and Cher are just too off-the-wall. I don't care if their new show succeeds or fails."

"I don't care what Chris says or how he feels," Vanoff rejoined. "I'm going to use a different format than Chris did and I've been assured by Sonny and Cher that they will give me all the cooperation I'll need." The cooperation came from people who had nothing to do with Cher's past. Aside from Bob Mackie, Ret Turner and Rena—all of whom pretty much worked exclusively for Cher—only two were hired from *Cher*: lighting director Jim Beam and (much to his surprise) "regular" Gailard Sartain. Director Bill Davis, who had done a stellar job on the final episodes of *Cher*, was replaced with Tim Kiley (*The Ed Sullivan Show*, *The Flip Wilson Show*). Art director Ray Klausen, who brought the second season of *Cher* to a whole new level of visual splendor, was replaced with Gene McAvoy and Jim Tompkins. Choreographer Anita Mann, who was comfortable working with Cher and wanted to continue, was replaced with Jaime Rogers (who, toward the series' end, took over directorial duties). And the new collection of writers chosen by Vanoff to replace the "old, the past" included Barry Silver, Stuart Gillard, Coslough Johnson, Bob Arnott and Jeannine Burnier.

Advertisers weren't afraid of the divorced Sonny and Cher. The impressive list included Revlon (*Cher*'s major sponsor), Buick, Chrysler, Coca Cola, Singer Sewing Machines, Quaker Oats, Avon Cosmetics and Burger King.

In the midst of all the tumult and sensational headlines—"Chaos: Confusion and Doubt Plague Comeback" declared *TV-Hotline*—on Sunday, February 1, 1976, at 8:00 p.m., *The Sonny and Cher Show* premiered in the time slot vacated by *Cher*—an unprecedented turn of events if ever there was one. "Ladies and gentleman, together again for the first time… Sonny and Cher," boomed the announcer's voice at the top of their premiere episode, and the hour that followed, chock-full of cameos (Jerry Lewis, Jim Nabors, Rona Barrett), rapid-fire editing and sight gags (Tony Orlando playing Sonny's supportive Aunt Rosa), was exciting.

There was music; Sonny and Cher's ironic opening number, the Captain and Tennille's "Love Will Keep Us Together," and Cher's not so ironic "Breaking Up Is Hard to Do," on-point comedy, and a glossy new, elaborately-designed cyclorama that spelled out SONNY AND CHER and featured an illuminated hand with crossed fingers for good luck (an appropriation of the long-running CBS game show *To Tell the Truth*'s logo).

"The new Sonny and Cher show should be highly entertaining but they are bucking long odds," observed an unnamed CBS executive in an extensive *Daily News* interview. "For one thing, they will still be in the restrictive Family Hour. That will limit their free-wheeling efforts, and the CBS censor will watch them just as carefully as he did when he had Cher's solo series under the microscope. For another thing, the show is running opposite *The Six Million Dollar Man*, which is entrenched as leader in that particular time slot. For the first couple of weeks, viewers may turn to Sonny and Cher out of curiosity, but then I foresee them switching back to Lee Majors and his series. In addition, the NBC network has quietly moved the well-done *Ellery Queen* detective series up against both shows. As I see it, the detective show will take viewers away from Sonny and Cher, too. I believe CBS made a major blunder by not scheduling Sonny and Cher at a later time or on a different night."

And, true to the executive's predictions, the very first Sonny and Cher show rated a lofty No. 7 in the Nielsen ratings. The second broadcast rated a respectable No. 9. It was, however, the third broadcast that told the truth; it came in at No. 38.

Neil Sedaka was a guest on the third broadcast. "I was delighted to be asked to be on the show. I watched *The Sonny and Cher Comedy Hour*, Cher's solo show, and now here I was on their new show. It was marvelous." On the program Sonny and Cher joined Sedaka for a five-song medley of his tunes. "I didn't choose the songs but I thought the choices were great—very eclectic. 'Calendar Girl' took me back to the beginning and 'Breaking Up Is Hard to Do' was on the charts at the time. It was a Neil Sedaka salute!" (Indeed it was: Cher chose Sedaka's "Solitaire" as her solo number.) Another song that Sedaka and Sonny and Cher performed together was the melancholy ballad "The Hungry Years."

"Not many people know this but Howie [Greenfield] and I wrote that song about Sonny and Cher and their breakup," reveals Sedaka. "It's a song about a show business couple who reach the top but are empty. They look back and long for the hungry years; the years when they were struggling, longing, and striving toward a goal. I don't remember if I ever even told Sonny and Cher that they were the inspiration for that song. Maybe I didn't need to: maybe it was clear to them."

All in all, *The Sonny and Cher Show* ran for almost a full year—from February 1976 to March 1977. In the span of just thirteen months the show played in three different time slots—Sundays at 8:00, Fridays at 9:00, and Mondays at 10:00. "Our show fell into the willy-nilly hands of the network brain trust," wrote Sonny in *And the Beat Goes On*. "They kept switching us from one time slot to another like a pawn in a chess game."

Series highlights included appearances by Tina Turner, the Jackson Five (featuring Michael Jackson)—now called "The Jacksons"—and Glen Campbell (all of whom had appeared on *Cher*), as well as Tom Jones, Debbie Reynolds, Diahann Carroll, Engelbert Humperdinck and the soul band the Sylvers. Outstanding Cher solos included "The Way We Were," "Something," "I Honestly Love You," and "Danny's Song," while Sonny and Cher shined bright on a string of spirited tunes, including a perfectly-pitched rendering of the Beatles' "The Two of Us" (a.k.a. "On Our Way Home") and "We Can Work It Out." Farrah Fawcett-Majors made her very first (post-*Charlie's Angels*) television appearance on the show. So did Cher's new bouncing baby boy, Elijah Blue Allman, and Sonny and Cher's longtime music arranger, friend and confidant Harold Battiste. Chastity was a regular as was comedian Ted Zeigler and mimes Shields and Yarnell (regulars on *The Sonny and Cher Comedy Hour*).

With the March 18, 1977 airing of the final episode of the series—an hour that featured clips from the past season—Sonny and Cher's tenure as television stars came to a close. "CBS has a marvelous relationship with Sonny and Cher," said CBS's new president Robert Wussler at the time. "But, for the moment, their entertainment career is headed toward nightclub appearances and records. However, I anticipate the day when they will both be back on television."

"I thought the Sonny and Cher reunion series was a good idea," says George Schlatter. "Though, the truth of the matter is that you can't ever really go back. You can't make wrong things right. People have to, if they hope to flourish, keep moving forward."

"I think it was time for them to pack it up and go do something else," remembered Bob Mackie in 2000. "They were trying to do what they used to do and it just wasn't funny anymore."

Lee Miller has the final word: "I watched the very first episode of *The Sonny and Cher Show* and I never watched it again. After I saw the show I said to myself, 'That show is going to last for all of five episodes.' It lasted a bit longer than that, but what did it matter? From the very beginning it looked like a dead duck. Cher looked unhappy, and I personally heard from people who were working on the show that she was. The fun of doing a TV variety series—and for that mater of working with Sonny—was totally gone for her. And it showed on her face.

Previous Page: Dance, sister, dance! Clad in her "Road Runner on acid"-style get-up, Cher was lowered from the ceiling on a rope to perform one of the Cher show's most elaborate numbers: a medley of "Witchy Woman" and "Honky Talk Woman." (Photo Fair)

Above: And the winner is? "They were in competition to see who was going to wear the least," recalls producer George Schlatter of Raquel Welch and Cher–shown here performing "I'm a Woman." Below: The Showman and his Muse: Laverne shows up on Liberace's doorstep, demanding a personal tour of the icon's home. This marks the one and only occasion that Cher went on location. (J. Howard Collection; CBS-TV)

Above: on their second appearance, Labelle noted that Cher wasn't quite herself. There was a reason: the strain of her on-off relationship with Gregg Allman—as played out in the tabloids. Below: A revealing pantsuit and a flop album. Despite the beautiful cover portrait—courtesy of Interview magazine's Bill King, no one bought the hotly anticipated, Jimmy Webb-produced Stars. The album "peaked" at No. 153 on the charts. (Photo Fair; TV Time)

Above: In her element: Cher, satin-clad, surrounded by feathers, and, belting out the appropriately-titled "Keep the Customer Satisfied." (Photo Fair)

Opposite: Cover Girl: During the run of her solo series, Cher appeared on the cover of over 200 magazines including Time (deemed "pornographic" and removed from newsstands in Florida).

Above: Hostess with the most-ess: Dancing in a geometrical, multi-colored jumpsuit (left) and holding court in a fire-engine red, embroidered velvet gown (right). The tan was the result of an impromptu three-day trip to Hawaii. (Nostalgia Network; J. Howard Collection)

Opposite: "She's got the best armpits in the business," Bob Mackie once said of Cher... even when lost in thought during a break in taping. (J. Howard Collection)

Above: Encore! Still gorgeous at 54,
Cher in 2000, out promoting Believe,
the biggest single and album of her entire
career. Below: Cher back in films (and still
singing) at the Los Angeles premiere
of 2010's Burlesque. (Photo Fair;
DFree /Shutterstock)

Frankly speaking, I always wondered if Nick Vanoff, who put the show together for them and encouraged them to do it, ever really believed that it would be a success. I wondered if he was just in it for the money, because it really was a profoundly stupid idea."

In a 2003 interview, *Sonny and Cher Comedy Hour* producer Chris Bearde revealed that the Nick Vanoff regime was ruthless. After it was clear that the show was failing, Vanoff attempted to find replacements for his hand-picked talent. "They called me up and asked me to come in and help," remembered Bearde. "I said, 'Under no circumstances will I work for you. Did you tell the guys that are working on the show with you that you are calling me to replace them?' They said 'no,' and I said, 'Then I'm not even going to entertain this conversation.' I got off the phone and called up everyone I knew that worked on *The Sonny and Cher Show*. I said, 'Are you aware that your boss is on the phone talking to people like me to come in and replace you?' I never heard back from any of them."

"They dropped our option," Sonny informed *The Washington Post* about *The Sonny and Cher Show*'s unceremonious cancellation after 33 episodes. "It didn't come as a surprise, but it *was* disappointing." Sonny and Cher received the news that their TV series was cancelled while on the road performing their brief, and as it turned out, aborted reunion tour.

"Television is a really, really tough business," observes journeyman photographer Julian Wasser. "Every single week you're starting all over again from the very beginning. It's not like a film that you finished a year or maybe even two years before, and all you have to do after the fact is go out and promote it. TV is constant. Everyone is always looking at the ratings and whatever the ratings are that week directly affects your experience working on the show—and with the people in charge of the show. Cher was huge in the '70s—with and without Sonny—and the '70s were a wonderful time, so creative and so free. But that world was slipping away when Sonny and Cher tried to reunite—and it's totally gone now—like it never happened. All that remains are the memories that people have, the stories they have to tell and the pictures that have been left behind."

Reflecting on her television years, Cher is of two minds. "I don't love the work I did on TV, but I'm not ashamed of it either," she observed in a 2001 two-hour syndicated radio broadcast called "The Cher Story." "It's all so long ago, and I don't remember it like other people do. A lot of things were going on in my life. The thing with Sonny, and me going it on my own and everything. I remember seeing an article in a British paper [*The London Observer*] and they were talking about me living in a mansion and having five cars and owning thousands of gowns and hundreds of pairs of shoes. It made me seem so shallow, so superficial. I read it and then I threw it in the garbage. And then I just sat and cried.

"The truth is that TV is a grind from beginning to end. You don't have a life. There are constant hassles, negotiations, things you can and can't do. I remember when [the second] Sonny and Cher show ended, it was such a relief. I had no idea what I was going to do, but at least I had free time to *think* about what I was going to do. What I did on television wasn't really important. It wasn't the cure for cancer. It wasn't even particularly polished; we were really just having fun. But it did provide people with an escape. For an hour, or maybe even just for five minutes, they were entertained. And I think that that's a good thing."

So was, it was thought, an album that came out while *The Sonny and Cher Show* was still on the air. *I'd Rather Believe in You*, Cher's second Warner Bros. album, was produced by Steve Barri (who the same year produced John Sebastian's "Welcome Back" and Rhythm Heritage's "Theme From S.W.A.T.", both No. 1 hits) and Michael Omartian. Under-promoted (uninventive ads read "Cher a little... Cher a lot...") and an uncontestable flop (the album never charted) *I'd Rather Believe in You* was, nevertheless, a modern-sounding, fully realized music project.

"Long Distance Love Affair" (B-side "Borrowed Time") was the collection's first and only single. An upbeat pop production with a driving bass drum and an irresistible guitar riff, the song told the story of what sounded like Cher and Gregg Allman's relationship. It didn't chart. Even though *Melody Maker* called it "an excellent song performed with gusto," and even though Cher performed it twice on *The Sonny and Cher Show*, the single, like the album, went completely unnoticed.

"I get more people complimenting me about that album than on so many other things that I've done that were way more successful," says Barri. "With that album we tried to present Cher as a straight singer. We wanted to get away from the novelty story songs that she had done before. Our game plan was to start with 'Long Distance Love Affair' and follow up in a big way with the ballad 'I'd Rather Believe in You'—which we all thought was fantastic and would take Cher to another level. But that never happened. It's a shame. We really thought the whole package would be a smash."

"I wrote 'Flashback' with Artie Wayne," remembers Alan O'Day, whose reflective song was included on *I'd Rather Believe in You*'s second side. "For me, 'Flashback' is a personal confession; filled with my own ideas and memories. I was really happy with Cher's recording of it. They included everything—all the spacey musical sound effects—that were present in my original demo. I thought it really came together nicely."

An even bigger flop than *I'd Rather Believe in You* was Sonny and Cher's one and only post-divorce "reunion" single—which was also released during the run of *The Sonny and Cher Show*. Entitled, appropriately enough, "You're Not Right for Me" (B-side "Wrong Number"), the song was written by Sonny and envisioned (by Warner Bros. and CBS) as a tie-in television product. But even with a filmed lip synch on *The Sonny and Cher Show*, "You're Not Right for Me" landed with a thud. The lack of interest guaranteed that a planned (post-divorce) Sonny and Cher reunion album would never happen.

EPILOGUE

The years that followed Sonny and Cher's tenure as television performers were filled with the realisation of long-held dreams and the discovery of new ones.

At the same time that the post-divorce *Sonny and Cher Show* was canceled, Sonny and Cher went out on the road to make good on their agreed upon touring commitments. Following a dry-run in Los Angeles in December 1976 they premiered their revived act on March 19, 1977 at the Blaisdell Memorial Center in Honolulu, Hawaii. The duo's fifteen-song set included "All I Ever Need Is You," "The Beat Goes On," and "I Got You Babe" as well as Cher singing her solo hits "The Way of Love" and a medley of "Gypsys, Tramps and Thieves," "Half-Breed" and "Dark Lady." Sonny even had a solo spot: "Laugh at Me" and there were home movies of Chastity during costume changes.

One particular night didn't go as planned. "Our whole show—all our comedy—is arranged so that I talk about something for a very long time and then at the end of it all, Cher hits me with a zinger," Sonny explained. "Well, on this particular night, Cher and I had an argument. So I get out there and am doing the act, rambling on for about ten minutes and when it came time for her to drop the bomb—she doesn't say a word! It's just me up there talking about nothing. This went on for the entire show! People were looking at us like 'what the hell is going on here?'"

Sonny and Cher's tour got middling reviews. When the show came to Long Island's Westbury Music Fair they held a press conference that offered a clear view of what was happening behind the scenes. Cher, dressed in her spectacular turquoise and gold opening-number gown, stood next to Sonny—with a scowl on her face. Sonny looked no better. "I didn't want to go on the road with him," Cher frankly admitted a year later, "but I had no choice. I still owe him about

$200,000 on the lawsuit he won after we divorced, and I'll find some other way to pay it off. I just can't handle any more of that."

1977 was also the year that Cher collaborated with Gregg Allman—still her husband but increasingly less so—on a collection of tunes, *Two the Hard Way*, that was released on her label, Warner Bros. "Move Me" was the first single by Allman and Woman. It didn't make a mark. Nor did a planned 29-day promotional tour of Europe. After just a week out on the road, Cher and Gregg returned to the States resigned to the fact that their combined talents had no audience. "Cher's fans came in tuxedos and gowns and my fans came in cut-offs wearing back packs," Allman later observed. He also had questions about the merits of Cher's vocals. "I'm really glad that she never asked me what I felt about her singing," he confessed in his 2012 autobiography. "I'm sorry; she isn't a very good singer."

They didn't make it as husband and wife either. In January of 1978 Cher was quietly (and it *was* quietly; the press, bored with the never-ending Cher and Gregg saga, barely covered it) granted a divorce. "Dead weight starts out as dead weight and ends up just the same," Cher said. She later observed: "I don't know why I waited so long."

Today, Cher remembers her creative partnership with Gregg Allman fondly. "I really loved being in the studio with Gregory. I really loved making [*Two the Hard Way*] but that album didn't stand a chance, did it? I mean, everybody hated that we were together. It just didn't stand a chance." Gregg Allman's view of the project is different. "It was terrible, just awful. That record sucked, man. That's the truth and I knew it as well as anyone else."

Two the Hard Way wasn't 1977's only disappointment. In the shadow of that failure came another: her third and final solo Warner Bros. album, *Cherished*. "Pirate" (B-side "Send the Man Over") was the album's first single—a return to the melodramatic story song format. It peaked at No. 93.

"Snuff hired me to write songs for *Cherished*," remembers Sandy Pinkard, whose biggest credit would come four years later with the No. 1 country tune "You're the Reason God Made Oklahoma," performed by David Frizzell and Shelly West. "I got together with a few of his in-house writers [John Durrill, Cloretta Kay Miller and Al Capps] and we wrote three songs: 'War Paint and Soft Feathers,' 'Dixie,' and 'Thunderstorm.' No one at Warner Bros. believed in the second single, 'War Paint and Soft Feathers,' or for that matter, the album. There was no promotion, no TV, no nothing. Still, what a great time it was for me to know that Cher was recording songs that I had written."

Today *Cherished*, a failure on all fronts and a collection of tunes that was skewered in *Rolling Stone* and *Creem*, remains a fan favorite—not for its music, but for the beautiful Harry Langdon cover photo. A head-to-toe shot (head to waist on the front cover, waist to feet on the back) Langdon's picture encapsulated

1970s Cher; long flowing hair, plaintive expression, jeans, silver high heels, and multi-colored Indian-inspired feathers. "*That* should have been the 'Half-Breed' album cover," observes an ardent Cher fan. "But it was four years too late and no one even knew that the album was out."

Snuff Garrett, apparently, agreed. "I had no idea why [Warner Bros.] contacted me to do that album. I told them that I thought it was too late to reclaim the sound that we had with 'Half-Breed' and all the other songs we did together. Cher wasn't into it at all and she complained about the material we had chosen. Her attitude was: 'I'm committed to Warners to do this, and I'll do it, but I ain't gonna like it.'"

1978 was the year that Cher filed to have her name legally changed—to just "Cher." Gone now, both legally and symbolically, were all of her previous incarnations; LaPiere, Sarkisian, Bono, and Allman. "I don't need any one else's name behind mine," she professed. "And no, it's not 'Ms. Cher' or 'Madame Cher,' it's just plain Cher." That year was also the year she returned to television. Her one-hour special was straightforwardly called *Cher... Special*.

"I was terrified when we were taping the show last week," Cher told Marilyn Beck. "I was really afraid I'd show I didn't have it, convinced that I was ugly, untalented, couldn't sing, that I had extended myself too far."

Unfortunately, more than one reviewer believed she had. *Variety* wrote: "Cher's first TV special seemed excessively self-indulgent and likely to turn off more people than it turned on. The big production number, Cher performing all the parts of *West Side Story*, turned out to be no musical treat. And from there on it was downhill..." *The Daily News*' Kay Gardella (usually a Cher fan) agreed. "To hear Cher's rasping, deep tones fight to reach the high notes in *West Side Story*, like a captain of a sinking ship shouting his last orders, is an experience not easily forgotten. It's an ego trip all the way. Cher bombs so badly that one wonders who the guiding force was behind this atrocious hour." Guests on Cher's special included Dolly Parton, Rod Stewart (in 2003 Stewart and Cher dueted on the jazz standard "Bewitched, Bothered and Bewildered") and the Tubes.

Just a year after *Cher... Special*, Cher was back on television in *Cher... and Other Fantasies*, an hour of song and dance that featured cameos by Lucille Ball, Andy Kaufman, Elliott Gould and Shelley Winters. *The New York Times* observed: "Long before the hour is over viewers may be wishing to return from Cher's fantasies to the real world."

When *Cher... and Other Fantasies* aired Cher was riding high with the No. 7 disco hit "Take Me Home" (B-side "My Song [Too Far Gone]"). "[Casablanca Records president] Neil [Bogart] came to me and told me that he wanted me to write a 'Last Dance' for Cher," remembers songwriter/producer Bob Esty, the man commissioned to take Cher from pop to disco. Esty had arranged Donna Summer's *Once Upon a Time* album and worked with Paul Jabara on both

Summer's "Last Dance" and Barbra Streisand's "Main Event". "It was a strange collaboration; Cher and me," says Esty. "She didn't like disco and she told me so, and I didn't see her as a disco star, and I told *her* so! But Neil had a vision of what she could be and we were both happy to oblige. My partner Michele Aller and I wrote 'Take Me Home' specifically for Cher. It was our idea of her. We thought if she were out and she met a guy that she liked she wouldn't play coy, she'd just go right up to him and say 'take me home.'"

And many people did. "Take Me Home," Cher's biggest hit since "Dark Lady", necessitated a casino and nightclub tour. Summed up by *Variety* as "a lush package and a well-conceived one in which Cher unveils both her new show and considerable portions of her anatomy," for Cher's very first solo outing—no Sonny, no Gregg, just Cher—she was backed by a band, four dancers, three back-up singers, and three female impersonators; J.C. Gaynor as Bette Midler, Russell Elliott as Diana Ross, and Claude Sacha as Cher. Her set included everything from "The Way of Love," and Stevie Wonder's "Signed, Sealed, Delivered, I'm Yours" to the Eagles' "Take It to the Limit" and "Easy to Be Hard" from *Hair*. "'Easy to be Hard' way my idea," says Take Me Home Tour musical director Fred Thaler. "I thought it would be interesting to do it differently than it had usually been performed, so I wrote out an arrangement, she gave me the okay, and it went right into the show. It was a knockout." Fresh from his directorial duties on the Broadway production *Platinum*, Thaler came away from the Take Me Home Tour with a lasting impression. "Having an image of Cher that was strictly from the tabloids, I was very surprised at what I encountered. She was hard-working, professional, warm-hearted, generous, intuitive and tireless."

"Cher's use of female impersonators was pretty daring for the time," says Chad Michaels, America's premier Cher impersonator. "Even though drag and impersonation were familiar to her gay fans, it left many of her straight audiences completely bewildered—especially when there were two Chers onstage. In my opinion Cher was taking a big chance using drag performers and I think she deserves credit for that. She was an inspiration to all of us."

But even with sold-out performances on both coasts—Atlantic City and Washington D.C. in the East; Los Angeles, San Francisco, Reno and Las Vegas in the West, and with performances expanding north and south—Toronto and Australia—Cher's lack of interest in continuing to perform on the nightclub circuit was becoming clear. "Oh, its okay," Cher indifferently informed *The Washington Post*'s Lynn Darling. "I really didn't want to do anything, you know, but they said I should. It's like I better do something alone quick or I never will. So I'm doing what my audience likes me to do. I mean I can't go on doing this forever. It would look really dumb for a 45-year-old woman to be out there doing what I do." (As it turned out, these were words spoken much too soon.)

Cher's apathy might have been due to the fact that, at the same time that she was performing in front of casino crowds and delivering disco tracks to Casablanca—Bob Esty also wrote and produced *Take Me Home's* follow-up album *Prisoner*—she was doing something she said was "much closer to my heart." In 1981 Cher offered herself up as lead singer of the band Black Rose. The album of the same name was released in the fall of 1980 by Casablanca—her final album for the label. Despite a raucous and rocking lead-off single, "Never Should've Started" (B-side "Young and Pretty"), and vigorous promotion—*The Merv Griffin Show*, *The Midnight Special*, *The Tonight Show*—the album and single completely died.

Black Rose was, in many ways, a partnership between Cher and band member Les Dudek. At the time Dudek was a coveted session guitarist (ironically, he played on the Allman Brothers' biggest hit "Ramblin' Man"), a Columbia Records solo recording artist, and member of DFK (the Dudek, Finnigan, Krueger Band). "Apparently Cher always had a dream to be the lead singer in a rock and roll band," says Dudek, who first met Cher at an open audition she held in L.A. He not only joined the band, he helped recruit other band members, suggested producer James Newton Howard, contributed one of the albums' catchiest songs, and became her romantic partner.

"I originally wrote 'You Know It' with Paul and Linda McCartney in mind," says Dudek. "I wanted to pitch it to them for Wings, but since Cher and I became somewhat of an item, and she needed some radio-friendly tunes [potential hits], I suggested we do it as a rock duet." Their collaboration was stellar; "You Know It" sounded just as good as the album's lead-off single. "It was a little high for her to sing, perhaps we should have dropped the key, but I thought it turned out pretty darned good. I heard it was going to be the second single, but that never happened."

"Les is the person I've had more fun with than anybody I ever knew," Cher later said. "He has a wonderful sense of humor. He's really carefree and not very materialistic at all. We just have a good time doing nothing—riding motorcycles and doing nothing." Paparazzi photos confirmed it; pictures of the couple—attending concerts, having late-night dinners, going to the movies—appeared in newspapers and magazines for the better part of two years.

"Someone from my publishing company called me and told me that Cher was at Sunset [Sound Recording Studios]," remembers Fred Mollin, whose tune "Fast Company," written with his brother Larry, appeared on Black Rose's second side. "I worked there a lot. They said she wanted to meet me so I went down and was brought into this little lounge off of Studio Two, which is where I did all my tracks. I was ushered in and there she was: sitting on Les Dudek's lap! She shook my hand and maybe said two words like 'great song.' That was it. I got nothing else. There was no chat, no enthusiasm; just dead silence. I made some small talk, and she and Les just looked at me. I felt like the third man, like they just wanted me to go away. After about a minute I just kind of said an embarrassed goodbye and backed my way out of the room."

Mollin's opinion of Cher's rendering of "Fast Company" was in line with his experience meeting her. "I must admit I wasn't really impressed with the outcome," says Mollin. "First of all the song is about drag racing. What the hell did Cher know about drag racing? Also, I thought it was a very masculine song, very hard-rocking and Springsteenesque. To me, Cher's singing, the mixing, the arrangement, especially the heavy ambient drums, all sounded forced and inauthentic."

Grammy Award-winning songwriter Allee Willis (best known for Earth, Wind and Fire's "September" and "Boogie Wonderland") also contributed a song to the Black Rose project. "I remember thinking that a strictly rock and roll album seemed a bit limiting for Cher," says Willis, who co-wrote "Young and Pretty" with Richard "T Bear" Gerstein (Cher covered Gerstein's "Love and Pain [Pain in My Heart]" on Take Me Home). "But I assumed that she was just going to do what she was going to do." Cher and Willis became friendly via Cher's mid-'80s select-friends-only yard sales; discreet events at which Cher "got rid" of everything from belts and handbags to hats and shoes. "I think Cher and I connected because we had something in common. We both were artistic [along with songwriting Willis is a performance artist and grand matron of the Museum of Kitsch] and because she appreciated that I recognized her as something above and beyond the rest. In my opinion she was the very first multi-media artist; someone who incorporated costumes, dance, music, and outrageous visual ideas into what could have just been good, catchy pop songs." (Cher continued to try and crack the rock market with "Dead Ringer for Love" [B-side "More Than You Deserve"], a UK-only duet with Meatloaf.)

Although no one but Cher seemed to care, throughout the latter part of the '70s Cher quietly pursued film roles. In 1975 Mike Nichols turned her down for a role in The Fortune. In 1978 Cher told Kay Gardella that her name was connected to three films that were in the first draft stage: Jane, A Tough One to Lose, and P.S. 74. At the time, she also described a Jon Peters project called Love Land, a "simple love story that I really want to do." None of the projects came to fruition. In 1979 Cher talked, at length, about developing The Enchanted Cottage, a film she said she had purchased the rights to remake. That project didn't materialize either. Neither did her prospective casting in the 1979 comedy The Fish That Saved Pittsburgh or 1980's Discoland—later re-titled Can't Stop the Music.

Undeterred, in fact more determined than ever to expand on her celebrity and follow her dream—a dream deferred, as it were—in 1981 Cher relocated to New York City. When the famed Dakota (where John Lennon and Aretha Franklin lived) unapologetically turned her away—"They told me they were afraid fans would hang outside by the gate"—she first took a suite at the Pierre

Hotel and then sublet apartments from Gene Simmons (of KISS) and Tom Cruise, both of whom she, for a time, dated.

Acting classes at Lee Strasberg's Actors Studio were part of her schedule. So were private tutoring sessions with Strasberg—who helped her hone her skills for an audition for *I'm Getting My Act Together and Taking it on the Road*.

Robert (*Nashville*) Altman was the man who changed the direction of Cher's career. After learning that she was in town and looking for work, the director asked her to read for his Broadway-bound production of *Come Back to the Five and Dime Jimmy Dean, Jimmy Dean*. She got the part of Sissy, a small-town, good-time girl with a secret. "I was the curiosity factor," Cher later observed. "Everyone wanted to see if I could act—especially up against people like Karen Black and Sandy Dennis. As far as I'm concerned Bob [Altman] is 25-feet high."

On Broadway *Jimmy Dean* received mixed reviews and only lasted for 52 performances, but Cher was on the "serious" acting map. Frank Rich of *The New York Times* said: "Cher gives a cheery, ingratiating, non-performance," while *The Daily News*' Rex Reed enthused: "Cher provides the play with the kind of naturalism it requires. If she learns to project with the same ease and grace, she will have a first-rate characterization to her credit."

Jimmy Dean served its purpose—in more than one way. Even before Altman's filmed version of the play reached theaters, following a matinee on March 17, 1982, director Mike Nichols came backstage to praise Cher's performance and ask if she had any interest in taking a small part in his latest project. The picture, she was told, would star Meryl Streep. Cher said "yes," on the spot—without seeing a script.

A downbeat film about the life and mysterious death of a blue-collar factory worker, 1983's *Silkwood* caught audiences, and Cher fans, off guard. No sequins, no feathers—not even very much makeup, Cher's small but memorable dramatic turn as Dolly Pelliker, Karen's would-be lesbian lover, was rewarded with a Best Supporting Actress Golden Globe Award and a Best Supporting Actress Academy Award nomination (she lost the Oscar to Linda Hunt for her role in *The Year of Living Dangerously*).

Just prior to filming *Silkwood* Cher released *I Paralyze*, her one and only nod to new-wave pop rock. It was hoped that this newest collection would bring her back to the top of the charts. It didn't. Even though the clever first single "I Paralyze" (B-side "Walk with Me") was written and produced by Olivia Newton-John's master technician John Farrar, and even though Cher appeared on *American Bandstand* and *Solid Gold* to promote it, *I Paralyze* made only a quick stop in stores before being relegated to the cut-out bin.

"I never did believe in 'I Paralyze' and I told everyone so," says David Wolfert, producer of eight of the album's nine tracks. "I thought the better choice for a first single would have been the flip, 'Walk with Me.' It had a bigger chance of becoming a success."

"I Paralyze" had actually been preceded by a British-only single from the album entitled "Rudy" (B-side "Do I Ever Cross Your Mind"). "That choice was just as bad as the first," reflects Wolfert. "I just didn't get it."

But he did get Cher. "Cher is in a category of female performers whose discipline is above and beyond the ordinary. A lot of our sessions went on to 3:00 a.m. We would start in the morning, break for lunch, and then start again in the evening. It wasn't fun; it was work. It was doing things over and over again until it was right. Throughout all our sessions, all the retakes and revisions, I never once got a 'can we go home now?' feeling from Cher. She was willing to do whatever she had to do, and do it for however long it took to get it right." (In the official Geffen Records biography for 1987's *Cher*, Cher is quoted as saying: "I hated my last album [*I Paralyze*]. I didn't have anything to contribute. I hated the whole experience and I didn't have any control over it.")

Mask made Cher an uncontestable movie star. Directed by Peter Bogdanovich (who wrote a 1966 cover story on Sonny and Cher for *The Saturday Evening Post*) the film told the true-life story of Rocky Dennis, a boy with a disfiguring facial disease. Cher played Rusty, Rocky's biker mom, a role that, with her penchant for rock and roll, long-haired men, motorcycles, and tattoos, fit her like a glove (she even got former boyfriend Les Dudek a small part in the film). But *Mask* premiered at the Cannes Film Festival under a cloud. Extraordinarily, Cher and director Peter Bogdanovich appeared at the festival holding separate press conferences and with dramatically different personal agendas.

"If I can live without it, he should be able to live without it," Cher informed *The Los Angeles Times* about Bogdanovich's gripe that two of what he believed were *Mask*'s key scenes were cut from the picture. "It doesn't surprise me that he would put his interests before the interests of the film."

Bogdanovich, who had broken ties with Universal Pictures over the issue, was also unhappy that Bruce Springsteen's music, music that the real Rocky Dennis loved, was replaced with music by Bob Seger. "I'm here to talk about the rights of artists," he informed. And to make his point, along with his press conference, Bogdanovich filed a lawsuit against Universal, and placed full-page ads in industry trade papers decrying creative freedom. (The 2009, Director's Cut edition of *Mask* contains the excised sequences as well as the original Bruce Springsteen score.) Despite the uncommon public squabbling—which included gripes by the real Rusty Dennis' mom who said she was grossly underpaid—Cher won the Best Actress Award at the 38th annual Cannes Film Festival (an award she shared with Argentine actress Norma Aleandro). "What's happening to me now reminds me of those old movies where the secretary trips and her glasses fall off and her boss exclaims, 'Why Miss Jones, you're beautiful.' It's like finally people can see that I'm just like everyone else; I have many different sides."

But the bickering that surrounded *Mask* left Academy Award voters with a sour taste in their mouths. Even with stellar reviews like *The New York Post*'s "A Cher delight! Cher's no-fuss acting style matches Rusty's passionate lifestyle," and *USA Today*'s "Cher takes a career role and gives a career performance," there was to be no Best Actress nomination for Cher that year. Though she may not have gotten a nomination, she did get an invitation to present an award: and she seized the moment. Responding to both her banishment and Academy voters' (assumed) discomfiture with her often flamboyant visual presentation, at the internationally televised event she emerged from the wings in a giant feather headdress, sequined bra, black cape and thigh-high boots. When she reached the podium she made her objective crystal clear: "As you can see, I *did* receive my Academy booklet on how to dress like a *serious* actress!" The crowd roared: Cher had won the fight. Pictures of her in her outlandish getup (standing beside an upstaged and bewildered-looking Don Ameche—who had actually *won* the Oscar that Cher presented) appeared on the covers of newspapers and magazines around the world.

After the unqualified success of *Mask*, the powers that be in Hollywood added another adjective to Cher's name: "bankable." Film roles were hers for the picking and, dutifully, she picked three film projects that she believed showcased her newly acknowledged versatility. *The Witches of Eastwick* had been a bestselling book. Cher took on the supporting role of Alexandra Medford, a single woman living in a small New England town, in part, because she was casual friends with the picture's star Jack Nicholson. *Witches*, directed by George Miller and co-starring Michelle Pfeiffer and Susan Sarandon, was a mix of comedy, gore and social satire that left audiences and critics generally unsatisfied.

"The film has enough flamboyance to hold your attention," observed Janet Maslin in *The New York Times*, "but beneath the surface charm there's too much confusion, and the charm itself is gone long before the film is over." Even so, Cher came away with a memorable film clip. Her dressing down of Nicholson was a soundbite that was played, again and again, when the picture was reviewed on television. Cher also used the clip, to great advantage, in her live concert act.

CHER TO NICHOLSON: I think—no I am positive—that you are the most unattractive man I have ever met in my entire life. In the short time that we've been together you have demonstrated every loathsome characteristic of the male personality—and even discovered a few new ones. You are physically repulsive, intellectually retarded, morally reprehensible, vulgar, insensitive, selfish, stupid, you have no taste, a lousy sense of humor, and you smell. You're not even interesting enough to make me sick!

Suspect, directed by Peter Yates, was a crime drama that was released in the fall of 1987. In it, Cher played Kathleen Riley, a beleaguered Washington D. C. public defender who attempts to put together the pieces of a complicated homicide. The film stretched the parameters of believability, but Cher, who shared screen time with Dennis Quaid and Liam Neeson, added another "real woman" character to her repertoire. *The Chicago Sun-Times* noted: "Cher does a convincing job of playing a lonely career woman," while *The Washington Post* pointed out one of the picture's problems: "Cher is trapped playing the one thing in the world she is *not*—dull."

Moonstruck, was the final film in Cher's 1987 triumvirate. Released in November, it was an instant hit. In the film Cher played Loretta Castorini, an Italian-American widow living in Brooklyn. An ensemble piece that also featured Nicolas Cage, Olympia Dukakis (who won the Best Supporting Actress Oscar), and Danny Aiello, the feel-good film struck a chord with audiences. *The Washington Post* called it "a great big beautiful valentine of a movie. An intoxicating romantic-comedy set beneath the biggest, brightest Christmas moon you ever saw," while *The Christian Science Monitor* observed: "the acting is as real and warm as the characters themselves. And the streets, shops and living rooms of Brooklyn have never seemed more inviting." But Cher, one and all agreed, was *Moonstruck*'s Krupp Diamond: the center-jewel in the crown called *Moonstruck*. "Cher is absolutely brilliant. It's the best work she's ever done," raved Roger Ebert. "Cher's never been better, don't miss her in this film," proclaimed *The Wall Street Journal*, while New Jersey's *Home News* surmised: "Cher's performance is likable, honest, funny, smart and natural—and different from any of the other characters she has played in films. She is simply wonderful." And she was nominated for a Best Actress Academy Award.

There was, however, competition. While *Moonstruck* was enchanting audiences, *Fatal Attraction* was terrifying them. Many film fans (and even many Cher fans) believed that Glenn Close's equally praised tour-de-force performance was the more substantial. Close agreed. In a televised interview with Barbara Walters, Walters asked her directly: "Do you think you should win the Best Actress Award?" Her response was instant: "Yes. *I* should win." (With Cher and Close as front runners, few journalists took note of that year's other nominees; Meryl Streep in *Ironweed*, Holly Hunter in *Broadcast News* and Sally Kirkland in *Anna*.)

But Cher wanted to win the Oscar, too. And she campaigned vigorously. Although she'd made the cover of *Time* in 1975, in '87 and '88, she appeared on the cover of *Time*'s rival *Newsweek*, as well as a host of other high-circulation magazines including *Los Angeles, New Woman, Ms., Us, People, Film Review, Cosmopolitan, In Touch, Celebrity,* and *Premiere*. There were television interviews on MTV, VHI, *Good Morning America, The Today Show,* and, most notably, *The Barbara Walters Special*. Her endorsement deal with the Health & Tennis Corporation—owners of Jack LaLanne Health Spas—was also useful. Although she had signed as a company spokesperson two years earlier, during 1987 and '88, both print and TV ads, which featured her in quick edits, free-associating about life, health, and fitness, were stepped-up.

The perfectly-timed November 1987 release of the album *Cher* made Cher *even more* visible; perhaps too much so. Would there be a Cher backlash? After all, Academy voters were proud of saying that their coveted votes were not for sale: to anyone.

Oscar night was a tense one, but Cher didn't spend the day waiting for night to come. Early on the morning of April 11, 1988 she was whisked from her Beverly Hills home to the bustling downtown streets of L.A. There, in a suite of nondescript offices, she signed contracts that solidified a deal with Parfums, Inc., to manufacture, market, and distribute a line of products under the umbrella *Uninhibited*. It was to be Cher's signature perfume—sold in both high-end specialty stores as well as mass-market chain outlets.

Cher arrived at the Oscar ceremony characteristically late with daughter Chastity, Elijah and boyfriend Rob Camilletti (eighteen years her junior and dubbed "Bagel Boy" because he once worked in a Brooklyn bakery). "When Paul Newman announced the winner he took a deep breath and in that second I thought, 'Well, I didn't win,'" Cher later recalled. "It doesn't take a breath to say 'Cher' so I was resigned to being a loser."

But she wasn't a loser. Cher's name was announced as the winner of the Best Actress Academy Award. At the podium she thanked the Academy, her family, and Meryl Streep, who was a friend and had also been nominated (cameras caught Streep blowing Cher a kiss and mouthing the word "bravo"). As always, Cher ended her Oscar acceptance speech with a soundbite: "I don't think this award means that I am somebody... but maybe I'm on my way."

On her way was, of course, an understatement. At the same time she was being toasted in the film industry, Cher was reestablishing herself the music world. Her nineteenth album, *Cher* was a collection of pop/rock tunes released on Geffen Records—her former boyfriend's label. The lead-off single, "I Found Someone" (B-side "Dangerous Times") was bolstered by an exciting music video. "My body was never better than when I did that video," Cher later observed, and it may have been true. In the video, which prominently featured her boyfriend Rob, she looked and sounded fabulous. "I Found Someone" rose to No. 10 on the Pop charts, and the follow-up single "We All Sleep Alone" (B-side "Working Girl), directed by Cher and paid for by Jack LaLanne Health Spas, made it to No. 14. With it, a whole new generation of music-buyers—people who had no memory of Cher the '60s "hippie," or Cher the '70s "glamour goddess"—discovered her.

The promotional activities attendant to *Cher* included an appearance on the top-rated *Saturday Night Live* as well as an expansive *New York Times Magazine* profile and a ten-page Q & A with *Playboy*. However, it was an appearance she made on *Late Night with David Letterman* that would not only be talked about, but forever burned into the public consciousness. On *Letterman* Cher was reunited with Sonny Bono. There was electricity in the air as Sonny and Cher chatted about old times, her new music, and, finally, took to the stage for a rough, but no less moving, impromptu rendition of "I Got You Babe." "Everybody was crying that night," Cher later recalled. "I don't know, I think it meant something for people to see us together again."

When Cher released her second Geffen Records album, *Heart of Stone*, she was ready to hit both the charts and the road. The Heart of Stone Tour was an expansive endeavor that reintroduced Cher to America and Europe. It also brought home what was already obvious; Cher *had* realized her dream of becoming a legitimate rock and roll star. She sold out arenas everywhere from Orlando, Florida to Minneapolis, Minnesota. From Dublin, Ireland to Sydney, Australia. "Cher's concerts are so lavishly Cher-centric they make Madonna's [who she had an ongoing public feud with] look modest," surmised *The Daily News*. And when demand for tickets exceeded supply, more dates were added.

Heart of Stone's lead-off single was the decidedly non-rock "After All (Love Theme from Chances Are)" (B-side "Dangerous Times"). Written by Dean Pitchford and composed by Tom Snow (Cher sang Snow's "Let This Be a Lesson to You" on *Take Me Home*, as well as "Holdin' Out for Love" written by Snow and Cynthia Weil on *Prisoner*), Cher's newest release was a ballad performed with Chicago's former lead singer Peter Cetera. It went to No. 1 on the Adult Contemporary chart and No. 6 on the Pop chart.

"I love what Cher did with 'After All,' and I love that she still uses it in her act," says Tom Snow. "That song was played constantly at proms, memorials and weddings. People really loved it. When Dean and I wrote it we had no idea that Cher and Peter were going to get it. We were just told to write a good love song for the movie *Chances Are*. Needless to say we were thrilled that two of the biggest music stars of the time recorded it." (Although it was a top-ten hit and a staple in her concert act, Cher and Cetera never filmed a music video for "After All" and have never performed the song together live.)

The anthemic "If I Could Turn Back Time" (B-side "I Found Someone") was *Heart of Stone*'s second single. The song rose to No. 3 and was accompanied by a music video that featured Cher dressed in fishnets, boots and a G-string. The video was banned from MTV. "It's really weird. The video has been in heavy rotation for six weeks and now MTV has decided to ban it," Cher said at the time. "I don't get it. But if that's what they have to do, that's what they have to do."

Heart of Stone's two follow up singles "Just Like Jesse James" (B-side "Starting Over") and "Heart of Stone" (B-side "All Because of You") went to No. 8 and No. 20 respectively. And Cher came at the music market from another angle. The two songs from *Heart of Stone* shared the charts with a tune from the film *Mermaids*—"The Shoop Shoop Song (It's in His Kiss)," a cover of the 1964 Betty Everett hit, topped off at No. 33.

More music and another tour followed. *Love Hurts*, Cher's third Geffen Records album, was released in June of 1991. The first single "Love and

Understanding" (B-side "Trail of Broken Hearts") went to No. 17. The follow-up, "Save Up All Your Tears" (B-side "A World without Heroes") went to No. 37. And the Love Hurts Tour, once again, took Cher and her music to all the major arenas in America. "It's my job to make myself ten feet tall," she told *Entertainment Tonight* during the tour's first dates. "The energy it takes is incredible, but so is the feeling I get when I'm out there in front of the crowds."

Back in theaters, Cher's highly anticipated follow-up to *Moonstruck, Mermaids,* offered her a second chance to display her comedic skills. In the film she played Rachel Flax, a decidedly unconventional, modern-minded woman dealing with her two daughters (Winona Ryder and Christina Ricci) in the 1960s. "Cher is deliciously trashy—kitsch in high heels. She is the most ravishingly otherworldly of modern actresses," observed *The Washington Post*. While *The New York Times* opined: "*Mermaids* is a stylish sitcom... a smooth, unexceptional entertainment."

Given the fact that *Mermaids* had reached theaters only after the flight of two directors (Lasse Hallstrom and Frank Oz) and the dismissal of an actor (Emily Lloyd), in 1991 *Fan Fare* columnist Hilary de Vries asked Cher about the growing perception that she was difficult to work with. "I don't know if I'm difficult to work with, I just don't know," was her (uncharacteristically) defensive response. "Ask some directors or studio heads. I don't care if I am. I've always worked uphill. I loved working with Mike Nichols [*Silkwood*] and Robert Altman [*Come Back to the Five and Dime Jimmy Dean, Jimmy Dean*]. I really loved working with Richard Benjamin [*Mermaids*]. I didn't like Peter Yates [*Suspect*] or George Miller [*The Witches of Eastwick*]—there was no real connection there. I didn't like Frank Oz [*Mermaids'* second director] and I didn't like Peter Bogdanovich [*Mask*]. So there are two directors I disliked intensely, two I had no connection with, and three that I really loved. My average is okay." That same year, the year that Sonny's autobiography *And The Beat Goes On* hit stores—and was excerpted in *The National Enquirer*—Cher sat down and chatted with Oprah. When Oprah asked her to respond to some of Sonny's allegations, Cher, clearly disturbed, disclosed that she had contacted Sonny's representatives and asked for an apology and a retraction. (Neither was forthcoming.)

The year before *Mermaids'* release, Cher expanded on her charitable endeavors. Along with the Children's Craniofacial Organization—an organization she aligned herself with after filming *Mask*, she also donated her time, money and person to Mothers and Others for a Livable Planet, the United Armenian Fund Relief Organization, the American Foundation for AIDS Research, Operation Helmet (an organization that supplies helmet upgrades to troops), TAPS (The Tragedy Assistance Program for Survivors) and Children of the Night (a rescue organization for children forced into prostitution).

In 1992 Robert Altman contacted Cher and asked her if she would do him a favor. The director of *Come Back to the Five and Dime Jimmy Dean, Jimmy Dean* (the play and the movie), wanted her to do a "walk on" in his latest entertainment-industry treatise *The Player*. Cher agreed. With the *Cher* show's Ret Turner as her date, she made a cameo, as herself, arriving at a black-and-white-only formal event—wearing a blood-red off-the-shoulder sequined gown.

Two years later, in 1994, Altman asked Cher to do it again, this time in *Pret-à-Porter* (*Ready to Wear*), his "behind the scenes" look at the fashion industry. Cher obliged. Six years would pass between *Mermaids* and Cher's next two pictures—*Faithful* and *If These Walls Could Talk*—both released in 1996. Cher attributed her absence from the screen to her battle with Epstein-Barr virus a.k.a. Chronic Fatigue Syndrome. "I was sick for a really long time; almost three years," she informed *USA Today*. "You never lose it and it really took the life out of me."

Faithful was a movie-from-a-play written by Chazz Palminteri, co-produced by Robert De Niro and directed by Paul Mazursky. Cher, as housewife Margaret O'Donnell, spends almost the entire film tied to a chair while her husband (Ryan O'Neal) hires a hitman (Chazz Palminteri). *Faithful* flopped. The film, which cost $13 million and only made back $2 million, was pulled from theaters after just two weeks. "I felt really sorry for Chazz," Cher later said. "That film started out as one thing and ended up something all together different."

If These Walls Could Talk, an HBO tele-movie, was, on the other hand, appreciated. An ambitious trilogy of mini-films, each dealing with the issue of abortion, Cher acted in and directed the segment in which she appeared. "I can't remember anything of this depth," she told the Associated Press at the time. "I don't think you could get away with anything like this on network TV." HBO's senior vice president agreed: "I don't believe there is a TV studio in the world that would have financed this picture." In *If These Walls Could Talk* Cher played Dr. Beth Thompson, a sympathetic practitioner who deals with a conflicted young woman. The picture was unsparing in its details. "The only thing we fought [with HBO] about was how loud the suction machine would be," said Cher, referring to the apparatus her character uses to perform abortions. "That sound was very upsetting to people." While promoting the film, Cher made a personal admission. "I've had a few abortions. I've also had four miscarriages. And I've had two children. I know every angle of motherhood: I know the anguish of wanting children and not being able to carry them, I know the joy of having them, and I know the anguish of having to make the decision not to have a child. I'm not pro-abortion by any means. But I believe that it's the woman's right to choose."

Another personal matter that Cher spoke a great deal about at the time was plastic surgery. "I had my nose done. I had my tits done. I wore braces," she told *The Cable Guide*'s Jay Gissen. "I'm not embarrassed to say the stuff that I've had done, because I don't really care what people think about it."

But to many eyes it appeared that Cher had done much more. Although a British doctor confirmed that she had not, as was reported, had two of her ribs removed to create a smaller waist, or had cheek implants ("I've had these cheeks all my life") rumors of face lifts, Botox injections (comedienne Joan Rivers made the Botox rumors an essential part of her stand-up act) as well as her newly pouty lips, and fuller bust, expanded the story. In *Cher: If You Believe*, writer Mark Bego observed: "An entire generation of her fans, who had grown up loving her bigger nose and unique jagged-tooth smile, were suddenly seeing Cher as someone entirely different than the woman American television audiences had once fallen in love with." Perhaps, but it didn't much matter. In fact, as pivotal a figure as she was in the beauty-and-age-obsessed entertainment industry, the fine-tuning of Cher's physical appearance enabled her to continue in her chosen profession.

It was the "new and improved" Cher (*People* magazine featured her on its cover under the headline "Ooh! La la... or Oops? Plastic Surgery of the Stars!") that kept moving forward. When her three-album deal with Geffen came to a close, and even though she called her five years with the label "my favorite time as a singles artist, because I was getting to do songs that I really loved... songs that really represented *me*," Cher signed with Warner Bros. Records' UK division.

1995's ironically titled *It's a Man's World*—the album art showed a picture of Cher as Eve complete with apple and snake—was a downbeat collection of songs that came and went without much notice; at least in America. In Britain the album reached No. 10 and produced four top 40 hits: "One by One" (No. 7), "Walking in Memphis" (No. 11; for which Cher filmed an exciting video that featured her in "Elvis" drag), "The Sun Aint Gonna Shine Anymore" (No. 26), and "Not Enough Love in the World" (No. 31). Cher's British success was cemented with the British-only No. 1 album *Cher's Greatest Hits 1965-1992*. ("The Shoop Shoop Song [It's in His Kiss]" from *Mermaids*, also topped the charts in Britain.)

With her popularity at an all-time high in Britain ("Love Can Build a Bridge," a Comic Relief charity single she performed with Chrissie Hynde, Neneh Cherry and Eric Clapton also went to No. 1) Cher, for a time, relocated to London. A remix of "One by One" had become a dance/club hit in both Britain and America, so executives at Warner Bros. encouraged her to record an album entirely composed of dance/club music. *Believe* was the album and single that would bring Cher back—worldwide. It would, in fact, incredibly, make her (at 52) bigger than she had ever been before.

Recorded in England, and released globally, "Believe," the single, topped charts in 23 countries including England, France, Germany and Australia. In America the single went to No. 1, the album went to No. 4, and when it was all said and done, *Billboard* deemed "Believe" the top-selling song of 1999. And then the awards documented the fact. The shimmery, instantly-memorable "Believe," whose centerpiece was Cher's digitally enhanced vocal—"the Cher effect"—won the Grammy (Cher's first) for Best Dance Music Recording and was nominated for Record of the Year (it lost out to Santana's "Smooth"). At the

World Music Awards Cher performed and then took home the Legend Award. To date, "Believe" has the distinction of being one of fewer than 30 all-time singles to have sold ten million (or more) copies worldwide, and in Britain it remains the best-selling single, of all time, by a female artist. (In September 2012 sixteen-year-old singing sensation Ella Henderson mesmerized TV viewers when she transformed the tune into a plaintive, love-lost ballad on Britain's top-rated talent competition *The X Factor*. Cher's Twitter response: "...tears came 2 my eyes! So touching! A great version of a great song!")

"'Strong Enough' was the first song I recorded for [*Believe*]," Cher explained of *Believe*'s self-explanatory second single. "The producers told me they set out to write a 'Cher song' and 'Strong Enough' was what they came up with." A feminist anthem set to a dance beat, Cher and METRO (her team of producers; Mark Taylor, Brian Rawling, and Paul Barry) worked hard to give the song a time-specific—circa 1975—authenticity. "The boys [METRO] tried a whole bunch of different ways to do it, but I told them their ideas weren't going to work. Finally they bit the bullet and did it the way they did it in the old days [used real strings and horns] and it was perfect."

"Perfect," but not a hit on the scale of "Believe." Even with heavy promotion and *two* colorful music videos, "Strong Enough" (Cher called it "an 'I Will Survive' for the '90s") proved to be relatively weak—at least in the States, where it only made it to No. 57 (it went to No. 5 in England). *Believe*'s subsequent singles "All or Nothing," (No. 38) and "Dov'è l'amore" (English: "Where's The Love"; No. 104) also charted lower than hoped.

Still, and regardless, throughout 1999 Cher was everywhere. At the top of the year, on January 31, she sang "The Star Spangled Banner" at the Super Bowl in front of a television audience that topped 75 million (the song was later issued on a promo-only CD). Her face was on the cover of magazines that ranged from *Tattoo* and *CD Review* to *People* and *Entertainment Weekly*. And, as fate would have it, before the year ended, her image returned to both the small and big screen.

"I got the part because I wasn't a huge Cher fan," says Renee Faia, who, following a national search for Sonny and Cher lookalikes (more a publicity stunt than an actual search), was cast as Cher in the television adaption of Sonny's autobiography, *And the Beat Goes On*. "Rather than just focusing on her looks or mannerisms I was interested in portraying her emotional inner life."

It proved to be a challenge. "The biggest thing I learned about Cher was that she was three distinct and different people: a self-conscious teenager, an unhappily married TV star, and then a self-assured post-Sonny award-winning actress. I totally immersed myself in the part, so much so that, although I wasn't aware of it, I kept talking and acting like Cher for weeks after we wrapped. My boyfriend was like, 'Renee, you're doing it again!'"

And The Beat Goes On: The Sonny and Cher Story received mixed reviews. *People* observed: "The film has the familiar monotonous rhythm of the showbiz biopic," while *Entertainment Weekly* called it "notably cheap-looking... and padded out by full-length versions of Sonny and Cher's hits."

Around the same time as *And The Beat Goes On: The Sonny and Cher Story* was broadcast, *Tea With Mussolini*—an ensemble piece directed by Franco Zeffirelli and starring Cher, Lily Tomlin, Joan Plowright, Maggie Smith and Judi Dench—made its way into theaters. Set in the 1930s, in the film Cher played Elsa Maxwell, a crass, wealthy Jewish-American singer. "Cher plays a role that allows her to be seen and create a vivid character while showing off what is best about her; her screen personality," observed *The San Francisco Chronicle*. While *The Chicago Sun Times* noted: "I liked the performances of all the women, including Cher. People forget what a really good actress she can be."

As part of her global domination of the media, along with her presence in films and her impersonation on television, 1999 was also the year that Cher embarked on her Do You Believe? Tour. For the very first time her live show encapsulated her entire career; from 1965's "I Got You Babe" (her comedic remake with MTV's Beavis and Butt-Head not withstanding) right up to her dawn-of-the-millennium triumph "Believe." The Do You Believe? Tour ran from June 1999 through March 2000 and grossed more than $160 million. It also received the support of her two harshest critics: her children. "I am so uncool to my kids," Cher said, "but the other day Elijah said, 'My friends and I actually thought your show was good.' That's better than a rave review in *The New York Times*."

Chastity, too, found the all-encompassing tour to be a revelation. "Seeing Mom's Believe concert gave me one of those rare opportunities to disconnect, to forget who I am, and be totally blown away by her. I had a ball watching the crowd—kids, old people, straights, gays—everybody, including myself, just loved her."

But there were those who no longer did. In January 1999 Cher fired Billy Sammeth, her manager of twenty years. Cher and Sammeth first met in 1977, when he was a talent agent working for Katz-Gallin (the managers who came in and lured her away from Dick Grant Intercom while she was still working on *Cher*). When Sammeth, whom Cher nicknamed "Bumper," went out on his own and launched the Bill Sammeth Organization, Cher followed.

"I did that on purpose [purchased a home and moved from L.A. to Northern California]," Sammeth told *The Daily Beast*, referring to Cher's complaint that he was inaccessible. "I didn't want to become a prisoner for Cher. I didn't want to become the live-in person in her life." And he wasn't: shortly after his move he was replaced with talent coordinator Roger Davies and personal manager Lindsay Scott.

On March 5, 1999, three months before the Do You Believe? Tour hit the road, Sammeth filed a Breach of Contract lawsuit demanding the fifteen percent commission due him for preliminary work done on the tour. Cher responded in court with a Determination of Controversy Petition that claimed she and Sammeth had a "handshake" arrangement, and that he had actually been "formally terminated" a year before his claim. The court case was a draw: Sammeth had to return monies collected from deals made in absence of a written agreement and Cher had to return exactly $24,595.54–the amount Sammeth put on his charge card when he accompanied her on a promotional trip to Europe.

Cher's foray into writing was also issued in 1999. Although she refused to write her autobiography, *The First Time*–whose narrowly-focused stories included "My First Shopping Spree," "My First Tattoo," and "My First Time a Sandwich Got Me in Trouble"–aided and abetted Cher's return to the top.

The improbably named *not.com.mercial* was the album that followed *Believe*. The highly personal collection of ten songs, eight of which she wrote, was issued in limited edition through the internet website ArtistDirect. Acoustic-heavy, pointedly political, downbeat, *not.com.mercial* included seriously-themed material. "Our Lady of San Francisco" dealt with homelessness, "Fit to Fly" was a celebration of American war veterans, "Sisters of Mercy" referenced Cher's own experience attending Catholic School and looked at organized religion's hypocrisy, and "(The Fall) Kurt's Blues" paid tribute to Kurt Cobain, someone she had never met, but someone whose unexpected early death affected her.

"*not.com.mercial* is probably the best work I've ever done," Cher observed at a 2000 music conference. "For years [after her record label passed on it] I used to just give it to friends as birthday presents, or at Christmas. Then the internet came along. And so now it's available to everyone." Today, *not.com.mercial* remains the only album on which Cher writes, produces and is credited as music arranger.

But not all of Cher's "outside market" endeavors delivered a sense of satisfaction. *Uninhibited*, her signature perfume, was popular for a time–buoyed by heavy-promotion television and print ads–but was eventually discontinued. So was her mail-order home-decorating venture *Sanctuary*. Cher's *Aquasentials Skin Care* line seemed like a good idea, but few bought the concept, or the products. *Cher Fitness*, a two-part series of home exercise videos–one called *Body Confidence*; the other *A New Attitude*–also underperformed. So did *Forever Fit: The Lifetime Plan for Health, Fitness, and Beauty*, a book Cher co-authored with nutritionist Dr. Robert Haas, and *Cooking for Cher*, a collection of low-fat recipes written by Andrew Ennis, Cher and Joan Nielsen.

The biggest misstep in Cher's career, or at least the most embarrassing–not including having to bail boyfriend Robert Camilletti out of jail after he was accused of trying to run over a paparazzo–came in 1991, when she appeared in a series of endlessly aired infomercials for Lori Davis Hair Care Products. Although Cher's endorsement made the company millions, emboldening her to sell her *own* products via infomercial, the cheesy half-hour "tutorials" which featured Cher,

her sister, and Davis chatting about hair mousse, "cleansers" and conditioners, tarnished Cher's image. "Yes I fucked up, but does it negate every other thing I've ever done?" Cher asked *Entertainment Weekly*. For a time it seemed so. Undaunted, Cher proved an effective pitchwoman for the artificial sweetener Equal, and Blackglama mink furs. Another thing that Cher was effective at pitching was her own belongings. On October 3 and 4, 2006, Sotheby's and Julien's auction houses combined forces and put up for sale 784 lots of her personal effects.

"You might be interested to know why I'm doing this," Cher wrote in the *Property from the Collection of Cher* catalogue. "There's a scene in the film *Harold and Maude* in which he gives her a ring and she throws it in a lake and says, 'Now I'll always know where it is.' That's the way I feel about my treasures. They came from somewhere to me and now they go from me to you, and since you're choosing the pieces you really love, I know you'll take great care of them." Cher's auction, which included many of the Bob Mackie gowns she wore on *The Sonny and Cher Comedy Hour* and *Cher*, grossed $3.5 million dollars.

Living Proof was Cher's follow-up to *Believe*. Another collection of songs fashioned for the dance floor, the album spawned four singles: "The Music's No Good Without You," "Song for the Lonely," "A Different Kind of Love Song," and "Alive Again". None of the songs became hits. Living Proof: The Farewell Tour, however, was. "Yes, this is my final tour," Cher informed Diane Sawyer of TV's *Nightline*. "Why? Because I think it's all down hill from here. It won't get any better." The tour (later humorously dubbed the Never Can Say Goodbye Tour) hit the road in June of 2002 and didn't wind up until almost three years later, in April of 2005. When all was said and done (when aired on television the concert won an Emmy for Outstanding Variety, Musical or Comedy Special) Cher had performed 325 glamorous, spectacular and outrageous shows—and then decided to call it quits.

But had she? In 2008 Cher began a protracted series of negotiations with Caesars Palace, Las Vegas, a venue at which she had appeared many times—with and without Sonny. Caesars was interested in having her commit to a three-year series of shows that would be performed in their new state-of-the-art Colosseum theater. "So much technology changed after I stopped touring," Cher said. "I realized that there were huge advances in lighting, sound, and special effects. By staying in one theater I could present the biggest and best show that I had ever done in my life."

And so she did. On May 6, 2008 Cher made her debut, her post-Farewell Tour tour, as it were, complete with fourteen dancers, four aerialists, a five-man band, two background singers, and an ever-changing number of spectacular Bob Mackie-designed costumes. "It's the Cheriest Cher show of them all," observed *The Las Vegas Review-Journal*, and to those who saw it, it most certainly was. One hundred and ninety-two performances (and almost a full three years later) on February 5, 2011, Cher ended her Caesars run.

"It was fun doing it,' she frankly informed David Letterman, "and it will be fun *not* doing it." (Interestingly, when Cher wasn't onstage at the Colosseum, the auditorium was used by Elton John and Bette Midler—the two featured guests on the premiere episode of her solo variety series.)

Cher's former manager Billy Sammeth was less than congratulatory about her commitment to Caesars—and Vegas. "Look at Cher's career now. She's whored herself out to a city she despises," he told *The Daily Beast*'s Kevin Sessums. "She even had a big falling out with Steve Wynn [who played a pivotal role in Vegas' '90s resurgence] because she called Vegas 'Pig City' [a take on the city's nickname 'Sin City']. Don't tell me how ethical you are when you chose to go through the money door. That's it. Are you happy now? I don't think so. Nobody's putting you in movies anymore."

At the same time that she was back and forth and on and offstage at Caesars, and as incredible as it seems, someone did put Cher in a movie; a musical that was written and directed by her former lover (David Geffen's) former boyfriend Steve Antin.

Burlesque starred singing sensation Christina Aguilera (who, at nineteen, won the Best New Artist Grammy the same year that Cher won her very first Grammy for "Believe") as an aspiring singer/dancer and Cher as her older, more-knowledgeable mentor. *The New York Times* called it "achingly dull... a combination of a Disney tween program and a Lifetime [television network] weepie." Even *The Chicago Sun Times*' Roger Ebert, usually a Cher fan, gave the film, and Cher, a tempered review. "*Burlesque* shows Cher and Christina Aguilera being all they can be... and Cher looks exactly as she always does. Other people age; Cher has become a logo." Neither a flop nor a success (advance DVD sales were brisk) *Burlesque* offered Cher the chance to sing onscreen. "Welcome to Burlesque" was classic Cher, while "You Haven't Seen the Last of Me," a song that seemed to accurately sum up her life and career, was a power-ballad that was remixed and became a No. 1 dance/club hit. It also won a Golden Globe.

The list of men that Cher has dated over the years is a mostly familiar one. Along with David Geffen, Tom Cruise, Gene Simmons and Les Dudek, Cher has been linked with Val Kilmer, John Heard, Eric Stoltz, Ray Liotta, Ron Duguay, John Loeffler, Richie Sambora, Eric Clapton, Joshua Donnen and, most recently, Ron Zimmerman. Robert Camilletti is the man she continues to reference as the "love of my life."

"I got to know Cher a bit when she was with Rob," says one of Camilletti's friends. "I spent many nights with him, Cher and the kids at the Egyptian house. I've got to tell you that they were really, really in love. They really connected. It was a once in a lifetime thing."

Sonny Bono's-post Sonny and Cher life was also busy. In 1981 he married longtime girlfriend Susie Coelho. The marriage ended four years later. His

Italian eatery Bono lasted for a few years and provided his introduction to Mary Whitaker. They married and in 1988 became the proud parents of Chesare Elan, a boy (who would later come forward with his story of addiction to alcohol and the painkiller Oxycontin) and, in 1991, Chianna Maria, a girl. Christy Bono, Sonny's daughter from his first marriage to Donna Rankin, first worked on and off for her famous father and later opened two restaurants—Christy's and Nico's—both in the Long Beach section of Los Angeles.

In 1988 Sonny ran for and was elected mayor of Palm Springs, California. An unsuccessful bid for the Republican nomination to the U.S. Senate was next and then, in 1994, Sonny ran for and was elected to, the U.S. House of Representatives as the representative of California's 44th District.

Sonny Bono died in a skiing accident in Lake Tahoe, Nevada on January 5, 1998. He was 62. It was reported in the press that Sonny's escalating dependency on painkillers may have contributed to the accident (Mary Bono confirmed that Sonny was dependent on painkillers and mood stabilizers). Sonny's funeral took place during a week when there was little other news to report. Consequently it became an event. CNN broadcast the proceedings live and inter-cut it with commentary. "You'll have to excuse this little piece of paper in my hands, I've been writing this stupid eulogy for the past three days," Cher tearfully informed the assemblage, "and of course I know Sonny is just loving all of this."

The pageantry of Sonny's funeral had a downside—a stream of bad press aimed at Cher. Several journalists pulled up the many negative quotes that were on record and former manager Billy Sammeth called Cher's speech "a brilliant performance... she thought Sonny was nothing more than a used car salesman." Others thought she used the event to garner publicity. "When I heard that I thought, 'I just want to move to another country,'" she informed *Good Morning America*. "I've never, in my entire career, had to work to get publicity—I can get it anytime and anywhere. It's just stupid and really mean to say that."

Part of the problem, it seemed, was a hastily-arranged television special that Cher put together. *Sonny and Me: Cher Remembers* was a Prime Time hour-long broadcast on which Cher told stories, showed clips, and sang a song—Nat King Cole's "Nature Boy." "I'm not advertising anything. I'm not selling a record. It's something that's my life," Cher defended. But there were those that found the special unseemly and unnecessary—especially given the spectacle of Sonny's funeral. (Three months after Sonny's death, in a special election, his widow Mary ran for, and won, his congressional seat. When she ran again, two years later, she won a second term.)

2011 brought Sonny and Cher's daughter Chastity into the limelight: as she had never been before. Through *The Sonny and Cher Comedy Hour*, the *Cher* show, and *The Sonny and Cher Show*, she was a familiar face to American audiences—and beyond. A darling (it appeared) little girl who had blonde hair, button-brown eyes and two doting parents who just happened to be superstars. It wasn't a life that she was comfortable with.

"I remember when I was little, another little kid came up to me an said, 'I wish I were you,' and I thought, 'I wish I were *you—you* have two parents who aren't divorced, they don't have a problem with the way you dress, and you don't have to share them with the world.'"

It was the way that she wanted to dress that first caused her mother concern. "My clothes were always a negotiation with my mother. I was her first child, I was her daughter, and she had an idea of what she wanted me to be. I didn't fit it at all." When Chastity hit her teens something profound happened. "My body betrayed me. All of a sudden there were these big things [breasts]. They didn't feel like they belonged on me. I hated them." But, for the time being at least, and as confused as she may have been about the changes in her body, Chastity was still a female.

In 1989 the gay magazine *OutWeek* was the first to "out" Chastity as a closeted gay person. The tabloid press dutifully picked up the story and soon her life was reduced to salacious headlines. "Sonny Blames Cher for Gay Nightmare" declared *The Globe*, while *The Star* bellowed, "Cher's Lesbian Daughter Chastity in Late-Night Catfights with Gal-Pal Roommate." Chastity denied the charges. She gave an exclusive interview to *The National Enquirer* whose focus was her "heterosexuality." "I date men," she claimed. "I don't have a steady boyfriend—I go out with guys I find appealing, and I go out with them for however long we like each other."

But no one believed her. 1993's *Hang Out Your Poetry* was a collection of songs she performed with her band Ceremony. The conspicuously released Geffen Records entry (her mother's label) came and went without notice. Two years later, with Ceremony disbanded and with other female entertainers revealing their sexuality—k.d. lang, Melissa Etheridge, the Indigo Girls—Chastity publicly acknowledged that she was a lesbian. The April 1995 edition of *The Advocate*, America's most widely read gay magazine, said it all. Under a photo of a beaming Chastity were placed the words: "Chastity Out At Last." Three years later, after fully embracing gay causes (she wrote for *The Advocate* and became a spokesperson for GLAAD, the Gay and Lesbian Alliance Against Defamation), Chastity co-authored *Family Outing*, a collection of stories about people coming out to their families—including her own. A second gay-themed book, *The End of Innocence*, a chronicle of the challenges she faced while dealing with the terminal illness of a loved one, was released in 2003. Five years later still, Chastity stood by as her mother, who initially found it difficult to accept the fact that she had a gay daughter—"I had a very un-Cher-like reaction, but I got over it"— accepted the GLAAD Media Award for Woman of the Year.

In 2009 Chastity told her mother that she wanted to "transition" from male to female. "She was really supportive at first," Chastity recalled, "but then, a few weeks later, when she realized that I really meant it, that I was really going to go through with it, she had a really difficult time."

"It's hard because she's still my little girl," Cher admitted to *Parade*'s Dotson Rader. "But she's got an inner strength and she's a courageous person. She believes what she believes." Chaz's gender transition (his legal name change took place in 2010; from Chastity Sun Bono to Chaz Salvatore Bono—"Salvatore" in honor of his father) was thoroughly chronicled in the May 10, 2011 televised documentary *Becoming Chaz*, and the tie-in book *Transition: The Story of How I Became a Man*—in which he continued his transgender sensitivity and "awareness" campaign. As a man, Chaz became the first transgendered contestant on the top rated *Dancing with Stars*. (Fascinatingly, in *And the Beat Goes On*, years before Chaz's transition, Sonny wrote that throughout the length of Cher's pregnancy with Chastity, Cher was convinced that she was going to give birth to a son.)

Elijah Blue Allman's early days were spent at CBS Television City, where his mom was starring with her former husband in *The Sonny and Cher Show*. "Elijah has never known his father," Cher told Phil Donahue. When asked if she felt guilty she replied: "No. Elijah is *available* to see his father. I guess his father just doesn't want to see him."

Interested in music from an early age, when Elijah hit his teens he joined Cher on tour, playing backup guitar in her band (he and his mother share a memorable moment in Cher's "If I Could Turn Back Time" video). In 1991 Elijah joined his mother for a duet of the 1969 Tommy James and the Shondells hit "Crimson and Clover" (from the *A Walk on the Moon* soundtrack). In 2000 Elijah formed a rock band called Deadsy. Their self-tiled first album *Deadsy*, though spirited, was released independently and came and went without much notice. Their second album, *Commencement*, contained an opaque song entitled "Mansion World" which, considering the CD art—an illustration of a huge mansion with a scull lawn ornament and blood dripping down from the sky—may or may not have been a commentary on the wealthy and entitled world into which he was born. A third Deadsy album, *Phantasmagore*, made it into stores but didn't become a hit.

In 2003, after an intervention that was staged by his mother, Elijah went into treatment for heroin dependency and emerged sober. "It's weird, both my children had the same drug problems as their fathers—same drug of choice," Cher told *Vanity Fair*. "It jumped me and my sister. My father was a heroin addict and my sister's father was an alcoholic."

"Even with music, I always came from a place of art theory and philosophy," Elijah informed *Art News* about his switch from music to art. "Step-and-Repeat," his first exhibition, was displayed at Los Angeles' Kantor Gallery and included paintings and mixed media whose focus he said was: "The contemporary celebrity condition, its arc, and the cheapening of fame."

On July 8, 2011, Cher made her debut as "Janet"—a giraffe in *Zookeeper*, the story of a lonely man (Kevin James) who talks to the animals he tends to. That same year she appeared as a guest host, with Robert Osborne, on TCM (the Turner Classic Movies network); a film introduction hostess role she would repeat in 2013.

Cher's latest musical endeavor is the dance tune "Woman's World," a minute of which was first leaked and played at a Chicago nightclub, and then went viral. "I'm upset about the leak," Cher tweeted. "But it's not the end of the world." In response to the leak Cher and her label Warner Bros. unveiled "Woman's World" on Thanksgiving Day, 2012. Billed as an "early holiday gift," the song—replete with Vocoder effects, a chanting sing-song chorus, and swirling dance beats—picked up where "Believe" left off, and offered a continuation of Cher's certainty of the inner strength of the brokenhearted: particularly women.

Cher's newest collection of tunes is scheduled for a third quarter 2013 "roll out." Her first collection of music in eleven years, the album will contain two songs written for Cher by Pink, as well as her collaborations with producer Timbaland and standby hit-maker Diane Warren. (A much-anticipated duet with Lady Gaga entitled "The Greatest Thing" was recorded but pulled by Gaga and her producer RedOne at the final hour.)

And so Cher, the recipient of Glamour magazine's Lifetime Achievement Award (at the ceremony she told the largely female audience that one of the biggest lessons she has learned is that "... 'no' is just a word... you don't have to believe it...") has penciled in 2013 as yet another year in which she'll give her fans what they want: a comeback. Up to now, Cher's 87-year-old mother, Georgia Holt, has played a part in this. On April 30, 33 years after it was first recorded, Holt's album Honky Tonk Woman (which features a duet with her famous daughter) was released. The project was cross-promoted in a televised Mother's Day special, Dear Mum, Love Cher, as well as on a host of other broadcasts including Ellen, Jay Leno and Access: Hollywood. An inveterate Twitter user (she has more than one million followers) Cher tweets about everything—from her daily activities and her music to religion and politics (she is a staunch Obama supporter; on November 6, 2012, following Obama's re-election, Cher tweeted: "OMG! I'm so happy! This is one of the great nites of my life!!! Tears are streaming down my face! Women we have a champion!!!"). Cher even tweets about her own death.

Following what the press dubbed "The Cher Death Hoax"—"American recording artist Cher dies at 65. Found dead in her Malibu Home"—a rumor picked up and tweeted by Kim Kardashian (who has more than sixteen million followers) Cher waited a day and responded as she always does: matter of factly. "Well here I am tweeting from the hereafter! It's very blue up here and thank God they gave me a view of the sea... Let's tweet later because even though I'm just a spirit I'm hungry!"

Cher, as always, has the last word.

TV OR NOT TV

The new appreciation, indeed the new *knowledge* of Sonny and Cher's expansive television work—the work that brought Cher from star to superstar—began in the summer of 1996 with TV-Land's airing of episodes of both *The Sonny and Cher Comedy Hour* and the post-divorce *Sonny and Cher Show*. In 1998 the music channel VHI followed suit and aired (an edited version) of Cher's 1975 special with Elton John, Bette Midler and Flip Wilson, as well as twelve half-hour edited versions of *Cher* as part of their *VHI Flashback* series of programming.

V.I.E.W. Video was the first to bring Sonny and Cher's work to the home-video market. In 2003 the company released *The Sonny and Cher Nitty Gritty Hour*, an edited version of the hour-long pilot for *The Sonny and Cher Comedy Hour*.

"It's really a great show," says V.I.E.W. Video president and founder Bob Karcy. "We've repackaged it a couple of times [in 2009 it was repackaged and re-titled *The Sonny and Cher Hour*] and changed the artwork to better position it in the marketplace." He also changed the format of the show. "We made the decision to release the video without the comedy sketches for two reasons," says Karcy. "First; we wanted the focus to be on music, that's what our video catalogue is about. Second; viewed today, we felt that a large part of the comedy material was politically incorrect. Of course, at the time it was done it was all done it the spirit of fun, but times have changed. The comedy on the pilot episode did not sit well with me or my staff."

R2 Entertainment released *The Sonny and Cher Ultimate Collection* the same year as *The Sonny and Cher Nitty Gritty Hour*. A comprehensive nine-episode overview, the *Ultimate Collection* is, by far, the most representative—including both pre- and post-divorce shows, producer interviews, station promos, music videos, and (limited) commentary by Cher. The set also features an early

Sonny and Cher appearance on the short-lived *Barbara McNair Show*. Today, distribution (broadcast) rights for Sonny and Cher's television work is handled by Paul Brownstein Productions, Inc. *Cher* and *The Sonny and Cher Show* are owned by Apis Productions, Inc. (Cher's production company), while *The Sonny and Cher Comedy Hour* is jointly owned by Blye-Bearde Productions (producers Allan Blye and Chris Bearde's company), Apis Productions, and the beneficiaries of the estate of Sonny Bono.

The final entry in the Sonny and Cher television cannon is R2 Entertainment's *The Sonny and Cher Christmas Collection*. Issued in 2004, the holiday themed three-episode set features two Christmas episodes from the pre-divorce *Sonny and Cher Comedy Hour* and one from the post-divorce *Sonny and Cher Show*. Cher's solo television work—the 29-episode *Cher* series (including the *Cher* special) as well as her two 60-minute specials; ABC's *Cher... Special* (1978) and NBC's *Cher... and Other Fantasies* (1979), have yet to be released on DVD. One of the challenges, it seems, is the complicated and costly process of acquiring the rights to redistribute and sell copyrighted music. "Broadcast rights and the right to 'sell' are two totally different things," says Enrique Rodriguez, Jr., a lawyer whose specialty is broadcast television. "As far as Cher's solo television series goes, it would be very costly to acquire the rights to sell DVDs that include all the songs that she sang. I mean she sings songs from the Beatles catalogue, from the Rolling Stones, from Michael Jackson, from Elton John. All that material costs money: substantial money. Very few companies, especially today, would be willing to put up the money needed to bring all those shows—and all that music—to market."

Perhaps, but it hasn't kept fans from creating a lucrative Cher and Sonny and Cher black market. Each and every *Sonny and Cher Comedy Hour* and *Sonny and Cher Show* episode is available on the bootleg circuit, while about half of *Cher's* 29 episodes are also available.

"I know there's a huge Cher black market out there," says a person who works for Cher's company. "But that's just the way it is. There's a black market for just about everyone in show business—the only difference with Cher is that there is so much more to sell illegally! More power to them. It's a testament to the interest that Cher's fans take in every aspect of her career."

NOTES

Much of this book is based on first-hand interviews conducted over several years. All were recorded, transcribed and archived. The text also includes references culled from books, periodicals, scripts, recordings and video broadcasts. The "notes" provide additional citations and references for significant quotes and not-generally-known information that, if placed in the text, would prove too lengthy and/or confusing. Quotes culled from author interviews are designated "AI."

INTRODUCTION

1. "I'm scared": Rowland Barber, *TV Guide*, Apr. 5, 1975.
2. "Cher is an original": Nicholas von Hoffman, *The Washington Post*, Feb. 28, 1975.
3. "Everything seems," "My mother always told me": Morton Moss, *The Los Angeles Herald-Examiner*, Mar. 30, 1975.

PART ONE: CHERILYN

Chapter 1: The Sicilian and the "Indian"

1. "Our life together": Rowland Barber, *TV Guide*, Apr. 5, 1975.
2. "A hot plate, lice, and cold drafts": Jane Ardmore, *Photoplay*, Mar. 1975.
3. Holt's alcoholic father and early childhood: Ibid.
4. Sarkisian's early life and work: Tony Bowen, *Motion Picture*, Feb. 1975
5. "Haunted House": Ibid.
6. "A third time": John J. Miller, *Pageant*, Sept. 1975.
7. "My mother was": Sony Pictures press conference, 2010.
8. Jean and Santo Bono's courtship and marriage: Sonny Bono, *And the Beat Goes On*, 1991.
9. Marriage to Donna Rankin, "doomed": Ibid.
10. "When I first saw": *The Barbara Walters Special*, 1988.
11. Virginity: *Playboy*, Dec. 1988.

Chapter 2: I Got You Babe

1. "Sonny called me up": AI, Randy Sterling.

2. "In one night": *Sonny and Cher Live* LP, Kapp Records, 1971.
3. "I took the tempo": AI, Les Reed.
4. "a nice, colorful": *The New York Times*, unknown date, 1967.
5. "Cher is onscreen": Vincent Canby, *The New York Times*, Aug. 9, 1969.
6. "After seeing": Jane Ardmore, *Photoplay*, Feb. 1973.
7. "We were getting a little old": George Carpozi, *Motion Picture*, Jun. 1973.
8. "The cool people thought we were square": Claire Safran, *Redbook*, Feb. 1973.
9. "Appealing to all audiences": *Billboard*, unknown date, 1974.
10. "I used to get fan mail": AI, Gary Chowen.
11. "My first meeting," "to me": AI, Allan Blye.
12. "a huge fight": AI, anonymous.
13. "I've always liked Sonny and Cher": Cecil Smith, *Los Angeles Times*, Aug. 22, 1973.
14. At the taping: Victoria Price, *Vincent Price: A Daughter's Biography*, 2000.

Chapter 3: Gypsys, Half-Breeds and Dark Ladies

1. "For me, modern furniture": John Peter, *Look*, Nov. 4, 1969.
2. Description of home: Ibid.
3. "Sonny takes the credit": Vicki Pellegrino, *Cher!*, 1975.
4. Tijuana marriage: Ibid.
5. "First I was Sonny's girlfriend": Rowland Barber, *TV Guide*, Apr. 5, 1975.
6. "We put in a year": Jane Ardmore, *Photoplay*, Nov. 1973.
7. "Sonny kept saying": Judy Fayard, *Life*, Mar. 17, 1972.
8. "I fought him all the way": Ibid.
9. "I thrive on it": Dick Adler, *TV Guide*, Mar. 18, 1972.
10. Arranged appearance: Ibid.
11. "I never knew," "when Cher heard it": AI, Jimmy Dale.
12. "I have no idea," "Back in Oklahoma": AI, John Durrill.
13. "I was very pleased": AI, Dick Holler.
14. "I wrote": AI, Alan O'Day.
15. "The first time," "The first ending," "I first approached": AI, Durrill.

16. "I remember": Dean Ferguson and Johnny "Lauderdale" Danza, *About.com*, 2000.
17. "You wouldn't believe": Starkey Flyth, Jr., *The Saturday Evening Post*, Jul. 1973.
18. Possessions, "you're standing there": Ibid.
19. "Talking about their good works": Henry Ehrlich, *Good Housekeeping*, May 1972.
20. "own everything": Jane Ardmore, *Photoplay*, Sept. 1972.
21. "brilliant marriage": AI, Lenny Roberts.
22. "I loved Cher's version," "it sounded": AI, Neil Sedaka.
23. "perfectly imperfect": AI, anonymous.
24. "We had a schedule," "Siamese twin thing": Nellie Blagden, *McCalls*, Jun. 1974.
25. "He was very domineering": Mark Bego, *Cher*, 1986.
26. "By the time I moved": Brenda Shaw, *Motion Picture*, Jul. 1974.

Chapter 4: I Got Someone Else Babe

1. "This was Bono," "My first knowledge": AI, Roberts.
2. "I went to San Francisco": Rona Barrett, *Rona Barrett's Gossip*, Oct. 1975.
3. "Happy to be free": Lyn Tornabene, *Ladies' Home Journal*, Jul. 1974.
4. "One short ugly guy": Richard Schickel, *Time*, Mar. 27, 1975.
5. Geffen's childhood: Tom King, *The Operator*, 2000.
6. "It didn't take long": Nellie Blagden, *People*, Mar. 25, 1974.
7. "I asked him to buy it": Jane Ardmore, *Photoplay*, Oct. 1974.
8. "I just don't understand": Eileen Barber, *Photoplay*, May 1975.
9. Expenditures: "Vulnerable Vamp," *Forbes*, Mar. 1, 1975.
10. "Dave turns me on," "There is no bitterness": Mary Porter, *Screen Stars*, Jul. 1974.
11. Conversion to Judaism: George Carpozi, *Cher*, 1975.
12. "I'm a late bloomer," Legal filings: Ibid.
13. "I took her": *Screen Stars*, unknown date (1975).
14. "Cher became cold": Michael St. John, *The National Star*, Mar. 9, 1974.
15. "To take it apart" "If anyone wants": John J. Miller, *Motion Picture*, Jun.1974.
16. Letters to CBS: Ibid.
17. "They were streaming down," "pointed head": Andy Warhol, *Interview*, Dec. 1974.
18. Cher and Geffen attend *Grease*: AI, Barbara Johnson.

Chapter 5: Laugh at Me

1. "For a while I was wondering": John J. Miller, *Motion Picture*, Jun. 1974.
2. "Sonny has always been ahead of his time": Jane Ardmore, *Photoplay*, Sept. 1972.
3. Custom tailored material: *TV Guide*, Sept. 7, 1974.
4. "I didn't like it": Bob Williams, *New York Post*, Jun. 13, 1975.
5. "I think": Will Tusher, *TV Radio Mirror*, Mar. 1975.
6. "No one wanted," "it wasn't his fault": AI, Allan Blye.
7. "I'd love to put all the blame": Sue Cameron, *Hollywood Reporter*, Dec. 9, 1974.
8. "I would very much like": George Carpozi, *Cher*.

Chapter 6: *New* Teamwork

1. "Sonny was in his dressing room": Jane Ardmore, *Photoplay*, Sept. 1972.
2. "I'm sure it will": *Screen Stars*, Jul. 1974.
3. "I thought hard," "They're funny," "I'm so thrilled": Morton Moss, *The Los Angeles Herald-Examiner*," Mar. 30, 1975.
4. "Maybe the first time": Julie Baumgold, *Esquire*, Feb. 1975.
5. Greeted by telegrams: AI, anonymous.
6. "A drab overflowing": Claire Safran, *Redbook*, Feb. 1973.
7. "She had it all done up": AI, Ret Turner.
8. "Not only did she love it": AI, George Schlatter.
9. "They didn't": Bob Mackie, Archive of American Television, Jun. 29, 2000.
10. Off their radar: George Schlatter's *Cher* notebook.
11. "old and new," "have her on": Vera Servi. *Chicago Tribune*, Feb. 9, 1975.
12. "It's the difference," "no mention": Nicholas von Hoffman, *The Washington Post*, Feb. 28, 1975.
13. "Hammer and nails": Tom King, *The Operator*, 2000.
14. "George did a really good job" AI, Rona Barrett.
15. "At the time," "Cher requested me": AI, Schlatter.
16. "She is frighteningly new": Carol Troy, *Village Voice*, Mar. 3, 1975.
17. "George was a domineering": AI, Digby Wolfe.
18. Rainer Dart and *Beaches*: BWW News Desk, Aug. 20, 2009
19. "I can't say": Cecil Smith, *The Los Angeles Times*, Feb. 16, 1975.

Chapter 7: The Star Treatment

1. "One of my best": John Engstead, *Star Shots*, 1978.
2. "During rehearsal," "She asked": Bob Mackie, Archive of American Television.
3. "Draws beautifully," "I took care": Ray Aghayan, Archive of American Television.
4. "Going to": AI, Lily Tomlin.
5. "Had her heart set," "People always said": AI, Turner.
6. "I understand": Morton Moss, *The Los Angeles Herald-Examiner*, Mar. 30, 1975.
7. "Cher came to me": Doris Klein Bacon, *Coronet*, Jun. 1974.
8. "Breaking up the planes": Vicki Pelligrino, *Cher!*
9. "Ben was a terrific guy": AI, Turner.
10. "When I'm home": Doris Klein Bacon, *Coronet*, Jun. 1974.
11. "When Cher was broken out": AI, anonymous.
12. "Really knows," "Has a great body," "square look": Doris Klein Bacon, *Coronet*, Jun. 1974.
13. "People would always ask," "We used Rena": Michael Schmidt, *Details*, Aug. 1989.
14. "In my experience": George Schlatter's *Cher* notebook.

Chapter 8: A Cast of Characters

1. "It's quite a jump": Unknown date, 1974.
2. "This is the first time": Carol Troy, *Village Voice*, Mar. 3. 1975.
3. "First you mesh": Harry F. Water, *Newsweek*, Feb. 24, 1975.
4. "It's the only thing": Andy Warhol, *Interview*, Dec. 1974.
5. "The idea of Laverne's hairdo": Michael Schmidt, *Details*, Aug. 1989.
6. "Laverne was sort of": Bob Mackie, Archive of American Television.
7 "Today, nobody remembers": AI, Turner.
8. "The only thing": AI, Wolfe.
9. "I've got to admit": AI, Schlatter.
10. "What I saw in Cher," "The Cher series logo," "George is": AI, Lee Miller.
11. Three program ideas: George Schlatter's *Cher* notebook.
12. "Until Cher": Nicholas von Hoffman, *The Washington Post*, Feb. 28, 1975.
13. "The monologue that I do": Vera Servi, *Chicago Tribune*, Feb. 9, 1975.
14. "From black": First season *Cher* scripts.
15. "Just standing there": Richard Schickel, *Time*, Mar. 17, 1975.

PART TWO: CHER (FORMERLY OF SONNY AND CHER)

Chapter 9: Let Me Entertain You

1. "By the time": AI, Schlatter.
2. "Rented space": AI, Miller.
3. "for some reason": Rowland Barber, *TV Guide*, Apr. 5, 1975.
4. "the audience had to wait": AI, Bo Kaprall.
5. "For those of you": *Cher* broadcast, Feb. 12, 1975.
6. "Once I stopped singing": Rowland Barber, *TV Guide*, Apr. 5, 1975.
7. Geffen assisted: Tom King, *The Operator*, 2000.
8. "I looked like death": *In The Know*, Jan. 1976.
9. Personal pitch: AI, Schlatter.
10. "I just loved": John J. Miller, *Motion Picture*, Aug. 1975.
11. "I can't think": "Star-Studded Special Welcomes Cher Back," *TV Week*, Feb. 8, 1975.
11. "greatest transition": Morton Moss, *The Los Angeles Herald-Examiner*, Mar. 30, 1975.

Chapter 10: "In It Up to My Neck"

1. "She was a most," "It was all so stupid": George Carpozi, *Cher*, 1975.
2. David Geffen called: Steve Dunleavy, *The National Star*, Mar. 8, 1975.
3. "We were aware": Steve Dunleavy, *The National Star*, May 17, 1975.
4. Cher's concession: George Carpozi, *Cher*, 1975.
5. "no small feat": Richard Schickel, *Time*, Mar. 7, 1975.
6. "Wednesday was fitting": Cher, *The First Time*, 1998.
7. "Offstage": AI, Donna Schuman.
8. "Cher and I were close": AI, Miller.
9. "embarked on": Tatum O'Neal, *A Paper Life*, 2004.
10. Trip to Hawaii: Army Archer's "Hollywood," unknown date.
11. "With all due respect": Bob Knight, *Variety*, Feb. 19, 1975.
12: "Tatum kept interrupting": AI, anonymous.
13. Sonny and Raquel at party, "Cher is without a doubt": *And the Beat Goes On*, 1991.
14. "I started": AI, Tony Charmoli.
15. "Cher relishes": Claire Safran, *Redbook*, Feb. 1973.
16. "When I was little": *Rona Looks At...*, TV special, 1975.
17. "I think my looks": Doris Klein Bacon, *Coronet*, Jun. 1974.
18. "That number was," "Raquel was," "I told

George": AI, Wayne Rogers.
19. "Look, this industry": Robert Kerwin, *Photoplay*, Apr. 1977.
20. "Stick It": *Cher*, script #101.

Chapter 11: Up, Up... and Away

1. "Working Marcel": AI, Wolfe.
2. "Cher and the Osmonds": AI, Schlatter.
3. "The company": Rowland Barber, *TV Guide*, April 5, 1975.
4. "I'd seen that": AI, Wolfe.
5. "Cher voice can": Harry F. Waters, *Newsweek*, Feb. 24, 1975.
6. "I thought the comedy": AI, Rona Barrett.
7. "Dropped by studio": AI, anonymous.
8. "David, as brilliant": Fred Robbins, *Forum*, Mar. 1981.
9. "so much in love": AI, anonymous.
10. "We were all": AI, Ruth Pointer.
11. "The first thing," "Though Art": AI, Dee Dee Wood.
12. "getting married": Amanda Murrah Matesky, *TV-Radio Mirror*, Nov. 1975.
13. "Sometimes I don't": Ann Moore, *TV-Radio Mirror*, Oct. 1975.
14. "I was there": AI, Julian Wasser.
15. "Cher is about to": Nicholas von Hoffman, *The Washington Post*, Feb. 28, 1975.
16 "The Fashion Awards": Unknown date, *TV Guide*.

Chapter 12: Magazine Queen

1. "We always over filmed": AI, Schlatter.
2. "Cher was such": Mark Bego, *Cher: If You Believe*, 2001.
3. "The show is pretty sloppy": J.R. Young, *TV Guide*, May 3, 1975.
4. "It could be": AI, Lily Tomlin.
5. "Lily's talent was": AI, Schlatter.
6. "All I remember": AI, Tomlin.
7. "The Jackson Five": AI, Wood.
8. "They were great": AI, Miller.
9. "The picture was more": George Carpozi, *Cher*, 1975.
10. "really quite": Will Tusher, *TV-Radio Mirror*, Mar. 1975.
11. "Under threat": *The New York Times*, Mar. 30, 1975.
12. "I remember": AI, Wolfe.
13. "She reminds": George Bernard, *Motion Picture*, Apr. 1975.

14. "Those magazines," "stupid": Phil Donahue, TV broadcast, 1979.
15. "In the early": "Self Made Woman," *Vox*, Aug. 1991.
16 "When an artist": J. Randy Taraborrelli, *Cher*, 1986.
17. "I don't know how": Dean Ferguson and Johnny "Lauderdale" Danza, *About.com*, 2000
18. "I took": Jay Grossman, *Rolling Stone*, Nov. 8, 1973.
19. "That was," "To this day": AI, Wood.

Chapter 13: A Sunday Night Staple

1. "Cher was someone": AI, Schlatter.
2. "We were all": AI, Nona Hendryx.
3. "very special woman": Cleveland Amory, *TV Guide*, Ap. 5, 1975.
4. Stapleton interview: Loretta Mars, *TV-Radio Mirror*, Nov. 1974.
5. "I was working," "all the sets": AI, Turner.
6. "I was really," "at the time": AI, Kris Kristofferson.
7. "I absolutely," "Cher and I": AI, Rita Coolidge.
8. "to tell the truth," "I'm not really": AI, Billy Swan.
9. "reggae was," "I remember": AI, Wood.

Chapter 14: Belly Button Bickering

1. "the family viewing": Michael Ryan, *TV Guide*, Dec. 6, 1975.
2. "not violent," "Chastity goes": Morton Moss, *The Los Angeles Herald-Examiner*, Mar. 30, 1975.
3. "Cher always had": AI, Schlatter.
4. "I object": "Cher in Cincinnati." *Variety*, Feb. 26, 1975.
5. "when I first": Eugenie Ross-Leming and David Standish, *Playboy*, Oct. 1975.
6. "I was the first": Brant Mewborn, *After Dark*, Feb. 1979.
7. "we have no problem": Bob Williams, *New York Post*, Jun. 13, 1975.
8. "with all": AI, Schlatter.
9. "Should the tiniest": Thomas Meehan, *The New York Times*, Aug. 10, 1975.
10. "floor-show": Janine Gressel, *The Seattle Daily News*, Feb. 14, 1975.
11. "In retrospect": AI, Schlatter.
12. Poll results: *Rona Barrett's Hollywood*, Sept. 1975.
13. "One time": Michael Schmidt, *Details*, Aug. 1989.
14. "All the taping": AI, Miller.
15. "With your stringy hair": "Random Notes."

Rolling Stone, Jun. 5, 1975.
16. "easy to work with": AI, Miller.
17. "When we": AI, Schlatter
18. "the suit": AI, Jim Lapidus.
19. "Everyone loved": AI, Schlatter.

Chapter 15: All in the Family

1. "I asked Son": Eugenie Ross-Leming and David Standish, *Playboy*, Oct. 1975.
2. "Cher expressed surprise": Sonny Bono, *And the Beat Goes On*, 1991.
3. "Closer to Sonny": Chaz Bono, *Transition: The Story of How I Became a Man*, 2011.
4. "No longer wore dresses": *The View*, broadcast May 12, 2011.
5. "Chastity's actually happier": John J. Miller, *Motion Picture*, Jun. 1974.
6. "One of Chastity's pastimes": AI, Turner.
7. "Whenever Cher": AI, anonymous.
8. "It was so funny": Eileen Barber, *Photoplay*, May 1975.
9. "Cher was a wise": AI, Schuman.
10. "Tina and I": Michael Schmidt, *Details*, Aug. 1989.
11. "George suggested": AI, Wood.
12. "I lock myself away": *Newsweek*, Nov. 30, 1987.
13. "I don't remember": AI, Jimmy Webb.
14. "So many": AI, Turner.
15. "What a hoot": AI, Wood.

PART THREE: CHER BONO ALLMAN

Chapter 16: Ramblin' Man

1. First meeting: Tom King, *The Operator*, 2000.
2. "the best damn": *Rolling Stone*, unknown date.
3. "I remember it today": CBS Sunday Morning broadcast, Jan. 16, 2011.
4. "I looked": Elliot Mintz, *Viva*, Oct. 1977.
5. "We made a date," "everything was just awful": Eugenie Ross-Leming and David Standish, *Playboy*, Oct. 1975.
6. "In Macon at Bistro": Marguerite Schott, *Hollywood Reporter*, Feb. 18, 1975.
7. "Gregg hangs out": Will Tusher, *Hollywood Reporter*, Apr. 3, 1975.
8. "drawling whiskey flavored": Tim Cahill, *Rolling Stone*, Jan. 16, 1975.
9. "Cher wanted": AI, Schlatter.
10. "Gregg Allman": AI, Miller.
11. "Our relationship makes": Colin Dangaard,

The National Star. Jul. 22, 1975.
12. "In those days": AI, Turner.
13. "I enjoy": *Motion Picture*, 1975, unknown date.
14. Extra taping: *Cher* script.
15. Left with Gregg: AI, anonymous.

Chapter 17: Girls Will Talk

1. "Art Carney is": AI, Wolfe.
2. "I remember": AI, anonymous.
3. "A middle-aged man": Steve Tinny and Glenn Lovell, *The National Enquirer*. Jul. 25, 1975.
4. "Congratulations ad": *Hollywood Reporter*, April 28, 1975.
5. "Hearing intimate": Sue Cameron, *Hollywood Reporter*, May 28, 1975.
6. "As far as I'm": AI, Barrett.
7. "The papers have": Cher, "Rona looks at..." TV broadcast, 1975.
8. "Long time coming": AI, anonymous.

Chapter 18: "I Do," I Think

1. "Turning down": "People in the news." *The New York Times*, Jul. 2, 1975.
2. "The most awful": Cher, *The First Time*, 1998.
3. "One Sunday": Elliot Mintz, *Viva*, Oct. 1977.
4. "Only minutes" Rona Barrett, *Rona Barrett's Gossip*, Nov. 1975.
5. "I'm beginning": John J. Miller, *Motion Picture*, Oct. 1975.
6. "Before I knew": Leo Janos, *Ladies' Home Journal*, Aug. 1976.
7. "When I was sixteen": Eugenie Ross-Leming, and David Standish, *Playboy*, Oct. 1975.
8. "Gregg told me": Leo Janos, *Ladies' Home Journal*, Aug. 1976.
9. "The first time": Cher, as told to audience at Caesars Palace, Las Vegas, 2009.
10. "Coke, Lady Snow": Maxine Letterford, *Motion Picture*, Dec. 1975.
11. "It was grim": Elliot Mintz, *Viva*, Oct. 1977.
12. "I've always believed": Dick Grant Intercom press release.
13. "Listen I really," "Let's face it": John J. Miller, *Motion Picture*, Jan. 1976.
14. "Cher called": Sonny Bono, 1974 *Dinah!* TV broadcast.
15. "Geffen didn't agree": Tom King, *The Operator*, 2000.
16. "4th of July party": Robert Hofler, *Party Animals: A Hollywood Tale of Sex, Drugs, and Rock 'N' Roll Starring Allan Carr*, 2012.

17. "I think it was seeing": Leo Janos, *Ladies' Home Journal*, Aug. 1976.
18. "It's like having": Jim Jerome, *People*, Sept. 8, 1975.
19. "Helps me," "One night": Leo Janos, *Ladies' Home Journal*, Aug. 1976.
20. "She should ask," "Irving Shatz": George Carpozi, *Cher*, 1975.
21. "I'll wait until": Sonny Bono, 1974 *Dinah!* broadcast.
22. "A final request": "Cher Linked to James Arness' Daughter!" *Movie World*, Aug. 1975.
23. "I honestly": Eugenie Ross-Leming and David Standish, *Playboy*, Oct. 1975.
24. "were dining": Rona Barrett, *Rona Barrett's Gossip*, Nov. 1975.
25. "My network": Eugenie Ross-Leming and David Standish, *Playboy*, Oct. 1975.
26. "I always thought": AI, Barrett.
27. "came to my house": AI, Coolidge.
28. "Did not appear": AI, Schuman.

Chapter 19: New Album, Old Father

1. "We were just": Dean Ferguson and Johnny "Lauderdale" Danza, *About.com*, 2000.
2. "Nilsonny and Cher": Adam Block, *Creem*, Jul. 1975.
3. "Stars, or for that matter": AI, Jimmy Webb.
4. "I wrote": AI, Janis Ian.
5. "I really loved": Dean Ferguson and Johnny "Lauderdale" Danza, *About.com*, 2000.
6. "When I was on": Cher, *Mike Douglas* TV broadcast, 1979.
7. "It's the only": Andy Warhol, *Interview*, May, 1982.
8. "Cher's first": "Random Notes." *Rolling Stone*, Jun. 5, 1975.
9. "Cher is solid": *Women's Wear Daily*, 1975, unknown date.
10. "I can't listen": Eugenie Ross-Leming, David Standish, *Playboy*, Dec. 1988.
11. "That sounds like": John J. Miller, *Pageant*, Sept. 1975.
12 "After Georgia," "never thought she was": Tony Bowen, *Motion Picture*, Feb. 1975.
13. "During World War II": John J. Miller, *Pageant*, Sept. 1975.
14. "I didn't really": Eugenie Ross-Leming and David Standish, *Playboy*, Dec. 1988.

Chapter 20: All in the Family Too

1. "I found lots," "Cher's mother and sister": Cal York, "Remember You Heard it First in

Photoplay," *Photoplay*, unknown date (1975).
2. "Johnny came into": Tony Bowen, *Motion Picture*, Jul. 1975.
3. "The girls had fathers," "When Sonny and Cher": Jane Ardmore, *Photoplay*, Mar. 1975.
4. "I can be silly": Claire Safran, *Redbook*, Feb. 1973.
5. "I would have": Doris Klein Bacon, *Coronet*, Jun. 1974.
7. "The idea": Andy Warhol, *Interview*, Dec. 1974.
8. "Now I don't," "Well you see": Merv Griffin on the *Merv Griffin* show, 1979.
9. "It's difficult," "My mother used to": Hilary De Vries, *New York Newsday*, Nov. 3, 1991.
10. "Lets face it": Michael St. John, *Movie Life*, Aug. 1975.
11. "We are alike": Ellen Torgerson, *TV Guide*, Dec. 25, 1976.
12. Staged event: John J. Miller, *Motion Picture*, Nov. 1975.
13. "To see if I can": Barbra Wilkins, *People*, Aug. 11, 1975.
14. "Cher's phone," "there wasn't": John J. Miller, *Motion Picture*, Nov. 1975.
15. "I read": Eugenie Ross-Leming and David Standish, *Playboy*, Oct. 1975.
16. "There are a number": Stephen Traiman, *Billboard*, Apr. 5, 1975.
17. "Twenty years ago": Jeffrey Newman, *The National Enquirer*, Feb. 10, 1976.
18. "They all looked": Bob Mackie, Archive of American Television.
19. "Top ten shows": "Second Season Ratings Averages." *Variety*, Apr. 16, 1975.
20. "Everything seems": Alan Markfield, *The National Enquirer*, Mar. 25, 1975.

Chapter 21: Musical Chairs

1. "Joey Heatherton": *The National Star*, unknown date, 1975.
2. "I kept thinking": AI, Schlatter.
3. "I love it": Harry F. Water, *Newsweek*, Feb. 24, 1975.
4. "I happened to," "The first season": AI, Miller.
5. "Over budget": Richard Schickel, *Time*, Mar. 7, 1975.
6. "Oh, that": Bob Lardine, *Daily News*, Jan. 25, 1975.
7. "CBS continues": Eugenie Ross-Leming and David Standish, *Playboy*, Oct. 1975.
8. "All I know": Brant Mewborn, *After Dark*, Feb. 1979.
9. "I really want Sonny": Nancy Marks, *Movie*

Stars, Apr. 1976.
10. "I saw it," "A single": Joseph N. Bell, *Good Housekeeping*, Sept. 1975.
11. "I'm a producer": Schlatter, *TV Guide*, unknown date, 1975.
12. "I was certain," "Cher's an ingrate": Bob Lardine, *Daily News*, Jan. 25, 1975.
13. "People just don't": Barbara Wilkins, *People*, Aug. 11, 1975.
14. "Schlatter's pitch to Hawn": *Hollywood Reporter*, unknown date, 1975.
15. "just disappeared," "During our": AI, Miller.
16. "I was furious": AI, anonymous.
17. "I know": AI, Miller.

Chapter 22: Something for Everyone

1. "At the end": AI, Wolfe.
2. "Losing Jimmy": AI, Miller.
3. "out of hand," "I think it's healthy": Will Tusher, *Hollywood Reporter*, Apr. 3, 1975.
4. "That particular": AI, Schlatter.
5. "When I heard," "the contrast: AI, Klausen.
6. "I submitted," "Jim said," "first of all": AI, Mann.
7. "I was the first": AI, Ric Drasin.
8. "I thought": AI, Jim Morris.
9. "The FBI," "I really don't feel": John J. Miller, *Motion Picture*, Jan. 1976.
10. "We tried something": Kay Gardella, *Daily News*, Nov. 7, 1975.
11. "When they first": Cher, *The First Time*, 1998.
12. "Having the Rolling Stones": AI, Miller.
13. Angie Dickinson: Jack Martin, *The National Enquirer*, Sept. 2, 1975.
14. "There really is": Kay Gardella, *Daily News*, Nov. 7, 1975.
15. "The network was": AI, Schlatter.
16. "Ray and I met": AI, Paul Galbraith.
17. "I got the job," "I was finally more:" AI, Sartain.
18. "Otis and for that": AI, Schlatter.

PART FOUR: (ANOTHER) NEW BEGINNING

Chapter 23: Salute to a Friend

1. Banked footage, "Cher returned": *Cher* script.
2. "Scott Salmon": AI, Mann.
3. "Asian Brigade": *Sanford and Son: Behind the Scenes*, TV documentary, unknown date.
4. "Today I still": AI, Klausen.

5. "When we were," "Cher was definitely": AI, Pointer.
6. "I was there": AI, Rogers.
7. "Puppet Man," "There was always": AI, Mann.
8. "It wasn't as nuts," "She was such": AI, Rogers.
9. "severe arthritis": Sally Newton, *Movie Stars*, May 1976.

Chapter 24: Two for the Price of One

1. "Fourteen-hour day": Schlatter's *Cher* notebook.
2. "After I was": AI, Rogers.
3. "I always loved": AI, Galbraith.
4. "At the time": "Cher didn't show," "the levitation": AI, Mark Wilson.
5. "I remember": AI, Mann.
6. "The second time": AI, Pointer.
7. "Fainting": Cal York, "Remember You Heard it First in Photoplay," *Photoplay*, unknown date, 1975.
8. "As a woman," "We were all out": AI, Mann.
9. "Hollywood was kind of," Labelle learned of cut: AI, Hendryx.
10. "Space Madonna": Bob Mackie, *The Mike Douglas Show*, 1979.
11. "'500 Miles' is": AI, Klausen.
12. "I'm quite sure," "Chastity bluntly": Leo Janos, *Ladies' Home Journal*, Aug. 1976.
13. "On the show": AI, Schlatter.
14. "I hit the deck": Cher, *The Tonight Show*, 1979.
15. "Every week," "They first": AI, Mann.
16. "I remember Jean": AI, Klausen.
17. "I just didn't get": AI, Mann.
18. Cher onstage with Allman: *Jersey City News*, unknown date, 1975.
19. "I was at": AI, Tina Schultz.

Chapter 25: Witchy Woman

1. "Demand for tickets": James Gregory, *The National Enquirer*. Dec. 4, 1975.
2. "I saw Cher" AI, Sandy Griffin.
3. "We had a whole": AI, Turner.
4. "They think": Bob Mackie, Archive of American Television.
5. "While you're shooting," "I think": AI, Mann.
6. "It's some of": AI, Schlatter.
7. "I'm busier": Glenn Lovell, *The National Enquirer*, Sept. 2, 1975.
8. "If I had to pick": AI, Miller.
9. "I was really": AI, Klausen.
10. "Cher as everyone," "I remember": AI, Turner.
11. "Impressive in comedy": Will Tusher, *Hollywood Reporter*, Apr. 3, 1975.

12. "Just finished": Bob Lardine, *Daily News*, Jan. 25, 1975.

13. "That sketch": AI, Schlatter.

14. "That Witchy": AI, Mann.

15. "I remember": AI, Turner.

16. "It wasn't done": "Cher Recalls Spinners for Instant Replay:" *Jet*, Dec. 11, 1975.

17. "Well, I'm": Eugenie Ross-Leming, and David Standish, *Playboy*, Oct. 1975.

18. "When I was": Tim Cahill, *Rolling Stone*, Jan. 16, 1975.

Chapter 26: Who Becomes a Legend Most?

1. "Cher heard the news": Eugenie Ross-Leming, and David Standish, *Playboy*, Oct. 1975.

2. "The weekend," "He Really hurt": Barbara Wilkins, *People*, Sept. 27, 1976.

3. "They told me," "There comes," "I'm terribly afraid," "Marriage is such": John J. Miller, *Motion Picture*, Apr. 1976.

4. "That particular sketch": AI, Miller.

5. "I don't remember": AI, anonymous.

6. "Blindness is": *The National Star*, unknown date, 1975.

7. "Dealing with": AI, Miller.

8. "Uncle Ray": AI, Schlatter.

9. "I remember": AI, anonymous.

10. "I would love": Schlatter notebook.

11. "I had this guest": Rowland Barber, *TV Guide*, Jun. 5, 1976.

12. "I'm against": Gerald Greene, *TV-Radio Mirror*, Mar. 1975.

13. "Cold and distant": British TV Broadcast, unknown date, 1990s.

14. "Bowie's fee": Schlatter notebook.

15. "Cher was obviously": Lisa Robinson, *Creem*, Mar. 1976.

16. "Personality hassles": John J. Miller, *Motion Picture*, Jan. 1976.

17. "Things are going": John J. Miller, *Motion Picture*, Nov. 1975.

18. "Writers have": AI, Wolfe.

19. "I wrote": AI, Sartain.

20. "Cher was never": AI, Schlatter.

21. "I wasn't always": AI, Miller.

Chapter 27: Cher Shares "Cher"

1. "Can Cher's show": *Screen Stars*, unknown date, 1975.

2. Nov. 2 Nielsens: "Second Season Ratings Averages." *Variety*, Apr. 16, 1975.

3. "Why did a girl," "now at least": Kay Gardella, *Daily News*, Nov. 7, 1975.

4. "Right now": Bob Mallory, *The National Star*. Dec. 9, 1975.

5. "I was ready," "for the record": Eugenie Ross-Leming and David Standish, *Playboy*, Oct. 1975.

6. Roger Corman's offer: Will Tusher, *Hollywood Reporter*, Apr. 3, 1975.

7. "Most of our dolls," "When you're dealing": Rick Mitz, *Celebrity*, Jul. 1977.

8. "Cher arrived": Lisa Robinson, *Creem*, Sept. 1976.

9. "While she was": AI, Klausen.

10. "I thought": AI, Schlatter.

11. "The fans": Stephen Schaefer, *Photoplay*, Mar. 1976.

12. "Watching our daughters": Shirley Boone, *Photoplay*, Oct. 1974.

13. "I remember seeing": AI, Holler.

14. "Go dancing," "I was there": AI, Mann.

15. "No one ever": AI, Sedaka.

Chapter 28: It Was a Good Year

1. "After a while": Leo Janos, *Ladies' Home Journal*, Aug. 1976.

2. "Laverne and Gladys taping": Schlatter notebook.

3. "At 9:00 p.m.": Tony Bowen, *TV-Radio Mirror*, Dec. 1975.

4. "He liked me": Cher, *The First Time*, 1998.

5. "Alcohol", "It was no more": Glen Campbell and Tom Carter, *Rhinestone Cowboy*, 1994.

6. "All of a sudden": Rowland Barber, *TV Guide*, Apr. 12, 1975.

7. "I'm no bra burner": Leo Janos, *Ladies' Home Journal*, Aug. 1976.

8. "Even though," "I knew": AI, Miller.

9. "After we finished": AI, Klausen.

10. "The last show," "She didn't": AI, Turner.

11. "I remember": AI, Miller.

12. "For the solo," "After Cher": AI, Klausen.

13. "Being on Cher": AI, Janet Lennon.

14. "During most": AI, Kathy Lennon.

15. "There was no party": AI, anonymous.

Chapter 29: The Beat Goes On

1. "There was": AI, Klausen.

2. "On her own": Lisa Robinson, *Creem*, Mar. 1976.

3. "Cher endeared": Deana Richards, *In The Know*, Jul.1975.

4. "Tragic how": Marie Brenner, *New Times*, Feb. 1976.

5. "Cher's show": Bob Mackie, Archive of American Television.

6. "1.5 million", "I'm producing": Sander Vanocur, *The Washington Post*, Dec. 3, 1975.

7. "I remember": AI, Miller.

8. "Surrounded by": "Sonny and Cher Rejoin." *The New York Times*, Jan. 31, 1976.

9. "No I don't think": Archival news footage, 1975.

10. "You know why": Rowland Barber, *TV Guide*, Jun. 5, 1976.

11. "If you think," "It was still,": Don Shirley, *The Washington Post*, Dec. 24, 1975.

12. "Obviously": "Sonny and Cher Rejoin," *The New York Times*, Jan. 31, 1976.

13. "I wouldn't work," "I don't care": Jeffrey Newman, *The National Enquirer*, Feb. 10, 1976.

14. "The new Sonny and Cher": Sander Vanocur, *The Washington Post*, Dec. 3, 1975

15. Ratings, "This show is": Rowland Barber, *TV Guide*, Jun. 5, 1976.

16. "I liked the idea," "I get more": AI, Steve Barri.

17. "I wrote," "When you're": AI, O'Day.

18. "An excellent song": M.O., *Melody Maker*, Nov. 1976.

19. "I was thrilled," "Not many people": AI, Sedaka.

20. "CBS has a marvelous": CBS press release, 1977.

21. "I thought": AI, Schlatter.

22. "I think": Bob Mackie, Archive of American Television.

23. "The second" AI, Turner.

24. "I watched": AI, Miller.

25. "They dropped": Judy Bacharach, *The Washington Post*, May 13, 1977.

26. "Television is": AI, Wasser.

27. "I don't love": "The Cher Story" with host Casey Kasem, syndicated radio broadcast, 2001.

EPILOGUE

1. Sonny and Cher set list: *Cher...ing the Limelight*, Feb. 1977.

2. "Our whole show": *The Merv Griffin Show*, 1979.

3. "I didn't want": Marilyn Beck, *The Star Ledger*, Apr. 3, 1978.

4. "Dead weight": Liz Smith, *The Daily News*, unknown date, 1978.

5. "I really loved": Dean Ferguson and Johnny "Lauderdale" Danza, *About.com*, 2000.

6. "Cher's fans came": Elliot Mintz, *Us*, Jan. 10, 1978.

7. "Snuff hired," "Snuff told me": AI, Sandy Pinkard.

8. "I don't need": *Phil Donahue* broadcast, 1979.

9. "I was terrified": Marilyn Beck, *The Star Ledger*, Apr. 3, 1978.

10. "Cher's first TV special": *Variety*, Apr. 12, 1978.

11. "Cher's special bombs": Kay Gardella, *The Daily News*, Apr. 3, 1978.

12. "The show's flimsy": Tom Buckley, *The New York Times*, Mar. 3, 1979.

13. "Cher does," "tonight Cher gives": Kay Gardella, *The Daily News*, Mar. 3, 1979.

14. "Casablanca came," "It was a strange": AI, Bob Esty.

15. "Cher unveils": *Variety*, Jun. 20, 1979.

16. "Cher's use of ": AI, Chad Michaels.

17. "Oh, it's okay": Lynn Darling, *The Washington Post*, Jul. 16, 1979.

18. "I wrote," "someone from my publishing": AI, Fred Mollin.

19. "I remember thinking," "I was disappointed": AI, Allee Willis.

20. "I'll only get one chance": *Rona Barrett's Hollywood*, Jan. 1976.

21. "I hate L.A.": *New York Review*, February, 1982.

22. "It's like a": Unknown magazine source, 1982.

23. "I was the curiosity," "this gay club": Mark Bego, *Cher: If You Believe*, 2001.

24. "I never did": AI, David Wolfert.

25. "Cher gives a cheery": Frank Rich, *The New York Times*, Feb. 19, 1982.

26. "Cher proves": Mark Bego, *Cher: If You Believe*, Rex Reed, 2001.

27. "I'm out talking": *USA Today*, unknown date, 1982.

28. "If I can live with it": Stephen Silverman, *The New York Post*, May 28, 1985.

29. "What's happening to me," "a Cher delight": Mark Bego, *Cher: If You Believe*, 2001.

31. "The film has enough": Janet Maslin, *The New York Times*, Jun. 12, 1987.

32. "Cher does a convincing": Roger Ebert, *The Chicago Sun Times*, Oct. 23, 1987.

33. "Cher is trapped": Hal Hinson, *The Washington Post*, Oct. 23, 1987.

34. "a great big": Rita Kempley, *The Washington Post*, Jan. 15, 1988.

35. "The acting is": David Sterritt, *The Christian Science Monitor*, Jan. 29, 1988.

36. "Cher is absolutely": "*Siskel and Ebert at the Movies*" broadcast, unknown date, 1987.

37. "Cher's never been better": Julie Salamon, *Wall Street Journal*, Jan. 5, 1988.

38. "a winning": Andy Seiler, *Home News*, Jan. 15, 1988.

39. "to know me": *Cosmopolitan*, Feb, 1988.

40. "when Paul Newman": Mark Bego, *Cher: If You Believe*, 2001.

41. "My body was never better": *Hot Air*, 1991.

42. "I loved what Cher": AI, Tom Snow.

43. "they told me": Geffen Records, *Heart of Stone* publicity book, 1989.

44. "It's really weird": *Dateline* broadcast, unknown date, 1989.

45. "It's my job": *Entertainment Tonight* broadcast, unknown date, 1989.

46. "devilishly trash-kitsch": Hal Hinson, *The Washington Post*, Dec. 14, 1990.

47. "a stylish": Vincent Canby, *The New York Times*, Dec. 14, 1990.

48. "I don't know": Hilary de Vris, *Fan Fare*, Nov. 3, 1991.

49. "I was sick": Edna Gundersen, Feb. 6, 2008.

50. "a thin commonplace": Janet Maslin, *The New York Times*, Apr. 3, 1996.

51. "I felt really sorry": *New York Post*, unknown date, 1996.

52. "I've had a few": *Superpak Vol. I*, Jul. 2000.

53. "I can't remember," "I don't believe": AP Press Release, Sept. 11, 1996.

54. "My favorite time," "'Strong Enough' was": Dean Ferguson and Johnny "Lauderdale" Danza, *About.com*, 2000.

55. "Cher plays a role": Mick LaSalle, *San Francisco Chronicle*, May 14, 1999.

56. "I liked": Roger Ebert, *Chicago Sun Times*, May 14, 1999.

57. "I am so uncool": Michael Logan, *TV Guide*, Aug. 21, 1999.

58. "I did that on purpose": Jacob Bernstein, *The Daily Beast*, Jun. 25, 2010.

59. "Yes, this is": *Nightline* broadcast, unknown date, 2008.

60. "So much technology": Josiah Howard, Cher Caesars Palace Program, 2008.

61. "the Cheriest": Mike Weatherford, *Las Vegas Review-Journal*, May 15, 2008.

62. "It was fun": *Late Night With David Letterman* broadcast, 2011.

63. "Look at Cher's career": *The Daily Beast*, Feb. 13, 2012.

64. "achingly dull": Manohla Dargis, *The New York Times*, Nov. 23, 2011.

65. "Burlesque shows": Roger Ebert, *The Chicago Sun Times*, Nov. 23, 2011.

66. "the love of my life": Hilary de Vries, *Fanfare*, Nov. 3, 1991.

67. "I got to know": AI, anonymous.

68. "you'll have to excuse": CNN broadcast, Jan. 8, 1998.

69. "I got the part": AI, Renee Faia.

70. "a brilliant performance": *The Daily Beast*, Feb. 13, 2012.

71. "when I heard": *Good Morning America* broadcast, unknown date.

72. "I'm not selling": CBS News, Feb. 11, 2009.

73. "I remember": Chaz Bono interview on National Public Radio, May 10, 2011.

74. "The way I dressed": Chaz Bono, *Transition: The Story of How I Became a Man*, 2011.

75. "I'm scared": J. Randy Taraborrelli, *Cher*, 1989.

76. "I date men": Steve Herz and Patricia Towle, *The National Enquirer*, Feb. 13, 1990.

77. "I live in": *Contactmusic.com*, Nov. 5, 2011.

78. "I had a very": *Charlie Rose* broadcast, 1996.

79. "she was really": Chaz Bono, *Transition: The Story of How I Became a Man*, 2011.

80. "It's hard" Dotson Radar, *Parade*, Nov. 21, 2010.

81. "I'm sure": *The Daily Beast*, Feb. 13, 2012.

82. "Elijah has never": *Phil Donahue* broadcast, 1979.

83. "we have ended": Cara Sprunk, *Star*, January 2, 2012.

84. "It's weird": Kristina Smith, *Vanity Fair*, Dec. 2010.

85. "Even with music": *Art News*, Feb. 26, 2010.

86. "I met with Cher": Kara Warner, Sept. 26, 2011.

BIBLIOGRAPHY

Allman, Gregg. *My Cross to Bear*. New York: William Morrow, 2012.

Ames, Janice. "Cher's Mother Confides..." *Movie Life*, May. 1976.

Amory, Cleveland. "The Sonny and Cher Comedy Hour." *TV Guide*, Feb. 2, 1972.

Amory, Cleveland. "Cher." *TV Guide*, Ap. 5, 1975.

Amory Cleveland. "The Sonny and Cher Show." *TV Guide*, May 8, 1976.

Anderson, Jon. "Book Review." *The Chicago Tribune*. Jul. 22, 1999.

Archerd, Army. "Just For Variety." *Variety*, May 14, 1975.

Ardmore, Jane. "Sonny and Cher: Their Best Friend Tells All." *Photoplay*, Sept. 1972.

Ardmore, Jane. "Sonny and Cher Fighting!" *Photoplay*, Feb. 1973.

Ardmore, Jane. "Extra! Sonny Answers Divorce Rumors." *Photoplay*, Nov. 1973.

Ardmore, Jane. "Cher Living With Sonny Again." *Photoplay*, Oct. 1974.

Ardmore, Jane. "Her Mom's First Interview." *Photoplay*, Mar. 1975.

Bacharach, Judy. "Sonny's Story." *The Washington Post*, May 13, 1977.

Barber, Eileen. "Cher's Best Friend Talks About the Pain She Hides!" *Photoplay*, May 1975.

Barber, Rowland. "The Party's Over." *TV Guide*, Jun. 1, 1974.

Barber, Rowland. "Cher... Alone." *TV Guide*, Apr. 12, 1975.

Barber, Rowland. "The Lives and Loves of Salvatore and Cherilyn Part IV." *TV Guide*, Jun. 5, 1976.

Barnes, Ken. *The Best of Sonny and Cher: The Beat Goes On*. (CD booklet.) Atco Records, 1991.

Barrett, Rona. "Rona Talks to Cher Part I." *Rona Barrett's Gossip*, Sept. 1975.

Barrett, Rona. "Rona Talks to Cher Part II." *Rona Barrett's Gossip*, Oct. 1975.

Barrett, Rona. "Cher's Nine-Day 'Marriage' Isn't Over Yet!" *Rona Barrett's Gossip*, Nov. 1975.

Bascombe, Laura. "The Truth Behind the Sonny and Cher Split." *Photoplay*, May 1975.

Bascombe, Laura. ""How Sonny Made Cher and Allman Reconcile." *Photoplay*, Mar. 1976.

Baumgold, Julie. "The Winning of Cher." *Esquire*, Feb. 1975.

Behrens, Leigh. "Georgia Holt: I'm Learning to Love Myself." *Chicago Tribune*, Jul. 24, 1988.

Bernard, George. "We Spend a Day with Elvis's Girl." *Motion Picture*, Apr. 1975.

Bernstein, Jacob. "The Man Suing Joan Rivers." *The Daily Beast*, Jun. 25, 2010.

Black, James. "My Face is My Fortune." *Photoplay*, Oct. 1976.

Blagden, Nellie. "Cher Without Sonny: Can the Show Go On?" *People*, Mar. 25, 1974.

Blagden, Nellie. "What Really Happened to Sonny and Cher?" *McCall's*, Jun. 1974.

Block, Adam. "Drunk with John, George, Ringo and..." *Creem*, Jul. 1975.

Bego, Mark. "Cherchez La Cher." *New York*, Apr. 27, 1979.

Bego, Mark. *Cher*. New York: Pocket Books, 1986.

Bego, Mark. *Cher: If You Believe*. New York: Cooper Square Press, 2001.

Bell, Joseph N. "Cher: Super S tar! Super Mom?" *Good Housekeeping*, Sept. 1975.

Bond, Paul. "Cher's Anti-Romney Twitter Rant." *Hollywood Reporter*, May 8, 2012.

Bono, Chaz and Billie, Fitzpatrick, *Transition: The Story of How I Became a Man*. New York: Dutton, 2011.

Bono, Sonny. *And The Beat Goes On*. New York: Pocket Books, 1991.

Bowen, Tony. "Cher's Just Too Big for Her Britches." *Motion Picture*, Feb. 1975.

Bowen, Tony. "Cher's Mom Defends Her Against Father's Attack!" *Motion Picture*, Jul. 1975.

Bowen, Tony. "Hal Linden and Family." *TV-Radio Mirror*, Dec. 1975.

Breithaupt, Don and Breithaupt, Jeff. *Precious and Few*. New York: St. Martin's Griffin, 1996.

Brenner, Marie. "Final Tribute." *New Times*, Feb. 6, 1976.

Bronson, Fred. *The Billboard Book of Number One Hits*. New York: Billboard Books, 1992.

Burke, Wally. "Sonny Cheated Me... He Treated Me Like a Slave," *Photoplay*, Jun. 1974.

Cahill, Tim. "Nothing Matters But the Fever." *Rolling Stone*, Jan. 16, 1975.

Cameron, Sue. "Cher." *Hollywood Reporter*, Feb. 12, 1975.

Cameron, Sue. "Rona Looks at..." *Hollywood*

Reporter, May 28, 1975.

Campbell, Glen and Carter, Tom. *Rhinestone Cowboy*. New York: Villard Books, 1994.

Canby Vincent. "Chastity Begins Local Run." *The New York Times*, Aug. 9, 1969.

Carpozi, George. "Cher to Pose in the Nude." *Motion Picture*, Jun. 1973.

Carpozi, George. *Cher*. New York: Berkley Medallion Books, 1975.

Carson, Andrea. "Cher's Secret Dates are Driving Her Lover Wild!" *Modern Screen*, Aug. 1975.

Cavendish, Lucy. "Rock of Ages." *The Sunday Telegraph Magazine*, Feb. 28, 1999.

Cher. *The First Time*. New York: Simon & Schuster, 1998.

Coelho, Susie. *Secrets of a Style Diva*. New York: Thomas Nelson, 2006.

Cyclops. "Cher's Sonny, Wilbur's Fannie and Privacy." *The New York Times*, Mar. 2, 1975.

Dangaard, Colin. "Cher's New Husband a 'Terrific Lover.'" *The National Star*. Jul. 22, 1975.

Dangaard, Colin. "Only Liberace!" *The National Star*. Jul. 22, 1975.

Dangaard, Colin. "Chering a Joke." *The National Star*. Dec. 23, 1975.

Daniel, Winston. "Tatum..." *The National Star*. Mar. 8, 1975.

Darling, Lynn. "Cher: Gilded, Glamorous...." *The Washington Post*, Jul. 16, 1979.

De Vries, Hilary. "Cher Talks Tough." *New York Newsday*, Nov. 3, 1991.

Distel, Larry. "Cher Back in Special." *Register TV Magazine*, Feb. 9, 1975.

Douglas, Benjamin. "Who's Kidding Who?" *The National Star*, Dec. 30, 1975.

Dunleavy, Steve. "Death Party: 'They Just Left Robbie to Die.'" *The National Star*, Mar. 8, 1975.

Dunleavy, Steve. "This I Believe." *The National Star*, May 17, 1975.

Edelman, Rosemary. "It Ain't Easy Being a Star." *TV Guide*, Mar. 1, 1975.

Eden Barbara and Wendy Leigh. *Jeanie Out of the Bottle*. New York: Crowne Archetype, 2011.

Efron, Edith. "TV's Sex Crisis." *TV Guide*. Oct. 18, 1975.

Engstead, John. *Star Shots*. Vancouver, Canada: Clarke, Irwin & Company, Ltd, 1978.

Essex, David. *A Charmed Life*. Great Britain: Orion Books, 2002.

Farr, William. "Held in Drummer's Death." *Los Angeles Times*. Jun. 27, 1975.

Fayard, Judy. "The Changing of Cher." *Life*, Mar. 17, 1972.

Ferguson, Dean and Johnny Danza. "Cher: Back to the Dance Floor!" About.com, 2000.

Fiore, Mary. "Cher Talks About Cher." *Good Housekeeping*, Jan. 1976.

Fisher, William, T. "Cher Witness to Murder?" *Motion Picture*, Jun. 1975.

Flythe, Jr., Starkey. "That Amazing Creature the SonnyAndCher." *Saturday Evening Post*, Jul. 1973.

Gallo, Phil. "And The Beat Goes On." *Variety*, Feb. 21, 1999.

Gardella, Kay. "Stylish Cher Soars in Her Solo CBS Outing." *Daily News*. Feb. 13, 1975.

Gardella, Kay. "Great CBS Problem: What To Do with Cher's Navel." *Daily News*, Jul. 21, 1975.

Gardella, Kay. "Cher Won't Cover Up For The Family Hour." *Detroit Free Press*, Aug. 24, 1975

Gardella, Kay. "Cher A Loser This Season and Producer Tells Why." *Daily News*. Nov. 7, 1975.

Garr, Teri. *Speed bumps: Flooring it Through Hollywood*. New York: Hudson Street Press, 2005.

Gissen, Jay. "Cher Struck." *The Cable Guide*, March 1989.

Greene, Gerald. "A Bounty full of Laughs and Love." *TV-Radio Mirror*, Mar. 1975.

Gressel, Janine. "Janine Gressel." *The Seattle Daily News*, Feb. 14. 1975

Gregory, James. "Two Year Wait to Get Tickets to TV Shows." *The National Enquirer*. Dec. 4, 1975.

Grossman, Jay. "Singles: Half-Breed." *Rolling Stone*, Nov. 8, 1973.

Gundersen, Edna. "Cher Shares." *USA Today*, Feb. 6, 2008.

Han, Christina. "The Lash Couturier." *Vogue*, Sept. 2007.

Haralovich, Mary Beth and Rabinovitz, Lauren. *Television History and American Culture: Feminist Critical Essays*. London: Duke University Press, 1999.

Herz, Steve and Patricia Towle. "Branded a Gay, Cher's Daughter Chastity Fights Back." *The National Enquirer*, Feb. 13, 1990.

Hinckley, Robert. "Memo to Cher: Let Loose." *Daily News*, Aug. 25, 1989.

Hobson, Dick. "The Wizard of Glitter and Flash." *TV Guide*. Oct. 18, 1975.

Hodenfield, Chris. "As Bare as You Dare With Sonny and Cher." *Rolling Stone*, May 24, 1973.

Hofler, Robert. *Party Animals: A Hollywood Tale of Sex, Drugs, and Rock 'N' Roll Starring Allan Carr*. Cambridge, MA, Da Capo Press, 2012.

Homer, Ron. "Cher." *Ladies' Home Journal*, Sept. 1975.

Janos, Leo. "Cher's Troubled Year." *Ladies' Home*

Journal, Aug. 1976.

Jerome, Jim. "Gregg Allman Takes to the Road Again." *People*, Sept. 8, 1975.

Kelleher, Terry. "And The Beat Goes On." *People*, Feb. 22, 1999.

Kerwin, Robert. "The New Raquel Welch." *Photoplay*, Apr. 1977.

King, Tom. *The Operator*. New York: Random House, 2000.

Klein Bacon, Doris. "Cher: Super Chick of the '70s." *Coronet*, Jun. 1974.

Klein Bacon, Doris. "Cher's Hair Care-She Knows What's Best," *Coronet*, Jun. 1974.

Klein Bacon, Doris. "How the Super Bodies Stay That Way," *Coronet*, Jun. 1974.

Klein Bacon, Doris. "Keeping Cher in Two Inch Nails," *Coronet*, Jun. 1974.

Klein Bacon, Doris. "A Clean Skin is a Healthy Skin," *Coronet*, Jun. 1974.

Knight, Bob. "Cher is Back and a Winner." *Variety*, Feb. 19, 1975.

Lardine, Bob. "Only on Sunday." *Daily News*, Jan. 25, 1975.

Laurent, Lawrence. "All By Herself, Cher Tries a TV Series." *TV Channels*. Feb. 9, 1975.

Letterford, Maxine. "Cocaine: The Craze That's Sweeping Hollywood." *Motion Picture*, Dec. 1975.

Lipton, Lilly. "Violence is Obscene... Sex is Too Easy." *Photoplay*, Apr. 1977.

Logan, Michael. "Cher the Experience." *TV Guide*, Aug. 21, 1999.

Lovell, Glenn. "George Burns: Busier Now." *The National Enquirer*, Sept. 2, 1975.

Mackie, Bob and Bemer, Gerry. *Dressing For Glamour*. New York, A & W Publishers, 1979.

Mackie, Bob. *Unmistakably Mackie*. New York, Universe Press, 2001.

Mallory, Bob. "CBS Bosses Will Ax Cher's Show." *The National Star*. Dec. 9, 1975.

Mallory, Bob. "Cher's Unborn Baby Throws TV Show into Chaos." *The National Star*. Feb. 3, 1976.

Mars, Loretta. "Jean Stapleton: Prayer Saved Her Husband." *TV-Radio Mirror*, Nov. 1974.

Martin, Jack. ""Elvis Shoots up His Hotel Room." *The National Enquirer*, Sept. 2, 1975.

Matetsky, Amanda Murrah. "The Taming of Cher." *TV-Radio Mirror*, Nov. 1975.

Matetsky, Amanda Murrah. "Sally Struthers Dodges Her Marriage." *TV-Radio Mirror*, Nov. 1975

Markfield, Alan. "Cher Talks About Her New Love." *The National Enquirer*, Mar. 25, 1975.

Marks, Nancy. "Beaming Sonny Confirms Cher is with Him Again." *Movie Stars*, Apr. 1976.

Mayhew, George. "Cher Fights with Geffen Over That Male Superstar, *TV-Radio Mirror*, Oct. 1974.

Meehan, Thomas. "The Children's Hour After Hour." *The New York Times*, Aug. 10, 1975.

Mewborn, Brant. "Conversations with an All-American Vamp." *After Dark*, Feb. 1979.

Miller, John, J. "Cher Vows: 'No One is Going to Take Chastity Away!" *Motion Picture*, Jun. 1974.

Miller, John, J. "Elton John.": 'I Get Gratification out of Spending!'" *Motion Picture*, Aug. 1975.

Miller, John, J. "Cher's Father Talks about the People She's Hurting." *Pageant*, Sept. 1975.

Miller, John, J. "Gregg's a Better Boyfriend than a Husband..." *Motion Picture*, Oct. 1975.

Miller, John, J. "Cher's Two Men: the Battle Begins." *Motion Picture*, Nov. 1975.

Miller, John, J. "An Explosive Last Interview with Cher and Gregg." *Motion Picture*, Jan. 1976.

Miller, John, J. "Cher Terrified Over Plot to Murder Her Baby's Father!" *Motion Picture*, Apr. 1976.

Mintz, Elliot. "Gregg Allman: Cher's Ex Sings the Blues." *Viva*, Oct. 1977.

Mintz, Elliot. "Cher and Gregg: The Losing Fight to Save Their Marriage." *Us*, Jan. 10, 1978.

Mitz, Rick. "Cher and Other Dolls: Is all This Celebrity Fondling Healthy?" *Celebrity*, Jul. 1977.

Moore, Ann. "The Sally Struthers-Art Fisher Romance Fizzles!" *TV-Radio Mirror*, Oct. 1975.

Moss, Morton. "Agony and Ecstasy." *The Los Angeles Herald-Examiner*, Mar. 30, 1975

Musto, Michael. "The New Cher." *Us*, Nov. 11, 1980.

Newman, Jeffrey. "Sonny and Cher: Nothing but Trouble." *The National Enquirer*, Feb. 10, 1976.

Newton, Sally. "The Operation That Made Nancy a New Woman." *Movie Stars*, May. 1976.

North, Harry. "Public Service Announcements We Really Need." *Mad Super Special # 27*, 1978.

O'Neal, Tatum. *A Paper Life*. New York: Harper Collins, 2004.

O'Neal, Thomas. *The Emmys*. New York: Penguin Books, 1992.

Oppenheimer, Peer. "An Unpredictable Woman Named Cher." *Family Weekly*, Aug. 24, 1975.

Pellegrino, Vicki. *Cher*. New York: Ballantine Books, 1975.

Pence-Anderson, Penny. "Designing the Cher that Meets the Eye," *TV Showpeople*, Aug. 1975.

Peters, John. "The Flip Side of Sonny and Cher." *Look*, Nov. 4, 1969.

Petschek, Willa. "Cher Spectacular." *The London Observer*, Jan. 11, 1976.

Plaskin, Glenn. "Total Cher." *Daily News*. May 24, 1992.

Porter, Mary. "Cher Reveals Everything!" *Screen Stars*, Jul. 1974.

Price, Victoria. "Vincent Price: A Daughter's Biography." New York: St. Martin's Press, 2000.

Quirk, Lawrence. *Totally Uninhibited: Cher*. New York: William Morrow & Company, 1991.

Rader, Dotson. "Doing it Her Way." *Parade*, Nov. 21, 2010.

Rich, Frank. "Stage: Robert Altman Directs Cher." *The New York Times*, Feb. 19, 1982.

Richards, Deana. "Cher, Star of the Year... But Why?" *In The Know*, Jul. 1975.

Robins, Fred. "Talking Straight with Cher." *Forum*, Mar. 1981.

Robinson, Lisa. "Is Cher More Than Russ Mael?" *Creem*, Mar. 1976.

Robinson, Lisa. "Eleganza." *Creem*, Sept. 1976.

Ross-Leming, Eugenie and Standish, David. "Playboy Interview: Cher." *Playboy*, Oct. 1975.

Ross-Leming, Eugenie and Standish, David. "Playboy Interview: Cher." *Playboy*, Dec. 1988.

Rubenstein, Harold, R. "Bob Mackie." *Model's Circle*, Oct. 1975.

Ryan, Michael. "Does America Want Family Viewing Time?" *TV Guide*, Dec 6, 1975

Ryan, Michael. "Family Viewing Time: Has It Passed the Test?" *TV Guide*, Jun. 5, 1976.

Sandar, Lynne. "Why Sonny Had to Hide His Illegitimate Son!" *Movie Mirror*, Nov. 1974.

Sanders, Coyne Stevens. *Rainbow's End: The Judy Garland Show*. New York: Zebra Books, 1990.

Safran, Claire. "Sonny and Cher: Even When We Fight We Love." *Redbook*, Feb. 1973.

Sessums, Kevin. "Billy Sammeth, the Manager fired by Cher and Joan Rivers, Tells His Side of the Story." *The Daily Beast*, Feb. 13, 2012

Schaefer Stephen. "David Essex Rocks On." *Photoplay*, Mar. 1976.

Schickel, Richard. "Cher: Rags to Riches." *Time*, Mar. 7, 1975.

Schmidt, Michael. "I Got Clothes Babe." *Details*, Aug. 1989.

Schott, Marguerite. "Cher and Gregg's New Theme Song?" *Hollywood Reporter*, Feb. 18, 1975.

Servi, Vera. "Cher's Back." *Chicago Tribune*, Feb. 9, 1975.

Shaw, Brenda. "I Lived Intimately with Sonny and Cher." *Motion Picture*, Jul. 1974.

Shirley, Don. "Sonny's New Show: Cher Goes,

Glitter Stays." *The Washington Post*, Sept. 21, 1974.

Shirley, Don. "Cher: Great Expectations." *The Washington Post*, Dec. 24, 1975.

Silverman, Stephen. "The Life and Loves of America's Most Unconventional Superstar." *New York Post*, May 28, 1985.

Simmons, Patricia. "Special to Launch New TV Series." *TV Magazine*, Feb. 9, 1975.

Smith, Cecil. "Truman Capote on The Sonny and Cher Show." *The Los Angeles Times*, Aug. 22, 1973.

Smith, Cecil. "Cher Goes It Alone in New Variety Series." *Los Angeles Times*, Feb. 16, 1975.

Smith, Cecil. "Cher Works Her Magic with Talent And Dazzle." *Star Ledger*, Feb. 16, 1975.

Smith, Krista. "Forever Cher." *Vanity Fair*, Dec. 2010.

Smith, Robert G. "Cher's Clothes Cost up to $30,000 a Week." *The National Enquirer*, Sept. 5, 1975.

Sorensen, Jeff. *Lily Tomlin: Woman of a Thousand Faces*. New York: St. Martin's Press, 1989.

Spada, James. *The Divine Bette Midler*. New York: Macmillan Publishing Company, 1984.

Sprunk, Cara. "Chaz Bono: Betrayal." *Star*, Jan. 2, 2012.

Stein, Susan. "An Intimate Look inside Cher and Chastity's New World." *Motion Picture*, Apr. 1975.

St. John, Michael. "The Story of Why We Broke Up, By Sonny." *The National Star*, Mar. 9, 1974

St. John, Michael. "Cher's Sister Tells All." *Movie Life*, Aug. 1975.

Tinny, Steve and Lovell, Glenn. "Missed at the Emmys." *The National Enquirer*. Jul. 25, 1975.

Taraborrelli, J. Randy. *Cher*. New York: St. Martin's Press, 1986.

Taraborrelli, J. Randy. *Cher*. Great Britain: Pan Books, 1989.

Torgerson, Ellen. "Heather is Kind of a Rat." *TV Guide*, Dec. 25, 1976.

Tornabene, Lyn. "Cher's Own Story of Life without Sonny." *Ladies' Home Journal*, Jul. 1974.

Traiman, Stephen. "TV Musical Series Face Hard Times." *Billboard*, Apr. 5, 1975.

Troy, Carol. "Maintaining Cher." *Village Voice*, Mar. 3, 1975.

Troy, Carol. "Glitter Just For Cher." *The New York Daily News*, Jul. 13, 1975.

Tucker, Ken. "And The Beat Goes On." *EW.com*, Feb. 19, 1999.

Tusher, Will. "What is Cher Trying to Prove?" *TV-Radio Mirror*, Mar. 1975.

Tusher, Will. "Rambling Reporter." *Hollywood*

Reporter, Apr. 3, 1975.

Unger, Arthur. "Variety Shows Soft-Shoe Back" *The Christian Science Monitor*, Feb. 7, 1975.

Vanocur, Sander. "Together Again—On Screen." *The Washington Post*, Dec. 3, 1975.

Von-Hoffman, Nicholas. "Cher in a Step Beyond Chauvinism." *The Washington Post*, Feb. 28, 1975.

Warhol, Andy. "Cher at the Pierre." *Interview*, Dec. 1974.

Warhol, Andy. "Cher." *Interview*, May, 1982.

Warner, Kara. "Lady Gaga and Cher Make History." *MTV News*, Sept. 26, 2011.

Waters, Harry F. "Cher and Cher Alone." *Newsweek*, Feb. 24, 1975.

Weatherford, Mike. "Cher Revels in New Show." *Las Vegas Review-Journal*, May 15, 2008.

Weigler, Tom. "No Sonny Days for Cher." *TV Showtime*, Feb. 21, 1975.

Williams, Bob. "On the Air." *New York Post*, Jun. 13, 1975.

Wilkins, Barbara. "Cher Wings a TV Solo Where Sonny Crashed." *People*, Feb. 10, 1975.

Wilkins, Barbara. "Who Dresses Cher in Those Slinky Feathers?" *People*, Jun. 30, 1975.

Wilkins, Barbara. "It's Sonny and Susie: But the Saga with Cher Goes On." *People*, Aug. 11, 1975.

Wilkins, Barbara. "Cher, Gregg and Baby: Chastity Gets a New Brother." *People*, Sept. 27, 1976.

Young, J. R. "David Groh: 'That's The New Yorker in Me.'" *TV Guide*, May 3, 1975.

The following feature articles provided valuable information but were published without author credits:

"Allman Asked Me To Marry Him, Says Blonde." *The National Star*, Feb. 3, 1976.

"Another Cher Special... She Quits!" *Rona Barrett's Hollywood*, May, 1977.

"CBS Gets It's Cher." *Variety*, Feb. 19, 1975.

"Cher in Cincinnati." *Variety*, Feb. 26, 1975.

"Coast Jury Indicts Party Host in Death of a Rock Musician." *The New York Times*, Feb. 21, 1975.

"Cher, and Cher Alike." *The National Star*, Dec. 2, 1975.

"Cher Recalls Spinners for Instant Replay." *Jet*, Dec. 11, 1975.

"Cher Linked to Suicide of James Arness' Daughter!" *Movie World*, Aug. 1975.

"'Cher Remembers' Life with Sonny." CBS News, Feb. 11, 2009.

"Clean Up Your Act CBS Warns Cher... Her Answer!" *Movie World*, Mar. 1976.

"Elijah Blue's 'Step-and-Repeat' at Kantor Gallery." *Art News*, Feb. 26, 2010.

"Has Cher Gone Too Far?" *Rona Barrett's Hollywood*, Aug. 1975.

"Has Cher Gone Too Far? Your Answer: Yes and No!" *Rona Barrett's Hollywood*, Sept. 1975.

"Iris Rainer Dart to be Honored." BroadwayWorld.com Aug. 20, 2009

"Looks Like Cher Joy." *Daily News* (AP), Jul. 1, 1975.

"Married Nine Days 'Mistaken' Cher Sues For Divorce." *New York Post* (AP), Jul. 10, 1975

"Moss Arraigned on Coast." *The New York Times* (UPI), Jun. 27, 1975.

"On the Record." *People*, May 11, 1998.

"People in the News." *The New York Times*, Jul. 2, 1975.

"People in the News." *The New York Times*, Mar. 1, 1974.

"Random Notes." *Rolling Stone*, Jun. 5, 1975.

"Rona Barrett Talks to Cher." *Rona Barrett's Gossip*, Oct. 1975.

"Second Season Ratings Averages." *Variety*, Apr. 16, 1975.

"Second Season Ratings Leaders." *Variety*, Feb. 26, 1975.

"Self Made Woman." *Vox*, Aug. 1991.

"Sonny and Cher TV Show Canceled by CBS for Fall." *The New York Times*, Apr. 6, 1974.

"Sonny and Cher Rejoin." *The New York Times*, Jan. 31, 1976.

"Star-Studded Special Welcomes Cher Back." *TV Week*, Feb. 8, 1975.

"TV Moonlighting." *TV-Radio Mirror*, Oct. 1975.

"Tampa is Ordered to Stop Enforcing Obscenity Law." *The New York Times*, March 30, 1975.

"The Sonny Comedy Revue." *TV Guide*, Sept. 7, 1974.

"Vulnerable Vamp." *Forbes*, Mar. 1, 1975.

APPENDIX

THE PLAYERS

Director
Art Fisher (first season); Mark Warren,
Bill Davis (second season)

Producer
George Schlatter (Producer [first season],
Executive Producer [second season]);
Lee Miller (Executive in Charge of Production
[first season], Producer [second season]);
Don Reo, Allan Katz (Producers [second season])

Musical Director
Jimmy Dale (first season); Jack Eskew (second
season)

Special Musical Material
Billy Barnes & Earl Brown

Choreographer
Tony Charmoli, Dee Dee Wood (first season);
Anita Mann (second season)

Art Director
Robert Kelly (first season);
Ray Klausen (second season)
Set Decorator, Robert Checchi

Writers
Digby Wolfe, Don Reo & Alan Katz,
Iris Rainer, Pat Proft & Bo Kaprall,
David Panich, Ron Pearlman, Nick Arnold,
John Boni, Ray Taylor (first season);
Iris Rainer, Mort Scharfman, Nick Arnold,
Ron Pearlman, Tom Moore, George Bloom,
Jim Mulholland, Michael Barrie,
George Schlatter (second season)

Costumes
Bob Mackie (Cher); Ret Turner

Makeup
Ben Nye II (first season); Ben Nye II,
Jeff Hamilton (second season)

Wigs
Rena (Renata Leuschner)

Lighting
John Beam, V. Dale Palmer, Stich Cantrell

Publicity
Rogers-Cowan (first season); Dick Grant
Intercom (second season)

VIDEOGRAPHY

CHER: Episode Guide and Breakdown

Cher #1 (Special; Program No. 100)
Taped: 1/6-7-8/75; Aired: 2/12/75 (10:00 p.m.)
Starring: Elton John; *Guest Star*: Bette Midler;
Special Guest Star: Flip Wilson
Opening number: "Let Me Entertain You"—
Cher; "All in Love is Fair"—Cher; "Bennie
and The Jets"—Cher and Elton John; Trashy
Ladies medley: "Sister Kate," "Tangerine,"
"Ramona," "Lulu's Back in Town," "Put the
Blame on Mame," "Mary Had a Little Lamb,"
"Minnie The Moocher," "Rose of Washington
Square," "Second Hand Rose," "Mary," "Sweet
Georgia Brown,"—Cher, Bette Midler; "Lucy in
the Sky with Diamonds"—Elton John; Medley:
"Mockingbird," "Proud Mary," "Never Can Say
Goodbye," "Ain't No Mountain High Enough"—
Cher, Elton John, Bette Midler, Flip Wilson

Notes: Scheduled but not taped: Musical number
"Hello in There" performed by Bette Midler.
Taped but not aired: "Mable's Fables," a comedy
sketch featuring Cher and Bette Midler. Art
director Robert Kelly (and set decorator Robert
Checchi) won an Emmy Award for "Outstanding
Achievement in Art Direction or Scenic Design
for a Single Episode of a Comedy-Variety or Music
Series or a Comedy-Variety or Music Special."

Cher #2 (Premier; Program No.101)
Taped: 1/19-20/75; Aired: 2/16/75 (7:30 p.m.)
Starring: Tatum O'Neal; *Guest Star*: Wayne Rogers;
Special Guest Star: Raquel Welch
Opening number: "You're Nobody till Somebody
Loves You"—Cher; Medley: "Long Train
Runnin'," "Love the One You're With"—Cher;
"I'm a Woman"—Cher, Raquel Welch; "Let Me
Be There"—Cher, Wayne Rogers; "Girls Are

Smarter"—Cher, Tatum O'Neal; "Top Hat, White Tie and Tails"—Cher, Tatum O'Neal, Wayne Rogers, Tony Charmoli Dancers

Notes: Taped but not aired: Solo musical number "Feel Like Makin' Love" performed by Raquel Welch, and a Donna Jean Brodine comedy segment featuring Cher selling a product called "Stick It."

Cher #3 (102)
Taped: 1/30-31/ 75; Aired: 2/23/75
Starring: Nancy Walker; *Guest Stars:* the Osmonds; *Special Guest Star:* Jerry Lewis
Opening number: "Got to Get You Into My Life"—Cher; "Ain't Nobody's Business"—Cher; "He 'Aint Heavy He's My Brother"—Cher, Jerry Lewis; "I'm Still Gonna Need You," "Danny Boy," "Law and Order"— Osmond Brothers; Stevie Wonder medley: "You Are the Sunshine of My Life," "Signed, Sealed, Delivered," "Superstition," "Higher Ground," "For Once in My Life"—Cher, Osmond Brothers

Notes: Scheduled but not taped: An appearance by acclaimed Mime Marcel Marceau. The unaired Bette Midler / Cher "Mable's Fables" comedy segment from Show No. 1, was rewritten for Nancy Walker and Cher and featured in this episode.

Cher #4 (103)
Taped: 2/8-9/75; Aired: 3/2/75
Guest Star: Jack Albertson; *Special Guest Star:* Cloris Leachman
Opening number: "By Myself"—Cher; "Am I Blue?"—Cher; Medley: "I've Got the Music in Me," "Listen to the Music"—Cher; "The Men in My Little Girl's Life"—Cher, Jack Albertson; "Do a Take"—Cher, Jack Albertson, Cloris Leachman.

Notes: Jack Albertson won an Emmy Award for "Outstanding Continued or Single Performance by a Supporting Actor in a Variety or Music Series" for his performance on this episode. Cloris Leachman won an Emmy Award for "Outstanding Continued or Single Performance by a Supporting Actress in a Variety or Music Series" for her performance on this episode.

Cher #5 (104)
Taped: 2/22-23/75; Aired: 3/9/75
Starring: Teri Garr; *Guest Stars:* Pointer Sisters; *Special Guest Star:* Freddie Prinze

Opening number: "When You're Smiling"—Cher; "How Long Has This Been Going On?"—Cher; "Singin', Dancin', Clownin' Around"—Cher, Freddie Prinze; "Girls Are Smarter"—Cher, Pointer Sisters; "Live Your Life Before You Die"— Pointer Sisters; Big Band Era Medley: "On The Sunny Side of the Street," "Chattanooga Choo Choo," "Well, All Right," "Opus One," "I've Got a Gal in Kalamazoo"—Cher, Pointer Sisters, Freddie Prinze, Teri Garr, Dee Dee Wood Dancers

Notes: An in studio photo by Julian Wasser of Cher wearing the costume she wears for her solo "How Long Has This Been Going On?" was scheduled to be used on the cover of *Time,* but was replaced at the last minute by a previously published *Vogue* photo by Richard Avedon.

Cher #6 (105)
Taped: 3/1-2/75; Aired: 3/16/75
Starring: David Groh; *Guest Stars:* Jackson 5; *Special Guest Star:* Lily Tomlin
Opening number: "Friends"—Cher; "Since I Fell For You," "If"—Cher; "I Am Love," "The World is a Mess"— Jackson 5; Jackson 5 Medley: "I Want You Back," "I'll Be There," "Never Can Say Goodbye," "The Love You Save," "Dancing Machine"—Cher, Jackson 5

Notes: Taped but not aired: A comedy sketch entitled "Committee on Committees" featuring Cher and the Jackson 5.

Cher #7 (106)
Taped: 3/8-9/75; Aired: 3/23/75
Starring: Jimmie Walker; *Guest Star:* Teri Garr; *Special Guest Star:* Marty Feldman
Opening number: "You're No Good"—Cher; "My Love,"—Cher; No. 1 Hits Medley: "Half-Breed," "Gypsys, Tramps and Thieves," "Dark Lady"— Cher; "Ragtime Cowboy Joe"—Cher, Teri Garr

Notes: Before performing her Hits Medley Cher posed, in costume, for photos with and without Gregg Allman. The pictures appeared in *Time* and on the cover of *People.*

Cher #8 (No.107)
Taped: 3/15-16/75; Aired: 4/6/75
Starring: Ted Knight; *Guest Stars:* Labelle; *Special Guest Star:* Redd Foxx
Opening number: "Take Me Home, Country Roads"—Cher; "Never-Never Land"—Cher;

"What Can I Do For You?"—Cher, Labelle; "Lady Marmalade"—Labelle; "Attitude"—Cher, Redd Foxx

Cher #9 (108)
Taped: 3/22-23/75; Aired: 4/13/75
Starring: Billy Swan; Guest Stars: Kris Kristofferson and Rita Coolidge; Special Guest Star: Jean Stapleton
Opening number: "If You Wanna Get to Heaven"—Cher; "Many Rivers to Cross"—Cher; Medley: "This is Reggae Music," "Stir it Up"—Cher, Dee Dee Wood Dancers; Country Medley: "Oh, Lonesome Me," "Help Me Make It Through the Night," "Oakie From Muskogee"—Cher, Kris Kristofferson and Rita Coolidge; "Late Again (Gettin' Over You)"—Kris Kristofferson and Rita Coolidge; "Girls Are Smarter"—Cher, Jean Stapleton; "I Can Help"—Billy Swan

Cher #10 (109)
Taped: 4/4/75; Aired: 4/20/75
Starring: Linda Ronstadt; Guest Star: Nancy Walker; Special Guest Star: Liberace
Opening number: "I Can't Get No Satisfaction"—Cher; "Sunshine on My Shoulders"—Cher; Medley: "Drift Away," "Rip it Up"—Cher, Linda Ronstadt; "When Will I Be Loved?"—Linda Ronstadt; "The Way We Were"—Liberace; Medley: "The Trouble with Men," "To Keep Our Love Alive"—Cher, Nancy Walker

Cher #11 (110)
Taped: 4/17-18/75; Aired: 4/27/75
Starring: Kate Smith; Guest Stars: Ike and Tina Turner, Chastity Bono; Special Guest Star: Tim Conway
Opening number: "All I Really Want to Do"—Cher; "Relationships"—Cher, Kate Smith; "Shame, Shame, Shame"—Cher, Tina Turner; "Nutbush City Limits"— Ike and Tina Turner Revue; "What Kind of Fool am I?"—Kate Smith; Beatles Medley: "Help," "With a Little Help from My Friends," "All You Need is Love," "Day Tripper," "Yellow Submarine," "I Want to Hold Your Hand," "Here Comes the Sun," "Let It Be," "We Can Work It Out," "When I'm Sixty Four," "Eleanor Rigby," "Hey Jude"—Cher, Ike and Tina Turner Revue, Kate Smith, Tim Conway, Chastity Bono, Dee Dee Wood Dancers

Cher #12 (111)
Taped: 4/24-25/75; Aired: 5/4/75
Starring: Charo, Chastity Bono; Guest Star:

Art Garfunkel, Jimmy Webb; Special Guest Star: McLean Stevenson
Opening number: "Where You Lead"—Cher; "America"—Cher, Charo, Dee Dee Wood Dancers; "You Are So Beautiful"—Cher, Chastity; Medley: "All I Know," "Beautiful Balloon"—Cher, Art Garfunkel, Jimmy Webb; "Bridge Over Troubled Waters"—Art Garfunkel; "Malaguena"—Charo

Cher #13 (112)
Taped: 5/1-2/75; Aired: 5/11/75
Guest Stars: Dennis Weaver, Gregg Allman; Special Guest Star: Carol Burnett
Opening number: "For Once in My Life"—Cher; "Geronimo's Cadillac"—Cher; "Don't Mess Up a Good Thing"—Cher, Gregg Allman; "Prairie Dog Blues"—Dennis Weaver; "Midnight Rider"—Gregg Allman, Cher, Dee Dee Wood Dancers; Legendary Ladies medley: "Ladies of the Silver Screen," "I'm Following You," "Nagasaki," "G. I. Jive," "Lonely at the Top"—Cher, Carol Burnett

Cher #14 (113)
Taped: 5/8-9-10/75; Aired: 5/18/75
Starring: Teri Garr; Guest Stars: Hudson Brothers, Chastity Bono; Special Guest Star: Art Carney
Opening number: "Great Balls of Fire"—Cher; "Hernando's Hideaway"—Cher, Dee Dee Wood Dancers; Medley: "My Sweet Lord," "Oh, Happy Day"—Cher; "My Blue Heaven"—Cher, Art Carney; "Rendezvous"—Hudson Brothers

June 8, 15, 22, and 29 were filled with repeats from the series. Show #1 (Cher's Special) was repeated on Monday August 25 at 10:00 p.m.

Second Season

The larger part of Cher's second season was filmed out of sequence and in bits and pieces. Second season episodes are presented in the order in which the shows were aired (not taped).

Cher #15 (204)
Taped: 8/6-7-8/75; Aired: 9/7/75
Starring: Smothers Brothers; Guest Stars: Muppets, Eulle Gibbons; Special Guest Star: Bill Cosby; Featuring: Jim Morris, Ric Drasin, Bill Grant, Don Peters, Don Peters
Opening medley: "Where You Lead," "How Sweet it is to Be Loved by You,"—Cher; "Send in the Clowns,"—Cher; "Something"—Cher, Sweetums;

"Smoke Gets in Your Eyes"—Tom Smothers; "Yo-Yo Man"—Smothers Brothers; Shape Up America Finale: "He'll Do"—Cher, "Shape Up America"—Cher, Bill Cosby, Muppets, Smothers Brothers, Gailard Sartain, Eulle Gibbons

Notes: Taped but not aired: A comedy spoof of *The Six Million Dollar Man* TV series featuring Cher, Bill Cosby and Jack Harrell.

Cher #16 (206)
Taped: 9/4-5-6/75; Aired: 9/14/75
(New Time-8:00 p.m.)
Starring: Edward Asner; *Guest Stars*: Pointer Sisters; *Special Guest Star*: Redd Foxx; *Featuring*: Pat Morita
Opening medley: "Yesterday," "Crocodile Rock"—Cher; "Love Song"—Cher (featuring Scott Salmon); "Bet You Got a Chick on the Side"—Pointer Sisters; Elton John medley: "Saturday Night's Alright For Fighting," "Bennie and the Jets," "Daniel," "Rocket Man," "Don't Let the Sun Go Down on Me," "Take Me to the Pilot," "Goodbye Yellow Brick Road"—Cher, Pointer Sisters

Cher #17 (203)
Taped: 7/30-31-8/1/75; Aired: 9/21/75
Starring: Wayne Rogers; *Special Guest Star*: Nancy Walker
Opening medley: "Feeling Good," "I Feel the Earth Move,"—Cher; "Until It's Time for You to Go"—Cher; Medley: "Puppet Man," "It's Your Thing"—Cher, Anita Mann Dancers

Notes: Taped but not aired: a "Cher's Talent Showcase" segment featuring musician John Hresc and Cher performing "Old McDonald Had a Farm" and "Yearning and Turning."

Cher #18 (205)
Taped: 8/27-28/75; Aired: 9/28/75
Starring: Hudson Brothers; *Guest Star*: Mark Wilson; *Special Guest Star*: Captain Kangaroo; *Featuring*: Chastity Bono)
Opening number: "Can You Tell Me How to Get to Sesame Street?"—Cher; "When You Wish Upon a Star"—Cher, Chastity; "Lonely School Year"—Hudson Brothers

Notes: Taped but not aired: A Cher / Hudson Brothers duet entitled "Nothing Nicer Than a Nonsense Song."

Cher #19 (208)
Taped: 9/18-19-20/75; Aired: 9/5/75
Guest Stars: Labelle; *Special Guest Star*: Mac Davis
Opening number: "Take Me Home Country Roads"—Cher; "Five Hundred Miles"—Cher; "Are You Lonely?"—Cher, Labelle; "Messin' with My Mind"—Labelle; "I Still Love You (You Still Love Me)"—Mac Davis; Mack Davis medley: "Stop and Smell the Roses," "One Hell of a Woman," "In the Ghetto," "Baby Don't Get Hooked On Me," "I Believe In Music"—Cher, Mac Davis; Rolling Stones medley: "It's Only Rock and Roll (But I Like It)," "Under My Thumb," "It's All Over Now," "Ruby Tuesday," "Jumpin' Jack Flash"—Cher

Notes: Taped but not aired: Solo musical number "Can I Talk to You Before You go to Hollywood?" performed by Labelle.

Cher #20 (207)
Taped: 9/10-11-12/75; Aired: 10/12/75
Starring: Anthony Newley; *Special Guest Stars*: Ike and Tina Turner Review
Opening number: "There'll be Some Changes Made"—Cher; "You Turn Me On"—Cher; "Take a Little Dab of Hope"—Cher, Anthony Newley; "Country Side of Life"—Cher, Tina Turner; "Quilp"—Anthony Newley; "River Deep, Mountain High"—Tina Turner; "Baby, Get it On"—Ike and Tina Tuner Revue; Revival Meeting medley: "Brother Love's Traveling Salvation Show," "Resurrection Shuffle," "Saved"—Cher, Ike and Tina Turner Revue, Anthony Newley, Anita Mann Dancers

Notes: Art director Raymond Klausen (and set decorator Robert Checchi) won an Emmy Award for "Outstanding Achievement in Art Direction or Scenic Design-Single Episode of a Comedy-Variety or Musical Series or a Comedy-Variety or Musical Special."

Cher #21 (210)
Taped: 10/8- 9-10/75; Aired: 10/26/75
Guest Stars: Smothers Brothers, Steve Martin; *Special Guest Star*: Ted Knight
Opening medley: "Stars," Keep the Customer Satisfied"—Cher; "If You Could Read My Mind"—Cher; "I'm in Love with Barbara Walters"—Ted Knight

Cher #22 (211)
Taped: 10/15-16-17/75; Aired: 11/2/75

Starring: Teri Garr, Martin Mull; *Special Guest Star:* George Burns
Opening medley: "Rainy Days and Mondays," "On the Sunny Side of the Street"–Cher; "Lime House Blues"–Cher, Anita Mann Dancers; "I Ain't Got Nobody"–Cher, George Burns; Burns and Allen medley: "The Baby Song," "Where Did You Get That Girl?"–Cher, George Burns; "The Humming Song"–Martin Mull

Notes: Scripted and scheduled for taping but not taped: "Can't Lose What You Never Had" a musical number by the Allman Brothers Band, and an (undecided) duet featuring Cher and the Allman Brothers Band.

Cher #23 (209)
Taped: 9/25-26-27/75; Aired: 11/9/75
Guest Stars: Spinners, Steve Martin; *Special Guest Star:* Wayne Newton
Opening number: "Ain't Nobody's Business"–Cher; "Do Right Woman, Do Right Man"–Cher; Medley: "Witchy Woman," "Honky Tonk Woman"–Cher, Anita Mann Dancers; "Feelings"–Wayne Newton; "Could It Be I'm Falling in Love?"–Spinners; Medley: "Rock-a-Bye Your Baby with a Dixie Melody," "The Birth of the Blues," "Your Nobody 'Till Somebody Loves You"–Cher, Wayne Newton

Notes: Taped but not aired: A medley of "Mighty Love," and "Games People Play" performed by the Spinners, and "Then Came You" performed by the Spinners and Cher.

Cher #24 (202)
Taped: (All segments previously recorded: Ray Charles on 8/6-7-8/75; Muppets, Chastity on 7/30-31–8/1/75); Opening number on 9/4/75); Aired: 11/16/75
Guest Star: Muppets; *Special Guest Star:* Ray Charles and the Raelettes (featuring Chastity Bono)
Opening medley: "Happy Together," "Love Will Keep Us Together,"–Cher; "I Am... I Said"–Cher; "Georgia on My Mind"–Cher, Ray Charles; "That Old Black Magic"–Cher, Sweetums; "Living for the City"–Ray Charles; "It's Not Easy Being Green"–Ray Charles, Kermit the Frog; Ray Charles medley: "Look What They've Done to My Song, Ma," "Take Me Home Country Roads," "Just for a Thrill," "Hit the Road Jack," "What'd I Say?"–Cher, Ray Charles, Raelettes

Notes: Taped but not aired: "America the Beautiful," a musical number performed by Ray Charles.

Cher #25 (201)
Taped: 9/18-19-20/75; Aired: 11/23/75
Starring: Tony Randall; *Guest Star:* Steve Martin; *Special Guest Star:* David Bowie
Opening number: "When Will I Be Loved"–Cher; "A Song for You"–Cher; Medley: "Silver Dollar," "More of her on the Chair"–Cher, Tony Randall; "Can You Hear Me?"–Cher, David Bowie; "Fame"–David Bowie; Medley: "Young Americans," "Song Sung Blue," "One Is the Loneliest Number," "Da Doo Ron Ron," "Wedding Bell Blues," "Maybe," "Maybe Baby," "Day Tripper," "Blue Moon," "Only You," "Temptation," "Ain't No Sunshine When She's Gone," "Young Blood," "Young Americans"–Cher, David Bowie

Notes: Taped but not aired: A comedy segment featuring Tony Randall and Gailard Sartain entitled "War Toys" and a comedy segment featuring Gailard Sartain entitled "Forest Ranger."

Cher #26 (212)
Taped: 10/29-30-31/75; Aired: 11/30/75
Starring: David Essex; *Special Guest Star:* Jerry Lewis
Opening medley: "I Feel a Song Coming On," "Sing"–Cher; "Rhinestone Cowboy," "Trashy Ladies"–Cher; "The Long and Winding Road"–Cher, David Essex; "Hold Me Close"–David Essex

Cher #27 (214)
Taped: 11/12-13-14/75; Aired: 12/7/75
Guest Stars: Frankie Avalon, Frankie Valli, Dion DiMucci; *Special Guest Star:* Pat Boone
Opening medley: "An Old Fashioned Love Song," "I Dig Rock and Roll Music"–Cher; "Abraham, Martin and John"–Cher, Dion; "I Almost Lost My Mind"–Cher, Pat Boone; "One Hell of a Woman"–Frankie Avalon; Medley: "Swearin' to God," "My Eyes Adored You"–Frankie Valli; "The Wanderer"–Dion; "Magnificent Sanctuary Band"–Pat Boone; 1960s medley: "I Dig Rock and Roll Music," (Cher), "April Love" (Pat Boone), "Love Letters in the Sand" (Cher, Boone), "Venus" (Frankie Avalon), "De De Dinah" (Cher, Avalon), "Lets Hang on to What We've Got" (Frankie Valli), "Working My Way Back to You" (Cher and Valli), "Ruby, Baby"

(Dion), "Runaround Sue" (Cher, Dion), "All I Really Want to Do" (Cher), "The Beat Goes On" (Cher, Boone, Dion, Avalon, Valli); featuring the Anita Mann Dancers

Notes: Taped but not aired: A "Beehive Blackout" comedy segment featuring Cher.

Cher #28 (213)
Taped: 11/5-6-7/75; Aired: 12/14/75
Starring: Hal Linden; *Guest Star:* Ruth Buzzi; *Special Guest Star:* Glen Campbell
Opening medley: "Georgia on my Mind," "Sweet Georgia Brown"—Cher; "Trashy Ladies"—Cher; Glenn Campbell medley: "By the Time I Get To Phoenix," "Wichita Lineman," "Galveston," "Gentle on My Mind"—Cher, Glen Campbell; "Country Boy (You've Got Your Feet in L.A.)"— Glen Campbell; Hospital Finale: "Marsha Welby's Happy Hospital," "Psychomatic Tango," "My Heart is in Your Hands," "Rhythm of the Operating Room"—Cher, Buzzi, Campbell, Linden, Sartain, Anita Mann Dancers

Cher #29 (215)
Taped: 11/26-28/75; Aired: 12/21/75
Starring: Hudson Brothers, Chastity Bono; *Guest Stars:* Lennon Sisters; *Special Guest Star:* Redd Foxx
Opening medley: "White Christmas," "We Need a Little Christmas"—Cher; "Some Children See Him"—Cher; "Here Comes Santa Claus"— Hudson Brothers; Medley: "Star Carol," "Jingle Bells"—Lennon Sisters; Christmas medley: "Winter Weather," "I've Got Your Love to Keep Me Warm," "Let it Snow," "Santa Baby," "Santa Claus is Coming to Town," "Hawaiian Christmas," "Christmas Island," "Christmas in Trinidad," "Silent Night"—Cher, Lennon Sisters, Hudson Brothers, Redd Foxx, Chastity Bono

Cher Specials
"Cher... Special"
Aired: 4/3/1978, ABC. 60 Minutes
Guests: Dolly Parton, Rod Stewart, the Tubes
West Side Story medley: "Jet Song," "Maria," "A Boy Like That," "I Have a Love," "I Feel Pretty," "Maria," "America," "Somewhere"—Cher; "My Sweet Lord,"—Cher; "Two Doors Down," "People Get Ready"—Dolly Parton; "Hot Legs"—Rod Stewart; "Mondo Bondago"—the Tubes.

"Cher...and Other Fantasies"
Aired: 3/7/1979, NBC. 60 Minutes

Guests: Lucille Ball, Elliott Gould, Andy Kaufman, Shelly Winters
"Ain't Nobody's Business," "Take Me Home," "Love and Pain," "How Long Has This Been Going On?" "Feel like a Number"—Cher

"Cher: Live in Monte Carlo"
Aired: 1980, Showtime. 60 Minutes
"T'Aint Nobodies Business," "Signed Sealed, Delivered," "Fire," "Easy to be Hard," "The Way of Love," "Ain't No Mountain High Enough," "Friends," Medley: "Jail House Rock," "Dream Lover," "Great Balls of Fire," "Rockin' Robin," "Johnny be Good," "Dedicated to the One I Love," "Hand Jive," "Honky Tonk Woman," "Old Time Rock and Roll"; "Take It to the Limit," "Take Me Home," "Takin' it to the Streets," "Whole Lotta' Love"—Cher

"Cher: A Celebration at Caesars Palace"
Aired: 4/21/1983. Showtime, 90 Minutes
"Could I Be Dreaming?," "Signed, Sealed, Delivered," "You Make My Dreams Come True," "Fire," "Knock on Wood," "Those Shoes," "Out Here on My Own," "Take it to the Limit," "Lookin' for Love in All the Wrong Places," "When Will I be Loved?," "More Than You Know," "Fame"—Cher

"Cher: Extravaganza Live at the Mirage"
Aired: 1992, CBS. 60 Minutes. DVD.
"I'm No Angel," We all Sleep Alone," "Bang Bang (My Baby Shot Me Down)," "I Found Someone," Take It to the Limit," "If I Could Turn Back Time," "Perfection," "Fire Down Below," "Takin' it to the Streets," "After All (Love Theme From Chances Are)," "Hold On," "Many Rivers To Cross," "Tougher than the Rest"—Cher.

"Sonny and Me: Cher Remembers"
Aired: 5/20/1998, CBS. 60 Minutes
"Nature Boy"—Cher; "I Got You Babe," "The Beat Goes On"—Sonny and Cher.

"Cher: Live in Concert"
Aired: 12/1999, Home Box Office, 90 Minutes. DVD.
"I Still Haven't Found What I'm looking For," "All or Nothing," "The Power," We all Sleep Alone," "I Found Someone," "The Way of Love," Medley: "Half-Breed," "Gypsys, Tramps and Thieves," "Dark Lady"; "Take Me Home," "After

All (Love Theme From Chances Are)," "Walking in Memphis," "Just Like Jesse James," "The Shoop Shoop Song (It's In His Kiss)," "Dov'e L'amore," "Strong Enough," "If I Could Turn Back Time," "Believe"—Cher

. "Cher: The Farewell Tour"
Aired: 3/2003. CBS, 90 Minutes. DVD.
"I Still Haven't Found What I'm Looking For," "Song for the Lonely," "All or Nothing," "I Found Someone," "Bang Bang (My Baby Shot Me Down)," Medley: "The Beat Goes On," "Baby Don't Go," "I Got You Babe," "All I Really Want to Do"; Medley: "Half-Breed," "Gypsys, Tramps and Thieves," "Dark Lady"; "Take Me Home," "The Way of Love," "After All (Love Theme From Chances Are)," "Just Like Jesse James," "Heart of Stone," "The Shoop Shoop Song (It's in His Kiss)," "Strong Enough," "If I Could Turn Back Time," "Believe"—Cher

Sonny and Cher Episode Guide

"The Sonny and Cher Show" CBS-TV, 8:30 p.m. 60 Min. Sundays

1. 8/1/1971: *Guests:* Jimmy Durante
2. 8/8/71: Ken Berry
3. 8/22/71: Merv Griffin
4. 8/29/71: Phyllis Diller, Fanny
5. 9/5/71: Grass Roots

The Sonny and Cher Comedy Hour CBS-TV, 10:00 p.m. 60 Min. Mondays

6. 12/27/1971: *Guests:* Carol O'Connor, Glen Ford, Harvey Korman, Robert Merrill
7. 1/3/72: Tony Curtis, Dinah Shore
8. 1/17/72: Kate Smith
9. 1/24/72: Lorne Greene, Chad Everett
10. 1/31/72: Tony Randall, Honey Cone
11. 2/7/72: Jean Stapleton, Mike Connors
12. 2/14/72: Burt Reynolds
13. 2/21/72: Art Carney
14. 2/28/72: Ken Berry, Ralph Edwards
15. 3/6/72: Sandy Duncan
16. 3/13/72: George Burns, David Clayton-Thomas
17. 3/20/72: Merv Griffin, Miss. Universe

Repeat broadcasts ran for ten weeks

Second Season: (8:00 p.m. Fridays)

18. 9/22/1972: Jerry Lewis, Supremes
19. 9/29/72: Chad Everett, Bobby Sherman
20. 10/6/72: Tony Curtis, Barbara McNair
21. 10/13/72: Jimmy Durante, Gilbert O'Sullivan, Robert Goulet
22. 10/20/72: Temptations
23. 10/27/72: William Conrad, Rick Springfield
24. 11/3/72: Lorne Greene, Williams Brothers
25. 11/10/72: Bobby Darrin
26. 11/17/72: Ken Berry, the New Seekers
27. 11/24/72: Jim Brown, Bobby Vinton
28. 12/1/72: Andy Griffith

New Time: (8:00 p.m. Wednesdays)

29. 12/20/1972: William Conrad, Earl Brown Singers
30. 12/27/72: Carroll O'Connor
31. 1/27/73: Jean Stapleton
32. 1/10/73: Marc Spitz
33. 1/24/73: Mike Connors
34. 1/31/73: Merv Griffin, Larry Storch, Mike Curb Congregation
35. 2/1/73: Jim Nabors
36. 2/14/73: Joe Namath, Hugh Hefner, Playboy Playmates
37. 2/21/73: Danny Thomas
38. 2/28/73: Don Adams
39. 3/7/73: John Byner
40. 3/14/73: Tennessee Ernie Ford, Capt. John Nasmith
41. 3/21/73: William Conrad, Jean Stapleton, Chad Everett, Lyle Waggoner, Tennessee Ernie Ford

Repeat broadcasts ran for eight weeks

Third Season:

42. 9/12/1973: Howard Cosell, Chuck Connors, Miss Universe, Miss USA
43. 9/19/73: Danny Thomas, Telly Savalas
44. 9/26/73: Bobby Vinton, Frankie Valli and the Four Seasons, Dick Clark, Chuck Berry, Jerry Lee Lewis, Ed Byrnes
45. 10/3/73: Truman Capote, John Davidson
46. 10/10/73: Jack Palance, Ed McMahon
47. 10/17/73: Dennis Weaver
48. 10/24/73: Jim Nabors
49. 10/31/73: Jerry Lewis
50. 11/7/73: Andy Griffith, Billy Jean King, Bob Guccione and Penthouse Pet
51. 11/14/73: Douglas Fairbanks, Jr., Kris

Kristofferson and Rita Coolidge
52. 11/28/73: Little Richard, Brenda Lee, Herman's Hermits, the Temptations
53. 12/5/73: Vincent Price, the Temptations
54. 12/12/73: Ken Berry, George Foreman
55. 12/19/73: William Conrad
56. 1/9/74: O. J. Simpson, Teddy Nelly
57. 1/16/74: Danny Thomas
58. 1/23/74: Robert Goulet, Carol Lawrence, Miss World
59. 1/30/74: Sally Struthers, Jackson 5
60. 2/13/74: Ricardo Montalban, Jeanette Nolan, Defranco Family
61. 2/20/74: Joe Namath, Righteous Brothers
62. 2/27/74: Joel Grey
63. 3/6/74: Sally Struthers, Merv Griffin

Repeats ran through May 29, 1974

The Sonny and Cher Show CBS-TV, 8:00 p.m. 60 Min. Sundays

1. 2/1/1976: *Guests*: Raymond Burr, Richard Thomas, Jim Nabors, Don Meredith
2. 2/8/76: Raymond Burr
3. 2/15/76: Neil Sedaka
4. 2/22/76: Jim Nabors
5. 2/29/76: Don Knotts, Chastity Bono
6. 3/7/76: McLean Stevenson
7. 3/21/76: Gabriel Kaplan, Frankie Avalon
8. 3/28/76: Debbie Reynolds, Smothers Brothers
9. 4/4/76: Diahann Caroll, Tony Randall
10. 4/11/76: George Gobel
11. 4/18/76: Andy Griffith, Sherman Hemsley

Repeat broadcasts ran through August 22, 1976

Second Season:

12. 9/26/1976: Ruth Buzzi, Rona Barrett, Charo, Wayne Rogers, Don Knotts, Shields and Yarnell, Smothers Brothers, Barbara Eden
13. 10/3/76: Smothers Brothers, Barbara Eden
14. 10/10/76: Bob Hope, The Jacksons
15. 10/17/76: Wayne Rogers, Charo
16. 10/24/76: Donny and Marie, Ruth Buzzi, Alex Karras
17. 10/31/76: Jim Nabors, Hudson Brothers, Shields and Yarnell
18. 11/7/76: Betty White, Ed McMahon, the Sylvers
19. 11/17/76: Jack Albertson, Steve Lawrence

20. 11/21/76: Redd Foxx, Tom Jones, Shields and Yarnell
21. 12/5/76: Andy Griffith, Twiggy
22. 12/12/76: Jim Nabors, Debbie Reynolds
23. 12/26/76: Don Knotts, Joey Heatherton
24. 1/2/77: John Davidson, Karen Valentine
25. 1/14/77: Farrah Fawcett, Debbie Reynolds, Don Knotts
26. 1/21/77: Flip Wilson, Betty White, Ken Berry
27. 1//28/77: Engelbert Humperdinck, Ruth Buzzi, Don Knotts, William Conrad, Barbi Benton
28. 2/4/77: Farrah Fawcett-Majors, Glen Campbell, Don Knotts
29. 2/18/77: Muhammad Ali, Marilyn McCoo and Billy Davis, Lyle Waggoner
30. 2/25/77: Peter Graves, Anne Meara, Dr. Joyce Brothers, Shields and Yarnell
31. 3/4/77: George Gobel, Charo
32. 3/11/77: Tina Turner, David Steinberg, Shields and Yarnell
33. 3/18/77: Clips from the past season featuring the series' high and low points.

Sonny Bono Episode Guide

The Sonny Comedy Revue ABC-TV, 8:00 p.m. 60 Min. Sundays

1. 9/22/1974: *Guests*: Sally Struthers, Howard Cosell, Jackson 5
2. 9/29/74: McLean Stevenson, Joey Heatherton, Spinners
3. 10/6/74: James Brolin, Barbara Eden, Temptations
4. 10/13/74: Glen Campbell, Twiggy, Temptations
5. 10/20/74: Jim Nabors, Charo, Penthouse Pet of the Year
6. 10/27/74: Karen Valentine, Clifton Davis, Carrie McDowall
7. 11/3/74: Juliet Prowse, Steve Allen, Billy Preston
8. 11/10/74: Loretta Switt, Ed McMahon, Smokey Robinson
9. 11/17/74: Jill St. John, Hudson Brothers
10. 11/24/74: Cloris Leachman, Frankie Avalon, Alex Karras
11. 12/8/74: Ken Berry, Barbara Feldon, Rufus
12. 12/15/74: Spinners
13. 12/22/74: Lucie Arnaz

One repeat episode aired on December 29, 1974

Cher (Official) Music Videos

1979. "Hell on Wheels"
1981. "Dead Ringer for Love" (with Meatloaf)
1987. "I Found Someone"
1988. "We All Sleep Alone"
1988. "Main Man"
1989. "If I Could Turn Back Time"
1989 "Just Like Jesse James"
1989. "Heart of Stone"
1990 "The Shoop Shoop Song" (It's in His Kiss)
1991. "Love and Understanding"
1991. "Save Up All Your Tears"
1993. "I Got You Babe" (with Beavis and Butt-head)
1995. "Walking in Memphis"
1995. "Love Can Build a Bridge" (with Chrissie Hynde, Neneh Cherry featuring Eric Clapton)
1996. "One By One"
1998. "Believe"
1999. "Strong Enough"
1999. "All or Nothing"
1999 "Dov'e L'Amore"
2001. "Piu Che Puoi" (with Eros Ramazzotti)
2001. "The Music's No Good Without You"
2002. "Song for the Lonely"
2011. "You Haven't Seen the Last of Me"

DISCOGRAPHY

Cher (Original Solo Albums)

All I Really Want to Do
(Imperial; 1965) Producer: *Sonny Bono*
All I Really Want to Do / I Go To Sleep / Needles and Pins / Don't Think Twice, It's All Right / She Thinks I Still Care / Dream Baby / The Bells of Rhymney / Girl Don't Come / See See Rider / Come and Stay with Me / Cry Myself to Sleep / Blowin' in the Wind

The Sonny Side of Cher
(Imperial; 1966) P: *Sonny Bono*
Bang Bang (My Baby Shot Me Down) / A Young Girl (Une Enfante) / Where Do You Go / Our Day Will Come / Elusive Butterfly / Like a Rolling Stone / Ol' Man River / Come To Your Window / The Girl from Ipanema / It's Not Unusual / Time / Milord

Cher
(Imperial; 1966) P: *Sonny Bono*
Sunny / Twelfth of Never / You Don't Have to Say You Love Me / I Feel Something in the Air / Will You Love Me Tomorrow / Until It's Time for You to Go / Cruel War / Catch the Wind / Pied Piper / Homeward Bound / I Want You / Alfie

With Love, Cher
(Imperial; 1967) P: *Sonny Bono*
You Better Sit Down Kids / But I Can't Love You More / Hey Joe / Mama (When My Dollies Have Babies) / Behind the Door / Sing for Your Supper / Look at Me / There But for Fortune / I Will Want for You / The Times They Are A-Changin'

Backstage
(Imperial; 1968) P: *Sonny Bono, Harold Battiste, Jr., Denis Pregnolato*
Go Now / Carnival / It All Adds Up to Now / Reason to Believe / Masters of War / Do You Believe in Magic / I Wasn't Ready / A House is Not a Home / Take Me For a Little While / The Impossible Dream / The Click Song / A Song Called Children

3614 Jackson Highway
(Atco; 1969) P: *Jerry Wexler, Tom Dowd, Arif Madrin*
For What It's Worth / (Just Enough to Keep Me) Hangin' On / (Sittin' On) The Dock of the Bay / Tonight I'll Be Staying Here with You / I Threw It All Away / I Walk on Gilded Splinters / Lay Baby Lay / Please Don't Tell Me / Cry Like a Baby / Do Right Woman, Do Right Man / Save the Children

Cher
(Kapp; 1971) P: *Snuff Garrett*
The Way of Love / Gypsys, Tramps and Thieves / He'll Never Know / Fire and Rain / When You Find Out Where You're Goin' Let Me Know / He Ain't Heavy, He's My Brother / I Hate to Sleep Alone / I'm in the Middle / Touch and Go / One Honest Man

Foxy Lady
(Kapp; 1972) P: *Snuff Garrett, Sonny Bono*
Living in a House Divided / It Might as Well Stay Monday (From Now On) / Song for You / Down, Down, Down / Don't Ever Try to Close a Rose / The First Time / Let Me Down Easy / If I Knew Then / Don't Hide Your Love / Never Been Spain

Bittersweet White Light

(MCA; 1973) P: *Sonny Bono*

By Myself / I Got it Bad and That Ain't Good /
Am I Blue / How Long Has This Been Going On
/ The Man I Love / Jolson Medley: Sonny Boy,
My Mammy, Rock-a-Bye Your Baby with a Dixie
Melody / More Than You Know / Why Was I
Born / The Man That Got Away

Half-Breed

(MCA; 1973) P: *Snuff Garrett*

My Love / Two People Clinging to a Thread /
Half-Breed / The Greatest Song I Ever Heard /
How Can You Mend a Broken Heart / Carousel
Man / David's Song / Melody / The Long and
Winding Road / This God-Forsaken Day /
Chastity Sun

Dark Lady

(MCA; 1974) P: *Snuff Garrett*

Train of Thought / I Saw a Man and He Danced
with His Wife / Make the Man Love Me / Just
What I've Been Looking For / Dark Lady / Miss
Subway of 1952 / Dixie Girl / Rescue Me /
What'll I Do / Apples Don't Fall Far from
the Tree

Stars

(Warner Bros.; 1975) P: *Jimmy Webb*

Love Enough / Bell Bottom Blues / These Days
/ Mr. Soul / Just This One Time / Geronimo's
Cadillac / The Bigger They Come the Harder
They Fall / Love Hurts / Rock and Roll
Doctor / Stars

I'd Rather Believe in You

(Warner Bros.; 1976) P: *Steve Barri,
Michael Omartian*

Long Distance Love Affair / I'd Rather Believe
in You / I Know (You Don't Love Me) / Silver
Wings and Golden Rings / Flashback / It's a
Cryin' Shame / Early Morning Strangers / Knock
on Wood / Spring / Borrowed Time

Cherished

(Warner Bros.; 1977) P: *Snuff Garrett*

Pirate / He Was Beautiful / War Paint and Soft
Feathers / Love the Devil Out of Ya / She Loves
to Hear the Music / L.A. Plane / Again / Dixie /
Send the Man Over / Thunderstorm

Take Me Home

(Casablanca; 1979) P: *Bob Esty, Ron Dante*

Take Me Home / Wasn't It Good / Say the Word
/ Happy Was the Day We Met / Get Down
(Guitar Groupie) / Pain in My Heart / Let This
Be a Lesson to You / It's Too Late to Love Me
Now / My Song (Too Far Gone)

Prisoner

(Casablanca; 1979) P: *Bob Esty*

Prisoner / Holdin' Out for Love / Shoppin' /
Boys and Girls / Mirror Image / Hell on Wheels
/ Holy Smoke / Outrageous

I Paralyze

(CBS; 1982) P: *David Wolfert, John Farrar*

Rudy / Games / I Paralyze / When the Love is
Gone / Say What's On Your Mind / Back on the
Street Again / Walk with Me / The Book of Love
/ Do I Ever Cross Your Mind

Cher

(Geffen; 1987) P: *Michael Bolton, Jon Bon Jovi,
Richie Sambora, Desmond Child, Peter Asher, Jon Lind*

I Found Someone / We All Sleep Alone / Bang
Bang / Main Man / Give Our Love a Fightin'
Chance / Perfection / Dangerous Times / Skin
Deep / Working Girl / (It's Been) Hard Enough
Getting Over You

Heart of Stone

(Geffen; 1989) P: *Peter Asher, Michael Bolton, John
Kalodner, Jon Lind, Diane Warren, Guy Roche*

If I Could Turn Back Time / Just Like Jesse
James / You Wouldn't Know Love / Heart of
Stone / Still in Love With You / Love on a
Rooftop / Emotional Fire / All Because of You
/ Does Anybody Really Fall in Love Anymore /
Starting Over / Kiss to Kiss

Love Hurts

(Geffen; 1991) P: *John Kalodner, Peter Asher, Steve
Lukather, Guy Roche, Diane Warren, Richie Zito,
Bob Rock*

Save Up All Your Tears / Love Hurts / Love
and Understanding / Fires of Eden / I'll Never
Stop Loving You / One Small Step / A World
Without Heroes / Could've Been You / When
Love Calls Your Name / When Lovers Become
Strangers / Who You Gonna Believe

It's a Man's World

(Warner Bros.; 1995) P: *Craig Kostich*

Don't Come Around Tonight / What About the
Moonlight / The Same Mistake / The Gunman /

The Sun Ain't Gonna Shine Anymore / Shape of Things to Come / It's a Man's World / Walking in Memphis / Not Enough Love in the World / One By One / I Wouldn't Treat a Dog (The Way You Treated Me) / Angels Running / Paradise is Here / I'm Blowin' Away

Believe
(Warner Bros.; 1999) P: *Mark Taylor, Todd Perry, Junior Vasquez, Brian Rawling, Rob Dickins*
Believe / The Power / Runaway / All or Nothing / Strong Enough / Dov'e L'Amore / Takin' Back My Heart / Taxi Taxi / Love is the Groove / We All Sleep Alone

not.com.mercial
(Artist Direct; 2000) P: *Cher, Bruce Roberts*
Still / Sisters of Mercy / Runnin' / Born With The Hunger / (The Fall) Kurt's Blues / With or Without You / Fit to Fly / Disaster Cake / Our Lady of San Francisco / Classified 1A

Living Proof
(Warner Bros.; 2002) P: *Rob Dickins, Johan Aberg, Nigel Butler, Chapman, Chris Cox, Anderson* Hansson, Tony Moran, Bruce Roberts, Wayne Rodriguez, Stargate, Mark Taylor
(This Is) A Song For The Lonely / A Different Kind of Love Song / Rain, Rain / Love So High / Body to Body, Heart to Heart / Love is a Lonely Place Without You / Real Love / Love One Another / You Take it All / When The Money's Gone

Live! The Farewell Tour
(2003; Rhino / WEA) P: *Cher, Roger Davies, Lindsay Scott*
I Still Haven't Found What I'm Looking For / Song for the Lonely / All or Nothing / I Found Someone / Bang Bang / All I Really Want to Do / Half-Breed / Gypsys, Tramps and Thieves / Dark Lady / Take Me Home / The Way of Love / After All / Just Like Jesse James / Heart of Stone / The Shoop Shoop Song / Strong Enough / If I Could Turn Back Time / Believe

Cher with Others (Albums)

Allman and Woman (Cher with Gregg Allman)
(Warner Bros.; 1977) P: *Gregg Allman, Johnny Sandlin, John Haeny*
Move Me / I Found You Love / Can You Fool / You Really Got a Hold on Me / We're Gonna

Make It / Do What You Gotta Do / In for the Night / Shadow Dream Song / Island / I Love Makin' Love to You / Love Me

Black Rose (Cher with Black Rose)
(Casablanca; 1980) P: *James Newton Howard*
Never Should've Started / Julie / Take it from the Boys / We All Fly Home / 88 Degrees / You Know It / Young and Pretty / Fast Company

Cher Guest Vocalist (Albums)

Gene Simmons by Gene Simmons
(Casablanca; 1978)
Song: "Living in Sin" (Duet with Gene Simmons)

Foxes (Soundtrack)
(Casablanca; 1980)
Song: "Bad Love"

Dead Ringer by Meatloaf
(Epic; 1981)
Song: "Dead Ringer for Love"
(Duet with Meatloaf)

Mermaids (Soundtrack)
(Geffen; 1990)
Songs: "The Shoop Shoop Song (It's in His Kiss), "Baby I'm Yours"

The Beavis and Butt-head Experience
(Geffen; 1993)
Song: "I Got You Babe" (Duet with Beavis and Butt-head)

The Glory of Gershwin
(Mercury; 1994)
Song: "It Ain't Necessarily So."

For Our Children
(Kid Rhino; 1996)
Song: "A Dream is a Wish Your Heart Makes"

Sing America
(Warner Bros.; 1999)
Song: "Star Spangled Banner"

VH1 Divas Live
(Arista; 1999)
Songs: "Proud Mary," "If I Could Turn Back Time" ("Proud Mary"; Duet with Tina Turner)

A Rosie Christmas

(Columbia; 1999)
Song: "Christmas (Baby Please Come Home)"

A Walk on the Moon
(Sire; 1999)
Song: "Crimson and Clover" (duet with Elijah
Blue Allman)

Stilelibero by Eros Ramazzotti
(BMG; 2000)
Song: "Piu che puoi" (duet with Eros Ramazzotti)

**As Time Goes By: The Great American
Songbook 2**
(J Records; 2003)
Song: "Bewitched, Bothered and Bewildered"
(Duet with Rod Stewart)

Burlesque (Soundtrack)
(RCA; 2010)
Songs: "Welcome to Burlesque," "You Haven't
Seen the Last of Me"

Cher (Solo Singles)

"Ringo I Love You" / "Beatle Blues"
(Annette; 1964. *Cher as Bonnie Jo Mason*)
"Dream Baby" / "Stan Quetzal" (Imperial; 1965.
Cher as Cherilyn)
"All I Really Want to Do" / "I'm Gonna Love
You" (Imperial; 1965)
"Where Do You Go" / "See See Blues"
(Imperial; 1965)
"Bang Bang (My Baby Shot Me Down)" / "Our
Day Will Come" (Imperial; 1966)
"Alfie" / "She's No Better Than Me"
(Imperial; 1966)
"I Feel Something in the Air" / "Come to Your
Window" (Imperial; 1966)
"Sunny" / "Will You Love Me Tomorrow"
(Imperial; 1966)
"Behind the Door" / "Magic in the Air"
(Imperial; 1966)
"Mama (When My Dollies Have Babies)" /
"Dream Baby" (Imperial; 1966)
"Hey Joe" / "Our Day Will Come"
(Imperial; 1967)
"You Better Sit Down Kids" / "Elusive Butterfly"
(Imperial; 1967)
"The Click Song" / "But I Can't Love You More"
(Imperial; 1968)
"Take Me For a Little While" / "Song Called
Children" (Imperial; 1968)

"Yours Until Tomorrow" / "The Thought of
Loving You" (Atco; 1969. *Promo: Non album songs.*)
"Chastity's Song (Band of Thieves)" / "I Walk on
Gilded Splinters" (Atco; 1969)
"For What It's Worth" / "(Just Enough To Keep
Me) Hangin' On" (Atco; 1969)
"The First Time" / "You've Made Me So Very
Happy" (Atco; 1969)
"Superstar" / "Superstar" (Atco; 1970. *Promo:
Non album song*)
"Classified 1-A" / "Don't Put It On Me"
(Kapp; 1971)
"Gypsys, Tramps and Thieves" / "He'll Never
Know" (Kapp; 1971)
"The Way of Love" / "Don't Put It On Me"
(Kapp; 1971)
"Living in a House Divided" / "One Honest
Man" (Kapp; 1972)
"Don't Hide Your Love" / "The First Time"
(Kapp; 1972)
"Am I Blue" / "How Long Has This Been Going
On" (MCA; 1973)
"Half-Breed" / "Melody" (MCA; 1973)
"Dark Lady" / "Two People Clinging to a
Thread" (MCA; 1974)
"Train of Thought" / "Dixie Girl" (MCA; 1974)
"I Saw a Man and He Danced With His Wife" /
"I Hate To Sleep Alone" (MCA; 1974)
"Carousel Man" / "When You Find Out Where
You're Going Let Me Know" (MCA; 1974)
"Rescue Me" / "Dixie Girl" (MCA; 1974)
"I Hate to Sleep Alone" / "I Saw A Man and He
Danced With His Wife" (MCA; 1974)
"A Woman's Story" / "Baby I Love You"
(Warner-Spector; 1974)
"Geronimo's Cadillac" / "These Days"
(Warner Bros.; 1975)
"Long Distance Love Affair" / "Borrowed Time"
(Warner Bros.; 1976)
"Pirate" / "Send the Man Over"
(Warner Bros.; 1977)
"War Paint and Soft Feathers" / "Send The Man
Over" (Warner Bros; 1977)
"Take Me Home" / "My Song (Too Far Gone)"
(Casablanca; 1979)
"Take Me Home" (12" *Picture Disc*, Casablanca; 1979)
"It's Too Late (To Love Me Now)" / "Wasn't It
Good" (Casablanca; 1979)
"Hell On Wheels" / "Git' Down (Guitar
Groupie)" (Casablanca; 1979)
"Holdin' Out For Love" / "Boys and Girls"
(Casablanca; 1979)
"Rudy" / "Do I Ever Cross Your Mind"

(Columbia; 1982. *UK only release.*)

"I Paralyze" / "Walk With Me" (Columbia; 1982)

"I Found Someone" / "Dangerous Times" (Geffen; 1987)

"I Found Someone" / "Dangerous Times" (12" *Picture Disc*, Geffen U.K.; 1988)

"We All Sleep Alone" / "Working Girl" (Geffen; 1988)

"We All Sleep Alone" / "Working Girl" / "I Found Someone" (12" *Picture Disc*, Geffen U.K.; 1988)

"Skin Deep" / "Perfection" (Geffen; 1988)

"Main Man" / "(It's Been) Hard Enough Getting Over You" (Geffen; 1988)

"If I Could Turn Back Time" / "Some Guys" (Geffen; 1989)

"If I Could Turn Back Time" / "Some Guys" / "Kiss to Kiss" (12" *Picture Disc*, Geffen U.K.; 1989)

"Just Like Jesse James" / "Starting Over" (Geffen; 1989)

"Just Like Jesse James" / "I Found Someone" / "Starting Over Again" (12" *Picture Disc*, Geffen U.K.; 1989)

"Heart of Stone" / "All Because of You" (Geffen; 1990)

"Heart of Stone" / "All Because of You" / "Working Girl" (12" *Picture Disc*, Geffen U.K., 1990)

"You Wouldn't Know Love" / "Kiss to Kiss" / "Bang Bang" / "Heart of Stone" (Geffen; 1990. CD single)

"The Shoop Shoop Song (It's in His Kiss)" / "Love On A Rooftop" (Geffen; 1990)

"Love and Understanding" / "Trail of Broken Hearts" (Geffen; 1991)

"Save Up All Your Tears" / "A World Without Heroes" (Geffen; 1991)

"Love Hurts" / "One Small Step" / "Just Like Jesse James" (Geffen; 1992. CD single)

"When Lovers Become Strangers" / "When Lovers Become Strangers" (Geffen; 1992. *Promo only.*)

"Could've Been You" / "Love and Understanding" (Geffen; 1992. *UK only release.*)

"Could've Been You" / "Love and Understanding" / "Save Up All Your Tears" (12" Picture Disc Geffen U.K.; 1992)

"Oh No Not My Baby" / "Love on a Rooftop" / "Love Hurts" / "Main Man" (Geffen; 1992. *UK only release.*)

"Many Rivers to Cross" / "Who You Gonna Believe" (Geffen; 1993. *UK only release.*)

"Many Rivers to Cross" / "Tougher Than the Rest" / "Fire Down Below" / "Takin' it to the Streets" (Geffen; 1993. *UK only release.*)

"Whenever You're Near" / "Could've Been You" / "I'll Never Stop Loving You" (Geffen; 1993. *UK only release.*)

"Whenever You're Near" / "Could've Been You" / "I'll Never Stop Loving You" / "You Wouldn't Know Love" (12" Picture Disc, Geffen U.K.; 1993)

"Walking in Memphis" / Remixes (WEA; 1995. *UK only release.*)

"Not Enough Love in the World" / "One By One Remix" (WEA; 1996. *UK only release.*)

"One By One" / "I Wouldn't Treat a Dog (The Way You Treated Me)" (Reprise; 1996)

"The Sun Ain't Gonna Shine Anymore" / Remix (Reprise; 1996. *UK only release.*)

"Paradise Is Here" / Remixes (Reprise; 1996)

"Believe" / Remixes (WEA; 1999)

"Strong Enough" / Remixes (WEA; 1999)

"All Or Nothing" / Remixes (WEA; 1999)

"The Star Spangled Banner" (Warner Bros. 1999. *DJ promo.*)

"Dov'e L'Amore" / Remixes (WEA; 2000)

"The Music's No Good Without You" / Remixes (WEA; 2001)

"Song For The Lonely / Remixes (WEA; 2002)

"A Different Kind of Love Song" / Remixes (WEA; 2002)

"Alive Again" / "When You Walk Away" (WEA; 2002. *Germany only release.*)

"When the Money's Gone" / "Love One Another" (Geffen; 2003)

"Woman's World" (Warner Bros. ; 2012)

Cher With Others (Singles)

"A Love Like Yours" / ("Just Enough To Keep Me) Hangin' On" (Warner-Specter; 1974. *Duet with Nilsson.*)

"Move Me" / "Love Me" (Warner Bros.; 1977. *Duet with Gregg Allman billed as Allman and Woman.*)

"Never Should've Started" / "Young and Pretty" (Casablanca; 1980. *Cher is lead singer for band Black Rose.*)

"Dead Ringer For Love" / "More Than You Deserve" (Epic; 1981. *Duet with Meatloaf. No. 5 in Great Britain but not released as a single in America.*)

"After All (Love Theme from Chances Are)" / "Dangerous Times" (Geffen; 1989. *Cher and Peter Cetera. The song reached No. 6 on the American charts.*)

"I Got You Babe" / "Mental *@%#!" / "Fire

Down Below" (Geffen; 1993. *Cher with Beavis and Butt-head. UK only release.*)

"Bewitched, Bothered and Bewildered" (J Records; 1993. *Rod Stewart with Cher. Promo only.*)

"It Aint' Necessarily So" / "I'll Build a Stairway to Paradise" / "The Gettysburg Address" (Mercury; 1994. *Cher and Larry Adler. German only release.*)

"Love Can Build a Bridge" Remixes (London Records; 1995. *Cher, Chrissie Hynde, Neneh Cherry with Eric Clapton. No. 1 in Great Britain but not released as a single in America.*)

"Piu che puoi" / Remixes (BMG; 2000. *Eros Ramazzotti and Cher. Italy and Holland only release.*)

"The Greatest Thing" / (Unknown as of May 2013. *Cher and Lady Gaga.*)

"I'm Just Your Yesterday" (MPG; 2013. Cher, Georgia Holt.)

Sonny and Cher (Original Albums)

Look At Us
(Atco; 1965) P: *Sonny Bono*
I Got You Babe / Unchained Melody / Then He Kissed Me / Sing C'est La Vie / It's Gonna Rain / 500 Miles / Just You / The Letter / Let It Be Me / You Don't Love Me / You've Really Got a Hold on Me Why Don't They Let Us all in Love

The Wondrous World of Sonny and Cher
(Atco; 1966) P: *Sonny Bono*
Summertime / Tell Him / I'm Leaving It All Up to You / But You're Mine / Bring it On Home to Me / Set Me Free / What Now My Love / Leave Me Be / I Look for You / Laugh at Me / Turn Around / So Fine

In Case You're in Love
(Atco; 1967) P: *Sonny Bono*
The Beat Goes On / Groovy Kind of Love / You Baby / Monday / Love Don't Come / Podunk / Little Man / We'll Sing in the Sunshine / Misty Roses / Stand By Me / Living for You / Cheryl's Goin' Home

Good Times (Soundtrack)
(Atco; 1967) P: *Sonny Bono*
I Got You Babe (Instrumental) / It's The Little Things / Good Times / Trust Me / Don't Talk to Strangers / I'm Gonna Love You / Just a Name / I Got You Babe

Chastity (Soundtrack)
(Atco; 1969) P: *Sonny Bono*

Chastity's Song (Band of Thieves) / Chastity's Overture / Motel 1 / Chastity Walk / Flowers (Love of a Family) / Chastity Love Theme / Chastity Titles / Motel 2 / Chastity Carousel / Mexico / Chastity (Closing Theme)

All I Ever Need is You
(MCA; 1971) P: *Snuff Garrett, Denis Pregnolato*
All I Ever Need Is You / Here Comes That Rainy Day Feeling / More Than Yesterday / Crystal Clear, Muddy Waters / United We Stand / A Cowboy's Work Is Never Done / I Love What You Did with the Love I Gave You / You Better Sit Down Kids / We'll Watch the Sun Coming Up (Shining Down on Our Love) / Somebody

Sonny and Cher Live
(Kapp; 1971) P: *Denis Pregnolato*
What Now My Love / The Beat Goes On / Once in a Lifetime / More Today Than Yesterday / Got to Get You Into My Life / Someday (You'll Want Me To Want You) / Danny Boy / Laugh at Me / Something / Hey Jude / I Got You Babe

Mama Was a Rock and Roll Singer, Papa Used to Write All Her Songs
(MCA; 1973) P: *Sonny Bono, Denis Pregnolato, Michael Rubini*
It Never Rains in Southern California / I Believe in You / I Can See Clearly Now / Rhythm of Your Heartbeat / Mama Was a Rock and Roll Singer Papa Used to Write All Her Songs (Part 1 & 2) / By Love I Mean / Brother Love's Traveling Salvation Show / You Know Darn Well / The Greatest Show on Earth / Listen to the Music

Sonny and Cher Live in Las Vegas Vol. II
(MCA; 1973) P: *Denis Pregnolato*
All I Ever Need is You / Medley: I Can See Clearly Now, You've Got a Friend, Where You Lead / Gypsys, Tramps and Thieves / Brother Love's Traveling Salvation Show / You and I / Superstar / Bang Bang (My Baby Shot Me Down) / Medley: You Better Sit Down Kids, A Cowboy's Work is Never Done / I Got You Babe

Sonny and Cher (Singles)

"Love is Strange" / "Do You Wanna Dance" / "Let the Good Times Roll" (Reprise; 1964. *Sonny and Cher as Caesar and Cleo.*)

"The Letter" / "Spring Fever" (Vault; 1964. *Sonny and Cher as Caesar and Cleo.*)

"Just You" / "Sing C'est La Vie"
(Atco; 1965)
"Baby Don't Go" / "Walkin' the Quetzal"
(Reprise; 1965)
"I Got You Babe" / "It's Gonna Rain"
(Atco; 1965)
"Laugh at Me" / "Tony" (Atco; 1965.
Sonny Bono Solo.)
"But You're Mine" / "Hello" (Atco; 1965)
"Where Do You Go" / "See See Blues"
(Imperial; 1965)
"What Now My Love" / "I Look For You"
(Atco; 1966)
"Have I Stayed Too Long" / "Leave Me Be"
(Atco; 1966)
"Little Man" / "Monday" (Atco; 1966. Also
recorded in French and Italian for European markets.)
"Living For You" / "Love Don't Come"
(Atco; 1966)
"The Beat Goes On" / "Love Don't Come"
(Atco; 1967)
"A Beautiful Story" / "Podunk" (Atco; 1967)
"Il Cammino Di Ogni Speranza" / "L'Umanita"
(Atlantic; 1967. Italy only release.)
"Plastic Man" / "It's the Little Things"
(Atco; 1967)
"Cara Cara" / "Fantasie" (Atlantic; 1967. Italy
only release.)
"It's the Little Things" / "Don't Talk to
Strangers" (Atco; 1967)
"Good Combination" / "You and Me" (Atlantic;
1967. Italy only release.)
"You Gotta' Have a Thing of Your Own" / "I Got
You Babe" (Atco; 1968)
"Circus" / "I Would Marry You Today"
(Atco; 1968)
"You're a Friend of Mine" / "I Would Marry You
Today" (Atco; 1969)
"Real People" / "Somebody" (Kapp; 1971)
"All I Ever Need is You" / "I Got You Babe"
(Kapp; 1971)
"A Cowboy's Work is Never Done" /
"Somebody" (Kapp; 1972)
"When You Say Love" / "Crystal Clear/Muddy
Waters" (Kapp; 1972)
"Mama Was a Rock and Roll Singer Papa Used
to Write All Her Songs (Part 1)" / "Mama Was a
Rock and Roll Singer Papa Used to Write All Her
Songs (Part 2)" (MCA; 1973)
"The Greatest Show on Earth" / "You Know
Darn Well" (MCA; 1973)
"You're Not Right For Me" / "Wrong Number"
(Warner Bros.; 1977)

Sonny Bono (Solo Album)

Inner Views
(Atco; 1967) P: Sonny Bono
I Just Sit There / I Told My Girl to Go Away / I
Would Marry You Today / My Best Friend's Girl
is Out of Sight / Pammie's on a Bummer

Sonny Bono (Solo Singles)

"Ecstasy" / Unknown. (Dig; 1955.)
"Wearing Black" / "One Little Answer"
(Specialty; 1959. Sonny Bono as Don Christy.)
"Wearing Black" / "You Don't Have to Tell Me"
(Fidelity; 1960. Sonny Bono as Don Christy.)
As Long As You Love Me" / "I'll Always Be
Grateful" (Name Records; 1960. Sonny Bono as
Don Christy.)
"As Long as You Love Me" / "I'll Always Be Grateful"
(Go Records; 1960. Sonny Bono as Don Christy.)
"Don't Shake My Tree" / "Mama Come Get
Your Baby Boy" (Sawmi; 1961. Sonny Bono as
Ronny Sommers.)
"Shake Me Up" / "Mr. Pawnshop" (Go Records;
1961. Sonny Bono as Prince Carter.)
"Calling All Cars" / "Good Ship Love"
(Zen; 1962. Sonny Bono as Davey Summers.)
"I'll Change" / "Try it Out on Me" (Highland;
1963/1965)
"Laugh at Me" / "Tony (Sonny's Group)" (Atco; 1965)
"The Revolution Kind" / "Georgia and John
Quetzel" (Atco; 1965. UK only release.)
"My Best Friend's Girl is Out of Sight" /
"Pammie's on a Bummer" (Atco; 1967)
"I Told My Girl to Go Away" / "Misty Roses"
(Atco; 1967)
"Comin' Down the Chimney" / "One Little
Answer" (Specialty; 1962 [re-issue of same-titled
1959 single by "Little Joey with Little Tootsie"].
Sonny Bono as Sonny Bono and Little Tootsie.)
"Rub Your Nose" / "Laugh at Me" (MCA; 1973)
"Our Last Show" / "Classified 1A" (MCA; 1974)

Georgia Holt (Solo Album)

Honky Tonk Woman
(MPG; 2013) P: Unknown
I'm Just Your Yesterday / (Feat. Cher) / I Sure
Don't Want to Love You / Movin' On / Las
Vegas Blues / I Bought the Love That You Gave
Me / I Wonder Where You Are Tonight / Love
Me Tender / You Can't Go Home Again /
Homecoming Queen / Crying Time

FILMOGRAPHY

Cher

Wild on the Beach
(1965; with Sonny Bono) Director: Maury Dexter
Cast: Frankie Randall, Sherry Jackson, Jackie
and Gayle

Good Times
(1967; with Sonny Bono) D: William Friedkin
C: George Sanders, Norman Alden, Larry Duran

Chastity
(1969) D: Alessio de Paola
C: Barbara London, Stephen Whittaker,
Tom Nolan

*Come Back to the Five and Dime Jimmy Dean,
Jimmy Dean*
(1983) D: Robert Altman
C: Sandy Dennis, Karen Black, Kathy Bates

Silkwood
(1983) D: Mike Nichols
C: Meryl Streep, Kurt Russell, Diana Scarwid

Mask
(1985) D: Peter Bogdanovich
C: Eric Stoltz, Sam Elliott, Estelle Getty

The Witches of Eastwick
(1987) D: George Miller
C: Jack Nicholson, Susan Sarandon,
Michelle Pfeiffer

Suspect
(1987) D: Peter Yates
C: Dennis Quaid, Liam Neeson, John Mahoney

Moonstruck
(1987) D: Norman Jewison
C: Nicolas Cage, Olympia Dukakis,
Danny Aiello

Mermaids
(1990) D: Richard Benjamin
C: Bob Hoskins, Winona Ryder, Michael Schoeffling

The Player
(1992; cameo) D: Robert Altman
C: Including: Whoopi Goldberg, Tim Robbins,
Peter Gallagher

Pret-a-Porter (Ready to Wear)
(1994; cameo) D: Robert Altman
C: Including: Julia Roberts, Sophia Lauren,
Lauren Bacall

Faithful
(1996) D: Paul Mazursky
C. Chazz Palminteri, Ryan O'Neal, Paul Mazursky

If These Walls Could Talk
(1996; TV-Movie) D: Nancy Savoca, Cher
C: Demi Moore, Sissy Spacek, Shirley Knight

Tea with Mussolini
(1999) D: Franco Zeffirelli
C: Maggie Smith, Judi Dench, Lily Tomlin
Stuck on You
(2003) D: Bobby Farrelly, Peter Farrelly
C: Matt Damon, Greg Kinnear, Eva Mendes

Burlesque
(2010) D: Steven Antin
C. Christina Aguilera, Alan Cumming,
Cam Gigandet

Zookeeper
(2011; Voice) D: Frank Coraci
C: Kevin James. Rosario Dawson, Leslie Bibb

Sonny Bono

Wild on the Beach
(1965; with Cher) Director: Maury Dexter
Cast: Frankie Randall, Sherry Jackson,
Jackie and Gayle

Good Times
(1967; with Cher) D: William Friedkin
C: George Sanders, Norman Alden,
Larry Duran

Murder on Flight 502
(1975; TV-Movie) D: George McCowan
C: Ralph Bellamy, Polly Bergen,
Farrah Fawcett

Escape to Athena
(1979) D: George P. Cosmatos
C: Roger Moore, Telly Savalas, David Niven

Murder in Music City
(1979; TV-Movie) D: Leo Penn
C: Morgan Fairchild, Lee Purcell, Claude Akins

The Vals
(1985) D: James Polakof
C: Jill Carroll, Elena Statheros, Chuck Connors

Balboa
(1986) D: James Polakof
C: Tony Curtis, Carol Lynley, Jennifer Chase

Troll
(1986) D: John Carl Buechler
C: Noah Hathaway, Michael Moriarty, Shelly Hack

Dirty Laundry
(1987) D: William Webb
Leigh McCloskey, Jeanne O'Brien, Robbie Rist

Hairspray
(1988) D: John Waters
C: Ricki Lake, Jerry Stiller, Ruth Brown
Under the Boardwalk
(1989) D: Fritz Kiersch
C: Keith Coogan, Danielle von Zerneck,
Richard Joseph Paul

Sonny and Cher (Tele-Movie)

And the Beat Goes On: The Sonny and Cher Story
(1999; TV-Movie based on Sonny Bono's
autobiography) D: David Burton Morris
C: Renee Faia as Cher, Jay Underwood as Sonny,
Laura Johnson as Georgia LaPiere